Richard Anthony Proctor

Familiar Science Studies

Richard Anthony Proctor

Familiar Science Studies

ISBN/EAN: 9783337034474

Printed in Europe, USA, Canada, Australia, Japan

Cover: Foto ©Suzi / pixelio.de

More available books at **www.hansebooks.com**

FAMILIAR SCIENCE
STUDIES

BY

RICHARD A. PROCTOR

AUTHOR OF

'ROUGH WAYS MADE SMOOTH' 'THE POETRY OF ASTRONOMY'
'THE EXPANSE OF HEAVEN' ETC.

'Let knowledge grow from more to more'
TENNYSON

London

CHATTO & WINDUS, PICCADILLY

1882

· LONDON : PRINTED BY
SPOTTISWOODE AND CO., NEW-STREET SQUARE
AND PARLIAMENT STREET

PREFACE.

THE ESSAYS in the present volume are taken chiefly from the *Times, Scribner's Magazine,* the *Gentleman's Magazine, Belgravia,* the *Contemporary Review,* and the *Cornhill.* I have little to say of them that I have not already said of other essays of mine which have been republished in book form. My object in writing them has been to give clear and simple but also correct accounts of scientific matters likely to be interesting to the general public.

RICHARD A. PROCTOR.

LONDON : *December* 1881.

CONTENTS.

NOTES ON INFINITY.

WERE it not for the infinities by which he is surrounded, man might believe that all knowledge is within his power— at least, that every kind of knowledge is, to a greater or less degree, masterable. Men have analysed, one by one, the mysteries which surround the very great and the very little. On the one hand they have penetrated farther and farther into the star-depths, and have brought from beyond the remotest range of the telescope information not only as to the existence, but as to the very constitution of the orbs which people space. We know the actual elements which build up worlds and suns on the outskirts of our present domain in space ; and that domain is widening year by year, and century by century, as telescopes of greater power are constructed and greater skill acquired in their use. On the other hand, men have not only analysed the minutest structure of organic matter, have not only dealt with the movements of molecules and even of atoms, but they have inquired into the motions taking place in a medium more ethereal than matter as commonly understood—a medium utterly beyond our powers of direct research, and whose characteristics are only indirectly inferred from the study of effects produced by its means. Such is the extreme present range of man's researches in the direction of the vast on the one hand and the minute on the other ; and at first sight this range seems to include all that is or can be. For if the portions of the universe to which man cannot now penetrate, or may never be able to penetrate, resemble in the general characteristics of their structure and constitution the portions which he can examine, then, though he may examine but a part, he has in reality sampled the whole. And again, if the intimate structure of matter forming the visible universe, and the structure of that far subtler matter which forms the ether of space, represent the ultimate texture—so to speak—of the universe, then in the analysis of the minute also man has attained a similar success. We might thus recognise the possibility of that which a French philosopher has called the 'Scientific Apotheosis of Man :' in this sense, that, so far as quality of knowledge is concerned (as distinct from range of knowledge), men may become as gods, knowing all things, and even in the fulness of time able to discern good from evil, distinguishing that real good which exists in what, with our present knowledge, seems like absolute evil.

But so soon as we consider the infinite, the absolute necessity, according to our conceptions, of infinity of space and time if not of matter and energy, we recognise not only that there is much to which our researches can never be extended, but that the knowledge which is unattainable infinitely transcends that which is attainable. Take, for instance, the infinity of space. If we could suppose that the extremest possible range of telescopic vision fell short to some degree only of the real limits of the universe, we might not unreasonably believe that the unattainable parts were not unlike the portions over which our survey extends. But when we consider what infinity of space really means, we are compelled to admit that the portion of the universe which we have examined, or can conceivably examine, is absolutely as nothing—a mere mathematical point—compared with the actual universe. This being so, it would be utterly unreasonable to suppose that what we know of the universe affords any measurable indication of the structure of the rest. The part we know being as nothing compared with the whole, to assume that the remainder resembles it, is as unreasonable as it would be for a man who had seen but a single thread of a piece of cloth to attempt to infer from it the pattern of the whole. If such a man assumed that the whole piece was of one colour and made throughout of the same kind of thread, he would be much in the position of the man of science who should assume that the infinity of space surrounding the finite portion which we have examined, consists throughout of systems of suns—single, multiple, and clustered—attended by systems of planets.

So again of the infinity of time. We know of certain processes which are taking place in that particular portion of time in which our lives are set, or over which our reasoning powers range ; inferring from the present what has happened in the remote past or will happen in the distant future. We trace back our earth to its beginning 'in tracts of fluent heat,' or pass farther back to what Huxley has called the 'nebulous cubhood' of the solar system, or even attempt to conceive how the system of multitudinous suns filling the depths of space may have been formed by processes of development. And looking forward to the future, we trace out the progress of processes arising from those earlier ones, recognising apparently the ultimate surcease of every form of life, the life of all creatures living upon worlds, of worlds themselves, of solar systems, of systems of such systems, and of even higher orders of systems. If time were but finite, if we could conceive either a beginning or an end of absolute time,we might fairly enough suppose that processes such as these, and the subordinate processes associated with them, were the fulfilment of time. But time being infinite, of necessity we have no more reason for supposing that what we thus recognise in our domain of time re-sembles what takes place in other portions of time, than a man who listened for a single second to a concerted piece of music would have for imagining that the notes he heard during that second were continued throughout the whole performance.

Combining the consideration of the infinity of space with that of the infinity of time, we have no better right to consider that we understand the operation of the mighty mechanism of the universe, than one who for less than a second should be shown the least conceivable portion of a mighty machine would have thereafter to assert that he understood its entire workings. The saying of Laplace (whom, however, Swedenborg anticipated) that 'what we know is little, while the unknown is immense,' may truly be changed into this, that the known is nothing, the unknown infinite ; for whatever is finite, however great, bears to the infinite a ratio infinitely small, or is to the infinite as nothing. A million, equally with a single unit, is as nothing compared with a number infinitely large ; a million years, equally with a single second, is as nothing compared with eternity. The whole of what modern astronomy calls the universe is, equally with the minutest atom, as nothing compared with infinite space. 'System of nature!' exclaims Carlyle justly ; 'to the wisest man, wide as is his vision, nature remains of quite infinite depth, of quite infinite expansion, and all experience thereof limits itself to some few computed centuries and measured square miles.'

Let us consider, however, whether, after all, we must admit that space is infinite or time eternal. Remembering that space and time are forms of thought, and that the ideas of infinite space and infinite time are inconceivable, may it not be that, though we cannot escape the inconceivable by rejecting these infinities, we may nevertheless be able to substitute some other conditions less utterly oppressive than they are ?

So far as time is concerned, no attempt has been made, so far as I know, in this direction. It does not seem easy to imagine how time can be regarded as other than infinite. We should have entirely to change our conception of time, for instance, before we could regard it as self-repeating.

We can readily conceive the idea of a sequence of events being continually repeated, and thus assign a cyclical cha-racter to occupied time. But if we thus imagined that all the events now taking place had occurred many times before and will occur many times again, always in the same exact sequence, the cycles thus imagined would only be new and larger measures of absolute time. Though infinitely ex-tended in duration, according to our conceptions, they could no more be regarded as bearing a measurable ratio to time itself than the seconds or minutes into which we divide the part of time in which we live bear a measurable ratio to the duration, past, present, and future, of the visible uni-verse.

I am not, indeed, prepared to admit that a more suc-cessful effort has hitherto been made, or can be made, to indicate the possibility that space may not be infinite. Some eminent masters of mathematical analysis, whose acumen and profundity are justly celebrated, have expressed their acceptance of certain views, presently to be described, which suggest the possibility that space may be finite; but I find nothing either in their reasonings on this special subject, or in their writings generally, to suggest that they have the same mastery of geometrical as they have of analytical relations in mathematics. Nay, I venture to say that no competent geometrician who examines their reasoning can fail to recog-nise a confusion of thought, an indistinctness of mental vision, so soon as they pass from the verbal and mathe-matical *expression* of space relations, to the consideration of those relations themselves. Before considering the position they endeavour to maintain, let us briefly inquire into the general considerations which present themselves when we contemplate the relations of space as they appear to our conceptions.

It must be admitted at the outset (and no doubt in this we may recognise a reason for the diversity of view which appears to exist), that no theory of the finiteness of space can possibly be more utterly inconceivable than the idea of infinite space itself. And by inconceivable I do not mean merely that which is beyond our power of picturing mentally; for many things which not only exist, but can be measured and gauged, cannot possibly be pictured in our minds. No man, for instance, can form a clear mental picture of the dimensions of our earth, still less of Jupiter's or of the Sun's ; while the distances of the stars—distances which dwarf even the dimensions of the Sun into insignificance—are, in the ordinary use of the words, absolutely inconceivable. Yet, though we cannot picture these dimensions, we find no difficulty in admitting their actual existence. They are merely multiples of dimensions with which we are already familiar. But absolute infinity of space is unlike aught that the mind of man has hitherto been able to conceive. Aristotle well indicated this in his celebrated argument for the finiteness of the universe, that argument of which Sir J. Herschel truly said that, though *unanswerable*, it never yet convinced mortal man. The straight line joining any two points in space, *be they where they may*, is finite, because it has two definite terminations ; therefore the universe itself is finite. Equally unanswerable, however, though also equally unsatisfactory, is the retort in favour of the infinity of space. The straight line joining any two points in space, *be they where they may*, can be produced to any distance in the same straight line,[1] in either direction, and

---

[1] It is singular that the elementary ideas of geometry are introduced at the very beginning of any inquiry into the subject of infinity of space. The three postulates of the geometry of the line and circle present to us :—First, Aristotle's argument for a finite universe : secondly, the counter-argument for infinity of space ; and thirdly, the thought of Augustine (commonly attributed to Pascal) that the universe has its centre everywhere and its circumference nowhere. Let it be granted, says the first postulate, that a straight line may be drawn from any one point to any other point ; the second says, let it be granted that any finite line may be produced to any distance in the same straight line ; the third, let it be granted that a circle may be described with any centre and at any distance from that centre. The first is Aristotle's statement ; the second is the counter-statement ; the third is equivalent

therefore no point on the produced line on either side can be regarded as its extremity ; such lines being therefore infinite, the universe is infinite.

But it may be well to consider what we mean by a straight line—the absolute straight line of geometry. It is held by many mathematicians that our conceptions of points, lines, surfaces, figures, and so forth, in space are entirely derived from our experience of material points, lines, surfaces, figures, and so on. Assuming this to be so, what is the conception of straightness in a line joining two points? It appears to me that when we trace back the conception to its origin, we find the idea of a straight line joining two points to be that of a line, such that, if the eye were so placed that the two points appeared to coincide, the line itself, thus seen endwise, would appear as a point. This, if not the only independent test that can be applied to any material line, in order to determine its straightness, is certainly the best. Stretching a fine thread is either not a perfect test or not an independent test. If the two points are on a flat surface we can stretch a string from one to the other, because the flat surface affords suitable resistance to the string's tendency to bend ; but the flatness of the surface is a quality of precisely the same kind as the straightness of the line, and unless we are assured that the surface is flat we cannot be sure that the stretched string is not curved. Without a supporting surface we may be absolutely certain that the string is curved,

to the assertion that every point in the whole of space may be taken as a centre, and that there are no limits whatever to the distance at which a circle may be described around any point as centre. In like manner with the definitions and axioms. The idea of infinity is implicitly involved, and all but explicitly indicated, in the definition of parallel straight lines ; and before we can accept the doctrine of the possible existence of a fourth dimension in space, through which doctrine alone (so far as can be seen) the infinity of the universe can be questioned, we must reject the axiom that two straight lines cannot enclose a space ; or rather the wider axiom which Euclid should have adopted (since he makes, in reality, repeated use of it), that two straight lines which coincide in two points coincide in all points.

however slightly ; for the string, having weight, hangs (no matter how strongly it may be pulled) in the curve called the catenary—no force, however great, being able to pull any string, however short, into *absolute* straightness. An objection might be urged, in like manner, against the visual test ; because air is a transparent medium, and no finite portion of air being ever of constant heat and density throughout, the rays of light must always be bent, however slightly, in traversing any portion of air, however minute—so that, in fact, we cannot look quite straight through even a stratum of air only a single inch in thickness. The visual test, however, is independent, and, imagining vision to take place through a vacuum, we can at least conceive this test being absolutely perfect. The idea, then, of a finite straight line may be regarded as that of a line which, looked at endwise, would appear as a point. And we may extend this conception to lines of indefinitely enormous length. Thus, suppose there are two stars optically close together, though really separated by many million times the distance which separates our sun from us, and that, owing to the motion of one or both they draw optically nearer together until at length they appear as one, and this by so perfect an accordance of direction that, if telescopic power could be enormously increased, the centres of their two discs would be optically coincident : then a straight line joining these two centres would be one which, if it were a material line visible through the substance of the nearer star, would be optically reduced to a point—*supposing for the sake of argument that the two stars, after being carried by their proper motions into the required positions, were reduced to rest.*

The italicised words may seem unnecessary, but in point of fact they are only a part of what is necessary ; by themselves they are absolutely insufficient. If a telescopist living for a few odd millions of years could from a fixed standpoint watch two stars gradually approaching by their proper motion until they apparently coincided, one lying at an enormous distance beyond the other, and at that very instant those swiftly moving stars were brought to rest, they would not really be in a straight line with the observer's eye. For he would see the nearer in the direction it had many years ago, when its light began the journey towards him ; while he would see the farther in the direction which it had at a much more remote epoch. And it would be these two positions, which the two stars occupied, not at the same time, but at times widely remote, which would be in a right line with the observer's eye. If two stars really *were* brought by their proper motions into a straight line with the eye of an observer at a remote station, they would not seem to be coincident, and if they were then suddenly reduced to rest the observer would see them still apparently in motion, drawing nearer and nearer together until they apparently coincided.

We see, then, that this optical test of the straightness of the line joining two points requires that the points should be at rest.

I may here digress for a few moments to notice one very singular consequence of the effect of motion just mentioned. Conceive the production of a straight line joining two points to be effected under the visual test, the eye itself being the tracing point. The eye is first placed so that the nearer point (close to the eye) is coincident apparently with the more remote, and then the eye recedes with infinite velocity, or at least with a velocity exceeding many million times the velocity of light. Then it would seem at first as though the eye must of necessity travel in a straight line ; but in reality this would only be the case if the two points were either absolutely or relatively at rest. If *not*, then, paradoxical though it may seem, it is nevertheless true that the eye would have to travel in a series of whorls forming a mighty, spiral, the path of the eye at a very great distance from the two points being almost at right angles to a really straight line joining the eye and the centre of gravity of the moving points (around which they would make their . revolutions).

The relation here considered is rather a singular one in itself (apart, I mean, from all question of infinity). It may be illustrated by a phenomenon which occurred in December 1874, and will occur again in December 1882—a transit of Venus. Suppose we see the disc of Venus at any instant projected as a round black spot on the very centre of the Sun's face. Then one would say at the first view that at that moment the eye and the centres of the Sun and Venus were in a straight line. But this would not be exactly the case. For we see the Sun at any moment, not in his real direction, but in that towards which he lay some nine minutes before, light having taken that time in travelling to us from him ; and we see Venus at any moment, not in her real direction, but in that towards which she lay when the Sun's light passed *her*. As her distance from us varies widely, so the displacement due to the journey light has to take from her to reach us varies widely in relative amount, though, being always small, ordinary observation perceives no remarkable irregularity in her motions.[1] When she is

[1] If light did not travel with a velocity enormously exceeding that of the planets in their orbits, they would seem to move very irregularly (at least, until the cause of the irregularity had been discovered) ; we should sometimes see Mars, for example, where he was a month or so before, sometimes where he was a year or so before—*i.e.*, sometimes twenty or thirty millions of miles, sometimes two or three hundred millions of miles, from his true place. As it is, light crosses the greatest distance separating us from Mars in about twenty minutes, and the least in about four minutes, so that the irregularity in his apparent motions never amounts to more than the distance he traverses in about 16 minutes, or a little more than 14,000 miles. If light travelled at the same rate as sound, it would have been absolutely impossible for men to interpret the apparent planetary motions, and the most erroneous ideas would inevitably have prevailed respecting the real motions. Even if the velocity of light had amounted to 20 or 30 miles per second, instead of its real value—about 186,000 miles per second—the true theory of the planetary movements would have seemed absolutely inconsistent with what the eyes would have seen. Even as it is, astronomy is directly opposed to the doctrine that seeing is believing. We see every celestial body, not where it is, but where it was. It is hardly

between the Earth and Sun, light takes about $2\frac{1}{4}$ minutes in reaching us from Venus ; and therefore we see her where she was $2\frac{1}{4}$ minutes before. All that we can say, then, from the observed fact that Venus is seen at any moment, apparently at the very centre of the Sun's disc, is that a straight line from the eye to the place Venus occupied $2\frac{1}{4}$ minutes before is in the same direction as a straight line from the eye to the sun eight minutes before the moment of the observation. But the Earth is at the moment itself on the axis of Venus's shadow cone. This axis, then, cannot be a straight line. Similar reasoning applies to all the planets, including the Earth. They do not throw straight shadows into space. This is the point to which I have wished to lead the reader's attention. The axis of a planet's shadow is the path which would be pursued by the eye in the case before considered, if the planet were taken for the nearer and the Sun for the more remote of the two objects ; and instead of this axis of the shadow lying, as one would expect, upon straight lines extending radially from the Sun, it is curved with a constantly increasing deflection, until in depths very remote from the sun it actually sweeps out figures shaped almost like circles ! The shadow travels radially just as the light from the Sun does, simply because it lies between regions of light both receding radially from the Sun. Hence the place reached by the shadow which *had* been just behind a planet in one part of its course will lie in the same direction from the Sun, only at a much greater distance, when the planet has performed any part of its circuit or any number of circuits. This being true for every position of the planet, it follows readily that when we connect together the various positions reached by the outward-travelling shadow, at any moment, they form a mighty shadow-spiral extending in a series of whorls infinitely into space, or at least to a distance corresponding to that which light has

necessary to remark that astronomy, in predicting the motions of the celestial bodies, as well as the occurrence of eclipses, transits, occultations, and so on, takes this circumstance fully into account.

traversed since first the planet became an opaque body, or the Sun began to pour light upon the planet (whichever of these two events was the later)—in other words, *since first the planet cast a shadow.* Thus, let $p_1 p_2 p_3 p_4$ be the path of a planet about the Sun S, and let the planet be at p_1, then the shadow extends outwards from p_1. Let us see what

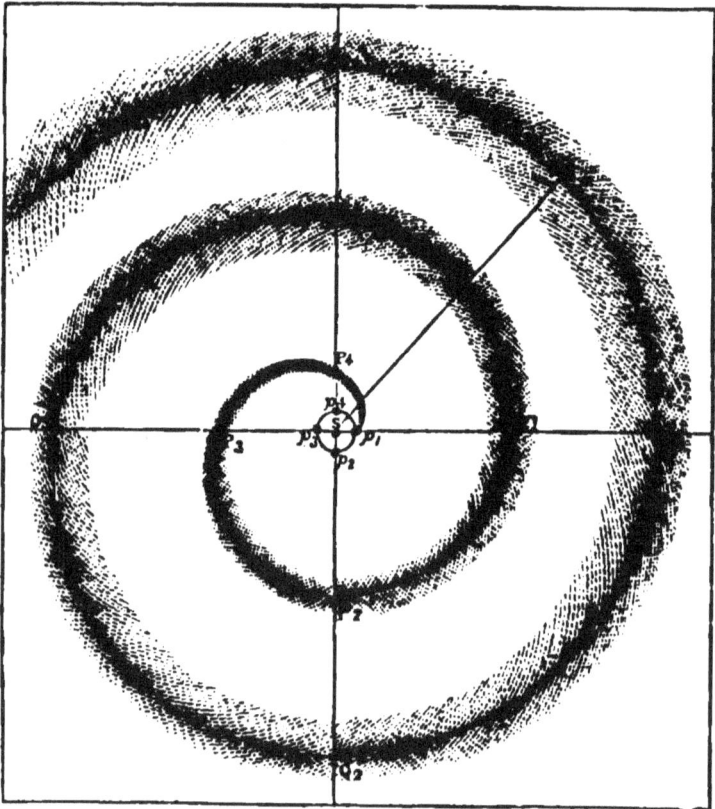

Shape of a Planet's shadow.

shape it will have. The shadow which had been behind the planet when last at p_1 has gone to P_1, $p_1 P_1$ being the distance traversed by light during one revolution of the planet. That which was behind the planet when last at p_2 has gone to P_2, $p_2 P_2$ being the distance traversed by light in three-quarters of a revolution. Similarly, we get P_3 for the place reached by the shadow which had been behind the planet when last at p_3, p_3 P_3 being the distance traversed by light during half a revolution ; and P_4 for the place reached by the shadow which had been behind the planet when last at p_4, p_4 P_4 being the distance traversed by light in a quarter of a revolution of the planet. The shadow's axis then lies along the curve p_1 P_4 P_3 P_2 P_1. But this is not the whole shadow. The shadow which had been behind the planet when last time but one at p_1, has been all the time travelling outwards, and is now at Q_1, P_1 Q_1 being equal to p_1 P_1 ; and similarly we get other points of another whorl Q_4 Q_3 Q_2 Q_1, the radial breadth a b, between the two whorls being everywhere equal to the distance traversed by light during one revolution of the planet. Outside this whorl there is another, another beyond that, and so on for as many whorls, in all, as the planet has made revolutions since it first began to cast a shadow. The radial breadth between two successive whorls is always the distance traversed by light during a revolution of the planet, and as the distance of the whorls increases this breadth bears a smaller and smaller proportion to the size of the whorl, whose shape therefore becomes more and more nearly circular, though of course there is always the gap P_1 Q_1 between the two ends. In the case of our earth this gap is equal to light's journey in a year, or to about one-third of the distance separating us from the nearest fixed star ; yet the greatest radius of the whorl corresponding to the year 881 of our era exceeds the least in no greater degree than 1,000 exceeds 999.

It is strange to reflect that this mighty shadow-whorl is even now conveying into depths of space, so remote that to our conceptions their distance is infinite, a material record of the actual beginning of our earth's existence as a shadow-throwing body. All the other planets of our own system, and whatever worlds there are circling around the multitudinous suns peopling space, have in like manner their vast whirling shadows, various in shape according to the varying motions of the planets, and greater or less in their extension according to the greater or less duration of planetary life. These mighty interlacing shadows are all the time in motion with a velocity altogether beyond our conceptions, yet so minute, compared with the dimensions of the shadow, that hundreds of years produce no appreciable change in the *shape* of the remoter whorls. It will be understood, of course that the shadows are not such shadows as human vision could perceive. Neither light-waves nor the absence of light-waves in the æther of space could be recognised as we recognise light and darkness. Only when some opaque object is placed in any region of space can ordinary vision determine whether light is passing there or not. Moreover, the shadows I have been speaking of are not black shadows even in this sense. They are only regions of space where the light which would else have arrived from the Sun has been to some finite, but very small, degree reduced through the interposition of a planet. Yet it is easy to conceive that beings living in the universe of æther, as we live in our universe of matter, might clearly perceive these shadows—these regions where the æther is less or more disturbed by the undulations forming what we call light ; and if we adopt the thought of Leibnitz, that the universe is the sensorium of God, then these mighty interlacing shadows swiftly rushing through His omnipresent brain convey to His mind such evidence as their shape and nature can afford respecting the past history of the worlds peopling space. Here, also, let this strange point be noted. If a Being thus sentient, through and by all space, conceived the idea of straight lines after the manner described above— regarding, to wit, the prolongation of the line joining two points as that line in space from every point of which *at the moment* the two points would seem as one—then in His mind straight lines would correspond with the shadow axes just dealt with, and would only be really straight if the points were at rest. To His conceptions, then—always on the assumption I have just made—the straight line joining the sun and earth would, if produced far enough, become almost circular, and form an endless spiral. Still referring to His conceptions of such a line, not to the real shadows before dealt with, it would not matter whether the line joining the earth and sun were produced beyond the earth or beyond the sun ; in either case it would extend outwards into space in an infinite series of whorls. Thus two mighty series of interlacing whorls [1] would be mistakenly conceived of as a straight line.

It is something like this error which the advocates of the new ideas concerning space suggest as possibly affecting the ordinary geometrical conceptions respecting straight lines and so falsifying all our ideas respecting the universe. Conceive, they say, the primary geometrical ideas of creatures living in a world of one dimension. They would know nothing of breadth or thickness, but of linear extension only. And we can readily imagine that such creatures might conceive their world infinite in extension ; because all lines in it must be supposed capable of being indefinitely produced, still remaining in it. Yet in reality the universe in which such creatures existed might be finite even as respects its single dimension ; for the line in which these imaginary creatures lived might be curved, and, returning into itself, be limited in actual length. Thus while a line could be infinitely produced in this singly dimensioned world, the world itself in which such infinite extension of lines could be effected would be finite. Conceive, again, the case of a world of two dimensions only—length and breadth without thickness. The creatures in this world would be mere surfaces, and their ideas would necessarily be limited to surfaces. All those portions of our geometry which relate to plane figures and plane curves would lie within their grasp, while

---

[1] The student of geometry will not need to be told that a spiral formed in the manner illustrated in the figure is what is called the spiral of Archimedes, and that for completeness it requires the second infinite series, travelling the other way round, but in other respects precisely like the first series, whorl for whorl. Each whorl of one series cuts each whorl of the other once, and once only.

not only would they be unable to deal with questions relating to solids or curved surfaces, or curved lines not lying
in one plane, but the very idea of a third dimension
would be utterly inconceivable by them. Now, while these
creatures might have, as we have, the conception of straight
lines, and might postulate, as we do, that such lines when
finite may be indefinitely produced, so that they would have
ideas like ours respecting infinite extension in length and
breadth, it might very well be that the surface in which they
lived, being curved and re-entering into itself, would no
more be infinite than the surface of a globe or an egg.
Moreover, and this is a point very specially insisted upon by
those whose reasoning I am reproducing, it might well be
that different portions of the curved surface in which they
resided might be differently curved (as the end of an egg is
differently curved from the middle parts), and geometrical
relations derived from the experience of creatures living in
one portion of this curved surface might not by any means
correspond with those which they would have deduced had
their lot been cast in another portion of the same surface.
For instance, in the case of two triangles belonging to one
portion of the surface, two sides enclosing an angle of
one might be severally equal to two sides enclosing an angle
of the other, and the perfect equality of the two triangles
might be tested by superposition in our region of this surface
world ; but a triangle having two sides and the enclosed
angle respectively equal to those of another in a different
part of that world, might not admit of being superposed on
this last. This can easily be shown by drawing two triangles,
one on the end of an egg and the other on the middle of
the egg, each triangle having two sides of given length and
at a given inclination : it will be found that if the corresponding pieces of shell are cut out they cannot be exactly
superposed. Not only is this so, but if two triangles, each
having two sides of given length and at a given inclination,
be drawn in different positions on the middle of the egg,
they cannot be superposed, simply because at that part of

the egg the curvatures in different directions are different. A line drawn lengthwise with respect to the egg belongs to a larger curve than a line drawn square to it. On the contrary, at the two ends of the egg, and there alone, the curvatures in all directions are alike, and therefore at either of these spots triangles of the kind described could be superposed, but not elsewhere. Thus the geometry of one part of such a surface differs essentially from the geometry of other parts, and creatures living on a portion of a surface of that kind would be altogether mistaken in supposing that throughout · their world the same geometrical laws held which experience derived from their own region of that world seemed to suggest.

The application of all this is obvious. We live in a world of three dimensions, and cannot conceive the existence of a fourth dimension. Length, breadth, and thickness seem, of necessity, to be the only possible measures of space. But as creatures living in a world of one dimension would be mistaken in assuming, as they unquestionably would, that there could be no other dimension—as, again, creatures living in a world of two dimensions would be mistaken in assuming that a third dimension was impossible— so may we be mistaken in assuming that there can be no other dimension than length, breadth, and thickness. Hence those who adopt the reasoning I have described believe in the possible existence of a fourth dimension in space. Nor can any reason be perceived why a fifth or sixth dimension or an infinite number of dimensions, may not be regarded as possible, if the reasoning be only admitted on which has been based the possibility of a fourth dimension.

Again, as creatures living in a world of one dimension or of two dimensions might mistakenly imagine their world infinite in extension in its single dimension or in its two dimensions—whereas in one case it might be any closed curve, and in the other any continuous curved surface—so may we also be mistaken in supposing our world infinite in extension throughout its three dimensions. It may in some

way (which we can no more conceive than creatures possessed with the idea that they lived in a world of two dimensions could conceive the idea of the curvature of their world,
which, of course, involves really a third dimension) possess
a kind of curvature which makes it a world of four dimensions (or more), and may be no more infinite than the circuit of a ring or the surface of a globe is infinite.

Yet again, the geometry of creatures living on a curved
line or on a curved surface, but who supposed they lived on
a straight line or a plane surface, would *pro tanto* be inexact.
For instance, creatures living on the surface of a sphere
enormously large compared with their own dimensions,
would readily deduce the relation that the three angles of a
triangle are equal to two right angles, for their plane geometry would be as ours ; yet this relation would not be strictly
true for their world, the three angles of a triangle described
on a spherical surface being constantly in excess of two
right angles. In like manner the relations of our geometry, linear, plane, and solid, may be inexact. The lines
we consider straight lines may in reality be curved. Our
parallel lines may in reality, if only produced far enough,
meet on both sides, just as two parallel lines marked on a
sphere meet necessarily if produced, and in fact enclose a
space. Or, instead of that, a contrary relation may hold,
and whereas, according to our present geometry, a straight
line through a given point must occupy a certain definite
position if it is not to meet another straight line (in the same
plane), however far it may be produced, it *may* be that in
reality the former line might be swung round through some
finite though small angle, and in every one of the positions it
thus assumed possess the property of parallelism, never meeting the other line, however far both might be produced.[1]

---

[1] This is no mere *reductio ad absurdum*. Lobatchowsky, who has
been compared by a skilful student of the new ideas with Copernicus,
has framed a system of geometry on this very assumption. Before
quoting Professor Clifford's account of Lobatchowsky's work in this
direction, I venture to quote Clifford's remarks on the general question,
in order that the reader may not imagine that what I have said above

Thus, by conceiving the possibility of a fourth dimension in space, we find ourselves freed from the difficulties which our present geometrical conceptions force upon us. The universe need no longer be regarded as infinite. The straight lines which had been so troublesome are no longer troublesome, because they are no longer straight, but share the curvature of space. We may produce them as much as we please, but they all come round to the same point again.

respecting the new geometry is drawn from my own imagination only. I remind the reader that Professor Clifford was a skilful analytical mathematician, and that he was professedly expounding the ideas of Helmholtz, Riemann, Lobatchowsky, and others of admitted skill in mathematics. ' The geometer of to-day,' says Clifford, ' knows nothing about the nature of actually existing space at an infinite distance ; he knows nothing about the properties of this present space in a past or a future eternity. He knows, indeed, that the laws assumed by Euclid are true with an accuracy that no direct experiment can approach, not only in this place where we are, but in places at a distance from us that no astronomer has conceived ; but he knows this as of Here and Now ; beyond his range is a There and Then of which he knows nothing at present, but may ultimately come to know more. So there is a real parallel between the work of Copernicus and his successors on the one hand, and the work of Lobatchowsky and his successors on the other. In both of these the knowledge of immensity and eternity is replaced by knowledge of Here and Now. *And in virtue of these two revelations* ' (the italics are mine), ' *the idea of the Universe, the Macrocosm, the All, as subject of human knowledge, and therefore of human interest, has fallen to pieces.*' Now the work of Lobatchowsky is thus described by Clifford : ' He admitted that two straight lines cannot enclose a space, or that two lines which once diverge go on diverging for ever. But he left out the postulate about parallels ' (viz. that there is one position, and one only, in which a straight line drawn through a point is parallel to a given straight line). ' Lobatchowsky supposed instead that there was a finite angle through which the second line might be turned after the point of intersection had disappeared at one end before it reappeared at the other.' This angle depends on the distance of the point from the line in such sort that the three angles of a triangle shall always be less than two right angles by a quantity proportional to the area of the triangle. ' The whole of this geometry,' proceeds Clifford, ' is worked out in the style of Euclid, and the most interesting conclusions are arrived at.'

This at least will happen 'on the supposition that the curvature of all space is nearly uniform and positive' (that is, of the same nature as the curvature of a nearly globe-shaped surface considered with reference to the portion of space enclosed within it ; for, considered with reference to 'all outside,' the curvature of a globe is negative). Professor Clifford thus sums up the benefits arising from these new ideas on the supposition just mentioned :—

'In this case, the universe, as known, is again a valid conception, for the extent of space is a finite number of cubic miles. And this comes about in a curious way. If you were to start in any direction whatever, and move in that direction in a perfectly straight line, according to the definition of Leibnitz, after travelling a most prodigious distance, to which ' the distance of the nearest star[1] ' would be only a few steps, you would arrive at—this place. Only, if you had started upwards, you would appear from below. Now, one of two things would be true. Either, when you had got half-way on your journey, you came to a place which is opposite to this, and which you must have gone through, whatever direction you started in' (just as, in whatever direction an insect might travel from any point on a sphere, he would pass through the point opposite from his starting-place, and that when he was half-way round) ; ' or else all paths you could have taken diverge entirely from each other till they meet again at this place ' (just as the various paths by which an insect might proceed from any point on an anchor ring, moving always directly forwards, would all bring him back to his starting-place, but would have no other point in common). ' In the former case, every two straight lines meet in two points ; in the latter, they meet only in one. Upon this supposition of a positive curvature, the whole of geometry is far more complete and interesting; the principle of duality, instead of half-breaking down over metric relations, applies to all propositions without exception. In fact, I do not mind confessing that I personally have often found relief from the

---

[1] I have here departed from the text, but, that I may not be suspected of vitiating the passage, I quote Clifford's exact words : 'a most prodigious distance,' he says, 'to which the parallactic unit—200,000 times the diameter of the earth's orbit—would be only a few steps.' I must confess I cannot see the advantage of inventing a word, and giving a roundabout explanation of it, when the thing really signified is extremely simple. Science does not require to be thus fenced round from ordinary apprehension by sesquipedalian verbal stakes.

dreary infinities of homaloidal space' (that is, space where straight lines are straight, and planes plane; from the Greek ὁμαλός, *level*) 'in the consoling hope that, after all, this other may be the true state of things.'

Now, with all respect for the distinguished mathematicians who have adopted the method of reasoning which I have briefly sketched, and which Professor Clifford thus eloquently sums up, I submit that the whole train of reasoning is geometrically objectionable, and that the very words in which those who adopt it are compelled to clothe their arguments and to express their conclusions should suffice to show this. To begin with, although it is unquestionably true that our ideas respecting the geometrical point, line, plane, circle, and so forth, are originally derived from experience, they in truth transcend experience. Thus, as the ancient geometers are said to have drawn figures on sand to illustrate their reasoning, and these figures were necessarily altogether imperfect representations of the figures as geometrically defined, we can imagine a gradually increasing accuracy in draughtsmanship, until at length only such lines as Rutherford has been able to draw on glass—10,000, if I remember rightly, to the inch—might be used, or even lines very much finer. Yet the lines so drawn only differ in degree, so far as their departure from geometrical perfection is concerned, from the lines drawn on sand. We can imagine a continual increase of fineness until at length the errors from exactness would be less than those ethereally occupied spaces, between the ultimate atoms of bodies, which lie beyond the range of our microscopes. We might conceive a yet further increase of fineness, until irregularities in the actual constitution of the ether itself took the place of the gross irregularities of the lines once drawn on the sand. Or such irregularities might in turn be conceived to be reduced to their million-millionth parts. Yet we are still as remote as ever from the geometrical line, simply because that is a conception suggested by ordinary lines, not a reality which can under any circumstances actually exist. And so of the straightness of lines, the planity of surfaces, and

other like geometrical conceptions : they are transcendental-
isms suggested (only) by experience, not in reality comparable
with them any more than infinity of space is comparable
with mere immensity.   To say, therefore, that geometrical
lines, surfaces, and so forth, may be imperfect because space
itself may be discontinuous, is to assert of them that possibly they may not be geometrical lines, but only exceedingly
delicate lines of the ordinary kind.   To say again that
geometrically straight lines may have their straightness
vitiated by the curvature of space, is to say that they are
not geometrically straight lines, but curved.   I was about to
say that it is as inconceivable that a straight line can, when
produced far enough, return into itself, as to say that two
things of any kind being added to two other things of the
same kind, make three or five things of that kind, and not
four ; but I remember that, among other objections to the
validity of our primary conceptions, one has been urged
against the mistaken notion that *ex necessitate* two and two
make four.   There may be regions of space or portions of
eternity where, when two things are added to two, the sum
is greater or less than four, and where in general our fundamental ideas about number may be altogether incorrect ;
and in those or other regions or times straight lines may be
curved, and level surfaces uneven.   Space also may there
and then be discontinuous, the interstices being neither void
nor occupied space ; and time may proceed discontinuously,
being interrupted by intervals which are neither void nor
occupied time.   It can only be in those regions of space
and in those portions of eternity that beings exist who can
conceive the possibility of the creatures spoken of by
Helmholtz, Clifford, and others, as having only length without breadth or thickness, or only length and breadth without
thickness. *Here* and *now* I apprehend that, though we may
speak of such creatures, we cannot possibly conceive of them
as actually existent.

We might on this account, indeed, dismiss the one-dimen-
sioned and two-dimensioned creatures and their mistaken

notions, which cannot possibly affect ourselves who are unable to conceive either them or their notions. But we may
admit for the sake of argument the possible existence and
the possible mistakes of such creatures, and yet find no
reason whatever to admit the possibility of a fourth dimension in space. Take the creatures living in a surface. So
long as the experience of such creatures was not opposed to
the requirements of plane geometry, their conceptions and
their experience would alike conform to the relations of *our*
plane geometry. But if, after gradually widening their experience, they discovered that these relations were not
strictly fulfilled—that, for instance, the three angles of a
triangle were appreciably greater than two right angles when
the triangle was very large—the existence of a third dimension would present itself to their conceptions, simply because
it had in effect, as their geometricians would explain, become
sensible to their experience. Its possibility would never
have been beyond their power of conception, and it is not
at all clear that such creatures, even without the lessons of
actual experience, might not conceive the possible existence
of matter on one side or the other of the surface in which
they lived. In fact, it is not easy to see what should prevent
them. Moreover, when they had made the discovery of a
third dimension in their own world, by finding in fact that
the surface in which they lived was not plane, they would be
unable to 'find relief from the dreary infinities of homaloidal
space in the consoling hope' that their world, being curved,
might therefore contain a finite number of square miles.
They would simply have found that what had seemed the
universe to them was in point of fact not the universe; that
the infinities of length and breadth which they had imagined
as existing in their world lay really outside of it, in company
with another infinity of which they had before (on Helmholtz's assumption as to their mental condition) formed no
conception. If we are really to admit with Helmholtz and
Clifford the possible existence of creatures of one dimension
or of two dimensions, and also to accept as certain the

theory of these mathematicians that creatures of this kind could form no conception of dimensions other than those of their own persons, then we must accept all the consequences of these (unfortunately inconceivable) conceptions. Not only must we assert with Helmholtz and Clifford that these creatures would have been mistaken at first in supposing their world necessarily infinite in the dimensions it possessed, but we must admit that they would have been mistaken later in supposing that the finiteness of their world was any proof of the finiteness of length and breadth. They would quite erroneously have come to the conclusion that they had mastered their old difficulties about infinite extension in these dimensions. The consoling hope which would buoy them up after their discovery would be an entirely deceptive one. Their world would be simply a spherical, spheroidal, or otherwise-shaped surface in space, surrounded on all sides by infinities, not only of length and breadth, but of depth also. Their second mistake would, in fine, be as preposterous as would have been the theory, could sane geographers ever have entertained it, that when our own earth had been shown to be a globe, the plane of the horizon had been proved not to be infinite, but to contain a finite number of square miles. If we must accept so much of the argument advanced by Helmholtz and supported by Clifford, the true analogue of the reasoning of the bi-dimensionists, on the part of us who are tri-dimensionists, would be *this*—that we may one day discover the part of the universe we inhabit to be finite, the length and breadth and depth of our universe lying within the real infinities of length and breadth and depth, while to these infinities a fourth infinity, of a kind which we are at present unable to conceive, would by that discovery have been added to those which we already find sufficiently overwhelming. Thus the ' consoling hope ' of Professor Clifford, rightly apprehended, is in reality but a fresh cause of despair.

In fact, it is easy to perceive on *à priori* grounds that this must be the case. For if we imagine a linear creature of advanced ideas arguing with less thoughtful fellow-lines as to the existence of breadth as well as length, we see that his argument would run somewhat on this wise : 'You imagine mistakenly, my linear friends, that *all* points lie in our line ; but there may be, and I believe for my own part there are, points not in our line at all.' He would not say, 'on one side of it or on the other,' simply because the conception of sides to their linear universe could not have been formed by his hearers   So with the planar folk.   An advanced surface would reason that all lines and points were not necessarily in their world, but might be above or below their level.   This idea, of points outside the linear world in one case, or of points and lines outside the surface world in the other, would be an absolutely essential preliminary to any argument in favour of the possible curvature of a world of either kind, and therefore of the possible finiteness of either world.   We can only make the analogy complete by reasoning that possibly there may be points outside what we call space, thence prove the possible curvature of space, and so infer the finiteness of space.   But the possible finiteness of space established by the assumption that there may be points outside of it, is not consoling to those who find the infinities of homaloidal space dreary ; and the fourth dimension called upon to relieve us from the dreary infinities of length, breadth, and depth, would only introduce a more awful infinity, just as surface infinity is infinitely vaster than linear infinity, and infinity of volume infinitely vaster than infinity of surface.   Fortunately, length, breadth, and depth are the only conceivable infinities of space.   The fearful quadri-dimensional infinity is as one of the spirits from the vasty deep over which Glendower boasted that he possessed controlling power.   We may *speak* of infinities thus unknown, but, so far as conceiving them is concerned, 'they will not come when we do call for them.'

I have said that the very words in which the advocates of the new ideas respecting space are compelled, not only to clothe their arguments, but to express their ideas, suffice to show that those ideas are geometrically objectionable ; and, so far as their arguments are concerned, I think I have proved this. As for their conclusion, it seems only necessary to point out, that to say the extent of space is a finite number of cubic miles, is in reality equivalent to saying that it has a limiting surface : now, the mind is unable to conceive a surface which has not space on both sides of it. Thus there must, according to our conceptions, be space outside the surface supposed to include all space—which is absurd. I may add, though the argument is complete already, that whether a straight line as defined by Leibnitz can or cannot, when produced sufficiently far, return to the point to which it started, it is certain that the straight line as defined by Euclid cannot do so, nor can the straight line as conceived by Newton, or probably by any mathematician of geometrical tendencies. For Euclid defines a straight line as lying evenly between its extreme points ; and a straight line which extends from one point and after an enormous journey returns, no matter by what course, to a point close by its starting-point (not to carry it on to the starting-point itself) cannot possibly be regarded as lying evenly between the starting-point and the point close by, which points are its extremities. And Newton, as we know, regarded a straight line as produced by the continuous motion of a point tending continually in one unchanged direction ; whereas a point which, after—no matter how long after—leaving a fixed point, is found travelling towards that point, can certainly not be regarded as travelling in the same direction all the time, but, on the contrary, its course must in the interim have changed through four right angles.

But after all, the infinities which surround us—not only the infinities of time and space, but the infinities also of matter, of energy, and of vitality, the infinity of the minute as well as the infinity of the vast—though inexpressibly awful, are not in truth 'dreary.' It is, in fact, in such infinities alone that we find an answer to the misgivings that arise continually within us as our knowledge widens. Were the universe finite in extent or in duration, the discoveries by which science is continually widening her domain in space and time would perplex us even more than they do at present. We should have to believe in the constant enormous expenditure of forms of force which there is no replacing, and whose transmutation to other forms implies a real waste of energy, if only the total supply of force is finite. As the action of processes of evolution is more clearly recognised, and seen to extend over longer and longer periods of time, we should seem to be continually tending towards the belief that from the very beginning there has been *only* evolution. If time were regarded as finite, then the vast range of time over which the vision of science extends would seem dreary indeed, because, so far as the eye of science extends, no direct evidence of a First Cause could be perceived. So also of the minute. If men could really penetrate to the ultimate constitution of matter —if they could perceive the operations of Nature within the corpuscles—we should find no means of conceiving how possibly the seemingly wasted energies of the perceptible universe may have their use in processes affecting matter beyond our powers of perception. And it is only by imagining some such employment of the apparently lost energies of our universe that we can be led to the belief that our universe in turn receives constant supplies of energy from processes lost to our perceptions because of their vast- ness, as the processes taking place within the ether are lost to us because of their minuteness. Lastly, were it not for the infinities which are beyond our powers of conception, as well as of perception, we should be logically forced, as it seems to me, into direct antagonism to the doctrine of a Being working in and through all things and during all time. For, step by step, knowledge has passed onwards from the development of leaf and limb to the development of plant and animals, thence to the development of races and species, of flora and fauna, onwards still to the development of the earth and her fellow-worlds, the development of solar

systems; and science bides her time to recognise the laws
of development according to which systems of solar systems,
and even systems of higher orders, have come into existence.
In like manner, science has learned to look beyond the
death of individuals and races, to contemplate the death of
worlds, and systems of worlds, and systems of systems, to
the death eventually of all, and more than all, the known
portions of the universe.   Had we to do with the finite only,
in time and space, and in all that time and space contain,
we might well shudder at the dreary wastes thus presented
to us—space, time, matter, power, and vitality, all ultimately the spoil of Death.   Even if we could recognise a
Supreme Being existing amid these desolations, we could
not reverence mere immensity of extent and duration without control over the progress of events and without purpose
which could be conceived.   But seeing that it is not immensity, but infinity, we have to deal with, and perceiving that
our knowledge, no matter how widely it may extend its
domain, still has in reality but an evanescent range—for the
immense is nothing in presence of the infinite—we are no
longer forced to this 'abomination of desolation.'   Being
able to grasp the finite only, whereas the universe is infinite,
reason compels us to admit that we can know absolutely
nothing of the scheme of the universe.   It must ever remain
as unfathomable as the infinite depths of space, as immea-
surable as the infinite domain of time.   We may reject this
theory or that theory of supervision or control, or plan or
purpose, or whatsoever name we choose to give to the un-
knowable relations between all things and their God.   When
men assure us that God wills this, or designs that, or will
bring about somewhat else, and still more when men pretend
to tell us the nature or ways of God, we may, from the
teachings of Nature, be able utterly to reject the doctrines
thus propounded.   But we cannot go further, and reject the
general doctrine with which these special doctrines have
been associated.   We can say truly that the idea of a personal God, whatsoever attributes may be assigned to such a

Being, is not only unintelligible, but utterly unimaginable ; and that those who tell us that they can conceive of such a Being, know not what they say ; but we cannot reject the doctrine because it is inconceivable, for we have seen that we cannot reject the doctrines of infinity of time and infinity of space. Nay, so far are we from being justified in rejecting the belief in a Supreme Being because we cannot conceive such a Being, that, on the contrary, no being of which we could conceive could possibly be the God of the utterly inconceivable universe. That God must of necessity be Himself inconceivable. The most earnest believers, as well as the exactest students of science, can have but *faith* ; they cannot *know* :—

> For knowledge is of things we see,
> And thou, O Lord, art more than they.

SCIENCE AND RELIGION.

I REPEATEDLY receive letters, doubtless from well-meaning but certainly from altogether mistaken persons, telling me that they fear the tendency of science, especially in its more recent developments, is irreligious. In some of these communications a special reason is given for this strange opinion —namely, the inconsistency, real or imagined, between some of the results to which modern science unmistakably points, and certain ideas which have been derived from poetical descriptions found in the Bible. So far as this particular form of objection is concerned I am at no pains to formulate a reply. It would be as reasonable to do so, I conceive, as it would be seriously to answer such a question as this, 'How can the Darwinian theory of the descent of man be reconciled with Job's statement (Job xxx. 29), "I am a brother to dragons?"' or this, 'How can the views of modern medical men be reconciled with Job's assertion (Job xxx. 27), "My bowels boiled and rested not?"' Moreover, the world is not interested (or should not be) in hearing the views of science as to the real meaning of words which even the theologians, after all the time and trouble they have given to a matter lying specially within their province, are not at one in interpreting. But when the question is of the truth of those scientific views which are oppugned, or as to the bearing of science generally on religion, the case is different. Science may reasonably—though at some risk of using time unprofitably—answer questions relating to the validity of scientific reasoning or to the influence of scientific discoveries on the human mind.

Now, the great objection raised against modern science appears to be in the main this, that it enlarges unduly our ideas of the vastness of God's domain in space, of the immensity of the time periods during which He acts, and, in fine, of His inconceivable power and wisdom. We may admire the wisdom of the Almighty, as shown in the pebble or the rock, in the flower or in the tree, in the insect or the animal—nay, we may even so far extend our vision as to recognise the laws under which a stratum, or a forest, or a race of animals, perhaps even a continent, or a flora, or a fauna, had their origin and passed through the various stages of development. But we must not extend our survey further. To see God's hand in these, His wisdom in the laws by which they are formed, is to be religious and good ; but to trace His power and wisdom on a larger scale is to be irreligious and wicked. Evolution on the small scale we may admit without harm, but to see evolution in the development of a world or a world-system, and still more to see evolution throughout the entire universe as revealed to man, this is 'to set God on one side in the name of Universal Evolution.'

It is unfortunate that those who take this view of the general scope of modern scientific research had not been careful at an earlier date to announce, when admitting the growth of a tree, a forest, or a flora, of an animal, a race, or a fauna, according to natural laws, and even explaining (as many of them did) the wonderful nature of the laws according to which such growths took place, that they wished it to be clearly understood that in thus recognising the action of law, they were rejecting the idea that the Almighty fashioned the plant or the animal, the forest or the race, the flora or the fauna, or indeed aught animate or inanimate, the development of which man is able to study through all its stages. Because, if it had been clearly understood that wherever they recognised growth and development as the results of law, they were assured such results could not possibly be attributed to the Almighty, science might, perhaps (though it seems unlikely), have been deterred from researches leading to the

distressing conclusion that there is development according
to law on the greater scale as well as on the less—nay, that
to all appearance law prevails throughout the entire domain
of the Almighty in space, and during the entire period of
time in which He acts—that is, throughout infinity of space,
and during eternity of time.

As regards the actual evidence of the vastness of space
and the immensity of time throughout which the action of
law extends, it may suffice to say that only those who are
absolutely steeped in ignorance (or drenched in dullness
of comprehension) can for a moment entertain doubt.   Unless the evidence given by earth and heaven has been
specially devised to mislead man, or unless the reasoning
powers bestowed on man by God have been given but to
lead him astray (conceptions alike blasphemous and unreasonable), there can be no manner of doubt that on the
one hand the universe is infinitely larger that it was supposed to be before the days of Copernicus and Kepler,
Galileo and Newton; or that, on the other hand, our
earth has lasted, and will last, thousands of times as long as
had been supposed before its structure had been examined ;
the·solar system millions of times as long as had been supposed before its movements had been studied; the galaxy of
stars yet longer ; the higher order of systems to which that
galaxy belongs for periods so vast that to all intents and
purposes they extend (in our conception) to absolute
eternity—in the past as in the future.

As to the influence which a result such a this should have
upon men's minds, it should perhaps suffice to say that
those who believe that the Almighty is all-wise as well as
all-powerful ought not to fear lest the discovery of truth
from the study of His universe shall produce evil effects.

But I go much further than this, and say that of all
possible forms of teaching, those derived from or based
upon science must be most beneficial in the religious sense
—not using the word science and religion in their ordinary
narrow significance, but in their widest and noblest. ' Doubt-

less,' as Herbert Spencer has well said, 'science is anta-
gonistic to the superstitions that pass under the name of
religion ; but not to the essential religion which these superstitions merely hide. Doubtless, too, in much of the science
that is current there is a pervading spirit of irreligion, but
not in the true science which has passed beyond the superficial into the profound.' Or, as Huxley has even more
pointedly remarked, 'True science and true religion are
twin-sisters, and the separation of either from the other is
sure to prove the death of both. Science prospers exactly
in proportion as it is religious, and religion flourishes in
exact proportion to the scientific depth and firmness of its
basis. The great deeds of philosophers have been less the
fruit of their intellect than of the direction of that intellect
by an eminently religious tone of mind. Truth has yielded
herself rather to their patience, their single-heartedness, and
their self-denial than to their logical acumen.'

But we may fairly go even further than this. We need
not be content to defend, or merely to justify, or even to
laud, science in its relation to religion. We may assert without fear of valid contradiction that the neglect of science is
irreligious. For what is such neglect (where men have time
and leisure for the work) but the refusal to study the works
of the Creator ? And in what position, logically, does a man
stand who praises the Creator in words, but declines to
study His creation ? 'Suppose,' says Spencer, 'a writer was
daily saluted with praises couched in superlative language.
Suppose the wisdom, the grandeur, the beauty of his works
were the constant topics of the eulogies addressed to him.
Suppose those who unceasingly uttered these eulogies on
his works were content with looking at the outside of them,
and had never opened them, much less tried to understand
them. What value should we put upon their praises ? What
should we think of their sincerity ? Yet, comparing small
things to great, such is the conduct of mankind in general
in reference to the universe and its cause.'

The study of science implies the belief that God's works

D

are worth study, the fullest recognition that the Author of those works is worthy of our reverence. It is the truest kind of homage, in that it is not homage expressed merely in words, but homage shown in work, in service, in sacrifice. The man of science, in fine, refuses to offer to the Almighty 'the unclean sacrifice of a lie,' but he offers Him instead (in the search for truth), the sacrifice of time, of labour, and of thought. His very questions imply his fullness of faith :—

This is his homage to the mightier powers,
To ask his boldest question, undismayed
By muttered threats that some hysteric sense
Of wrong or insult will convulse the throne
Where wisdom reigns supreme.

A MENACING COMET.

THE comet which was seen in the southern hemisphere during the earlier part of the year 1880 attracted more attention, when it had passed from view, than it did during the brief period of its visibility. In fact, when its movements were considered, it was found to be, in some respects, one of the most interesting comets ever seen by man. Views advanced respecting it—not by fanciful theorisers, but by mathematicians of eminence by no means prone to adopt wild and startling ideas—suggest the possibility, nay, even some degree of probability, that this comet may bring danger to the solar system. There is not, indeed, any reason to fear that any violent shock or sudden collision will disturb the movements of the sun or of the planets. Astronomy has long since learned that comets are not to be feared on account of any direct effects which their encounter with any member of the solar system could produce. But there are indirect effects which, while leaving the sun and every member of his family unchanged in position and undisturbed as to their motions, would seriously affect all creatures living on our earth and whatever other planets may at the present time be inhabited. It is the possibility that hereafter, and perhaps at no very distant period, the comet of 1880 may produce such effects as these, that I have now to discuss. I may remark that most of the considerations which I shall here present have been suggested to me since I discussed the subject in my lectures in Australia and the United States.

Soon after the comet of 1880 was discovered, the observations showed that the comet was passing away from
its point of nearest approach to the sun.   This point,
passed probably on 27th January 1880, was found to be
singularly near to the sun.   Only in two other cases had a
comet been recorded as coming so near to the sun at its
perihelion passage.   The comet of 1668, according to the
rough observations made at Goa, in India, had an orbit passing within 40,000 or 50,000 miles of the sun's surface.   The
orbit of the comet of 1843 passed within some 190,000
miles of the solar surface ; but according to certain estimates, the comet passed even nearer to the sun than this.
The comet of February 1880 passed within about the same
distance of the sun as that of 1843.

But this was not all.   A careful study of the observations made on the comet of the year 1880, showed that it
travelled on a path very similar to that pursued by the
comet of 1843 while in the neighbourhood of the sun.
Now, with regard to those parts of the path of either comet
(assuming they are really different bodies) which lie far
away from the sun, the astronomer can form no definite
opinion.   It may seem strange, perhaps, to those unfamiliar
with the subject of cometic astronomy, to hear that the
astronomer knows more about one part of a comet's path
than about another.   For it is known that a body like a
comet travelling round the sun in a closed orbit—that is,
in an oval or ellipse—would continue always to pursue
that path unless disturbed by the planets, and such disturbances as the planets can produce are not only slight in
themselves (in almost every case), but their effects are
calculable with great accuracy.   So that it might appear
as though when the astronomer had determined the track
of a comet along any portion of its orbit, he had determined
the orbit itself, and knew thenceforward what would be the
movements of the comet for a period practically illimitable.
A comet, one would suppose, must in this respect be similar
to a planet, and it is well known that the orbit of Uranus

was recognised long before that planet had traversed even
a tenth of its circuit; while the orbit of Neptune has formed
one of the items in our books of astronomy for the last
quarter of a century, though even now the planet has not
traversed a quarter of its orbit since first discovered.
But as a matter of fact the astronomer is often quite
unable to determine the position of the remoter parts of
a comet's orbit, while he may have very satisfactory knowledge as to the position of the part nearest to the sun.
For, most of the larger comets travel on paths of great
eccentricity. Now, the sun occupies that focus of a
comet's path which lies nearest the part of the path where
the comet is seen, and the comet moves with great velocity
round this part of its path, changing its position with respect
to the sun very quickly. If we could determine either the
exact shape of this part of the path, or the *exact* velocity of
the comet's motion at any point of it, we should be able to
infer the shape of the whole path. But a very slight error
in determining the position of the comet on any day, causing a correspondingly small error in determining, either
the shape of the orbit near the sun, or the comet's velocity
in that orbit, will introduce a very large error in the estimated position of the remoter parts of the comet's path.
As the comet's head has not, like a planet, a well-defined
disc, and the nucleus is generally irregular in shape, it becomes difficult to determine the exact position of the centre
of gravity. Then the comets of most eccentric orbit remain for a short time only in view. Thus the periods of
most of those comets have not been satisfactorily determined, and it is no unusual thing to hear that one eminent
mathematician (Oppolzer, for instance) has assigned a
period of seven or eight thousand years to a comet, while
another of equal skill (Hind, let us say) has assigned to the
same comet a period of only seven or eight hundred years,
or perhaps a period of seventy or eighty thousand.

The comet of 1843 affords a striking example of such
diversity of opinion. The most careful investigation of

that comet's path was perhaps that made by Professor Hubbard of Washington, who assigned to the comet a period of 533 years. But, as Professor Newcomb well remarks, the velocity corresponding to this period is so near the velocity which would correspond to a period of 5000, or 50,000, or an infinite number of years, that the difference does not exceed the uncertainty of the observations. That is, an orbit of infinite extent, so far as the remote parts were concerned, would satisfy the observations made on the comet in the nearer part of its course. On the other hand, a period much shorter than 533 years would serve almost equally well to reconcile all the observations. It was re-marked at a recent meeting of the Astronomical Society of London, that all sorts of periods have been found for the comet, ranging from seven years to 600 years. Thirty-seven years was one of the periods suggested.

I believe, but have not the book by me for reference, that in his Familiar Lectures Sir John Herschel adopts this very period of 37 years as the one which in his judgment seems to accord best with the observations. This period would have brought back the comet early in the year 1880. As the comet seen in February 1880 not only appeared at the right time, according to this view, but according to several skilful computers, travelled in the same path, a certain high degree of probability is suggested in favour of the theory that the comet of 1880 and that of 1843 are one and the same body. Mr. Hind, the Superintendent of the Nautical Almanac, is one of the mathematicians who has found the orbits of the two comets to be alike. 'He treated the question from several points of view, using observations by Dr. Gould at Cordoba, and by Mr. Ellery at Melbourne, as well as the rough places sent over by Mr. Gill, of the Cape Town Observatory, and in each case he obtained elements sensibly the same as those of the comet of 1843.' Professor Weiss, of Vienna, has computed the path which the comet of 1843 would have pursued in the heavens, on the assumption that the perihelion passage took place on January 27 this year; and he finds a very close agreement with the places given by Mr. Gill. Again, Mr. Hind, in a letter addressed to one of the secretaries of the Astronomical Society of London, says : 'Professor Winnecke, judging from a comparison of the places deduced from the orbit of the great comet of 1843 with Gould's position on 4th February, and Gill's later rough ones, appears to be of opinion that the identity of the comets of 1843 and 1880 hardly admits of a doubt.' And lastly, Dr. Gould, of Cordoba, from the positions observed by himself on February 6, 12, and 18, deduces a set of elements agreeing closely with those found by Mr. Hind, ' and bearing a striking resemblance to those found by Hubbard for the comet of 1843.'

But the result thus apparently established is so remarkable and (as will presently appear) so important in its bearing on our views respecting the future of the comet or comets in question, that we must pause to consider a little more closely the evidence bearing upon it. We shall find that a part of this discussion of the evidence bears also on the results which the movements of the comet may be expected to bring about.

In the first place, it is to be remembered that Hubbard's value of the period of the comet of 1843 is that which on the whole accords best with the observations. Hubbard himself called special attention to the large changes which might be made in the period without doing actual violence to the observations. He showed that a period of 175 years, for instance (taking that period because there was and is some reason for regarding the comet of 1843 as identical with that of 1668), will accord very fairly with the observations. Dr. Gould goes a little further, and shows that the period of 37 years, which is at present chiefly in question, involves no important correction of any single observation made on the comet of 1843. But still a period of over 500 years was certainly indicated by the evidence then obtained; and while a period of 200, or 175, or 150 years, may be admitted, a period of less than 100 years would make all the observations of 1843 erroneous *in the same direction.* This is a very important consideration. It must be explained that even the period of 533 years selected by Professor Hubbard does not account *exactly* for all the observations of 1843. The positions calculated from that period are some a little different in one direction, others a little different in another direction, from the observed positions. But the differences are, on the whole, reduced to a minimum by this value. In this latter respect it is to be preferred to all others ; but any period from 150 years upwards possesses the former quality of giving differences now in one direction, now in the other, between the calculated and the observed places of the comet. When we note, however, that a period of 37 years would cause all the calculated positions to err in the same direction,[1] the importance of this consideration is obvious. But it is in some degree diminished, as Dr. Gould points out (and as Professor Hubbard had earlier noticed), when we note that such systematic discordances would necessarily exist if the part of the comet regarded as the centre of gravity were not so in reality.

But while we do not seem absolutely precluded from accepting this period of about 37 years (more exactly 36 years $10\frac{2}{3}$ months) by the observations made in 1843, there seems to be a valid objection against the assumption of so short a period, in the circumstance that a comet so remarkable in appearance, returning to perihelion at such short intervals, ought to have been seen many times within the historical period. Now the comet of 1668 has been

[1] The astronomer will understand that I do not use the word direction here with any reference to the position of the comet on the sky, but mean that the differences all have the same relation to the estimated orbit of the comet. In the case of the longer period, one discrepancy would be such as to suggest a lengthening, while another would be such as to suggest a shortening of the estimated period ; in the case of a period of 37 years, every discrepancy would be such as to indicate a lengthening of the period. In other words, the discrepancies would be systematic,

supposed to be identical with that of 1843, and so has that
of 1702, about which, however, very little is known. Dr.
Gould also considers that the comet of 1538 may have been
the same comet which was seen in 1843 ; and he asks
whether the observations of the second comet of 1806 may
not be compatible with the orbit of that comet. But we
can certainly reject the second comet of 1806 (the first is
out of the question) as having had a very different orbit.
We may also reject the comet of 1702. Mr. Hind says he
can say with confidence that the comet of 1695 cannot be
the same body as the comet of 1843. The comet of the
year 1668 is the only one which can be regarded as moving
in the required orbit.

Now, although it is likely enough that a comet moving
in so eccentric an orbit as that along which the comet of
1843 travels, might escape detection at any particular return to the sun's neighbourhood, yet we can hardly imagine
that it would be unseen for so long a period as 175 years
(from 1668 to 1843), if it really completed the circuit of its
orbit in 37 years. It must be remembered that the comet
of 1843 was a very remarkable object. Not only had it
a tail of amazing length (sixty-five degrees on the heavens,
and 150 millions of miles in actual length), but its head was
exceedingly brilliant ; insomuch that it was seen as a bright
body within less than two degrees (about four sun-breadths)
from the sun. It is true that the comet of the year 1880
was not nearly so striking in appearance. ‘No nucleus was
at any time seen,’ says Dr. Gould, ‘the head appearing
cloudlike and filmy and elongated in the direction of the
tail, which it did not very much surpass in brightness.’ He
remarks on the great faintness of both tail and head and the
inordinate length of the tail, which was thirty-five degrees
long on 2nd February, and thirty-seven degrees long when
last seen on 14th February, when it was seen with great
difficulty, and was nearly of the same brightness throughout
its length. It was brightest on 7th or 8th February, when
its length was about forty degrees and its greatest breadth

a degree and a half, but its brightness was not superior to that of the Milky Way in Taurus.   It must be remembered, however, that the great diminution of the comet in brightness since 1843 (assuming the comet of the year 1880 to be really the same object) would lead us to believe that at its returns before 1843 the comet was even brighter than in that year, and would increase rather than diminish the difficulty we are considering.   If the comet is continually diminishing in splendour, yet could be seen close to the sun in 1843, how utterly improbable it seems that at any previous visit it could have escaped detection.

This being the case, while yet the evidence is clear that the comets of 1843 and 1880 travel in the same path if they are not one and the same comet—at any rate in the same path so far as the portion of the path nearest to the sun is concerned—we are led, or rather forced, to one of two conclusions.   Either the track of the comet of 1843 is traversed by another comet and possibly by several others, or else the period of this comet has undergone a remarkable diminution.

Now, although it appears likely enough that the enormous meteor flights known to follow in the track of certain comets, and possibly in the track of every comet, might be visible as cloudlike objects, nothing has yet shown that a meteoric swarm would appear as a comet with a nucleus, head, and tail.   It must be remembered that the tail of a comet is something quite distinct from the meteoric train. It not only lies always in a different position, but is constantly and rapidly shifting in position.   Moreover, so far as can be judged from spectroscopic analysis, the tail of a comet is not constituted of multitudes of small bodies shining, as a meteoric flight would shine, by simply reflecting sunlight. It seems unlikely, then, though it cannot be said to be altogether impossible, that a comet should be followed at a great distance by another travelling in the same track.   Thus we are led to adopt as a more probable interpretation of observed facts respecting the comets of 1843 and 1880, that they really are the same object, but that the period, formerly long, has been reduced to 37 years, and may be reduced still further. At any rate, this view must be regarded as worthy of consideration, if it shall appear that there is anything in the circumstances under which the body travels which might lead to a great diminution of its period.

The idea that the comet of 1880 may be identical, not only with that of 1843, but with that of 1668, the period having been reduced from 175 years to 37, was suggested at the Astronomical Society in April 1880 by Mr. Marth, a mathematician of great skill, and well known for the zeal with which he attacks problems relating to the movements of the satellites of Saturn and Mars. He says :—

Supposing the comet of 1843 is the same as that of 1668, it would not be very wonderful that it should reappear after 37 years instead of 175 years. The velocity of a body moving in the solar system depends simply on its distance from the sun and on the period of revolution.[1] If the velocity is reduced by a resisting medium, there will be a reduction of the period, and there is nothing whatever unreasonable in the supposition that, however weak the corona may be, its resistance would have a very great effect upon the motion of a comet which rushes through it : so that I should not be at all surprised if it should turn out that this comet of 1880 is the same as the comet of 1843 and that of 1668, and that its revolution has been so much affected that possibly it may return in, say, seventeen years.

Now, if this theory of the comet of 1880 be the true one, we are somewhat more nearly interested in the matter than we are in most theories respecting comets. If already the comet experiences such existence in passing through the corona when at its nearest to the sun that its period undergoes a marked diminution, the effect must of necessity be increased at each return, and after only a few —possibly one or two—circuits, the comet will be absorbed by the sun. It will be remembered that Sir Isaac Newton recognised the possibility that this might happen to a comet

---

[1] I have altered the wording here and further on, in such a way as to avoid the use of technical expressions, but without altering the sense of the passage.

having such an orbit as that of the comet of 1680 (generally known as Newton's comet), and that he had considered the consequences might be full of danger to this earth. Yet he only dwelt on the danger arising, as he judged, from the addition of so much fuel to the solar fires. We know now that the real danger lies, not from the absorption of so much matter as may exist in a comet's head and nucleus, but from the conversion of the momentum of the swiftly rushing mass of the comet into heat, the thermal equivalent of its mechanical energy. Now at present, assuming the period of the comet to be thirty-seven years, the velocity of the nucleus when nearest to the sun must exceed 300 miles per second. As to the mass of the comet's head we can form no opinion. But we know that the relatively insignificant comet of 1866, called Tempel's—a comet which required a telescope to make it visible—is followed by millions of millions of meteoric masses, and that when our earth passes through this system of meteors, though they enter her atmosphere with a velocity of only about 39 miles per second, they are converted into glowing vapour in their passage through it. If we consider how far more densely aggregated the meteoric masses must be which form the nucleus, head, and train (not tail, *bien entendu*) of the comet of 1843, how much larger the individual meteors, and that the velocity at the time of their final absorption could not be less than ten times that with which the November meteors enter the earth's atmosphere, it will be evident that the danger of which Sir Isaac Newton spoke so impressively in his celebrated letter is by no means altogether fanciful. I have for my own part been long of opinion that the periodical increase of such stars as Mira (the Wonderful Star) in the Whale, and Eta of the ship Argo, is due to the motion of some large comet, followed by a meteoric train, about these two stars. I have indicated fully, in my 'Pleasant Ways in Science,' the reasons which induce me to believe that the outburst of the so-called 'new star' in the Northern Crown in 1686 is to be similarly explained. Without saying

that I consider there is absolute danger of a similar outburst
in the case of our own sun when the comet of 1843 shall
be absorbed by him (a result which will, in my opinion,
most certainly take place), I will go so far as to express my
belief that if ever the day is to come when 'the heavens
shall dissolve with fervent heat,' the cause of the catastrophe
will be the downfall of some great comet on the sun. I
believe the passage even of the head of a comet over the
earth would do little harm, for the simple reason that the
velocity with which the meteoric masses forming the head
would travel at the earth's distance from the sun would be
too small to lead to any very mischievous result. If the
shower of meteoric masses were very dense, the meteors
themselves being of the larger sort and so able to break
their way through the earth's atmosphere, the shower might
kill a few of the earth's inhabitants, or even many hundreds.
But there would be no widespread destruction of life. It
would be altogether otherwise, I believe, if a comet of
the larger sort fell into or were absorbed by the sun.
The danger would lie in the sun's own might, not in the
comet or its attendant train. The bodies forming the
head, nucleus, and train of the comet, would fall in immense numbers with enormous velocity, and each with
mighty momentum on the sun's fiery surface. Possibly
(in my opinion, probably) their most destructive work
would be accomplished below that surface, under the
still more stupendous[1] attractive energy of that smaller
because more condensed orb within, which I take to be the
true ruling centre of the solar system. It might well be
that the effects thus produced would be but transient. In a

---

[1] In one sense the attractive energy of the sun is the same, whether
his globe is as large as it appears to be or is enormously condensed
near the centre. But there is far greater potential energy in a condensed sun than in a rarer sun of the same mass. At the visible surface of the sun, solar gravity is some 29 times that at the surface of the
earth ; but if the entire mass of the sun were (for example) contained
in a globe no larger than the earth, gravity at the surface of such an
orb would be no less than 324,000 times greater than terrestrial gravity.

few weeks, possibly in a few days or even hours, the sun, excited for a while to intense heat and splendour, would resume his usual temperature, his usual lustre. Such, indeed, was the nature of the change which affected the so-called 'new star' in the Northern Crown. For a day or two it shone out with several hundred times its usual lustre, and doubtless it poured forth during those few days several hundred times its usual heat. Then gradually its fires cooled, its lustre diminished, and after a few weeks had passed it shone as it had shone before for hundreds of years, with the lustre of a ninth magnitude star only. But it is certain that, if there are planets circling around that remote sun, and if the ordinary light and heat of that orb sufficed for the requirements of the inhabitants of those orbs, the abnormal light and heat during the outburst in 1866 must have destroyed all living creatures from the face of each one of those worlds. It is equally certain that, if at any time a great comet falling directly upon the sun should, by the swift rush of its meteoric components, excite the frame of the sun to a lustre far exceeding that with which he at present shines, the sudden access of lustre and of heat would prove destructive to every living creature, or at any rate to all the higher forms of life upon this earth. And though in a few days the sun might resume his ordinary lustre, and no longer glow with abnormal heat, he would pour his rays on a family of worlds in which not one of the higher forms either of vegetable or animal life would remain in existence.

METEORIC DUST.

MR. A. C. RANYARD, secretary of the Astronomical Society, has recently called attention to the evidence which our earth's surface affords of her passage through meteoric systems. Meteoric dust has been collected on the summits of snow-covered mountains. In the snows of Scandinavia and Finland, or those lying far within the Arctic circle, hundreds of miles from any human habitation, particles of meteoric iron have been found. Iron dust has been gathered in ice-holes in Greenland. Nay, in matter raised from the bottom of deep oceans magnetic particles have been detected, which must have been deposited there recently, and can no otherwise have come there but from the air above those oceans, nor have reached that air except from interplanetary space. It is true that all this might have been confidently foreseen. We know in other ways that meteoric matter is constantly falling upon the earth. Yet there is a strange interest in the actual recognition of this cosmical dust. What Humboldt said of the larger meteoric masses which have fallen visibly upon the earth from inter-planetary space is true (with slight change) of these more subtle signs of the earth's passage through cosmical dust :—
'Accustomed to know non-telluric bodies solely by measure-ment, by calculation, and by the inferences of our reason, it is with a sense of wonder that we touch, weigh, and sub-mit to chemical analysis metallic and earthly masses apper-taining to the world without.'
I have had occasion, in discussing the shooting stars of

November 25-27 (the later November system, as it may be called), to consider the history of recent research into meteoric and cometic systems, already one of the most fruitful subjects of astronomical inquiry, and likely, unless I mistake, to lead to yet more important inferences and conclusions than have yet been even suggested. Mr. Raynard's speculations—for as yet we fear they can hardly be called theories—invite to a consideration of the results of those inquiries the history of which we have already given. Until it had been shown that meteors and comets are associated (in some way as yet not clearly understood), the only evidence we could obtain about meteoric systems was by the earth's actual encounter with them. As she circles year by year round her wide orbit, 185 million miles in diameter, her small globe (for in this relation it is almost infinitely minute) encounters such meteors as may happen to be crossing any point of her track at the moment of her arrival there. Multitudes of cosmical bodies may cross that track without her encountering them ; and moreover, for every meteor track which crosses the earth's there must be millions which do not. Thus even of meteor-systems which the earth can, on occasion, encounter, we may remain for ages ignorant, while of those which the earth never can encounter we must for ever remain ignorant, unless we can learn something of them in another way. The astronomer may detect the comet along whose track one of those meteor-systems, 'fathomless by man,' pursues its course around the sun. Then, though we may never know certainly the nature of that system, we may be able to infer its existence, and perhaps form some more or less probable surmise respecting its importance. And from the general evidence collected by astronomers about comets and comet systems, with such theories as they may hereafter be able to establish respecting the meteoric and cometic nature of certain solar appendages, we may learn the laws according to which the meteor families attending on the sun are distributed. But it is clear that our knowledge respecting meteors must for a long while be derived chiefly from the study of those meteors which actually reach the earth either as aerolites, as fireballs, or as shooting stars. In other words, our more intimate knowledge of meteors must be limited to those few meteoric systems which cross the ring of space traversed by the earth in her annual motion around the sun. How exceedingly minute the number of systems thus encountered must be when compared with the total number (even supposing the distribution uniform, instead of being, as it probably is, far denser near the sun than at the earth's distance) can be inferred from the consideration that if the earth's track—that is, the ring of space swept by her whole body and its atmospheric envelope—were represented by a circle of wire a yard in diameter, the thickness of the wire would be less than 1-600th part of an inch. Remembering this, and also that it is not the whole even of this relatively fine ring in space which is occupied by observers of meteors at any given instant, but only the minute portion of it which the earth at that instant occupies ; that the meteors which fall on the sunlit half of the earth are never seen, unless now and then an exceptionally large mass forces its way through the earth's atmospheric envelope ; that on the dark or night half of the earth few are on the look-out for meteors—we perceive that our knowledge of the meteoric systems in the solar domain must long remain exceedingly imperfect, nay, by comparison with the real vastness of the subject, must be all but evanescent.

But the same considerations which might well make astronomers despair of mastering this difficult subject enhance our wonder at the facts actually ascertained respecting meteor systems encountered by the earth. Already we have evidence that in her circuit round the sun she encounters more than 200 meteor systems, or, more strictly, that she passes through the orbits of so many systems. Again, from calculations based on the average number of shooting stars observed per hour at single stations, Professor Newton, of Yale College, United States, has estimated that in a

E

single year the earth encounters as many as 400 millions of meteors, from the largest aerolite down to the smallest body which could be seen in a good telescope as a shooting star, if by chance it passed athwart the telescopic field of view. Without laying stress on these numbers, we may say that, roughly, about a million meteors are gathered up by the earth every day, more than 40,000 per hour, and (on the average, it will be understood) some 10 or 12 per second. As almost all of these bodies enter the earth's atmosphere with velocities compared with which that of a rifle-bullet is as rest, it follows that, however minute the majority of these meteoric visitants may be, the very least of them striking man or animal in any vital spot would cause death. But fortunately we are protected from all risk of this sort by a very efficient shield—the soft and yielding air, the resistance of which turns all save the largest meteors into vapour before they have penetrated even its outermost layers. The condensation of the metallic vapours into the finest possible metallic dust, and the eventual subsidence of this dust upon the earth's surface, explain, doubtless, the detection of metallic particles in regions far remote from human habitation—or rather, we might have been certain, even had no meteoric particles been detected by Reichenbach, Phipson, Nordenskjöld, and others, that they must exist in Arctic snows and glacial crevices, on mountain summits and at the sea-bottom.

Whether, however, we can safely pass from the sure ground of these known facts to the inferences which have been recently suggested, we may be permitted to doubt. Mr. Ranyard, for instance, submits that the facts go to show that meteoric matter falling in the lapse of ages must materially contribute to the matter of the earth's crust. He goes further. Not only does the total meteoric downfall, in his opinion, add appreciably to the matter of the earth's crust, but the excess of the downfall on the northern hemisphere of the earth may, he considers, account for the preponderating mass of the continents in the northern hemisphere of the earth, and for the fact that nearly all the peninsulas taper towards the south. This excess of northern meteoric downfall must of necessity bear a very small proportion to the total downfall. For it is certain that nearly all the meteoric families travel in closed orbits around the sun. It has, indeed, never been proved that any now come from interstellar space, though probably some do. Of those that do visit our solar systems from without, rather more would salute the northern than the southern hemisphere of the earth, simply because the solar system pursues a somewhat northerly course in its journey through interstellar space. But manifestly, if a small proportion only of our meteoric visitants come from outside the solar domain, and among such visitors those from the north exceed those from the south in a certain degree only, the actual excess of meteoric downfall on the earth's northern hemisphere over that on the southern must be very slight compared with the total meteoric downfall. But even the total downfall would not at its present rate, or even at the present rate increased a thousandfold, cause the earth's crust to grow appreciably in the lapse of ages—understanding by ages thousands of years. It has been shown by Professor Alexander Herschel that the average weight of shooting stars visible to the eye must be estimated rather by grains than by ounces, and the telescopic shooting-stars which form nine-tenths of the total, according to Professor Newton's estimate, are of course far smaller. But assigning even to each meteor a weight of 1lb.—an utterly inadmissible estimate—let us consider at what rate the earth's crust would grow. The earth has a surface of 200 million square miles, and about 400 million meteors fall upon it per annum. That gives two meteors, or 2lb. weight of matter, added to each square mile in a year. There are more than three million square yards in a square mile, so that 1,500,000 years would be required at the present rate of meteoric downfall to add 1lb. of meteoric matter to each square yard of the earth's surface. Such added matter, uniformly spread over the surface, would be utterly inappreciable so far as the thickness of the earth's crust is concerned.   In a thousand millions of years at that rate, which far exceeds the real rate, the crust of the earth would not be increased in thickness by a single foot.   The excess of increase in the northern hemisphere would not be one foot in a billion of years.   We must assuredly look to some other cause for the preponderating mass of the continents in the northern hemisphere.

So, also, of the suggested addition of large quantities of gas to our atmosphere.   Doubtless some meteors carry many times their own volume of occluded gas, and as they are vaporised during their rush through the air this gas is given off.   Very important effects may result from this process, since relatively minute additions of gaseous matter to our atmosphere may sensibly affect creatures which depend on that atmosphere for their existence.   But that atmospheric pressure can be sensibly modified from day to day, or in longer intervals, by the addition of gases occluded in meteors, the entire annual supply of which, if wholly gaseous and if all added in a single instant, would not increase the height of the barometer by a hair's breadth, is a proposition physically inadmissible.   We need not care, however, to consider doubtful details such as these, where the general relations involved and the conclusions which admit of being demonstrated are so important and so interesting as those involved in the recent discoveries of meteoric astronomy or deducible from them.

BIELA'S COMET AND METEORS.

IT was expected by astronomers that some time during the week ending November 30, 1879, the earth would pass through a flight of meteorites following in the track of one of the most remarkable comets ever discovered by astronomers. In 1878 it had been thought not improbable that there might be such a display, though the earth crossed the comet's path (or passed very near to it) before the head of the comet had passed the crossing point; but in 1879 a display was far more confidently expected, because in the interval the comet had passed that point, and the earth passes through the train of the comet not very far behind the head. Yet there were circumstances connected with this comet which, while greatly enhancing the interest of the expected display, rendered astronomers doubtful on what day it was likely to occur, what would be its nature, and in what parts of the earth it might be most favourably seen.

In the first place, the comet itself is in that list of missing comets at the head of which stands Lexell's, the famous lost comet of 1778. Discovered in 1826 by Biela, whose name it bears (though according to the customary arrangement it should be called Gambart's, after the astronomer who first calculated its orbit), it was seen again in 1832, returned in 1839, but was not seen because its course in the heavens passed too near the sun's place, was seen in 1846, and again in 1852, for the last time. Whether it returned in 1859 in such a form that, under favourable conditions, it would have been visible is not known, for the conditions were as unfavourable then as in 1839. But in 1866 it should have been seen, and again in 1872 ; whereas on both those occasions, though most carefully searched for by experienced astronomers (including some professional observers) using excellent telescopes, no trace of Biela's comet was recognised. Now, it should be remembered that each time the comet had returned astronomers were better able to determine its true orbit. Even during the time of its visibility in 1826 Gambart so successfully calculated its motion that it was readily detected at its return in 1832, very near to its calculated position. Not only so, but he was able to calculate its motion before 1826 in such sort as to show that it was the comet seen by Montaigne in March 1772, and later, up to April 3, by Messier. Gambart identified it also with a comet seen by Pons on November 10, 1805, when, being near the earth and under conditions otherwise favourable, it presented a conspicuous appearance, having an apparent diameter equal to about a fourth of the moon's. From calculations made in 1805, when Biela's comet was watched for several weeks by Pons, Olbers, and others, astronomers were led to believe that it was identical with the object seen by Montaigne in 1772, but they did not then succeed either in proving this or in calculating the true orbit of the comet. So soon, however, as it was proved that the comet of 1826 was the same which, three revolutions before, had been seen in 1805, and five revolutions before that again, in 1772, astronomy had this comet fairly in the net. Seven revolutions and fairly exact observations in 1772 and 1805, with very good observations in 1826, gave its period very accurately, and its actual path in space with a very fair degree of correctness. Its re-discovery in 1832 not only showed this to be the case, but gave astronomers an opportunity to still more accurately determine its path. Hence it was still more readily re-discovered in 1846, though in the interval since 1832 it had made two circuits of its orbit. Then, if a slight accident had not befallen the comet and occasioned doubts as to its stability, astronomers would have become

still more confident about its motion. So far, indeed, as
its orbital movement was concerned they were so, and the
calculated path for the next return in 1852 was given with
a degree of precision not before equalled, though surpassed
for the next (observable) returns in 1866, when, however, as
we have said, the comet was not detected.

But secondly, the accident just referred to and the subsequent loss of the comet have suggested doubts as to the
nature of the meteor shower to be expected when the earth
passes through its track. Every year when the earth passes
—about August 11—through the track of the comet of 1862
shooting stars belonging to the comet's train, the so-called
Perseids, may confidently be looked for. In the case of the
November meteors called Leonides, which must not be con-
founded with the November meteors following Biela's comet,
astronomers are equally confident that for several years after
the head of Tempel's comet (the second of the year 1866)
has passed our way, there will be a shower of shooting stars
on the night of November 13-14. But that is chiefly because we have no reason to suspect that either of these
comets is likely to be dissipated. The case is different with
Biela's comet. In 1846, when Sir John Herschel said 'all
seemed to be going on quietly and comfortably,' this comet
was suddenly found to have become divided into two distinct
comets, 'each with a head and coma and a little nucleus of
its own.' When the change happened is not known. It
may readily have escaped attention for some time. In fact,
we know that the change had occurred before it was detected in Europe. For on January 13, 1846, Lieutenant
Maury, of the Washington Observatory, reported officially
that the comet was double ; while Professor Wichmann,
who had a good view of the comet on the 14th, did not
then detect its duplicity, though on the following night, independently, of course, of any information from America,
he saw that the comet was divided. 'What domestic
trouble caused the secession,' says Herschel quaintly, 'it is
impossible to conjecture ; but the two receded further and

further from each other up to a certain moderate distance, with some slight degree of mutual communication, and a very odd interchange of light—one day one head being brighter and another the other—till they seem to have finally agreed to part company.' The oddest part of the story, however, is yet to come. The year 1852 brought round the time for their re-appearance, and behold, there they both were, at about the same distance from each other and both visible in one telescope. It should be mentioned, however, that the distance between the comets in 1852 was very much greater than in 1846—in fact, nearly eight times as great, the *maximum* distance attained in 1846 being only 157,000 miles, whereas in 1852 the distance had increased to 1,250,000 miles.

When we couple this partial disintegration of the comet with the circumstance that, despite the increased accuracy with which astronomers have been able to calculate its orbit, they failed to detect it in 1866 and 1872, we perceive that Biela's comet is not one to be trusted. The partial disintegration of 1846 had probably degenerated into total dissipation before 1866. After the unavailing search in 1872, few hoped to see any signs of the comet again, at least in the ordinary form. But it was known that the orbit of the comet intersects the earth's, or passes at any rate so close to the earth's orbit that if this comet, like others, has a meteor train, a display might be looked for when the earth is passing the place of nearest approach. In passing we may pause to correct the entirely erroneous notion that the meteoric train of a comet is the comet's tail. A mathematician of repute has taken up this idea, apparently from misunderstanding some passages in descriptions by astronomers, and has even based on it a theory of comets' tails as made up of flights of masses like bricks or even paving-stones ; but in reality the tail of a comet lies one way, the train of meteoric attendants another way, and there is not a particle of evidence to show that the tail of any comet even contains meteors, far less that it is composed of such bodies. We were not to

pass through the tail, however, but through the track of
Biela's comet in November 1872, and there were reasons
for believing that a display of shooting stars would be seen
during the last week of November or the first in December.
I invited general attention to the matter, and wrote towards
the end of October 1872 :—

'There will probably be a display of meteors following the track
of Biela's comet' (which, though unseen, must have crossed the earth's
path early in September). 'At any rate, the skies should be carefully
watched. The shower of meteors (should any occur) will fall in such
a direction that shooting stars might be looked for at any time of the
night. Those belonging to Biela's comet could be very readily distinguished from others, because their tracks would be seen to radiate from
the constellation Cassiopeia. So that should any one observe, on any
night between November 25 and December 5, a shooting star following
such a track, he will have the satisfaction of knowing that in all probability he has seen a fragment or follower of a comet which has divided
into two, if not three, distinct comets, and has followed up that process
of dissipation by dissolving altogether away.'

The predictions thus made in 1872 might have been repeated with more confidence, under somewhat similar conditions, in 1879, for in 1872 they were abundantly fulfilled. On
the night of November 27, 1872, there was a very remarkable
display of shooting stars. Professor Grant, of the Glasgow
Observatory, counted that evening between 5h. 30m. and 11h.
50m. no less than 10,579 meteors. Four observers in Italy,
parcelling out the heavens between them, counted in 6½ hours
33,400. The greatest number were seen between 7h. and
9h., and between 6h. 35m. and 6h. 56m. the whole of the
sky around the region whence the meteors radiated seemed
occupied by a meteoric cloud. This region was in that part
of the constellation of Andromeda where the feet of the
Chained Lady are supposed to be, and near enough to the
part of Cassiopeia whence attendants of Biela's comet
should radiate, to leave no doubt that these were really followers of that dissipated object. Indeed, Professor Grant
found that the meteors of longest track radiated from Cassiopeia. Then came one of the strangest episodes of this

strange story. Klinkerfues telegraphed to Pogson, of Madras, to examine the part of the southern heavens opposite that from which the flight of meteors had fallen on the earth, to see if any trace of the retreating flight of meteors could be recognised. He did so, and there—near the star Theta, on the Centaur's shoulder, he saw two cloud-like objects, which were certainly not star-clouds (or nebulæ), since they were moving athwart the stellar heavens. Many supposed that Pogson had re-detected Biela's comet, and that the comet had really touched the earth on November 27. But the comet was at least ten weeks' journey farther forward ; and it was shown that Pogson's clouds could not even be identified with the meteor flight through which the earth passed on November 27, but, assuming them to be travelling on a parallel course (which was not proved), must have been more than three days' journey behind the meteor-cloud.   .

That is the latest news we have had about the missing comet, except that during the last week of November 1877 many meteors were seen which were apparently following in the comet's track, though so far behind (nearly two-thirds of a circuit) that the comet might be, perhaps, more correctly described as following them. A few of the Biela meteors were seen in 1878 when the comet itself was rather more than four months' journey from the place of nearest approach to the earth's track, which place lies, be it understood, close to the part of the earth's track which she passes on the 27th of November. This part of its path the dissipated and disintegrated comet must have passed early in April 1879, and therefore it was not likely that the shower of Andromedes (as the Biela meteors are called), should one be sèen, would be so rich or remarkable as the shower seen in 1872. It will be observed that in estimating the epoch of the comet's passage past the point of nearest approach we assume that, dissipated though the comet is, it is still travelling in fragments along the orbit determined by Gambart in the first instance, and subsequently more exactly by mathematicians provided with more complete materials for effecting the necessary computations. We may reject altogether the idea that it was a portion of the comet itself, as distinguished from its train of meteoric attendants, which was traversed by the earth on November 27, 1872, or watched by Pogson on December 2 and 3. If the meteoric train of the comet is dense enough to be visible, in retreat, after producing a shower such as that of November 27, it should be worth while to look out for it as it approaches. The clouds seen by Pogson in the early morning of December 2 and 3, 1872, retreating southwards, would certainly have been seen during the whole of the night for a week or two before the display of November 27, approaching from the north. This, indeed, is the only way in which a meteor stream can be expected to be seen by reflected sunlight—namely, by looking for it when greatly foreshortened.

The moon was nearly full on the night when the display was expected, and few meteors were seen. Probably had the night been dark and clear, many more—possibly thousands—would have been seen, but unquestionably the display would not have been what was anticipated.

MOVEMENTS OF JUPITER'S CLOUD-MASSES.

IF Jupiter be regarded as a planet resembling our earth in condition, we find ourselves compelled to believe that processes of a most remarkable character are taking place on that remote world. It is singular with what conplacency the believers in the theory that all the planets are very much alike accept the most startling evidence respecting disturbances to which some among those brother worlds of ours must needs on that hypothesis have been subjected. Mighty masses of cloud, such as would suffice to enwrap the entire globe on which we live, form over large regions of Jupiter or Saturn, change rapidly in. shape, and vanish, in the course of a few minutes ; and many are content to believe that what has thus taken place resembles the formation, motion, and dissipation of our own small clouds, though the sun pours but about a twenty-seventh part of the heat on Jupiter, and but about a hundredth part on Saturn, which we receive from his rays. The outline of Jupiter, as indicated by the apparent position of a satellite close to his disc, expands and contracts through thousands of miles, yet the theory that Jupiter is still intensely hot must not for a moment be entertained, though the expansion and contraction of the solid crust of a cool planet through so enormous a range would vapourise a portion of its mass exceeding many times the entire volume of our earth. Saturn is seen by Sir W. Herschel and Sir J. Herschel, by Sir G. Airy, Coolidge, the Bonds, and a host of other observers, to assume from time to time the square-shouldered aspect, a change which—to be discernible from our distant standpoint —would imply the expansion and contraction of whole zones of Saturn's surface through. 4000 or 5000 miles at least ; yet it is better to believe, it would seem, that these stupendous changes have affected the solid crust of a planet like our earth, than to admit the possibility that the outline we measure is not that of the planet itself, but of layers of cloud raised to a vast height in the deep atmosphere surrounding a planet still glowing with its primeval fires.

The phenomena I am now about to consider belong to the same category. They are utterly inexplicable, or only explicable by the most sensational assumptions as to the processes taking place on Jupiter, if we adopt the old theory of Jupiter's condition ; while if we regard Jupiter as an intensely-heated planet surrounded by and entirely concealed within a cloud-laden atmosphere several thousand miles in depth, they at once admit of the most simple and natural explanation.

It has, of course, long been known that the belts of Jupiter are phenomena of his atmosphere, not of his surface. The belts of lightest tint have been regarded as belts of cloud, and the darker belts as either the real surface of the planet seen between the cloud-belts, or else as lower cloud-layers, appearing darker because in shadow. Accordingly, when features of the belts have been watched in their rotational circuit, it has been clearly recognised that the rotation determined in this way is not necessarily or probably the true rotation of the planet itself. Further, it has been proved, beyond all possibility of question, that some at least among the spots upon the planet's belts have a motion of their own ; for whenever two spots in different Jovian latitudes have been observed, it has been almost constantly noticed that the one nearer the Equator has had a greater rotation rate than the other. Again, it has sometimes happened that instead of two spots, in different latitudes, a well-defined dark streak or opening, having its two extremities in different latitudes, has remained long enough to be observed during several rotations of the planet. In these cases it has been observed that the end of the streak nearest the Equator has travelled fastest, not only absolutely, but in longitude, insomuch that the position of the streak has notably altered.

Thus, in February 1860, Mr. Long, of Manchester, noticed across a bright belt an oblique dark streak. 'Its position' (I quote from a paper of my own written six years ago, when as yet the theory now before us was in its infancy) 'might be compared to that of the Red Sea on the globe of the earth, for it ran neither north nor south nor east and west, but rather nearer the former than the latter direction. The length of this dark space—of this rift, that is, in the great cloud-belt—was about ten thousand miles, and its width at least five hundred miles ; so that its superficial extent was much greater than the whole area of Europe.' It remained as a rift certainly until April 10, or for six weeks, and probably much longer. It passed away to the dark side of Jupiter, to return again after the Jovian night to the illuminated hemisphere, during at least a hundred Jovian days ; and assuredly nothing in the behaviour of terrestrial clouds affords any analogue to this remarkable fact. 'This great rift *grew*, lengthening out until it stretched across the whole face of the planet, and it grew in a very strange way ; for its two ends remained at unchanged distances from the planet's equator, but the one nearest to the equator travelled forwards (speaking with reference to the way in which the planet turns on its axis), the rift thus approaching more and more nearly to an east and west direction.' The rate of this motion was perhaps the most remarkable circumstance of all. M. Baxendell, one of the observers of the rift, and one of our most experienced telescopists, thus describes the changes seen in the belt :— 'Since Mr. Long first observed the oblique streak on February 29, it has gradually extended itself in the direction of the planet's rotation at the average rate of 3640 miles per day, or 151 miles per hour, the two extremities of the belt remaining constantly on the same parallels of latitude. The belt also became gradually darker and broader.'[1]

Apart from the evidence afforded by this rift respecting the swift motions of the cloud-masses enwrapping Jupiter (for a velocity of 151 miles per hour exceeds that of the most tremendous hurricanes on our earth), it has always seemed to me that this one series of observations should suffice of itself to show that the phenomena of Jupiter's cloud-laden atmosphere are not due to solar action. For the rift itself continued, and the changes affecting it continued, whether Jovian day was in progress or Jovian night. For one hundred Jovian days or more, and for one hundred Jovian nights, the great cloud-masses on either side of the rift remained in position opposite each other, slowly wheeling, but still continuing face to face, as their equatorial ends rushed onwards at a rate fourfold that of a swift train, even measuring their velocity only by reference to the ends remote from the equator, and regarding these as fixed. Probably the cloud-masses were moving still more swiftly with respect to the surface of the planet below.

Of course, it is just possible that a great dark rift, such as I have just described, might appear thus to change in position without any actual transference of the bordering cloud masses. Mr. Webb, speaking of a number of phenomena, of which those presented by the great rift of 1860 are but a few, says that ' they prove an envelope vaporous and mutable like that of the earth, without, however, necessarily inferring' [? implying] 'the existence of tempestuous winds : even in our own atmosphere, when near the dewpoint, surprising changes sometimes occur very quietly : a cloud-bank observed by Sir J. Herschel, 1827, April 19, was precipitated so rapidly that it crossed the whole sky from east to west at the rate of at least 300 miles per hour ;

[1] Two pictures of this belt—as seen March 12, 1860, and April 9, 1860—will be found In my article on ' Astronomy,' in the Encyclopædia Britannica, vol. ii. p. 808.

and alterations far more sudden are conceivable where everything is on a gigantic scale.' It does not seem to me altogether probable that more rapid alterations would affect cloud-banks covering millions of square miles, than occasionally affect terrestrial cloud-banks covering perhaps a few tens of thousands of square miles ; on the contrary, as small terrestrial clouds change relatively in a far more rapid way than large ones, and these than cloud-masses covering a county or a country, so it would seem that the changes affecting our largest cloud layers would be relatively far more rapid than those affecting cloud-masses which could (many times over) enwrap the whole frame of this earth on which we live. But apart from that, and apart also from the important consideration that all such processes as evaporation and condensation, so far as the sun brings them about, should proceed far more sluggishly in the case of a planet like Jupiter than in that of our earth (which receives some twenty-seven times as much heat from the sun, mile for mile of surface), it is utterly incredible that precipitation should have occurred so steadily and swiftly along one edge of the great rift, and condensation—with such exactly equal steadiness and swiftness—on the opposite edge, that, while the rift as a whole shifted its position during a hundred Jovian nights and days at the rate of 150 miles per hour, its sides should nevertheless remain parallel all the time. Such processes may be spoken of as possible, in the same sense as it is possible that a coin tossed fifty times in succession should always show the same face ; but we do not reckon such possibilities among scientific contingencies.

The motion of great rounded masses in the atmosphere of Jupiter is still more decisive not only as to the existence of a very deep atmosphere, but also as to the swift motions taking place in that atmosphere.

I would, in the first place, note that the very existence of belts in the Jovian atmosphere, and especially of variable belts, implies the great depth at which the real surface of the planet must lie below the visible cloud-layers. Atmospheric belts can only be formed where there are differences of rotational velocity. In the case of our own earth we know that the trade-wind zone and the counter-trade zone owe their origin to the difference of absolute rotational velocity between the equatorial parts of the earth and parts in high latitudes. In the case of Jupiter the difference of this kind is not sufficient to account for the observed belts,— partly because there are many, partly because they are variable, but principally because Jupiter is so much larger than the earth that much greater distances must be traversed in passing from any given latitude to another where the rotational velocity is so many miles per hour greater or less. Combining with these considerations the circumstance that the solar action which causes the atmospheric movements from one latitude to another, in the case of our earth, is reduced to one twenty-seventh part only of its terrestrial value, in the case of Jupiter, we must clearly look to some other cause for the difference of absolute rotational velocity necessary to account for the belts of Jupiter.

Now, it seems to me that we are thus at once led to the conclusion that the cloud-masses forming the belts of Jupiter are affected by vertical currents, uprushing motions carrying them from regions nearer the axis, where the absolute motion due to rotation is slower, to regions farther from the axis, where the motion due to rotation is swifter, and motions of downrush carrying them from regions of swifter to regions of slower rotational motion. This view seems certainly encouraged by what we find when we come to study more closely the aspect of the Jovian belts. The white spots—some small, some large—which are seen to form from time to time along the chief belts, present precisely the appearance which we should expect to find in masses of vapour flung from deep down below the visible cloud-surface of Jupiter, breaking their way through the cloud-layers, and becoming visible as they condense into the form of visible vapour in the cooler upper regions of the planet's atmo·

F

sphere. Then, again, the singular regularity with which
in certain cases the great rounded white clouds are set side
by side, like rows of eggs upon a string, is much more
readily explicable as due to a regular succession of uprushes of vapour, from the same region below, than as due
to the simultaneous uprushes of several masses of vapour
from regions set at uniform distances along a belt of Jupiter's
surface. The latter supposition is indeed artificial and improbable in the highest degree, and in several distinct
respects. It is unlikely that several uprushes should occur
simultaneously, unlikely that regions whence uprush took
place should be set at equal distances from each other, unlikely that they should lie along the same latitude parallel.
On the other hand, the occurrence of uprush after uprush
from the same region of disturbance, at nearly uniform intervals of time, is not at all improbable. The rhythmical
succession of explosions is a phenomenon, indeed, altogether
likely to occur under certain not improbable conditions,—
as, for instance, when each explosion affords an excess of
relief, if one may so speak, and is therefore followed by a
reactionary process, in its turn bringing in a fresh explosion.
Now, a rhythmical succession of explosions from the same
deep-seated region of disturbance would produce at the
upper level, where we *see* the expelled vapour-masses (after
condensation) a series of rounded clouds lying side by side.
For each cloud-mass—after its expulsion from a region of
slow (absolute) rotational motion, to a region of swifter
motion—would lag behind with reference to the direction of
rotational motion. The earlier it was formed the farther
back it would lie. Thus each new cloud-mass would lie
somewhat in advance of the one expelled next before it ;
and if the explosions occurred regularly, and with a sufficient
interval between each and the next to allow each expelled
cloud-mass to lag by its own full length before the next one
appeared, there would be seen precisely such a series of
egg-shaped clouds, set side by side, as every careful observer

of Jupiter with high telescopic powers has from time to time perceived.[1]

That these egg-shaped clouds are really egg-shaped— not merely oval in the sense in which a flat elliptic surface is oval—is suggested at once by their aspect. But it is more distinctly indicated when details are examined. It appears to me that considerable interest attaches to some observations which were made by Mr. Brett, in April, 1874, upon some of the rounded spots then visible upon the planet's equatorial zone. It will be thought that I am disposed, as a rule, to place too much reliance upon the observations and theories of Mr. Brett, seeing that on more than one occasion I have had to call attention to errors into which, in my judgment, he has fallen. For instance, I certainly do not think he has ever seen the solar corona when the sun was not eclipsed, though I have no doubt he saw what he described, which he supposed to be the corona, but which was in reality not the corona. Nor, again, do I accept '(though I do not think it worth while to discuss) his theory that Venus has a surface shining with metallic lustre, and is surrounded by a glassy atmosphere ; though in that case, again, his description of what he saw may be accepted as it stands, and all that we need reject is his interpretation thereof. In the case of Jupiter's white spots, Mr. Brett's skill as an artist enables us to accept not only his observations, but his interpretation of them, simply because the interpretation depends on artistic, not on scientific, considerations.

---

[1] Webb thus describes the egg-shaped clouds :—'Occasionally the belts throw out dusky loops or festoons, whose elliptical interiors, arranged lengthways and sometimes with great regularity, have the aspect of a girdle of luminous egg-shaped clouds surrounding the globe. These oval forms, which were very conspicuous in the equatorial zone (as the interval of the belts may be termed) in 1869-70, have been seen in other regions of the planet, and are probably of frequent occurrence. The earliest distinct representation of them that I know of is by Dawes, 1851, March 8, but they are perhaps indicated in drawings of the last century.'

'I wish,' he says, 'to call attention to a particular feature of Jupiter's disc, which' [the feature probably] 'appears to me very well defined at the present time, and which seems to afford evidence respecting the physical condition of the planet. The large white patches which occur on and about the equatorial zone, and interrupt the continuity of the dark belts, are well known to all observers, and the particular point in connection with them to which I beg leave to call attention is *that they cast shadows;* that is to say, the light patches are bounded on the side farthest from the sun by a dark border shaded off softly towards the light, and showing in a distinct manner that the patches are projected or relieved from the body of the planet. The evidence which this observation is calculated to afford refers to the question whether the opaque body of the planet is seen in the dark belts or the bright ones, and points to the conclusion that it is not seen at all in either of them, but that all we see of Jupiter consists of semi-transparent materials. The particular fact from which this inference would be drawn is, · that the dark sides of the suspended or projected masses are not sufficiently hard or sharply defined for shadows falling upon an opaque surface ; neither are they sharper upon the light background than upon the dark. The laws of light and shade upon opaque bodies are very simple and very absolute ; and one of the most rudimentary of them is that every body has its light, its shade, and its shadow, the relations between which are constant ; and that the most conspicuous and persistent edge or limit, in this association of elements, is the boundary of the shadow; the shadow being radically different from the shade, in that its intensity is uniform throughout in any given instance, and is not affected by the form of the surface on which it is cast, whereas the shade is distinguished by attributes of an opposite character. Now, if the dark spaces adjoining the light patches on Jupiter, which I have called shadows, are not shadows at all, but shades, it is obvious that the opaque surface of the planet on which the shadows should fall is concealed ; whereas if they are shadows their boundaries are so soft and undefined as to lead to the conclusion that they are cast upon a semi-transparent body, which allows the shadow to be seen indeed, but with diminishing distinctness towards its edge, according to the acuteness of its angle of incidence. Either explanation of the phenomenon may be the true one, but they both lead to the same conclusion, viz., that neither the dark belts nor the bright ones are opaque, and that if Jupiter has any nucleus at all it is not visible to us. It is obvious that the phenomena I have described would not be visible at the time of the planet's opposition, and the first occasion on which I noticed it was the night of the 16th of April last.'

This reasoning, so far as it relates to the laws of light and shade and shadow, is of course altogether sound. Nor are there any points requiring correction which in any degree affect the astronomical inferences deducible from what Mr. Brett actually saw. I may note that somewhat later Mr. Knobel observed the shadow of white cloud-masses, and as the shadow had not so much greater a length at that time, two months from opposition, as it had when the planet was much nearer opposition, he infers that the true explanation of the appearance has hardly been found. He appears to have overlooked the fact that the assumption made in the explanation is not that Jupiter has a semi-transparent atmosphere always equally translucent and penetrable to the same depth by the solar rays. When the shadow was shorter than it should have been, had the atmosphere been in the same condition as when Mr. Brett made his observation, it is probable that a layer of clouds interrupted the rays, and thus the shadow was much closer to the cloud-mass throwing it than it would have been had that layer not been there. Mr. Knobel's paper contains very striking evidence of the variability of Jupiter's atmosphere, or rather of the clouds which float in it. ' The greater distinctness of the satellites when near the edge,' he says, ' is a curious phenomenon which has been repeatedly observed by astro·

nomers, but which seems to require explanation.' 'On an occasion described the second satellite transited a dark limb which was' [seemed] 'most dark near the centre, and fainter towards the edge, yet the satellite was almost invisible when on the darkest part of the belt, and was bright and distinct when the background of the belt was faintest.' This practically proved that on the occasion in question the dark central part of the belt seemed darker than it really was by contrast with the bright belts on either side, while the edge seemed lighter than it really was by contrast with the dark sky on which the planet was projected.   In reality the part near the edge must have been darker than the part near the middle, or the satellite could not have appeared brighter when near the edge.   No doubt the darkness near the edge (which, by the way, my friend Mr. Browning tested photometrically, and demonstrated at my suggestion, eight years ago) was due to transparency, the darkness of the sky beyond being to some degree discernible through the edge.   But this transparency is not always to be observed to the same degree, or through the same extent of Jovian atmosphere as to depth.   Mr. Knobel proceeds, illustrating this the more effectively that he does so uninten-tionally :—' The third satellite, on March 25, 1874, appeared as a dark spot when in mid-transit, and on nearing the edge appeared as a bright spot without trace of duskiness. But on March 26, 1873 ' (observe the difference of years), 'the fourth satellite made the whole transit as a dark spot, and was not perceptibly less dark at egress than in mid-transit.'

It appears to me demonstrated by the evidence thus far noted, that in a semi-transparent atmosphere of enormous depth, surrounding Jupiter, there float vast cloud-masses, sometimes in layers, at others in irregular heaps, at others having well-rounded forms.   These cloud-masses undergo sometimes remarkable changes of shape, often forming or disappearing in a very short time, and thus indicating the inferior activity of the forces at work below them,—in other words, the intense heat of Jupiter's real globe. As to the actual depth of the semi-transparent atmosphere in which these cloud-layers and cloud-masses float, it would be difficult to express an opinion. We do not know how many cloud-layers there are, how thick any cloud-layer may be, how great may be the depth of the vast rounded masses of cloud whose upper surface (that is, the surface remotest from Jupiter's true surface) we can alone see under favourable conditions. But we can indicate a minimum than which the atmosphere's depth is probably not less; and from all the observations which I have examined as bearing on this point, I should be disposed to assign for that minimum at least 6000 miles. I am strongly of opinion that in reality the depth of the Jovian atmosphere is still greater. I cannot doubt that Jupiter has a solid or liquid nucleus, though this nucleus—glowing, as it must be, with a most intense heat—may be greatly expanded, yet I should conceive that, with the enormous attractive power residing in it, containing as it must nearly the whole mass of the planet, its mean density cannot be less than that of the earth. Now a globe of the mass of Jupiter, but of the same mean density as our earth, would have one-fourth of Jupiter's volume—the mean density of Jupiter, as at present judged, being equal to one-fourth that of the earth. The diameter therefore of such a globe would be less than the present diameter of Jupiter in the proportion that the cube root of unity is less than the cube root of 4, or as 1 is less than 1·5874. Say roughly (remembering that the atmosphere of Jupiter must have a considerable mass) the diameter of Jupiter's nucleus would, on the assumptions made, be equal to about five-eighths of his observed diameter, or to about 53,000 miles. This is less than his observed diameter by about 22,000 miles, or the radius of his nucleus would be less than his observed radius by about 11,000 miles, which therefore would be the probable depth of his atmosphere.

But we have still to consider the velocities with which rounded masses of cloud travel in the very deep atmosphere

of Jupiter. 'There is clear evidence,' I have pointed out
in the article 'Astronomy' of the 'Encyclopædia Britannica,' 'that spots on Jupiter are subject to a proper motion
like that which affects the spots on the sun. Schmidt, in
No. 1973 of the " Astronomische Nachrichten," gives a number of cases of such proper movements of spots, ranging in
velocity from about 7 miles to about 200 miles an hour. It
may be noted, also, that from a series of observations of one
spot, made between March 13 and April 14, 1873, with the
great Rosse reflector, a period of 9 h. 55 m. 4 s. was deduced
while observations of another spot in the same interval gave
a rotation period of 9 h. 54 m. 55·4 s.' The actual difference
of velocity would depend in this case on the actual latitudes
of the two spots which were not micrometrically measured.
Taking 200,000 miles as about the circumference of a
parallel of latitude passing midway between the spots (only
a very rough calculation need be made), we should find that
in a period of one rotation, or roughly of ten hours, one
spot gained on the other about 51 seconds, or roughly about
1–700th part of a rotation—that is, in distance (dividing
200,000 by 700) about 286 miles in ten hours, or nearly 29
miles an hour.

We have, however, instances of yet greater relative
proper motion among cloud-masses. One of these cases I
proceed to consider at length.

In June, 1876, two spots were visible upon the disc of
Jupiter, so distinct and isolated as to be well adapted for
measurement to determine the rate of the planet's rotation.
Mr. Brett, observing them first as illustrative of the phenomenon to which he had called attention in 1874, turned his
attention afterwards to their rate of motion. He would
seem not to have been aware of the fact that the proper
motion of bright spots and other markings on Jupiter was
already a recognised phenomenon ; for he asks whether his
'observations of these spots, forming a series extending
over a period of 286 hours 20 minutes, afford evidence of
proper motion, or whether, on the other hand, they tend to

cast any doubt on the accepted rotation of the planet.'
However, his observations are all the freer from the bias of
preconceived opinions. 'There were several peculiarities
about these two spots,' he says, 'which seemed to me to
give them an eminent claim to attention. They occurred
very near to the equator, and were very well defined, and
free from entanglement with other markings—an advantage
which they have maintained with singular uniformity throughout the period mentioned ; but the special peculiarity to
which attention is asked is that during an interval of five
days they remained in the same relative position without
any variation whatever. Their stability in respect of latitude during those five days is undoubted ; but the question
is whether or not they were equally stable in longitude.
This remark only applies to the first five days of the series,
because at the end of twelve days a certain deviation was
obvious. The distance between the two spots occupied
about 42 degrees of Jovian longitude, or about 33,000
miles. Their diameter was nearly equal, being estimated at
about one-fourteenth of the planet's diameter, or 6310
miles. The interval of time between these first two observations 'was 119 hours,—that is to say, twelve rotations of
the planet according to Airy's determination, during which
time their distance apart and their latitude remained constant.' Between the first and second observations the two
spots had gained '44 m. 6s. in time. Assuming Airy's
rotation, viz., 9 h. 55 m. 21 s., the spots have gained on
the planet's surface at the rate of 4 m. 2 s. in each revolution.'

Between the second observation and the third 'there
was an interval of seven days, or seventeen rotations of the
planet ; and the same two spots turn up again somewhat
earlier than the calculated time. It unfortunately happens,'
proceeds Mr. Brett, 'that on this occasion their configuration
had undergone some change ; but their dimensions and the
distance between them remain very much as before. The
most important circumstance respecting them is, that their

rate of progress shows a certain acceleration.' The change, however, in these seven days, is not such as to permit us to believe that the same pair of spots was under observation. If so, a change in latitude much more remarkable than the change in longitude had taken place ; for the one which was the most northerly by about 6000 miles at the beginning of the seven days was the most southerly by nearly the same amount at the end of that period. Considering that in the five days between the first and second observations no change of latitude took place, it may fairly be doubted whether a change of the kind and so rapid—amounting, in fact, to nearly 900 miles per day—could have taken place in the interval. Proper motions in latitude may indeed be regarded as not less likely to occur in the case of Jupiter than in that of the sun, where they certainly sometimes occur ; but all the observations hitherto made on Jupiter assure us that, in his case as in the sun's, proper motions in latitude would be very much slower than proper motions in longitude. We must be content with the evidence of proper motion afforded by the first five days of observation. (The fourth observation only followed the third by about twenty minutes.)

Now, taking this evidence as it stands, and making fair allowance for probable error in an observation of the sort, we may consider that during the 119 hours the two spots were gaining on the estimated rotation-period of the planet by about four minutes per rotation. As they both lie on the equatorial belt, we may take the circuit accomplished by each at about 267,000 miles, or, say, their rate at about 270,000 in ten hours, or 27,000 miles per hour. Hence the distance traversed in four minutes would be about 1800 miles, which would be about the gain per rotation. One-tenth of this, or 180 miles, would be the hourly gain, as compared with the estimated rotation-rate. Mr. Brett takes the least proper motion at 165 miles per hour.

He points out justly that the rotation-rate has been de-rived from observations of some such spots. So that in reality the only inference we can form is, that the rotation-rate derived from some spots is different from the rotation-rate derived from others, and that some spots (if not all) are certainly not constant in position with respect to the solid nucleus of the planet. That the spots observed by Airy, Mädler, and others, should have indicated a slower rate of rotation than those observed by Mr. Brett may fairly be ascribed to the fact that the former were at some distance from the equator, while these last were nearly equatorial. For matter thrown up from the equatorial parts of the true surface of the concealed planet would manifestly differ less in velocity from the superior ambient atmosphere into which they were driven than would masses expelled from higher latitudes. (It is probable that the same explanation applies also in the case of the sun.)

This conclusion, that the spots of Jupiter have rapid rates of relative motion, would of itself be of singular interest, especially when we remember that the larger white spots represent masses of cloud 5000 or 6000 miles in dia-meter. That such masses should be carried along with velocities so enormous as to change their positions relatively to each other, at a rate sometimes of more than 150 miles per hour, is a startling and stupendous fact. But it appears to me that the fact is still more interesting in what it suggests than in what it reveals. The movements taking place in the deep atmosphere of Jupiter are very wonderful, but the cause of these movements is yet better worthy of study. We cannot doubt that deep down below the visible surface of the planet—that is, the surface of its outermost cloud-layers—lies the fiery mass of the real planet. Outbursts, compared with which the most tremendous volcanic explo-sions on our earth are utterly insignificant, are continually taking place beneath the seemingly quiescent envelope of the giant planet. Mighty currents carry aloft great masses of heated vapour, which, as they force their way through the upper and cooler strata of the atmosphere, are converted into visible cloud. Currents of cool vapour descend towards the surface, after assuming no doubt vorticose motions, and sweeping away over wide areas the brighter cloud-masses, so as to form dark spots on the disc of the planet. And owing to the various depths to which the different cloud-masses belong, and whence the uprushing currents of heated vapour have had their origin, horizontal currents of tremendous velocity exist, by which the cloud-masses of one belt or of one layer are hurried swiftly past the cloud-masses of a neighbouring belt or of higher or low cloud-layers. The planet Jupiter, in fact, may justly be described as a miniature sun, vastly inferior in bulk to our own sun, inferior to a greater degree in heat, and in a greater degree yet in lustre, but to be compared with the sun—not with our earth—in size, in heat, and in lustre, and, lastly, in the tremendous energy of the processes which are at work throughout his cloud-laden atmospheric envelope.

It may be added that Mr. Todd, a well-known observer of Adelaide, New South Wales, has been able to trace the motions of satellites behind the parts of the planet near the edge, or, in other words, *through* those parts of the planet's atmosphere which have hitherto been regarded as belonging to the mass of the planet itself. Mr. Ellery of Melbourne also saw a sixth-magnitude star in February, 1879, through a portion of what seemed to be Jupiter's globe, but in reality was but the deep cloud-laden atmosphere.

THE ORIGIN OF THE WEEK.

'It may be assumed, with Ideler, that the week has originated from the length of the synodic months, . . . and that references to the planetary series, together with planetary days and hours, belong to an entirely different period of advanced and speculative culture.'— Humboldt (*Cosmos*).

I HAVE considered in my essay on the Sabbath[1] the origin of the seventh day's rest. The origin of the week, or time-measure of seven days, is a different matter, though of course associated with the question of the Sabbath. The observance of a day of rest once in each week may or may not have synchronised with or quickly followed the recognition of the week as a measure of time, but it certainly was not a necessary adjunct to the week. I propose now to consider how the week probably had its origin, presenting, as occasion serves, such subsidiary evidence as can be derived from history or tradition. Usually this and kindred subjects have been dealt with *à posteriori.* Observances, festivals, chronological arrangements, and so forth, known or recorded to have been adopted by various nations, have been examined, and an inquiry made into their significance. The result has not been altogether satisfactory. Many interesting facts have been brought to light as research has proceeded, and several elaborate theories have been advanced on nearly every point of chronological research. Any one of these theories,

---

[1] 'Infinities Around us,' p. 290.

examined alone, seems to be established almost beyond dispute by the number of facts seemingly attesting in its favour; but when we find that for another and yet another theory a similar array of facts can be adduced, we lose faith in all theories thus supported. At least those only retain their belief in a theory of the kind who have given so much care to its preparation that they have had no time to examine the evidence favouring other theories.

On the other hand, there is much to be said in favour of an *à priori* method of dealing with ancient chronological arrangements. We know certainly how the heavens appeared to men of old times ; if occasion arise we can determine readily and certainly the exact aspect of the heavens at any given place and time ; we know generally the conditions under which the first observations of the heavens must have been made ; hence we can infer, not unsafely, what particular objects would have been first noted, or would have been early chosen as time-measures ; what difficulties would have presented themselves as time proceeded ; and how such difficulties would have been met.

The inquiry, let me remark at the outset, has an interest other than that depending on chronological relations. I know of none better suited to commend to our attention the movements of the heavenly bodies, which, as Carlyle has remarked, I think, though taking place all the time around us, are not half-known to most of us. As civilisation indeed progresses, the proportion of persons acquainted with the motions of the heavenly bodies becomes less and less ; both because artificial measures of time come more generally into use, and because fewer persons in proportion are engaged out of doors at night under conditions making the movements of the heavens worth observing. Even the increased interest taken of late in the study of astronomy has not tended, I believe, to increase the number who have a familiar acquaintance with the heavenly bodies and their motions. So soon as a student of astronomy sets up an observatory, indeed, he is more likely to forget what he already knows about ordinary celestial phenomena than to pay closer attention to them. If he wants to observe a particular star or planet, he does not turn to the heavens— one may almost say indeed, strange though it sounds, that the heavens are the last place he would think of looking at ; he simply sets the circles of his telescope aright, knowing that the star or planet he wants will then be in the field of view. The telescope is as often as not turned to the object before the door of the revolving dome has been opened—that is, while no part of the sky is in view.

It is precisely because in old times matters must have been entirely different, and familiarity with astronomical facts much more important to persons not themselves en- gaged in the study of astronomy, that the method of inquiry which I propose now to pursue respecting the origin of the week is so full of promise. If we will but put ourselves mentally in the position of the shepherds and tillers of the soil in old times, we can tell precisely what they were likely to notice, in what order, and in what way.

In the first place, I think, it will appear that some divi- sion of the month analogous to the week must have been suggested as a measure of time long before the year. Commonly the year is taken as either the first and most ob- vious of all time-measures, or else as only second to the day. But in its astronomical aspect the year is not a very obvious division of time. I am not here speaking, be it understood, of the exact determination of the length of the year. That, of necessity, was a work requiring much time and could only have been successfully achieved by astrono- mers of considerable skill. I am referring to the common- place year, the ordinary progression of those celestial phenomena which mark the changes of the seasons. As Whewell well remarks of the year, the repetition of similar circumstances at equal intervals is less manifest in this case [than in that of the day], and, the intervals being much lon- ger, some exertion of memory becomes requisite in order

that the recurrence may be perceived. A child might easily
be persuaded that successive years were of unequal length ;
or, if the summer were cold, and the spring and autumn
warm, might be made to believe, if all who spoke in its
hearing agreed to support the delusion, that one year was
two. Of course the recurrence of events characterising the
natural year is far too obvious to have been overlooked even
before men began to observe the heavenly bodies at all.
The tiller of the soil must observe the right time to plant
seeds of various kinds that they may receive the right proportion of the summer's heat ; the herdsman could not but
note the times when his flocks and herds brought forth their
young. But no definite way of noting the progress of the
year by the movements of the sun or stars [1] would probably
have suggested itself until some time after the moon's
motions had been used as means of measuring time. The
lunar changes, on the other hand, are very striking and obvious ; they can be readily watched, and they are marked by
easily determinable stages. 'It appears more easy,' says
Whewell, 'and in earlier stages of civilisation [it was] more
common, to count time by *moons* than by years.'

It has indeed been suggested that the moon's use as a
measurer of time was from the earliest ages so obvious that
the Greek words, *mēn* for month, *mēnē* for moon (less common, however, than *selēnē*), and the Latin *mensis* for month,
should be associated with the Latin verb *to measure* (*metior*,
mensus sum, &c.). Cicero says that months were called
menses, 'quia *mensa spatia conficiunt*,' because they complete
measured spaces. Other etymologists, says Whewell, connect these words 'with the Hebrew *manah*, to measure.'
Note also the measure of value, maneh,—'twenty shekels,
five-and-twenty shekels, fifteen shekels shall be your *maneh*,
or *mna*,' Ezek. xlv. 12. Again, the name *manna* is given to
the food found in the desert, by some interpreted ' a portion.'

---

[1] There are many reasons for believing, as I may one day take an
opportunity of showing in these pages, that the year was first measured
by the stars, not by the sun.

The word *mene*, or *mna*, in the warning, *Mene, tekel, phares*, was translated 'numbered.' With the same word is connected the Arabic *Al-manac*, or *Al-manach*. Whewell points out that 'if we are to attempt to ascend to the earliest conditions of language, we must conceive it probable that men would have a name for a most conspicuous object, *the moon*, before they would have a verb denoting the very abstract and general notion, to measure.' This is true ; but it does not follow that the moon may not have received a name implying her quality as a measurer long after she was first named. For the idea of using the moon as a measurer of time must as certainly have followed the conception of the abstract idea of measurement, as this conception must have followed the recognition of the moon as an object of observation. It is noteworthy, indeed, that in the Greek the moon has two names—one, more usual, *sēlēnē*, from which the Latins derived the name *luna;* the other, *mene*, certainly connected with *mēn*, for month. It seems almost certain that they, and those from whom they derived the usage, had come to regard the moon's quality as a time-measurer as distinct from her quality as an ornament of the night. To this second term for the moon Whewell's remark does not apply, or rather, his remark suggests the true explanation to be that very derivation of the words *mene, mensis, month, moon*, &c.,[1] from a word signifying 'to measure,' which he oppugns. Even if this view be rejected, we may yet regard the words signifying mensuration (measurement and numbering) as derived from a name for the moon, months, &c.—a circumstance which would indicate the recognised character of the moon as a time measurer even more significantly than the converse derivation.

It is noteworthy that of all the phenomena obvious to observation, the motions of the moon are those which most directly suggest the idea of measurement. The earth's

---

[1] To these may be added the Sanskrit *mâsa*, the Zend *mao*, the Persian *mah*, the Gothic *mena*, the Erse *mios*, and the Lithuanien *mienu*.

rotation on her axis is in reality much more uniform than
the moon's circling motion around the earth; but to
ordinary observation the recurrence of day and night
seems rather to suggest the idea of inequality than that of
the uniform subdivision of time. For the lengths of day
and night are seldom equal to each other, and are constantly
varying. The daily motions of the fixed stars are more
uniform than the moon's, and, if carefully noted, afford
an almost perfect uniformity of time-measurement. But
instruments of some kind are necessary to show that
this is the case. The moon, on the other hand, measures
off time in an obvious and striking manner, and, to ordinary observation, with perfect uniformity. In measuring time, the moon suggests also the idea of numerical
measurement. And measures of length, surface, volume,
and so forth, could more readily have been derived in
ancient times from the moon's motions than in any
other manner. In precisely the same way that now, in
Great Britain, all our measures,[1] without exception, are

---

[1] Even our measures of the value of money depend on the observed
motions of the stars. As I pointed out in my essay 'Our Chief Timepiece Losing Time' ('Light Science for Leisure Hours'), 'when we
come to inquire closely into the question of a sovereign's intrinsic value,
we find ourselves led to the diurnal motion of the stars by no very long
or intricate path.' For a sovereign is a coin containing so many grains
of gold mixed with so many grains of alloy. A grain is the weight of
such and such a volume of a certain standard substance,—that is, so
many cubic inches, or parts of a cubic inch, of that substance. An
inch is determined as a certain fraction of the length of a pendulum
vibrating seconds in the latitude of London. A second is a certain
portion of a mean solar day, and is practically determined by a reference to what is called a sidereal day,—the interval, namely, between
the successive passages by the same star across the celestial meridian of
any fixed place. This interval is assumed to be constant and is in fact
very nearly so. Strangely enough, the moon, the older measure of
time, is, by her attraction on the waters of this earth, constantly tending to modify this nearly constant quantity—the earth's rotation. For
the resistance of the tidal wave acts as a break, constantly retarding
the earth's turning motion,—though so slowly that 1,500 millions of
years would be required to lengthen the terrestrial day by one full hour.

derived from the daily motion of the stars, so in old times
the more obvious motions of the moon could have been
used, and were probably used, to give the measures required
in those days.

If, then, the names of the 'moon,' 'months,' and so forth,
were not originally derived from the idea of measurement, it
is nevertheless certain that the moon must, from the very
earliest times, have been regarded as, *par excellence, the
measurer.* The *à priori* reasons for expecting that the
moon's name, or one of her names, would be thus derived,
seem to me to add greatly to the probability of this derivation, which has been inferred from the actual co-existence
of such names as *mene* for the moon ; *men, mensis,* &c.
(see previous note), for the month ; *mna, maneh, mensus*
(root *mens*) for measurement.

The circling motion of the moon round the earth being
noted from the very earliest time, it is certain that, very
soon after, men would think of subdividing the moon's circuit. The nights when there was no moon would be distinguished in a very marked way from those in which the
moon was full or nearly so, and thus the lunar month would
be obviously marked off into two halves, each about a
fortnight in length. Something analogous to this first subdivision is to be recognised in a circumstance which I may
one day have to deal with more at length, the subdivision of
the year into two halves—one in which the Pleiades were
above the horizon and visible at sunset, the other when
they were below the horizon. There would be the bright
half and the dark half of the month (so far as the nights
were concerned), and it must be remembered that these
would not be unimportant distinctions to the men of old
time, nor mere matters of scientific observation. To the
shepherd, the distinction between a moonlit and a moon-
less night must have been very noteworthy. All his cares
would be doubled when the moon was not shining, all
lightened when she was nearly full. A poet in our time
singing the glories of the moonlit night might be apt to

forget the value of the light to the herdsman ; but in old times this must have been the chief thought in connection with such a night. Thus we find Homer, after describing the beauty of a moonlight night, in a noble passage (mistranslated by Pope, but nobly rendered by Tennyson), closing his description with the words—

'The shepherd gladdens in his heart.'

We can well understand, indeed, that according to tradition, the first astronomers in every nation were shepherds.

It might seem at a first view that the division of the months into two parts would be most conveniently marked by the moon (1) coming to full, and (2) disappearing. But apart from the consideration just mentioned, showing the probability that the first division would be into the bright half and the dark half, it is easily seen that neither the full phase, nor what is called technically 'new' (in reality the absolute disappearance of the moon), could be conveniently determined with anything like precision. The moon looks full a day or two before and a day or two after she really is full. The time of the moon's coming to the same part of the sky as the sun, again, though it can be inferred by noting when she first disappeared and when she first reappeared, is not obviously indicated,—or, which is the essential point, so manifested as to afford, *at the time*, an indication of the moon's reaching that special stage of her progress. If a clock were so constructed that time were indicated by the rotation of a globe half white half black, and so situated that the observer could not be certain when the white side was fully turned towards him, it is certain he would not observe that phase for determining time exactly. If he were not only uncertain when the black side was fully turned towards him, but could not ascertain this at all until some little time after the white side began to come into view again on one side (having disappeared on the other shortly before), he would be still less likely to observe the black phase as an epoch.

If we consider what the owner of such a timepiece would be apt to do, or rather woud be certain to do, we shall not be long in doubt as to the course which the shepherds of old time would have followed. The only phases which such a clock would show with anything like precision would be those two in which one half the globe exactly would be white and the other black. Not only would either of these be a perfectly definite phase marked unmistakeably by the straightness of the separating line between black and white, but also the rate of change would at these times be most rapid. The middle of the separating line, or terminator in the moon's case, is at all times travelling athwart the face of our satellite, but most quickly when crossing the middle of her disc. Apart, then, from the consideration already mentioned, which would lead the first observers to divide the month into a dark and a light half, the aspect of the moon's face so varied before their eyes as to suggest, or, one may say, to force upon them, the plan of dividing her course at the quarters, when she is half full increasing and half full diminishing.

Let us pause for a moment to see whether this first result, to which we have been led by purely *à priori* considerations, accords with any evidence from tradition. We might very well fail to find such evidence, simply because all the earlier and less precise ways of dividing time (of which this certainly would be one), giving way, as they must inevitably do, to more exact time-measures, might leave no trace whatever of their existence. It is, therefore, the more remarkable and in a sense fortunate, that in two cases we find clear evidence of the division of the lunar month into two halves, and in the precise manner above indicated. Max Müller, remarking on the week, says that he has found no trace of any such division in the ancient Vedic literature of the Hindoos, but the month is divided into two according to the moon—the *clear* half and the *obscure* half.[1] (Flam-

---

[1] It is noteworthy that in the Assyrian tablets lately deciphered by Mr. G. Smith (which are copies of Babylonian originals older probably

marion, from whom I take the reference to Max Müller, says, ' the *clear* half from new to full, and the *obscure* half from full to new ;' but this is manifestly incorrect, the half of the month from new to full having neither more nor less light by night than the half from full to new.) A similar division has been found among the Aztecs.

The next step would naturally be the division of each half, the bright and the dark half, into two equal parts. In fact this would be done at the same time, in most cases (that is, among most nations) that the month was divided into two. The division at half full increasing and half full decreasing would be the more exact ; but once made would afford the means of determining the times of ' full ' and ' new.' During the first few months after men had noticed closely the times of half full, they would perceive that between fourteen and fifteen days separated these times, so that 'full' and ' new ' came about seven days after the times of half-moon.

All this would be comparatively rough work. Herdsmen, and perhaps the tillers of the soil in harvest time, would perceive that the lunar month, their ordinary measure of time, was naturally divisible into four quarters two epochs (the half-moons) limiting which were neatly defined, while the intermediate two could be easily inferred. They would fall into the habit of dividing the months into quarters in this rough way long before they began to look for some connection between the length of the month and of the day, precisely as men (later, no doubt) divided the year roughly into four seasons, and the seasons into months, long before they had formed precise notions as to the number of months in years and seasons. We

than the books of Job and Genesis), we find in the account of the creation of the sun, moon, and stars, from which the account in Genesis was probably abridged, special reference to the moon's change from the horned to the gibbous phase—' At the beginning of the month, at the rising of the night, his horns are breaking through, and shine on the heaven ; on the ninth day to a circle he begins to swell.'

shall see presently that in each case, so soon as they tried to connect two measures of time—the month and day in one case, the year and month in the other—similar difficulties presented themselves. We shall see also that while similar ways of meeting these difficulties naturally occurred to men, these natural methods of dealing with the difficulties were those actually followed in one case certainly, and (to show which is the object of the present paper) most probably in the other also.

Men, at least those who were given to the habit of enumeration, would have found out that there are some 29½ days in each lunar month, not long after they had regarded the month as divided into four parts, and long before they had thought of connecting months and days together. After a while, however, the occasion of some such connection would arise. It might arise in many different ways. The most likely occasion, perhaps, would be the necessity of apportioning work to those employed as herdsmen or in tilling the soil. They would be engaged probably (so soon as the simplest of all engagements, by the day, required some extension) by the month. In fact one may say that certainly the hiring of labourers for agricultural and pastoral work must have been by the month almost from the beginning.[1]

---

[1] The earliest record we have of hiring is that contained in Genesis, chap. xxix. We read there that Jacob 'abode with Laban *the space of a month,*' serving him without wages. Then Laban said to Jacob, 'Because thou art my brother, shouldst thou therefore serve me for nought? tell me, what shall thy wages be?' At this time, it is worth noting, the number seven had come to be regarded as convenient in hiring, for Jacob said, 'I will serve thee seven years for Rachel thy younger daughter. . . . And Jacob served seven years for Rachel; and they seemed unto him but a few days, for the love he had to her.' It is obvious that the length of the service was regarded by the narrator as a special proof of Jacob's love for Rachel. For an ordinary wage a man would work seven days; for his love Jacob worked seven years. That this was so is shown by Laban's calling the term a week. After giving Leah instead of Rachel, he says, 'Fulfil her week, and we will

But from the beginning of hiring also, it must have become necessary to measure the month by days. Herdsmen and labourers could not have had their terms of labour defined by the actual observation of the lunar phases, though these might have shown them, in a rough sort of way, how their term of labour was passing on.

Thus, at length, a month of days and its subdivisions must have come into use. The subdivisions would almost certainly correspond with the quarters already indicated; and the week of seven days is the nearest approach in an exact number of days to the quarter of a month. Four periods of eight days exceed a lunar month by two and a-half days; while four periods of seven days exceed a lunar month by only one and a-half days.

Now there would be two distinct ways in which the division of the month into four weeks might be arrranged.

First, the month might be taken as a constant measure of time, and four weeks, of seven days each, suitably placed in each month, so that the extra day and a-half, or (nearly enough) three days in two months, could be intercalated. Thus in one month a day could be left out at the time of new moon, and in the next two days, one day alternating with two in successive months: if the remaining part of each month were divided into four equal parts of seven days in each, the arrangement would correspond closely enough with the progress of the months to serve for a considerable time before fresh intercalation was required. Two lunar months would thus be counted as fifty-nine days, falling short of the truth by one hour, twenty-eight minutes, and

give thee this also for the service which thou shalt serve with me yet seven other years. And Jacob did so, and fulfilled her week.' The week must have been a customary term of engagement long before this, or it would not be thus spoken of. Servants (the herdsmen of Abram's cattle, and the herdsmen of Lot's cattle) are mentioned somewhat earlier. The word 'week' is not used earlier than in the passage just quoted; and there is no reference to a weekly day of rest before the Exodus.

nearly eight seconds. On four lunar months the difference would be nearly three hours, and in thirty-two lunar months nearly one day. So that if in the first month two days, in the second one, in the third two, in the fourth one, and so on—in the thirty-first two, and in the thirty-second *two* (instead of one) were intercalated, the total error in those thirty-two months, or about two years and five calendar months of our present time, would be only about half-an-hour.

We find traces of a former arrangement by which the time of new moon was separated, as it were, from the rest of the lunar month. The occurrence of new moon marked in most of the old systems a time of rest and religious worship, probably, almost certainly, arising originally from the worship of the heavenly bodies as deities. But the chronological arrangements, probably connected with this usage at first, have left few traces of their existence. The usage presents manifest imperfections as part of a chronological system, and must soon have been abandoned by the more skilful of those who sought among the celestial bodies for the means of measuring time. The Greeks adopted such an arrangement as I have above indicated. 'The last day of each lunar month,' Whewell says, 'was called by them "the old and new," as belonging to both the waning and the reappearing moon, and their festivals and sacrifices, as determined by the calendar, were conceived to be necessarily connected with the same periods of the cycles of the sun and moon.' 'The laws and oracles,' says Geminus, 'which directed that they should in sacrifices observe three things, months, days, and years, were so understood.' With this persuasion, a correct system of intercalation became a religious duty. Aratus, in a passage quoted by Geminus, says of the moon—

> 'As still her shifting visage changing turns,
> By her we count the monthly round of morns.'

But the religious duty of properly intercalating a day every thirty-two months, to correct for the difference between two

lunar months and fifty-nine days, would seem not to have
been properly attended to, for Aristophanes in the 'Clouds'
makes the moon complain thus :—

'CHORUS OF CLOUDS.

' The moon by us to you her greeting sends,
But bids us say that she's an ill-used moon,
And takes it much amiss that you should still
Shuffle her days, and turn them topsy-turvy ;
And that the gods, who know their feast-days well,
By your false count are sent home supperless,
And scold and storm at her for your neglect.'

The second usage would be the more convenient. Perceiving, as they would by this time have done, that the
lunar month does not contain an exact number of days, or
of half-days, men would recognise the uselessness of attempting to use any subdivision of the month, month by
month, and would simply take the week of seven days as
the nearest approach to the convenient subdivision, the
quarter-month, and let that period run on continually, without concerning themselves with the fact that each new
month began on a different day of the week. In fact this
corresponds precisely with what has been done in the case
of the year.

The necessity of adopting some arrangement for periodi-
.cal rest would render the division of time into short periods
of unvarying length desirable. And, as herdsmen and labourers were early engaged by the lunar month, and afterwards by its subdivision the quarter-month, it is very probable that the beginning of each month would first be
chosen as a suitable time for a rest, while later one day in
each week would be taken as a rest day. This would not
be by any means inconsistent with the belief that from
very early times a religious significance was given to the
monthly and weekly resting days. Almost every observance
of times and seasons and days had its first origin, most probably, in agricultural and pastoral customs. It was only
after a long period had elapsed that arrangements, originally

adopted as convenient, became so sanctioned by long habit that a religious meaning was attached to them. Assuredly, whatever opinion may be formed about the Sabbath rest, only one can be formed about the 'new moon' rest. *That* certainly had its origin in the lunar motions and their relation to the convenience and habits of outdoor workers. It seems altogether reasonable, apart from the evidence *à priori* and *à posteriori* in favour of the conclusion, to adopt a similar explanation of the weekly rest, constantly associated as we find it with the rest at the time of new moon.

This explanation implies that the week would almost certainly be adopted as a measure of time by every nation which paid any attention to the subject of time-measurement. Now we know that no trace of the week exists among the records of some nations, while in others the week was at least only a subordinate time-measure. Among the earlier Egyptians the month was divided into periods of ten days each, and hitherto no direct evidence has been found to show that a seven-day period was used by them.[1] The Chinese divided the month similarly. Among the Babylonians the month was divided into periods of five days, six such periods in each month, and also into weeks of seven days. The same double arrangement was adopted by the Hebrews.

It is easy to show, however, that the division of the month into six equal or nearly equal parts, five days in each, was not arrived at in a similar way to the division into four parts, and was a later method. We have seen how the quarters of the lunar orbit are determined at 'half-full,' by the boundary between the light and dark half crossing the middle of the moon's disc. Content at first to determine this ocularly, observers would after a time devise simply

---

[1] Laplace asserts of the Egyptians that they used a period of seven days, but he misunderstood the account given by Dion Cassius, who referred to the astronomers of the Alexandrian School, not to the ancient Egyptians.

methods of making more exact determinations. Such
devices as Ferguson, the self-taught Scottish peasant, employed to determine the positions of the stars, would be
likely to occur to the Chaldæan shepherds in old times.
That astronomer (for he well merits the name, when we
consider under what disadvantages he achieved success)
constructed a frame across which slender threads could be
shifted, so that their intersections should coincide with the
apparent places of stars. A frame similarly constructed
might be made to carry four such threads forming a square,
which properly placed would just seem to enclose the
moon's disc, while a fifth thread parallel to two sides of the
square and midway between them could be made to coincide
with the straight edge of the half-moon,—and thus the
exact time of half-moon could be easily determined. Now
when the separating line or arc between light and darkness
fell otherwise, the fifth thread might be made to show exactly how far across this separating arc (that is, its middle
point) had travelled, and thence how far the month had
progressed,—*if* the observer had some little knowledge of
trigonometry. If he had no such knowledge, but were acquainted only with the simpler geometrical relations of lines
and circles, there would only be two other cases, besides
that of the half-moon, with which he could deal by this
simple method, or some modification of it. When the
middle point of the arc between light and darkness has
travelled exactly one-fourth of the way across the moon's
disc, the moon has gone one-third of the way from
'new' to 'full.' When that middle point has travelled
exactly three-fourths of the way across, the moon has gone
two-thirds of the way from 'new' to 'full.' Either stage
can be determined almost as easily with the frame and
threads, or some such contrivance, as the time of half-moon,
and similarly of the corresponding stages from 'full' to
'new.' Thus, including new and full, we have six stages
in the moon's complete circuit. She starts from 'new;'
when she has gone one-sixth of the way round, the advancing

arc of light has travelled one-fourth of the way across her disc ; when she has gone two-sixths round, it has travelled three-fourths of the way across : then comes 'full,' corresponding to half-way round ; then, at four-sixths of the way round, the receding edge is one-fourth of the way back across the moon's disc ; at five-sixths it is three-fourths of the way back ; and lastly she completes her circuit at 'new' again.   Each stage of her journey lasts one-sixth of a lunar month; or five days, less about two hours.   Thus five days more nearly represents one of these stages than a week represents a quarter of a lunar month.   For a week falls short of a quarter of a month by more than nine hours, while five days exceeds a sixth of a month by rather less than two hours.   Moreover while six periods of five days exceed a month by less than half-a-day, four weeks fall short of a month by more than a day and a-half.[1]

We can very well understand, then, that the division of the lunar month into six parts, each of five days, or into three parts, each of ten days, should have been early suggested by astronomers, as an improvement on the comparatively rough division of the month into four equal parts. We can equally understand that where the latter method had been long in use, where it had become connected with the system of hiring (one day's rest being allowed in each quarter-month), and especially where it had become associated with religious observances, the new method would be stoutly resisted.   It would seem that a contest between advocates of a five days' period and those of a seven days' period arose in early times, and was carried on with considerable bitterness.   There are those who find in the great pyramid of Egypt the record of such a struggle, and

---

[1] The five days' period has as great an advantage over the week in more exactly dividing the year, as it has in dividing the month, since, while fifty-two weeks fall short of a year by nearly a day and a quarter, seventy-three periods of five days only fall short of a year by a quarter of a day.   But the number 52 has the great advantage over 73 of being subdivisible into four thirteens.

evidence that finally the seven days' period came to be distinguished, as a sacred time-measure, from the five days' period, which was regarded doubtless as a profane though perhaps a more exact and scientific subdivision. In the Jewish religious system, however, both subdivisions appear.

A singular piece of evidence has quite recently been obtained respecting the week of the Babylonians, which, while illustrating what I have above shown about the week and the five days' period, seems to afford some explanation of the week of weeks. So far as I know, it has not been considered in this particular light before. We learn from Professor Sayce that the Babylonians called the 7th, 14th, 19th, 21st, and 28th days of each month *sabbatu,* or day of rest. Here clearly the 7th, 14th, 21st, and 28th correspond to the same day of the week; but how does the 19th fall into the series? It appears to me,—though I must admit that I only make a guess in the matter, knowing of no independent evidence to favour the idea,—that the 19th day of a month became a day of rest as being the forty-ninth day from the beginning of the preceding month. It was, in fact, from the preceding month, the seventh seventh day, or the sabbath of sabbaths. So to regard it, however,—that is, to make the 19th day of one month the forty-ninth from the beginning of the preceding,—it is necessary that the length of the month should be regarded as thirty days (the difference between forty-nine days and nineteen).

While in any nation the month and its subdivisions would thus, in all probability, be dealt with,—the week almost inevitably becoming, for a while at least, a measure of time, and in most cases remaining so long in use as to obtain an unshaken hold on the people from the mere effect of custom, —another way of dealing with the moon's motions would certainly have been recognised.

Watching the moon, night after night, men would soon perceive that she travels among the stars. It is not easy to determine, from *à priori* considerations, at what particular

stage of observational progress the stars, which are scattered
over the background on which the heavenly bodies travel,
would be specially noticed as objects likely to help men in
the measurement of time, the determination of seasons, and
so forth. On the whole it seems likely that the observation
of the stars for this purpose would come rather later than
the first rough determinations of the year, and therefore considerably later (if the above reasoning is just) than the determination of the month. The suitability of the stars for
many purposes connected with the measurement of time is
not a circumstance which obtrudes itself on the attention.
Many years might well pass before men would notice that
at the same season of the year the same stars are seen at
corresponding hours of the night ; for this is less striking
than the regular variation of the sun's altitude, &c., as the
year progresses. This would be true even if we assumed
that from the beginning certain marked star groups were recognised and remembered at each return to particular positions on the sky. But it is unlikely that this happened until
long after such rough observations as I have described above
had made considerable progress. There is only one group
of stars respecting which any exception can probably be
made,—viz., the Pleiades, a group which, being both conspicuous and unique in the heavens, must very early have
been recognised and remembered. But even in the case of
the Pleiades (though almost certainly it was the first
known star group, while most probably it was the object
which led to the first precise determination of the year's
length) a considerable time must have passed before the regular
return of the group, at times corresponding to particular
parts of the year of seasons, was recognised by shepherds
and tillers of the soil. Certainly the moon's motions must
have been earlier noted.

So soon, however, as men had begun to study the fixed
stars, to group them into constellations, and to watch the
motions of these groups athwart the heavens, hour by hour,

and (at the same hour) night by night, they would note with interest the motions of their special time-measurer, the moon, amongst the stars.

They would find first that the moon circuits the stellar heavens always in the same direction, namely, from west to east, or in the direction contrary to that of the apparent diurnal motion which she shares with all the celestial bodies. A very few months would show that, speaking generally, the moon keeps to one track round the heavens ; but possibly, even in so short a time, close observers would perceive that she had slightly deviated from the course she at first pursued. After a time this would be clearly seen, and probably the observers of those days may have supposed for a while that the moon, getting farther and farther from her original track, would eventually travel on a quite different path. But with the further progress of time, she would be found slowly to return to it. And in the course of many years it would be found that her path lies always, not in a certain track round the celestial sphere, but in a certain zone or band, some twenty moon-breadths wide—to which no doubt a special name would be given. It was in reality the mid-zone of the present zodiac, which is about thirty-five moon-breadths' wide. The central track of the moon's zone, which may be called the lunar zodiac, is in reality the track of the sun round the heavens. But the recognition of the moon's zone would long precede either the determination of the sun's path among the stars or that of the zodiac or planetary highway. The distinction between the sun and moon in this respect is well indicated in Job's words, ' If I beheld the sun when it shined, or the moon walking in brightness,' —the brightness of the sun preventing man from determining his real course till astronomy as a science had made considerable progress: whereas the track of the moon among the stars is obvious to every one who watches the moon, either from night to night or even for a few hours on any one night. The motions of the planets, again, and indeed the very recognition of these wandering stars, belong to an astronomy much more advanced than that which we have been here dealing with.

Watching the moon's progress along her zone of the stellar heavens night after night, the observers would perceive that she completes the circuit in less than a month. Before many months had passed they would have determined the period of these circuits as between twenty-seven and twenty-eight days. It is very likely that at first, while their estimate of the true period was as yet inexact, they would suppose that it lasted exactly four weeks. We must remember that the natural idea of the earlier observers would be that the motions of the various celestial bodies did in reality synchronise in some way; though how those motions synchronised might not easily be discovered. They would suppose, and as a matter of fact we know they did suppose, that the sun and moon and stars were made to be for signs and seasons and for days and months and years. To imagine that the celestial machinery contrived for man's special benefit was in any sense imperfect would have appeared very wicked. They would thus be somewhat in the position of a person for whom a clockmaker had constructed a very elaborate and ingenious clock, showing a number of relations, as the progress of the day, the hour, the minute, the second, the years, the months, the seasons, the tides, and so forth, but with no explanation of the various dials. The owner of the clock would be persuaded that all the various motions indicated on the dials were intended for his special enlightenment, though he would be unable for a long time to make out their meaning, or might fail altogether. So the first observers of the heavens must have been thoroughly assured that the movements of the sun, moon, planets, and stars were for measures of time, and therefore synchronised (though in long periods) with each other. We recognise a wider system (a nobler scheme, one might say, if this did not imply a degree of knowledge which we do not really possess) in the actual motions of the celestial bodies. But with the men of old times it was different.

H

Most probably, then, perceiving that the moon completes her circuit of the stellar heavens in a day or two less than a lunar month, they would suppose that it was *this* motion which the moon completes in twenty-eight days. Nor would they detect the error of this view so readily as the student of modern astronomy might suppose. The practice of carrying on cycle after cycle till a great number have been completed in order to ascertain the true length of the cycle, obvious though it now appears to us, would not be at all an obvious resource to the first observers of the heavens. Of course, if this method had been employed, it would soon have shown that the moon's circuit of the stellar heavens is accomplished in less than twenty-eight days. The excess of two-thirds of a day in each circuit would mount up to many days in many circuits, and would then be recognised,— while after very many months the exact value of the excess would be determined. This, however, is a process belonging to much later times than those we are considering. Watching the moon's motions among the stars during one lunation, the observer, unless very careful, would note nothing to suggest that she is travelling round at the rate of more than a complete circuit in twenty-eight days. If he divided her zone into twenty-eight equal parts, corresponding to her daily journey, and as soon as she first appeared as a new moon began to watch her progress through such of these twenty-eight divisions as were visible at the time (those on the sun's side of the heavens would of course not be visible), she would seem to travel across one division in twenty-four hours very nearly. As she herself obliterates from view all but the brighter stars, it would be all the more difficult to recognise the slight discrepancy actually existing,—the fact really being that she requires only twenty-three hours and about twenty-six minutes to traverse a station, a discrepancy large enough in time, but corresponding to very little progress on the moon's part among the stars. Then in the next month the observation would simply be repeated, no comparison being made between the moon's position among the stars when first seen in one month and that which she had attained when last seen in the preceding month. If this were done—and this seems the natural way of observing the moon's motions among the stars when astronomy was yet but young—the discrepancy between the period of circuit and four weeks would long remain undetected. So long as this was the case, the moon's roadway among the stars would be divided into twenty-eight daily portions.

Accordingly, we find, in the early astronomy of nearly all nations, a lunar zodiac divided into twenty-eight constellations or lunar mansions. The Chinese called the zodiac the Yellow Way, and divided it into twenty-eight *nakshatras.* These divisions or mansions were not neatly or precisely defined, but, precisely as we should expect from the comparative roughness of a system of astronomy in which alone they could appear at all, were irregular divisions, straggling far on either side of the ecliptic, which should be the central circle of the lunar roadway among the stars. The mansions were named from the brightest stars in each ; and we are told that the sixteenth mansion was named *Vichaca*, from a star in the Northern Crown, a constellation almost as distant from the ecliptic as the horizon is from a point half-way towards the point overhead.

A similar division of the older zodiac was adopted by Egyptian, Arabian, Persian, and Indian astronomers. The Siamese, however, only reckoned twenty-seven, with from time to time an extra one, called *Abigiteen*, or the intercalary mansion. It would appear, however, from some statements in their books, that they had twenty-eight lunar constellations for certain classes of observation. Probably, therefore, the use of twenty-seven, with an occasional intercalary mansion, belonged to a later period of their astronomical system, when more careful observations than the earlier had shown them that the moon circuits the stellar heavens in about twenty-seven and one-third days.

It is important to observe that astronomers were thus apt to change their usage, dropping either wholly or in great part the use of arrangements found to be imperfect. For, noting this, we shall have less difficulty in understanding how the twenty-eight lunar mansions of the older astronomy gave place entirely among the Chaldæans to the twelve signs of the zodiac—that is, the parts of the zodiac traversed day by day by the moon gave place to the parts of the zodiac traversed month by month by the sun. Because the Chaldæan astronomy has not the twenty-eight lunar mansions, it is commonly assumed that this way of dividing the zodiac was never used by them. But this conclusion cannot safely be adopted. On the contrary, what we have already ascertained respecting the Chaldæan use of the week, besides what we should naturally infer from *à priori* considerations, suggests that in the first instance they, like other nations, divided the zodiac into twenty-eight parts ; but that later, recognising the inaccuracy of this arrangement, they abandoned it, and adopted the solar zodiacal signs.

This corresponds closely with what the Persian astronomers are known to have done. We read that 'the twenty-eight divisions among the Persians (of which it may be noticed that the second was formed by the Pleiades, and called *Pervis*) soon gave way to the twelve, the names of which, recorded in the works of Zoroaster, and therefore not less ancient than he, were not quite the same as those now used. They were the Lamb, the Bull, the Twins, the Crab, the Lion, the Ear of Corn, the Balance, the Scorpion, the Bow, the Sea Goat, the Watering Pot, and the Fishes. The Chinese also formed a set of twelve zodiacal signs, which they named the Mouse, the Cow, the Tiger, the Hare, the Dragon, the Serpent, the Horse, the Sheep, the Monkey, the Cock, the Dog, and the Pig.

It appears to me not unlikely that the change from lunar to solar astronomy, from the use of the month and week as chief measures of time to the more difficult but much more scientific method of employing the year for this purpose, was the occasion of much ceremonial observance among the Chaldæan astronomers. Probably elaborate preparations

were made for the change, and a special time chosen for it.
We should expect to find that this time would have very
direct reference to the Pleiades, which must have been the
year-measuring constellation as certainly as the moon had
earlier been the time-measuring orb.   It has long seemed to
me that it is to this great change, which certainly took place,
and must have been a most important epoch in astronomy,
that we must refer those features of ancient astronomy
which have commonly been regarded as pointing to the
origin of the science itself.   I cannot regard it as a reasonable, still less as a probable assumption, that astronomy
sprang full formed into being, as the ordinary theories on
this subject would imply.   Great progress must have been
made, and men carefully trained in mathematical as well as
observational astronomy must for centuries have studied the
subject, before it became possible to decide upon those
fundamental principles and methods which have existed
from the days of the Chaldæan astronomers even until now.
As to the epoch of the real beginning of astronomy, then,
we have, in my opinion, no means of judging.   The epoch
to which we really can point with some degree of certainty
—the year 2170 B.C. or thereabouts—must belong, not to
the infancy of astronomy, but to an era when the science
had made considerable progress.

I have said that we should expect to find the introduction of the new astronomy, the rejection of the *week* as an
astronomical period in favour of the *year*, to be marked by
some celestial event having special reference to the Pleiades,
the year-measuring star-group.   Whether the *à priori* consideration here indicated is valid or not, may perhaps be
doubtful ; but it is certain the epoch above mentioned *is* related to the Pleiades in a quite unmistakable manner.   For
at that epoch, *quam proximè*, through the effects of that
mighty gyrational movement of the earth which causes what
is termed the precession of the equinoxes, the star Alcyone,
the brightest of the Pleiades and nearly central in the group,
was carried to such a position that when the spring began

the sun and Alcyone rose to their highest in the southern skies at the same instant of time.

Be this, however, as it may, it seems abundantly clear that quite early in the progress of astronomy, the more scientific and observant must have recognised the unfitness of the week as an astronomical measure of time. With the disappearance of the week from astronomical systems (the lunar 'quarters' being retained, however) the week may be considered to have become what it now is for ourselves, a civil and in some sense a religious time-measure. That it should retain its position in this character was to be expected, if we consider the firm hold which civil measures once established obtain among the generality of men, and the still greater constancy with which men retain religious observances. A struggle probably took place between astronomers and the priesthood when first the solar zodiac came into use instead of the lunar stations, and when an effort was made to get rid of the week as a measure of time. This seems to me to be indicated by many passages in certain more or less mythological records of the race through whom (directly) the week has descended to us. But this part of the subject introduces questions which cannot be satisfactorily dealt with without a profound study of those records in their mythological sense, and a thorough investigation of philological relations involved in the subject. Such researches, accompanied by the careful discussion of all such astronomical relations as were found to be involved, would, I feel satisfied, be richly rewarded. More light will be thrown on the ancient systems of astronomy and astrology by the careful study of some of the Jewish Scriptures, and clearer light will be thrown on the meaning of these books by the consideration of astronomical and astrological relations associated with them, than has heretofore been supposed. The key to much that was mysterious in the older systems of religion has been found in the consideration that to man as first he rose above the condition of savagery, the grander objects and processes of nature—earth, sea, and sky, clouds and rain, winds and storms, the earthquake and the volcano, but, above and beyond all, the heavenly bodies with their stately movements, their inextricably intermingled periods, their mystical symbolisms—all these must have appeared as themselves divine, until a nobler conception presented them as but parts of a higher and more mysterious Whole. In all the ancient systems of religion we have begun to recognise the myths which had their birth in those first natural conceptions of the Child-man. To this rule the ancient religious system of the Hebrew race was no exception; but from their Chaldæan ancestors they derived a nature-worship relating more directly to the heavenly bodies than that of nations living under less constant skies, and to whom other phenomena were not less important, and there- · fore not less significant of power, than the phenomena of the starry heavens. So soon as we thus recognise that Hebrew myths would, of necessity, be more essentially astronomical than those of other nations, we perceive that the Hebrew race was not unlike other early races in having no mythology, as Max Müller thought, but possessed a mythology less simply and readily interpreted than that of other nations. It would, however, take me far from my special subject at present to deal further with the considera- tions to which it has here led me. I may, however, before long endeavour to show reason for my belief.

THE PROBLEM OF THE GREAT
PYRAMID.

IN the preceding essay I endeavoured to trace out the probable origin of the week, as a measure of time, by a
method which has not hitherto, so far as I know, been followed in such cases.   I followed chiefly a line of *à priori*
reasoning, considering how herdsmen and tillers of the soil
would be apt at a very early period to use the moon as a
means of measuring time, and how in endeavouring so to
use her they would almost of necessity be led to employ
special methods of subdividing the period during which she
passes through her various phases.   But while each step of
the reasoning was thus based on *à priori* considerations, its
validity was tested by the evidence which has reached us
respecting the various methods employed by different nations
of antiquity for following the moon's motions.   It appears
to me that the conclusions to which this method of reasoning led were more satisfactory, because more trustworthy,
than those which have been reached respecting the week by
the mere study of various traditions which have reached us
respecting the early use of this widespread time-measure.
    I now propose to apply a somewhat similar method to a
problem which has always been regarded as at once highly
interesting and very difficult, the question of the purpose for
which the pyramids of Egypt, and especially the pyramids of
Ghizeh, were erected.   But I do not here take the full problem
under consideration.   I have, indeed, elsewhere dealt with it
in a general manner, and have been led to a theory respecting

the pyramids which will be touched on towards the close of the present paper. Here, however, I intend to deal only with one special part of the problem, that part to which alone the method I propose to employ is applicable—the question of the astronomical purpose which the pyramids were intended to subserve. It will be understood, there-fore, why I have spoken of applying a somewhat similar method, and not a precisely similar method, to the problem of the pyramids. For whereas in dealing with the origin of the week, I could from the very beginning of the inquiry apply the *à priori* method, I cannot do so in the case of the pyramids. I do not know of any line of *à priori* reasoning by which it could be proved, or even rendered probable, that any race of men, of whatever proclivities or avocations, would naturally be led to construct buildings resembling the pyramids. If it could be, of course that line of reasoning would at the same time indicate what pur-poses such buildings were intended to subserve. Failing evidence of this kind, we must follow at first the *à posteriori* method; and this method, while it is clear enough as to the construction of the pyramids themselves to speak unmistakably on this point, is not altogether so clear as to any one of the purposes for which the pyramids were built.

Yet I think that if there is one purpose among possibly many which the builders of the pyramids had in their thoughts, which can be unmistakably inferred from the pyramids themselves, independently of all traditions, it is the purpose of constructing edifices which should enable men to observe the heavenly bodies in some way not other-wise obtainable. If the orienting of the faces of the pyramids had been effected in some such way as the orienting of most of our cathedrals and churches—*i.e.*, in a manner quite sufficiently exact as tested by ordinary observation, but not capable of bearing astronomical tests, —it might reasonably enough be inferred that having to erect square buildings for any purpose whatever, men were likely

enough to set them four-square to the cardinal points, and
that, therefore, no stress whatever can be laid on this feature
of the pyramids' construction. But when we find that the
orienting of the pyramids has been effected with extreme
care, that in the case of the great pyramid, which is the
typical edifice of this kind, the orienting bears well the
closest astronomical scrutiny, we cannot doubt that this
feature indicates an astronomical purpose as surely as it indicates the use of astronomical methods.

But while we thus start with what is to some degree an
assumption, with what at any rate is not based on *à priori*
considerations, yet manifestly we may expect to find
evidence as we proceed which shall either strengthen our
opinion on this point, or show it to be unsound. We are
going to make this astronomical purpose the starting-point
for a series of *à priori* considerations, each to be tested by
whatever direct evidence may be available ; and it is practically certain that if we have thus started in an entirely wrong
direction, we shall before long find out our mistake. At
least we shall do so, if we start with the desire to find out as
much of the truth as we can, and not with the determination to see only those facts which point in the direction
along which we have set out, overlooking any which
seem to point in a different direction. We need not
necessarily be on the wrong track because of such seeming
indications. If we are on the right track, we shall see
things more clearly as we proceed ; and it may be that
evidence which at first seems to accord ill with the idea that
we are progressing towards the truth, may be found among
the most satisfactory evidence obtainable. But we must in
any case note such evidence, even at the time when it seems
to suggest that we are on the wrong track. We may push
on, nevertheless, to see how such evidence appears a little
later. But we must by no means forget its existence. So
only can we hope to reach the truth, or a portion of the truth,
instead of merely making out a good case for some particular theory.

We start, then, with the assumption that the great pyramid, called the Pyramid of Cheops, was built for this purpose, *inter alia,* to enable men to make certain astronomical observations with great accuracy ; and what we propose to do is to inquire what would be done by men having this purpose in view, having, as the pyramid builders had, (1) a fine astronomical site, (2) the command of enormous wealth, (3) practically exhaustless stores of material, and (4) the means of compelling many thousands of men to labour for them.

Watching the celestial bodies hour by hour, day by day, and year by year, the observer recognises certain regions of the heavens which require special attention, and certain noteworthy directions both with respect to the horizon and to elevation above the horizon.

For instance, the observer perceives that the stars, which are in many respects the most conveniently observable bodies, are carried round as if they were rigidly attached to a hollow sphere, carried around an axis passing through the station of the observer (as through a centre) and directed towards a certain point in the dome of the heavens. That point, then, is one whose direction must not only be ascertained, but must be in some way or other indicated. Whatever the nature of an astronomer's instruments or observatory, whether he have but a few simple contrivances in a structure of insignificant proportions, or the most perfect instruments in a noble edifice of most exquisite construction and of the utmost attainable stability, he must in every case have the position of the pole of the heavens clearly indicated in some way or other. Now, the pole of the heavens is a point lying due north, at a certain definite elevation above the horizon. Thus the first consideration to be attended to by the builder of any sort of astronomical observatory, is the determination of the direction of the true north (or the laying down of a true north-and-south line), while the second is the determination, and in some way or other the indication, of the angle of elevation above the north point, at which the true pole of the heavens may lie.

To get the true north-and-south line, however, the astronomer would be apt at first, perhaps, rather to make mid-day observations than to observe the stars at night. It would have been the observation of these which first called his attention to the existence of a definite point round which all the stars seem to be carried in parallel circles ; but he would very quickly notice that the sun and the moon, and also the five planets, are carried round the same polar axis ; —only differing from the stars in this, that, besides being thus carried round with the celestial sphere, they also move upon that sphere, though with a motion which is very slow compared with that which they derive from the seeming motion of the sphere itself. Now, among these bodies the sun and moon possess a distinct advantage over the stars. A body illuminated by either the sun or the moon throws a shadow, and thus if we place an upright pointed rod in sunlight or moonlight, and note where the shadow of the point lies, we know that a straight line from the point to the shadow of the point is directed exactly towards the sun or the moon, as the case may be. Leaving the moon aside as in other respects unsuitable, for she only shines with suitable lustre in one part of each month, we have in the sun's motions a means of getting the north-and-south line by thus noting the position of the shadow of a pointed upright. For being carried around an inclined axis directed northwards, the sun is, of course, brought to his greatest elevation on any given day when due south. So that if we note when the shadow of an upright is shortest on any day, we know that at that moment the sun is at his highest or due south ; and the line joining the centre of the upright's base with the end of the shadow at that instant lies due north and south.

But though theoretically this method is sufficient, it is open, in practice, to a serious objection. The sun's eleva-tion, when he is nearly at his highest, changes very slowly ;

so that it is difficult to determine the precise moment when the shadow is shortest. But the direction of the shadow is steadily changing all the time that we thus remain in doubt whether the sun's elevation has reached its maximum or not. We are apt, then, to make an error as to time, which will result in a noteworthy error as to the direction of the north-and-south line.

For this reason, it would be better for any one employing this shadow method to take two epochs on either side of solar noon, when the sun was at exactly the same elevation, or the shadow of exactly the same length,—determining this by striking out a circle around the foot of the upright, and observing where the shadow's point crossed this circle before noon in drawing nearer to the base, and after noon in passing away from the base. These two intersections with the circle necessarily lie at equal distances from the north-and-south line, which can thus be more exactly determined than by the other method, simply because the end of the shadow crosses the circle traced on the ground at moments which can be more exactly determined than the moment when the shadow is shortest.

Now, we notice in this description of methods which unquestionably were followed by the very earliest astronomers, one circumstance which clearly points to a feature as absolutely essential in every astronomical observing station. (I do not say 'observatory,' for I am speaking just now of observations so elementary that the word would be out of place.) The observer must have a perfectly flat floor on which to receive the shadow of the upright pointer. And not only must the floor be flat, but it must also be perfectly horizontal. At any rate, it must not slope down either towards the east or towards the west, for then the shadows on either side of the north-and-south line would be unequal. And though a slope towards north or south would not affect the equality of such shadows, and would therefore be admissible, yet it would clearly be altogether undesirable ; since the avoidance of a slope towards east or west would be made much more difficult if the surface were tilted, however slightly, towards north or south. Apart from this, several other circumstances make it extremely desirable that the surface from which the astronomers make their observations should be perfectly horizontal. In particular, we shall see presently that the exact determination of elevations above the eastern and western horizons would be very necessary even in the earliest and simplest methods of observation, and for this purpose it would be essential that the observing surface should be as carefully levelled in a north-and-south as well as in an east-and-west direction.

We should expect to find, then, that when the particular stage of astronomical progress had been reached, at which men not only perceived the necessity of well-devised buildings for astronomical observation, but were able to devote time, labour, and expense to the construction of such buildings, the first point to which they would direct their attention would be the formation of a perfectly level surface, on which eventually they might lay down a north-and-south or true meridional line.

Now, of the extreme care with which this preliminary question of level was considered by the builders of the great pyramid, we have singularly clear and decisive evidence. For, all around the base of the pyramid there was a pavement, and we find the builders not only so well acquainted with the position of the true horizontal plane at the level of this pavement, but so careful to follow it (even as respects this pavement, which, be it noticed, was only, in all probability, a subsidiary and quasi-ornamental feature of the building), that the pavement 'was varied in thickness at the rate of about an inch in 100 feet to make it absolutely level, which the rock was not.'[1]

[1] It seems to me not improbable that the level was de'ermined by simply flooding (though to a very small depth only, of course) the entire area to be levelled—not only the pavement level, but higher levels as the pyramid was raised layer by layer. By completing the outside of each layer first, an enclosed space capable of receiving the water

But now with regard to the true north-and-south direction, although the shadow method, carried out on a truly level surface, would be satisfactory enough for a first rough approximation, or even for what any but astronomers would regard as extreme accuracy, it would be open to serious objections for really exact work. These objections would have become known to observers long before the construction of the pyramid was commenced, and would have been associated with the difficulties which suggested, I think, the idea itself of constructing such an edifice.

Supposing an upright pointed post is set up, and the position of the end of the shadow upon a perfectly level surface is noted ; then whatever use we intend to make of this observation, it is essential that we should know the precise position of the centre of the upright's base, and also that the upright should be truly vertical. Otherwise we have only exactly obtained the position of one end of the line we want, and to draw the line properly we ought as exactly to know the position of the other end. If we want *also* to know the true position of a line joining the point of the upright and the shadow of this point, we require to know the true height of the upright. And even if we have these points determined, we still have not a *material* line from the point of the upright to the place of its shadow. A cord or chain from one point to the other would be curved, even if tightly stretched, and it could not be tightly stretched, if long, without either breaking or pulling over the upright. A straight bar of the required length could not be readily made or used : if stout enough to lie straight from point to point it would be unwieldy ; if not stout enough so that it bent under its own weight it would be useless.

Thus the shadow method, while difficult of application to give a true north-and-south horizontal line, would fail

would be formed (the flooding being required once only for each layer), and when the level had been taken, the water could be allowed to run off by the interior passages to the well which Piazzi Smyth considers to be symbolical of the 'bottomless pit.'

utterly to give material indications of the sun's elevation on particular days, without which it would be impossible to obtain in this manner any material indications of the position of the celestial pole.

A natural resource, under these circumstances—at least a natural resource for astronomers who could afford to adopt the plan—would be to build up masses of masonry, in which there should be tubular holes or tunnellings pointing in certain required directions. In one sense the contrivance would be clumsy, for a tunnelling, once constructed, would not admit of any change of position, nor even allow of any save very limited changes in the direction of the line of view through them. In fact, the more effective a tunnelling would be in determining any particular direction, the less scope, of course, would it afford for any change in the direc-tion of a line of sight along it. So that the astronomical architect would have to limit the use of this particular method to those cases in which great accuracy in obtaining a direction-line and great rigidity in the material indication of that line's position were essential or at least exceedingly desirable. Again, in some cases presently to be noticed, he would require, not a tubing directed to some special fixed point in the sky, but an opening commanding some special range of view. Yet again, it would be manifestly well for him to retain, whenever possible, the power of using the shadow method in observing the sun and moon ; for this method in the case of bodies varying their position on the celestial sphere, not merely with respect to the cardinal points, would be of great value. Its value would be enhanced if the shadows could be formed by objects and received on surfaces holding a permanent position.

We begin to see some of the requirements of an astrono-mical building such as we have supposed the earlier observers to plan.

First, such a building must be large, to give suitable length to the direction-lines, whether along edges of the building or along tubular passages or tunnellings within it.

Secondly, it must be massive in order that these edges and passages might have the necessary stability and permanence. Thirdly, it must be of a form contributing to such stability, and as height above surrounding objects (even though lying at considerable distances) would be a desirable feature, it would be proper to have the mass of masonry growing smaller from the base upwards. Fourthly, it must have its sides carefully oriented, so that it must have either a square or oblong base with two sides lying exactly north and south, and the other two lying exactly east and west. Fifthly, it must have the direction of the pole of the heavens either actually indicated by a tunnelling of some sort pointed directly polewards, or else inferable from a tunnelling pointing upon a suitable star close to the true pole of the heavens.

The lower part of a pyramid would fulfil the conditions required for the stability of such a structure, and a square or oblong form would be suitable for the base of such a pyramid. We must not overlook the fact that a complete pyramid would be utterly unsuitable for an astronomical edifice. Even a pyramid built up of layers of stone and continued so far upwards that the uppermost layer consisted of a single massive stone, would be quite useless as an observatory. The notion which has been entertained by some fanciful persons, that one purpose which the great pyramid was intended to subserve, was to provide a raised small platform high above the general level of the soil, in order that astronomers might climb night after night to that platform, and thence make their observations on the stars, is altogether untenable. Probably no fancy respecting the pyramids has done more to discredit the astronomical theory of these structures than has this ridiculous notion ; because even those who are not astronomers, and therefore little familiar with the requirements of a building intended for astronomical observation, perceive at once the futility of any such arrangement, and the enormous, one may almost say the infinite disproportion between the cost at which the raised small platform would have been obtained, and the small advantage which astronomers would derive from climbing up to it instead of observing from the ground level. Yet we have seen this notion not only gravely advanced by persons who are to some degree acquainted with astronomical requirements, but elaborately illustrated. Thus, in Flammarion's ' History of the Heavens,' there is a picture representing six astronomers in eastern garb, perched in uncomfortable attitudes on the uppermost steps of a pyramid, whence they are staring hard at a comet, naturally without the slightest opportunity of determining its true position in the sky, since they have no direction lines of any sort for their guidance. Apart from this, their attention is very properly directed in great part to the necessity of preserving their equilibrium. In only one point in fact does this picture accord with *à priori* probabilities—namely, in the great muscular development of these ancient observers. They are perfectly herculean, and well they might be, if night after night they had to observe the celestial bodies from a place so hard to reach, and where attitudes so awkward must be maintained during the long hours of the night.

It is perfectly clear, and is in fact one of the chief difficulties of the astronomical theory of the pyramids, that it would only be when these buildings were as yet incomplete that they could subserve any useful astronomical purposes ; nevertheless we must not on this account suffer ourselves at this early stage of our inquiry to be diverted from the astronomical theory by what must be admitted to be a very strong argument against it. We have seen that there is such decisive and even demonstrative evidence in favour of the theory that the pyramids were not oriented in a general, still less in a merely casual, manner, and this is, in reality, such clear evidence of their astronomical significance that we must pass further on upon the line of reasoning which we have adopted—prepared to turn back indeed if absolutely convincing evidence should be found against the theory of the astronomical *purpose* of the pyramids, but anticipating rather that, on a close inquiry, a means of obviating this particular objection may before long be found.

Let us suppose, then, that astronomers have determined to erect a massive edifice, on a square or oblong base properly oriented, constructing within this edifice such tubular openings as would be most useful for the purpose of indicating the true directions of certain celestial objects at particular times and seasons.

Before commencing so costly a structure they would be careful to select the best possible position for it, not only as respects the nature of the ground, but also as respects latitude. For it must be remembered that, from certain parts of the earth, the various points and circles which the astronomer recognises in the heavens occupy special positions and fulfil special relations.

So far as conditions of the soil, surrounding country, and so forth, are concerned, few positions could surpass that selected for the great pyramid and its companions. The pyramids of Ghizeh are situated on a platform of rock, about 150 feet above the level of the desert. The largest of them, the Pyramid of Cheops, stands on an elevation free all around, insomuch that less sand has gathered round it than would otherwise have been the case. How admirably suited these pyramids are for observing stations is shown by the way in which they are themselves seen from a distance. It has been remarked by every one who has seen the pyramids that the sense of sight is deceived in the attempt to appreciate their distance and magnitude. 'Though removed several leagues from the spectator, they appear to be close at hand; and it is not until he has travelled some miles in a direct line towards them, that he becomes sensible of their vast bulk and also of the pure atmosphere through which they are viewed.'

With regard to their astronomical position, it seems clear that the builders intended to place the great pyramid precisely in latitude 30°, or, in other words, in that latitude where the true pole of the heavens is one-third of the way from the horizon to the point overhead (the zenith), and where the noon sun at true spring or autumn (when the sun rises almost exactly in the east, and sets almost exactly in the west) is two-thirds of the way from the horizon to the point overhead. In an observatory set exactly in this position, some of the calculations or geometrical constructions (as the case may be) involved in astronomical problems, are considerably simplified. The first problem in Euclid, for example, by which a triangle of three equal sides is made, affords the means of drawing the proper angle at which the mid-day sun in spring or autumn is raised above the horizon, and at which the pole of the heavens is removed from the point overhead. Relations depending on this angle are also more readily calculated, for the very same reason, in fact, that the angle itself is more readily drawn. And though the builders of the great pyramid must have been advanced far beyond the stage at which any difficulty in dealing directly with other angles would be involved, yet they would perceive the great advantage of having one among the angles entering into their problems thus conveniently chosen. In our time, when by the use of logarithmic and other tables, all calculations are greatly simplified, and when also astronomers have learned to recognise that no possible choice of latitude would simplify their labours (unless an observatory could be set up at the North Pole itself, which would be in other respects inconvenient), matters of this sort are no longer worth considering, but to the mathematicians who planned the great pyramid they would have possessed extreme importance.

To set the centre of the pyramid's future base in latitude 30°, two methods could be used, both already to some degree considered—the shadow method, and the Pole-star method. If at noon, at the season when the sun rose due east and set due west, an upright A C were found to throw a shadow C D, so proportioned to A C that A C D would be one-half of an equal-sided triangle, then, theoretically, the point where this upright was placed would be in latitude 30°. As a matter of fact it would not be, because the air, by bending the sun's rays, throws the sun apparently somewhat above his true position. Apart from this, at the time of true spring or autumn, the sun does not seem to rise due east, or set due west, for he is raised above the horizon by atmospheric refraction, before he has really reached it in the morning, and he remains raised above it after he has really passed below—understanding the word 'really' to relate to his actual geometrical direction. Thus, at true spring and autumn, the sun rises to the north of east and sets slightly to the north of west. The atmospheric refraction is indeed so marked, as respects these parts of the sun's apparent course, that it must have been quickly recognised. Probably, however, it would be regarded as a peculiarity only affecting the sun when close to the horizon, and would be (correctly) associated with his apparent change of shape when so situated. Astronomers would be prevented in this way from using the sun's horizontal position at any season to guide them with respect to the cardinal points, but they would still consider the sun, when raised high above the horizon, or a suitable astronomical index

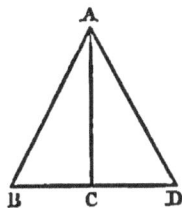

Fig. 1.

(so to speak), and would have no idea that even at a height of sixty degrees above the horizon, or seen as in direction D A, Fig. 1, he is seen appreciably above his true position.

Adopting this method—the shadow method—to fix the latitude of the pyramid's base, they would conceive the sun was sixty degrees above the horizon at noon, at true spring or autumn, when in reality he was somewhat below that elevation. Or, in other words, they would conceive they were in latitude 30° north, when in reality they were farther north (the mid-day sun at any season sinking lower and lower as we travel farther and farther north). The actual amount by which, supposing their observations exact, they would thus set this station north of its proper position, would depend on the refractive qualities of the air in Egypt. But although there

is some slight difference in this respect between Egypt and
Greenwich, it is but small; and we can determine from the
Greenwich refraction tables, within a very slight limit of
error, the amount by which the architects of the great pyramid would have set the centre of the base north of latitude 30°, if they had trusted solely to the shadow method.
The distance would have been as nearly as possible 1125
yards, or say three furlongs.

Now, if they followed the other method, observing the
stars around the pole, in order to determine the elevation
of the true pole of the heavens, they would be in a similar
way exposed to error arising from the effects of atmospheric
refraction. They would proceed probably somewhat in this
wise :—Using any kind of direction lines, they would take
the altitude of their Polar star (1) when passing immediately
under the pole, and (2) when passing immediately above the
pole. The mean of the altitudes thus obtained would be
the altitude of the true pole of the heavens. Now, atmospheric refraction affects the stars in the same way that it
affects the sun, and the nearer a star is to the horizon, the
more it is raised by atmospheric refraction. The Pole-star in
both its positions—that is when passing below the pole, and
when passing above that point—is raised by refraction,
rather more when below than when above ; but the estimated position of the pole itself, raised by about the mean
of these two effects, is in effect raised almost exactly as
much as it would be if it were itself directly observed
(that is, if a star occupied the pole itself, instead of merely
circling close round the pole). We may then simplify
matters by leaving out of consideration at present all
questions of the actual Pole-star in the time of the pyramid
builders, and simply considering how far they would have
set the pyramid's base in error, if they had determined
their latitude by observing a star occupying the position of
the true pole of the heavens.

They would have endeavoured to determine where the
pole appears to be raised exactly thirty degrees above the

horizon. But the effect of refraction being to raise every celestial object above its true position, they would have supposed the pole to be raised thirty degrees, when in reality it was less raised than this. In other words, they would have supposed they were in latitude 30°, when, in reality, they were in some lower latitude, for the pole of the heavens rises higher and higher above the horizon as we pass to higher and higher latitudes. Thus they would set their station somewhat to the south of latitude 30°, instead of to the north, as when they were supposed to have used the shadow method. Here again we can find how far they would set it south of that latitude. Using the Greenwich refraction table (which is the same as Bessel's), we find that they would have made a much greater error than when using the other method, simply because they would be observing a body at an elevation of about thirty degrees only, whereas in taking the sun's mid-day altitude in spring or autumn, they would be observing a body at twice as great an elevation. The error would be, in fact, in this case, about 1 mile 1512 yards.

It seems not at all unlikely that astronomers, so skilful and ingenious as the builders of the pyramid manifestly were, would have employed both methods. In that case they would certainly have obtained widely discrepant results, rough as their means and methods must unquestionably have been compared with modern instruments and methods. The exact determination from the shadow plan would have set them 1125 yards to the north of the true latitude ; while the exact determination from the Pole-star method would have set them 1 mile 1512 yards south of the true latitude. Whether they would thus have been led to detect the effect of atmospheric refraction on celestial bodies high above the horizon may be open to question. But certainly they would have recognised the action of some cause or other, rendering one or other method, or both methods, unsatisfactory. If so, and we can scarcely doubt that this would actually happen (for certainly they would recognise the theoretical

justice of both methods, and we can hardly imagine that
having two available methods, they would limit their operations to one method only), they would scarcely see any better way of proceeding than to take a position intermediate
between the two which they had thus obtained. Such a position would lie almost exactly 1072 yards south of true latitude 30° north.

Whether the architects of the pyramid of Cheops really
proceeded in this way or not, it is certain that they obtained
a result corresponding so well with this that if we assume
they really did intend to set the base of the pyramid in
latitude 30°, we find it difficult to persuade ourselves that
they did not follow some such course as I have just indicated
—the coincidence is so close considering the nature of the
observations involved. According to Professor Piazzi Smyth,
whose observational labours in relation to the great pyramid
are worthy of all praise, the centre of the base of this
pyramid lies about 1 mile 568 yards south of the thirtieth
parallel of latitude. This is 944 yards north of the position
they would have deduced from the Pole-star method ; 1
mile 1693 yards south of the position they would have deduced from the shadow method ; and 1256 yards south of
the mean position between the two last-named. The position
of the base seems to prove beyond all possibility of question
that the shadow method was not the method on which
sole or chief reliance was placed, though this method must
have been known to the builders of the pyramid. It does
not, however, prove that the star method was the only
method followed. A distance of 944 yards is so small in a
matter of this sort that we might fairly enough assume that
the position of the base was determined by the Pole-star
method. If, however, we supposed the builders of the
pyramid to have been exceedingly skilful in applying the
methods available to them, we might not unreasonably conclude from the position of the pyramid's base that they used
both the shadow method and the Pole-star method, but that,
recognising the superiority of the latter, they gave greater

weight to the result of employing this method. Supposing, for instance, they applied the Pole-star method three times as often as the shadow method, and took the mean of all the results thus obtained, then the deduced position would lie three times as far from the northern position obtained by the shadow method as from the southern position obtained by the Pole-star method. In this case their result, if correctly deduced, would have been only about 156 yards north of the actual present position of the centre of the base.

It is impossible, however, to place the least reliance on any calculation like that made in the last few lines. By *à posteriori* reasoning such as this one can prove almost anything about the pyramids. For observe, though presented as *à priori* reasoning, it is in reality not so, being based on the observed fact, that the true position lies more than three times as far from the northerly limit as from the southern one. Now, if in any other way, not open to exception, we knew that the builders of the pyramid used both the sun method and the star method, with perfect observational accuracy, but without knowledge of the laws of atmospheric refraction, we could infer from the observed position the precise relative weights they attached to the two methods. But it is altogether unsafe, or to speak plainly, it is in the logical sense a perfectly vicious manner of reasoning, to ascertain first such relative weights on an assumption óf this kind, and having so found them, to assert that the relation thus detected is a probable one in itself, and that since, when assumed, it accounts precisely for the observed position of the pyramid, therefore the pyramid was posited in that way and no other. It has been by unsound reasoning of this kind that nine-tenths of the absurdities have been established on which Taylor and Professor Smyth and their followers have established what may be called the pyramid religion.

All we can fairly assume as probable from the evidence, in so far as that evidence bears on the results of *à priori* considerations, is that the builders of the great pyramid preferred the Pole-star method to the shadow method, as a means of determining the true position of latitude 30° north. They seem to have applied this method with great skill, considering the means at their disposal, if we suppose that they took no account whatever of the influence of refraction. If they took refraction into account at all, they considerably underrated its influence.

Piazzi Smyth's idea that they knew the *precise* position of the thirtieth parallel of latitude, and also the *precise* position of the parallel, where, owing to refraction, the Pole-star would appear to be thirty degrees above the horizon, and deliberately set the base of the pyramid between these limits (not exactly or nearly exactly half-way, but somewhere between them), cannot be entertained for a moment by any one not prepared to regard the whole history of the construction of the pyramid as supernatural. My argument, let me note in passing, is not intended for persons who take this particular view of the pyramid, a view on which reasoning could not very well be brought to bear.

If the star method had been used to determine the position of the parallel of 30° north latitude, we may be certain it would be used also to orient the building. Probably indeed the very structures (temporary, of course) by which the final observations for the latitude had been made, would remain available also for the orientation. These structures would consist of uprights so placed that the line of sight along their extremities (or along a tube perhaps borne aloft by them in a slanting position) the Pole-star could be seen when immediately below or immediately above the pole. Altogether the more convenient direction of the two would be that towards the Pole-star when below the pole. The extremities of these uprights, or the axis of the upraised tube, would lie in a north-and-south line considerably inclined to the horizon, because the pole itself being thirty degrees above the horizon, the Pole-star, whatever star this might be, would be high above the horizon even when exactly under the pole. No star so far from the pole as to pass close to the horizon would be of use even for the work of orientation, while for the work of obtaining the latitude it would be absolutely essential that a star close to the pole should be used.

A line along the feet of the uprights would run north and south. But the very object for which the great astronomical edifice was being raised, was that the north-and-south line amongst others should be indicated by more perfect methods.

Now, at this stage of proceedings, what could be more perfect as a method of obtaining the true bearing of the pole than to dig a tubular hole into the solid rock, along which tube the Pole-star at its lower culmination should be visible? Perfect stability would be thus insured for this fundamental direction line. It would be easy to obtain the direction with great accuracy, even though at first starting the borings were not quite correctly made. And the further the boring was continued downwards towards the south, the greater the accuracy of the direction line thus obtained. Of course there could be no question whatever in such underground boring, of the advantage of taking the lower passage of the Pole-star, not the upper. For a line directly from the star at its upper passage would slant downwards at an angle of more than thirty degrees from the horizon, while a line directly from the star at its lower passage would slant downwards at an angle of less than thirty degrees; and the smaller this angle the less would be the length, and the less the depth of the boring required for any given horizontal range.

Besides perfect stability, a boring through the solid rock would present another most important advantage over any other method of orienting the base of the pyramid. In the case of an inclined direction line above the level of the horizontal base, there would be the difficulty of determining the precise position of points under the raised line; for manifest difficulties would arise in letting fall plumb-lines from various points along the optical axis of a raised tubing. But nothing could be simpler than the plan by which the horizontal line corresponding to the underground tube could be determined. All that would be necessary would be to allow the tube to terminate in a tolerably large open space ; and from a point in the base vertically above this, to let fall a plumb-line through a fine vertical boring into this open space. It would thus be found how far the point from which the plumb-line was let fall lay either to the east or to the west of the optical axis of the underground tunnel, and therefore how far to the east or to the west of the centre of the open mouth of this tunnel. Thus the true direction of a north-and-south line from the end of the tube to the middle of the base would be ascertained. This would be the meridian line of the pyramid's base, or rather the meridian line corresponding to the position of the underground passage directed towards the Pole-star when immediately under the pole.

A line at right angles to the meridian line thus obtained would lie due east and west, and the true position of the east-and-west line would probably be better indicated in this way than by direct observation of the sun or stars. If direct observation were made at all, it would be made not on the sun in the horizon near the time of spring and autumn, for the sun's position is then largely affected by refraction. The sun might be observed for this purpose during the summer months, at moments when calculation showed that he should be due east or west, or crossing what is technically termed the *prime vertical.* Possibly the so-called azimuth trenches on the east side of the great pyramid may have been in some way associated with observations of this sort, as the middle trench is directed considerably to the north of the east point, and not far from the direction in which the sun would rise when about thirty degrees (a favourite angle with the pyramid architects) past the vernal equinox. But I lay no stress on this point. The meridian line obtained from the underground passage would have given the builders so ready a means of determining accurately the east and west lines for the north and south edges of the pyramid's base, that any other observations for this purpose can hardly have been more than subsidiary.

It is, of course, well known that there is precisely such an underground tunnelling as the considerations I have indicated seem to suggest as a desirable feature in a proposed astronomical edifice on a very noble scale. In all the pyramids of Ghizeh, indeed, there is such a tunnelling as we might expect on almost any theory of the relation of the smaller pyramids to the great one. But the slant tunnel under the great pyramid is constructed with far greater skill and care than have been bestowed on the tunnels under the other pyramids. Its length underground amounts to more than 350 feet, so that, viewed from the bottom, the mouth, about four feet across from top to bottom on the square, would give a sky range of rather less than one-third of a degree, or about one-fourth more than the moon's apparent diameter. But, of course, there was nothing to prevent the observers who used this tube from greatly narrowing these limits by using diaphragms, one covering up all the mouth of the tube, except a small opening near the centre, and another correspondingly occupying the lower part of the tube from which the observation was made.

It seems satisfactorily made out that the object of the slant tunnel, which runs 350 feet through the rock on which the pyramid is built, was to observe the Pole-star of the period at its lower culmination, to obtain thence the true direction of the north point. The slow motion of a star very near the pole would cause any error in time, as when this observation was made, to be of very little importance, though we can understand that even such observations as these would remind the builders of the pyramid of the absolute necessity of good time-measurements and time-observations in astronomical research.

Finding this point clearly made out, we can fairly use the observed direction of the inclined passage to determine what was the position of the Pole-star at the time when the foundations of the great pyramid were laid, and even what

that Pole-star may have been. On this point there has
never been much doubt, though considerable doubt exists
as to the exact epoch when the star occupied the position in
question. According to the observations made by Professor
Smyth, the entrance passage has a slope of about 26° 27',
which would have corresponded, when refraction is taken
into account, to the elevation of the star observed through
the passage, at an angle of about 26° 29' above the horizon.
The true latitude of the pyramid being 29° 58' 51", corresponding to an elevation of the true pole of the heavens,
by about 30° ½' above the horizon, it follows that if Professor Smyth obtained the true angle for the entrance passage,
the Pole-star must have been about 3° 31½' from the pole.
Smyth himself considers that we ought to infer the angle for
the entrance passage from that of other internal passages,
presently to be mentioned, which he thinks were manifestly
intended to be at the same angle of inclination, though
directed southwards instead of northwards. Assuming this
to be the case, though for my own part I cannot see why we
should do so (most certainly we have no *à priori* reason for
so doing), we should have 26° 18' as about the required
angle of inclination, whence we should get about 3° 42' for
the distance of the Pole-star of the pyramid's time from
the true pole of the heavens. The difference may seem of
very slight importance, and I note that Professor Smyth
passes it over as if it really were unimportant ; but in reality
it corresponds to somewhat large time-differences. He
quotes Sir J. Herschel's correct statement, that about the
year 2170 B.C. the star Alpha Draconis, when passing below
the pole, was elevated at an angle of about 26° 18' above
the horizon, or was about 3° 42' from the pole of the heavens
(I have before me, as I write, Sir J. Herschel's original
statement, which is not put precisely in this way); and he
mentions also that somewhere about 3440 B.C. the same star
was situated at about the same distance from the pole. But
he omits to notice that since, during the long interval of
1270 years, Alpha Draconis had been first gradually ap-

proaching the pole until it was at its nearest, when it was
only about 3½' from that point, and then as gradually
receding from the pole until again 3° 42' from it, it follows
that the difference of nine or ten minutes in the estimated
inclination of the entrance passage corresponds to a very
considerable interval in time, certainly to not less than fifty
years. (Exact calculation would be easy, but it would be
time wasted where the data are inexact.)

Having their base properly oriented, and being about to
erect the building itself, the architects would certainly not
have closed the mouth of the slant tunnel pointing northwards, but would have carried the passage onwards through
the basement layers of the edifice, until these had reached
the height corresponding to the place where the prolongation
of the passage would meet the slanting north face of the
building. I incline to think that at this place they would
not be content to allow the north face to remain in steps,
but would fit in casing stones (not necessarily those which
would eventually form the slant surface of the pyramid, but
more probably slanted so as to be perpendicular to the axis
of the ascending passage). They would probably cut a
square aperture through such slant stones corresponding to
the size of the passage elsewhere, so as to make the four
surfaces of the passage perfectly plane from its greatest
depth below the base of the pyramid to its aperture, close
to the surface to be formed eventually by the casing stones
of the pyramid itself

Now, in this part of his work, the astronomical architect
could scarcely fail to take into account the circumstance
that the inclined passage, however convenient as bearing
upon a bright star near the pole when that star was due
north, was, nevertheless, not coincident in direction with the
true polar axis of the celestial sphere. I cannot but think
he would in some way mark the position of their true polar
axis. And the natural way of marking it would be to indicate where the passage of his Pole-star *above* the pole ceased
to be visible through the slant tube. In other words he

would mark where a line from the middle of the lowest face of the inclined passage to the middle of the upper edge of the mouth was inclined by twice the angle 3° 42' to the axis of the passage. To an eye placed on the optical axis of the passage, at this distance from the mouth the middle of the upper edge of the mouth would (*quam proximè*) show the place of the true pole of the heavens. It certainly is a singular coincidence that at the part of the tube where this condition would be fulfilled, there is a peculiarity in the construction of the entrance passage, which has been indeed otherwise explained, but I shall leave the reader to determine whether the other explanation is altogether a likely one. The feature is described by Smyth as ' a most singular portion of the passage—viz., a place where two adjacent wall-joints, similar, too, on either side of the passage, were *vertical* or nearly so ; while every other wall-joint, both above and below, was *rectangular* to the length of the passage, and, therefore, largely *inclined* to the vertical.' Now I take the mean of Smyth's determinations of the transverse height of the entrance passage as 47·23 inches (the extreme values are 47·14 and 47·32), and I find that, from a point on the floor of the entrance passage, this transverse height would subtend an angle of 7° 24' (the range of Alpha Draconis in altitude when on the meridian) at a distance 363·65 inches from the transverse mouth of the passage. Taking this distance from Smyth's scale in Plate xvii. of his work on the pyramid ('Our Inheritance in the Great Pyramid '), I find that, if measured along the base of the entrance passage from the lowest edge of the vertical stone, it falls exactly upon the spot where he has marked in the probable outline of the uncased pyramid, while, if measured from the upper edge of the same stone, it falls just about as far within the outline of the cased pyramid as we should expect the outer edge of a sloped end stone to the tunnel to have lain.

It may be said that from the floor of the entrance passage no star could have been seen, because no eye could be placed there. But the builders of the pyramid cannot reasonably be supposed to have been ignorant of the simple properties of plane mirrors, and by simply placing a thin piece of polished metal upon the floor at this spot, and noting where they could see the star and the upper edge of the tunnel's mouth in contact by reflection in this mirror, they could determine precisely where the star could be seen touching that edge, by an eye placed (were that possible) precisely in the plane of the floor.

I have said there is another explanation of this peculiarity in the entrance passage, but I should rather have said there is another explanation of a line marked on the stone next below the vertical one. I should imagine this line, which is nothing more than a mark such 'as might be ruled with a blunt steel instrument, but by a master hand for power, evenness, straightness, and still more for rect angularity to the passage axis,' was a mere sign to show where the upright stone was to come. But Professor Smyth who gives no explanation of the upright stone itself, except that it seems, from its upright position, to have had ' something representative of setting up, or preparation for the erecting of a building,' believes that the mark is as many inches from the mouth of the tunnel as there were years between the dispersal of man and the building of the pyramid ; that thence downwards to the place where an ascending passage begins, marks in like manner the number of years which were to follow before the Exodus ; thence along the ascending passage to the beginning of the great gallery the number of years from the Exodus to the coming of Christ ; and thence along the floor of the grand gallery to its end, the interval between the first coming of Christ and the second coming or the end of the world, which it appears is to take place in the year 1881. It is true not one of these intervals accords with the dates given by those who are considered the best authorities in Biblical matters,—but sc much the worse for the dates.

To return to the pyramid.

K

We have considered how, probably, the architect would plan the prolongation of the entrance passage to its place of opening out on the northern face. But as the pyramid rose layer by layer above its basement, there must be ascending passages of some sort towards the south, the most important part of the sky in astronomical research.

The astronomers who planned the pyramid would specially require four things. First, they must have the ascending passage in the absolutely true meridian plan; secondly, they would require to have in view, along a passage as narrow as the entrance tunnel, some conspicuous star, if possible a star so bright as to be visible by day (along such a tunnel) as well as by night; thirdly, they must have the means of observing the sun at solar noon on every day in the year; and fourthly, they must also have the entire range of the zodiac or planetary highway brought into view along their chief meridional opening.

The first of these points is at once the most important and the most difficult. It is so important, indeed, that we may hope for significant evidence from the consideration of the methods which would suggest themselves as available.

Consider:—The square base has been duly oriented. Therefore, if each square layer is placed properly, the continually diminishing square platform will remain always oriented. But if any error is made in this work, the exactness of the orientation will gradually be lost. And this part of the work cannot be tested by astronomical observations as exact as those by which the base was laid, unless the vertical boring by which the middle of the base, or a point near it, was brought into connection with the entrance passage, is continued upwards through the successive layers of the pyramidal structure. As the rock rises to a considerable height within the interior of the pyramid,[1] probably to quite

---

[1] The irregular descending passage long known as the well, which communicates between the ascending passage and the underground chamber, enables us to ascertain how high the rock rises into the pyra-

the height of the opening of the entrance passage on the northern slope, it would only be found necessary to carry up this vertical boring in the building itself after this level had been reached. But in any case this would be but an unsatisfactory way of obtaining the meridian plane when once the boring had reached a higher level than the opening of the entrance passage ; for only horizontal lines from the boring to the inclined tunnelling would be of use for exact work, and no such lines could be drawn when once the level of the upper end of the entrance passage had been passed by the builders.

A plan would be available, however (not yet noticed, so far as I know, by any who have studied the astronomical relations of the great pyramid), which would have enabled the builders perfectly to overcome this difficulty.

Suppose the line of sight down the entrance passage were continued upwards along an ascending passage, after reflection at a perfectly horizontal surface—the surface of still water—then by the simplest of all optical laws, that of the reflection of light, the descending and ascending lines of sight on either side of the place of reflection, would lie in the same vertical plane, that, namely, of the entrance passage, or of the meridian. Moreover, the farther upwards an ascending passage was carried, along which the reflected visual rays could pass, the more perfect would be the adjustment of this meridional plane.

To apply this method, it would be necessary to tempo· rarily plug up the entrance passage where it passed into the solid rock, to make the stone-work above it very perfect and close fitting, so that whenever occasion arose for making one of the observations we are considering, water might be poured into the entrance passage, and remain long enough standing at the corner (so to speak) where this passage and the suggested ascending passage could meet, for Alpha Dra-

mid at this particular part of the base. We thus learn that the rock rises in this place, at any rate, thirty or forty feet above the basal plane.

conis to be observed down the ascending passage. Fig. 2 shows what is meant. Here D C is the descending passage, C A the ascending passage, C the corner where the water would be placed when Alpha Draconis was about to pass

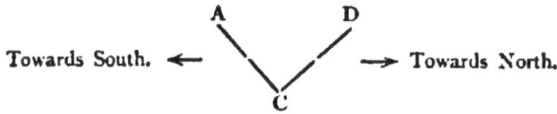

FIG. 2.

below the pole. The observer would look down A C, and would see Alpha Draconis by rays which had passed down D C, and had been reflected by the water at C. Supposing the building to have been erected, as Lepsius and other Egyptologists consider, at the rate of one layer in each year, then only one observation of the kind described need be made per annum. Indeed, fewer would serve, since three or four layers of stone might be added without any fresh occasion arising to test the direction of the passage C A.

It is hardly necessary to remind those who have given any attention to the subject of the pyramid that there is precisely such an ascending passage as C A, and that as yet no explanation of the identity of its angle of ascent with the angle of descent of the passage D C has ever been given. Most pyramidalists content themselves by assuming, as Sir E. Beckett puts it, ' that the same angle would probably be used for both sets of passages, *as there was no reason for varying it*,' which is not exactly an explanation of the relation. Mr. Wackerbarth has suggested that the passages were so adjusted for the purpose of managing a system of balance cars united by ropes from one passage to another ; but this explanation is open, as Beckett points out, to the fatal objection that the passages meet at their lowest point, not at their highest, so that it would be rather a puzzle ' to work out the mechanical idea.' The reflection explanation is not only open to no such objections, but involves precisely such an application of optical laws as we should expect from men as ingenious as the pyramid builders certainly were. In

saying this, let me explain, I am not commending myself
for ingenuity in thinking of the method, simply because such
methods are quite common and familiar in the astronomy
of modern times.

While I find this explanation, which occurred to me even
while this paper was in writing, so satisfactory that I feel
almost tempted to say, like Sir G. Airy of his explanation of
the Deluge as an overflow of the Nile, that ' I cannot entertain the slightest doubt' of its validity, I feel that there
ought to be some evidence in the descending passage itself
of the use of this method. We might not find any traces of
the plugs used to stop up, once a year or so, the rock part
of the descending passage. For they would be only temporary arrangements. But we should expect to find the
floor of the descending passage constructed with special
care, and very closely fitted, where the water was to be received.

Inquiring whether this is so, I learn not only that it is, but
that another hitherto unexplained feature of the great
pyramid finds it explanation in this way,—the now celebrated ' secret sign.' Let us read Professor Smyth's account
of this peculiar feature :—

' When measuring the cross-joints in the floor of the entrance passage, in 1865, I went on chronicling their angles, each one proving to
be very nearly at right angles to the axis, until suddenly one came
which was *diagonal*; another, and that was diagonal too ; but, after
that, the rectangular position was resumed. Further, the stone material carrying these diagonal joints was harder and better than elsewhere
in the floor, so as to have saved that part from the monstrous excavations elsewhere perpetrated by some moderns. Why, then, did the
builders change the rectangular joint angle at that point, and execute
such unusual angles as they chose in place of it, in a better material of
stone than elsewhere ; and yet with so little desire to call general attention to it, that they made the joints fine and close to that degree that
they escaped the attention of all men until 1865 A.D.? The answer
came from the diagonal joints themselves, on discovering that the stone
between them was opposite to the butt end of the portcullis of the first
ascending passage, or to the hole whence the prismatic stone of con-
cealment through 3000 years had dropped out almost before Al Mamoun's

eyes. Here, therefore, was a secret sign in the pavement of the entrance-passage, appreciable only to a careful eye and a measurement by
angle, but made in such hard material that it was evidently intended to
last to the end of human time with the great pyramid, and *has* done so
thus far.'

Whether Professor Smyth is right in considering that this
specially-prepared position of the floor was intended not for
any practical purpose, but to escape the notice of the care-
less, while yet, when the right men 'at last, duly instructed,
entered the passage,' this mysterious floor-sign should show
them where a ceiling-stone was movable, on perceiving
which they 'would have laid bare the beginning of the whole
train of those sub-aërial features of construction which are
the great pyramid's most distinctive glory, and exist in no
other pyramid in Egypt or the world,' I leave the reader to
judge. I would remark, only, that, if so, the builders of the
pyramid were not remarkably good prophets, seeing that
the event befell otherwise, the ceiling-stone dropping out a
thousand years or so before the floor-sign was noticed ;
wherefore we need not feel altogether alarmed at their own
prediction (according to Professor Smyth), that the end of
the world is to come in 1881, even as Mother Shipton also is
reported to have prophesied. On the other hand, there
seem excellent reasons for adopting the above interpretation
of the secret sign ; as showing where the floor of the descending passage was purposely prepared for the reception
of water, on the still surface of which the Pole-star of the day
might be mirrored for one looking down the ascending passage.

Albeit, I cannot but think that this ascending passage
must also have been so directed as to show some bright star
when due south. For if the passage had only given the
meridian plane, but without permitting the astronomer to
observe the southing of any fixed star, it would have subserved only one-half its purposes as a meridional instrument.
It is to be remembered that, supposing the ascending passage
to have its position determined in the way I have described,
there would be nothing to prevent its being also made to

show any fixed star nearly at the same elevation. For it could readily be enlarged in a vertical direction, the floor remaining unaltered. Since it is not enlarged until the great gallery is reached (at a distance of nearly 127 feet from the place where the ascent begins), it follows, or is at least rendered highly probable, that some bright star was in view through that ascending passage.

Now, taking the date 2170 B.C., which Professor Smyth assigns to the beginning of the great pyramid, or even taking any date (as we fairly may), within a century or so on either side of that date, we find no bright star which would have been visible when due south, through the ascending passage. I have calculated the position of that circle among the stars along which lay all the points passing 26° 18' above the horizon when due south, in the latitude of Ghizeh, 2170 years before the Christian era ; and it does not pass near a single conspicuous star.[1] There is only one fourth magnitude star which it actually approaches—namely, Epsilon Ceti ; and one fifth magnitude star, Beta of the Southern Crown.

When we remember that Egyptologists almost without

---

[1] There is a statement perfectly startling in its inaccuracy, in a chapter of Blake's ' Astronomical Myths,' derived from Mr. Haliburton's researches, asserting that in the year 2170 B.C., the Pleiades were *'exactly at that height that they could be seen in the direction of the Southward-pointing passage of the pyramid.'* The italics are not mine. As this passage pointed 33⅔°, or thereabouts, below (that is south of) the equator, and the Pleiades were then some 3⅔° north of the equator, the passage certainly did not then point to the Pleiades. Nor has there been any time since the world began when the Pleiades were anywhere near the direction of the southward pointing passage. In fact they have never been more than 20° south of the equator. The statement follows immediately after another to the surprising effect that in the year 2170 B.C. ' the Pleiades *really* commenced the spring by their midnight culmination.' The only comment an astronomer can make on this startling assertion is to repeat with emphasis the word italicised by Mr. Haliburton (or Mr. Blake ?). The Pleiades being then in conjunction with what is now called the first point of Aries, culminated at noon, not at midnight, at the time of the vernal equinox.

exception assert that the date of the builders of the great pyramid *must* have been more than a thousand years earlier than 2170 B.C., and that Bunsen has assigned to Menes the date 3620 B.C., while the date 3300 B.C. has been assigned to Cheops or Suphis on apparently good authority, we are led to inquire whether the other epoch when Alpha Draconis was at about the right distance from the pole of the heavens may not have been the true era of the commencement of the great· pyramid. Now, the year 3300 B.C., though a little late, would accord fairly well with the time when Alpha Draconis was at the proper distance $3\frac{2}{3}°$ from the pole of the heavens. If the inclination of the entrance-passage is 26° 27', as Professor Smyth made it, the exact date for this would be 3390 B.C. ; if 26° 40', as others made it before his measurements, the date would be about 3320 B.C., which would suit well with the date 3300 B.C., since a century either way would only carry the star about a third of a degree towards or from the pole.

Now, when we inquire whether in the year 3300 B.C. any bright star would have been visible, at southing, through the ascending passage, we find that a very bright star indeed, an orb otherwise remarkable as the nearest of all the stars, the brilliant Alpha Centauri, shone as it crossed the meridian right down that ascending tube. It is so bright that, viewed through that tube, it must have been visible to the naked eye, even when southing in full daylight.

But thirdly we must consider how the builders of the pyramid would arrange for the observation of the sun at noon on every clear day in the year.

They would carry up the floor of the ascending passage in an unchanged direction, as it already pointed south of the lowest place of the noon-sun at mid-winter. They would have to enlarge the tunnel into a lofty gallery, to in-crease the vertical range of view on the meridian. It seems reasonable to infer that they would prefer so to arrange matters that the upper end of the gallery would be near the middle of the platform which would form the top of the pyramidal structure from the time when it was completed for observational purposes. The height of the gallery would be so adjusted to its length, that the mid-winter's sun would not shine further than the lower end of the gallery (that is, to the upper end of the smaller ascending passage). In fact, as the moon and planets would have to be observed when due south, through this meridional gallery, and as they range further from the equator both north and south than the sun does, it would be necessary that the gallery should extend lower down than the sun's mid-winter noon rays would shine.

As it would be a part of the observer's work to note exactly how far down the gallery the shadow of its upper southern edge reached, as well as the moment when the sun's light passed from the western to the eastern wall of the gallery, and other details of the kind ; besides, of course, taking time-observations of the moment when the sun's edge seemed to reach the edge of the gallery's southern opening ; and as such observations could not be properly made by men standing on the smooth slanting floor of the gallery, it would be desirable to have cross-benches capable of being set at different heights along the sloping gallery. In some observations, indeed, as where the transits of several stars southing within short intervals of time had to be observed, it would be necessary to set some observers at one part of the gallery, others at another part, and perhaps even to have several sets of observers along the gallery. And this suggests yet another consideration. It might be thought desirable, if great importance was attached (as the whole building shows that great importance must have been attached) to the exactness of the observations, to have several observations of each transit of a star across the mouth of the gallery. In this case, it would be well to have the breadth of the gallery different at different heights, though its walls must of necessity be upright throughout— that is, the walls must be upright from the height where one breadth commences, to the height where the next breadth commences. With a gallery built in this fashion, it would be possible to take several observations of the same transit, somewhat in the same way that the modern observer watches the transit of a star across each of five, seven, or nine parallel spider threads, in order to obtain a more correct time for the passage of the star across the middle thread, than if he noted this passage alone.

How far the grand gallery corresponds with these requirements can be judged from the following description given by Professor Greaves in 1638 : —' It is,' he says, 'a very stately piece of work, and not inferior, either in respect of the curiosity of art, or richness of materials, to the most sumptuous and magnificent buildings,' and a little further on he says, ' this gallery, or corridor, or whatever else I may call it, is built of white and polished marble (limestone), the which is very evenly cut in spacious squares or tables. Of such materials as is the pavement, such is the roof and such are the side walls that flank it ; the coagmentation or knitting of the joints is so close, that they are scarcely discernible to a curious eye ; and that which adds grace to the whole structure, though it makes the passage the more slippery and difficult, is the acclivity or rising of the ascent. The height of this gallery is 26 feet' (Professor Smyth's careful measurements show the true height to be more nearly 28 feet), 'the breadth of 6·870 feet, of which 3·435 feet are to be allowed for the way in the midst, which is set and bounded on both sides with two banks (like benches) of sleek and polished stone ; each of these hath 1·717 of a foot in breadth, and as much in depth.' These measurements are not strictly exact. Smyth made the breadth of the gallery above the banks or ramps, as he calls them, 6 feet 10½ inches ; the space between the ramps, 3 feet 6 inches ; the ramps nearly about 1 foot $8\frac{1}{14}$ inches broad, and nearly 1 foot 9 inches high, measured transversely, that is, at right angles to the ascending floor.

As to arrangements for the convenience of observers on the slippery and difficult floor of this gallery, we find that upon the top of these benches or ramps, near the angle where they meet the wall, 'there are little spaces cut in right-angled parallel figures, set on each side 'opposite one another, *intended no question for some other end than ornament.'*

The diversity of width which I have indicated as a desirable feature in a meridional gallery, is a marked feature of the actual gallery. 'In the casting and ranging of the marbles' (limestone), 'in both the side walls, there is one piece of architecture,' says Greaves, 'in my judgment very graceful, and that is that all the ceurses or stones, which are but seven (so great are these stones), do set and flag over one another about three inches ; the bottom of the uppermost course overlapping the top of the next, and so in order, the rest as they descend.' The faces of these stones are exactly vertical, and as the width of the gallery diminishes upwards by about six inches for each successive course, it follows that the width at the top is about $3\frac{1}{2}$ feet less than the width, 6 feet $10\frac{1}{2}$ inches, at the bottom, or agrees in fact with the width of the space between the benches or ramps. Thus the shadow of the vertical edges of the gallery at solar noon just reached to the edges of the ramps, the shadow of the next lower vertical edges falling three inches from the edges higher up the ramps, those of the next vertical edges six inches from these edges, still higher up, and so forth. The true hour of the sun's southing could thus be most accurately determined by seven sets of observers placed in different parts of the gallery, and near midsummer, when the range of the shadows would be so far shortened, that a smaller number of observers only could follow the shadows' motions ; but in some respects, the observations in this part of the year could be more readily and exactly made than in winter, when the shadows' spaces of various width would range along the entire length of the gallery.

Similar remarks would apply to observations of the moon, which could also be directly observed. The planets and stars of course could only be observed directly.

The grand gallery could be used for the observation of any celestial body southing higher than 26° 18' above the horizon ; but not very effectively for objects passing near the zenith. The Pleiades could be well observed. They southed about $63\frac{2}{3}°$ above the horizon in the year 2140 B.C. or thereabouts when they were on the equinoctial colure.[1] But if I am right in taking the year 3300 B.C. when Alpha Centauri shone down the smaller ascending passage in southing, the Pleiades were about 58° only above the horizon when southing, and therefore even more favourably observable from the great meridional gallery.

In passing I may note that at this time, about 3300 years before our era, the equinoctial point (that is, the point where the sun passes north of the equator, and the year begins according to the old manner of reckoning) was midway between the horns of the Bull. So that then, and then alone, a poet might truly speak of spring as the time —

> ' Candidus auratis aperit quum cornibus annum
>   Taurus,'

as Virgil incorrectly did (repeating doubtless some old tradition) at a later time. Even Professor Smyth notices the necessity that the pyramid gallery should correspond in some degree with such a date. ' For,' says he, ' there have been traditions for long, whence arising I know not, that the seven overlappings of the grand gallery, so impressively described by Professor Greaves, had something to do with the Pleiades, those proverbially seven stars of the primeval world,' only that he considers the pyramid related to *memorial*

---

[1] This date is sometimes given earlier, but when account is taken of the proper motion of these stars we get about the date above mentioned. I cannot understand how Dr. Ball, Astronomer Royal for Ireland, has obtained the date 2248 B.C., unless he has taken the proper motion of Alcyone the wrong way. The proper motion of this star during the last 4000 years has been such as to increase the star's distance from the equinoctial colure ; and therefore, of course, the actual interval of time since the star was on the colure is less than it would be calculated to be if the proper motion were neglected.

not *observing* astronomy, ' of an earlier date than Virgil's.' The Pleiades also, it may be remarked, were scarcely regarded in old times as belonging to the constellation of the Bull, but formed a separate asterism.

The upper end of the great gallery lies very near the vertical axis of the pyramid. It is equidistant, in fact, from the north and south edges of the pyramid platform at this level, but lies somewhat to the east of the true centre of this platform. One can recognise a certain convenience in this arrangement, for the actual centre of the platform would be required as a position from whence observation of the whole sky could be made. Observers stationed there would have the cardinal points and the points midway between them defined by the edges and angles of the square platform, which would not be the case if they were displaced from the centre. Stationed as they would be close to the mouth of the gallery, they would hear the time signallings given forth by the observers placed at various parts of the gallery; and no doubt one chief end of the exact time-observations, for which the gallery was manifestly constructed, would be to enable the platform observers duly to record the time when various phenomena were noticed in any part of the heavens.

This corresponds well with the statement made by Proclus, that the pyramids of Egypt, which, according to Diodorus Siculus, had been in existence during 3600 years, terminated in a platform upon which the priests made their celestial observations. The last-named historian alleges, also ('Biblioth. Hist.' Lib. I.), that the Egyptians, who claimed to be the most ancient of men, professed to be acquainted with the situation of the earth, the risings and settings of stars, to have arranged the order of days and months, and pretended to be able to predict future events, with certainty, from their observations of celestial phenomena. I think that it is in this association of astrology with astronomy that we find the explanation of what, after all, remains the great mystery of the pyramid—the fact, namely, that all

the passages, ascending, descending, and horizontal, constructed with such extreme care, and at the cost of so much
labour, in the interior of the great pyramid, were eventually
(perhaps not very long after their construction) to be closed up.
I reject utterly the idea that they could have been constructed
merely as memorials.   Sir E. Beckett, who seems willing to
admit this conception, rejects the notion that the builders of
the pyramid recorded 'standard measures by hiding them
with the utmost ingenuity.'   Is it not equally absurd to
imagine that they recorded the date of the great pyramid, by
construction, by those most elaborately concealed passages?
Why they should have concealed them after constructing
them so carefully, may not be clear.   For my own part, I
regard the theory that the Pyramid of Suphis was built for
astrological observations, relating to the life of that monarch
only, as affording the most satisfactory explanation yet
advanced of the mysterious circumstance that the building
was closed up after his death.   Supposing the part of the
edifice (fifty layers in all), which includes the ascending and
descending passages, to have been erected during his lifetime, it may be that some reverential or superstitious feeling
caused his successors, or the priesthood, to regard the building as sacred after his death—to be closed up therefore and
completed as a perfect pyramid, polished *ad unguem* from
its pointed summit to the lines along which the four faces
meet the smooth pavement round its base.   We might thus
explain why each monarch required his own astrological
observatory afterwards to become his tomb.   Be this as it
may, it is certain that the pyramids were constructed for
astronomical observations ; and it would, I conceive, be
utterly unreasonable to imagine that the costly interior
fittings and arrangements, 'not inferior, in respect of curiosity
of art or richness of materials, to the most sumptuous and
magnificent buildings,' were intended to subserve no other
purpose but to be memorials ; and that, too, not until, in
the course of thousands of years, the whole mass of the
pyramid had begun to lose the exactness of its original figure,

THE PYRAMIDS OF GHIZEH.

In my treatise called 'Myths and Marvels of Astronomy' there are two essays on the great pyramid, one dealing with the strange fancies which have been associated with this building by Professor Piazzi Smyth, Astronomer Royal for Scotland, the other advancing a theory respecting the building which seems to me, on the whole, more probable than any other. In the last essay of this present volume I have considered other relations which had not occurred to me when I wrote those papers. I do not now propose to go over the ground covered by my three former essays, but, following the practice which I have before adopted in like cases, to indicate at full length in the present essay only such points as I have noted since the other papers were written. If in such study as I have given to the subject in the interval I had found any evidence bearing unfavourably upon the views I have advanced in those papers, I should have judged it right to point out clearly and definitely the nature and weight of such evidence, and to withdraw, if the evidence suggested such a course, from positions taken up in error—not merely abandoning views which appeared erroneous, but pointing out such errors as I had recognised. Since, on the contrary, the evidence I have obtained and the points which I have noticed in relation to the pyramids, and especially to the great pyramid, appear strikingly to confirm the theory I advanced in the essay entitled 'The Mystery of the Pyramid,' it is but just to indicate the nature of this new or recently noted matter, even as I should have indicated any adverse evidence. If I should thus appear *tenax propositi,* I believe such persistence has its origin in a wish to be just and truthful (qualities which, as we know, Horace associated with tenacity of opinion). I think too that readers of my former papers on the pyramid may find as much interest as I have found myself in the new matter thus submitted to them, respecting the oldest remaining monuments of human labour (except such as are to be re-garded as subjects rather of palæontological than of anti-quarian research).

I will first run briefly through such matters of detail as are necessary preliminaries to any discussion respecting the pyramids, following the line laid down in Sir Edmund Beckett's treatise on Building. I may remark that much which he there points out, and especially the theory which he advances respecting the measures of length used in the construction of the great pyramid, was not known to me when I wrote the papers above mentioned. It appears to me that he makes out a very strong case for his theory. I must frankly admit that he by no means entertains a similar opinion respecting my own views as to the purposes for which the pyramid was constructed. He can find nothing, he tells me, to suggest the idea that the builders of the pyramids had any astrological ideas in view ; and so far as I can judge, he would not admit that even astronomy entered into the plans of the pyramid architects otherwise than as an adjunct to the work of building. I believe, how-ever, that Sir E. Beckett's objections to the astrological interpretation of the pyramids, or rather to the association of the astrological theory with the tomb theory, have their origin rather in the idea that such a theory would be asso-ciated with my astrological interpretation of the origin of the Sabbath, than in any circumstances known respecting the pyramids or their builders. I have certainly found nothing in Sir E. Beckett's reasonings respecting his own theory (which I consider the most probable theory of pyramid dimensions yet advanced) opposed to my own views, but, on the contrary, much which seems strongly to favour them. Whether the astrological theory has or has not much to be said in its favour is a point upon which I willingly leave others to decide. I think I shall be able here considerably to strengthen the evidence I formerly adduced to show that the pyramid's present features cannot well be accounted for on any other theory.

In the first place, Sir E. Beckett starts with the statement, almost amounting in itself to an admission of the astronomical significance of the pyramid relations, that the great pyramid was built in the year 2170 B.C., by Cheops as Herodotus calls him, but Suphis or Shufu, as he is named in hieroglyphics painted on large stones over the king's chamber. This, says Beckett, was in the time of Peleg, 'ages before the Israelites were in Egypt, whom some persons have hastily guessed to have been employed in building the pyramids'—an argument effective indeed against Professor Smyth and those followers of his who see in the pyramid a sort of stone Bible, but scarcely as against those who believe no more in the 239 years of Peleg's life than in the nine hundred odd years of Methuselah's, or in the literal interpretation of the six days of creation. If we are to start with the theory that, in the year B.C. 2348, there were eight living persons in the world, and that, less than two centuries later, a monarch, ruling a nation large enough to provide tens of thousands of workers, erected the greatest mass of stonework ever raised on the face of this earth by man, we need not trouble ourselves to explain how and why the great pyramid was built. We might as well admit at once that the pyramid was built under the direct personal superintendence of Uriel, the Archangel who has special charge over the astronomical relations of the solar system,

> The same whom John saw also in the sun;

who also explained earlier to an inquiring angel how, in the beginning,

L

145

FAMILIAR SCIENCE STUDIES.

This ethereal quintessence of Heav'n
Flew upward, spirited with various forms,
That roll'd orbicular, and turn'd to stars
Numberless, as thou seest, and how they move.

One idea is not a whit more untenable than the other.

Secondly, it is to be noted that according to some traditions the second pyramid, though somewhat smaller than the first, and altogether inferior in design, was begun somewhat earlier. I would invite special attention to this point. It is one of those perplexing details which are always best worth examining when we want to obtain a true theory. The second pyramid was certainly built during the reign of the builder of the first or great pyramid. It must have been built, then, with his sanction, for his brother, Chephren, according to Herodotus; Noun-shofo, or Suphis II., according to the Egyptian records. Enormous quantities of stone, of the same quality as the stone used for the great pyramid, were conveyed to the site of the second pyramid, during the very time when the resources of the nation were being largely taxed to get the materials for the great pyramid conveyed to the place appointed for that structure. It would appear, then, that there was some strong—in fact, some insuperable—objection to the building of one great pyramid, larger by far than either the first or second, for both the brothers. Yet nothing has ever been learned respecting the views of the Egyptians about tombs (save only what is learned from the pyramids themselves, if we assume that they were only built as tombs) which would suggest that each king wanted a monstrous pyramid sepulchre for himself. If we could doubt that Cheops valued his brother and his family very highly, we should find convincing proof of the fact, in the circumstance that he allowed enormous sums to be expended on his brother's pyramid, and a great quantity of labour to be devoted to its erection, at the time when his own was in progress at still greater expense, and at the cost of still greater labour. But if he thus highly esteemed his brother, and, regarding him as

the future ruler of Egypt, recognised in him the same almost
sacred qualities which the people of Egypt taught their
rulers to recognise in themselves, what was to prevent him
from combining the moneys and the labours which were
devoted to the two pyramids in the construction of a single
larger pyramid, which could be made doubly secure, and
more perfectly designed and executed ? Is anything whatever known respecting either the Egyptians or any race of
tomb-loving, or rather corpse-worshipping people, which
would lead us to suppose that a number of costly separate
tomb pyramids would have been preferred to a single, but
far larger, pyramid-mausoleum, which should receive the
bodies of all the members of the family, or at least of all
those of the family who had ruled in turn over the land ?
If we could imagine for a moment that Cheops would have
objected to such an arrangement, is it not clear that when
he died his successors would have taken possession of his
pyramid, removing his body perhaps, or not allowing it to
be interred there, *if* the sole or even the chief purpose
for which a pyramid was erected was that it might serve
as a gigantic tomb ?

We may indeed note as a still more fatal objection to
the theory that the chief purpose for which a pyramid was
built was to serve as the builder's tomb, that it would have
been little short of madness for Cheops to devote many
years of his life, enormous sums of money, and the labour
of myriads of his people, to the construction of a building
which might and probably would be turned after his death
to some purpose quite different from that for which he intended it. It is not to be supposed, and indeed history
shows it certainly was not the case, that the dynasties which
ruled over Egypt were more secure from attack than those
which ruled elsewhere in the East during those days. Cheops
cannot have placed such implicit reliance on his brother
Chephren's good faith as to feel sure that, after his own
death, Chephren would complete the pyramid, place
Cheops's body in it, and close up the entrance so securely

that none could find the way into the chamber where the body was laid. Cheops could not even be certain that Chephren would survive him, or that his own son, Mycerinus or Menkeres, would be able to carry out the purpose for which he (Cheops) had built the pyramid.

Apart, then, from that feature of the tomb theory which seems so strangely to have escaped notice—the utter wildness of the idea that even the most tomb-loving race would build tombs quite so monstrous as these—we see that there are the strongest possible objections against the credibility of the merely tombic theory (to use a word coined, I imagine, by Professor Piazzi Smyth, and more convenient perhaps than defensible). It seems clear on the face of things that the pyramids must have been intended to serve some useful purpose during the lifetime of the builder. It is clear also (all, indeed, save the believers in the religion of the great pyramid, will admit *this* point) that each pyramid served some purpose useful to the builder of the pyramid, and to him only. Cheops's pyramid was of no use to Chephren, Chephren's of no use to Mycerinus, and so forth. Otherwise we might be sure, even if we adopted for a moment the exclusively tombic theory, that, though Chephren might have been so honest as not to borrow his brother's tomb when Cheops was departed, or Mycerinus so honest as not to despoil either his uncle or his father, yet among some of the builders of the pyramids such honesty would have been wanting. It is clear, however, from all the traditions which have reached us respecting the pyramids, that no anxiety was entertained by the builder of any pyramid on this score. Cheops seems to have been well assured that Chephren would respect his pyramid, and even (at great expense) complete it ; and so of all the rest. There must, then, have been some special reasons which rendered the pyramid of each king useless altogether to his successor.

Nay, may we not go somewhat further, and, perceiving that Chephren's pyramid must have been built chiefly at his brother's cost, and nearly all of it during his brother's lifetime, may we not assume that the particular purpose which Chephren's pyramid subserved to Chephren only, was nevertheless such a purpose as in some way advanced the interests of the dynasty? Nothing in the history of the dynasty implies that the relations among its members were very much more cordial than those usually prevailing among kings and their relatives. It would have implied singular generosity on Cheops's part, renewed by Chephren towards Mycerinus, and by Mycerinus towards Asychis, thus to have helped in the erection of mere tombs for their several heirs while these were still dependent upon them. But if the fortunes of the dynasty were in some way involved, or supposed to be involved, in these structures, the case would be entirely altered. It is a characteristic feature of my theory respecting the pyramids, though it certainly was not the point which suggested the theory (and, as the reader of my " Myths and Marvels " is aware, was not even touched upon in my original presentation of the theory), that it explains, not merely satisfactorily but fully, this particular circumstance, viz., that it was worth the reigning king's while to have special attention paid to the construction, not merely of his brother's pyramid, but also of his eldest son's large pyramid, of his three other sons' small pyramids, and of his six daughters' still smaller pyramids. There seems reason to believe that all these were put in hand, so to speak, nearly at the same time, though the great pyramid of Cheops, owing to the enormous scale on which the preliminary works were constructed, was probably not actually begun till some time after the others. Very probably the three small pyramids beside the third, the largest of which is the fourth pyramid or the pyramid of Asychis, were all commenced during the lifetime of Cheops. Thus the relative dimensions of the several pyramids, as shown in the accompanying map, Fig. 3, would correspond to the relative importance attached by Cheops to the fortunes—always as associated with his—of the various members of his own family. This would explain, what has

hitherto been thought perplexing, the singularly reduced
scale on which the pyramid of Mycerinus is built, and the
still further and most marked reduction in the case of the
pyramid of Asychis. It is not at all likely that Mycerinus,
if building a pyramid for himself, would have been content
with a smaller pyramid than that of Cheops himself. On
the contrary, all that we know of human nature, and especially of the nature of the Egyptian kings, assures us that

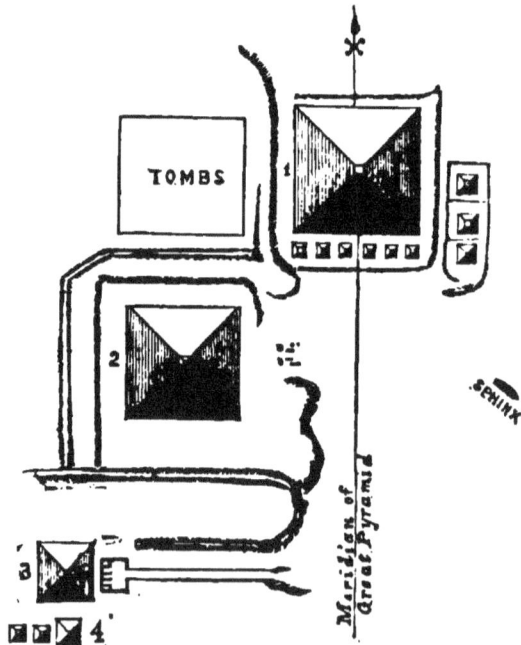

FIG. 3.

each successive monarch would have endeavoured to surpass his predecessors. On the other hand, if Cheops
assigned the proportions of a series of pyramids, one for
each member of his family, he would naturally arrange them
in order of magnitude as we see them in Fig. 3. To his
brother and next heir, his right hand probably in the government of Egypt, he would assign a pyramid second only in
dimensions to his own, though greatly inferior in quality.
To his eldest son, young doubtless when the pyramids were

begun, he would assign a much smaller pyramid (No. 3) ;
but as this son was to succeed Chephren as king, Cheops
would give him, like Chephren, a separate enclosure ; while
to his younger sons and to his daughters he would assign
pyramids not only smaller, but enclosed within the same
area as his own. Space seems to have been left for
Chephren's family, should he have any ; but it appears he
had no children. To Asychis, his grandson, Cheops would
assign a pyramid about as large as those of his own younger
sons. It is noteworthy, by the way, that the linear dimensions of the pyramid of Asychis are less than those of the
pyramid of Mycerinus, in the same degree that those are
less than the linear dimensions of the pyramid of Cheops.
Most certainly this distribution of the dimensions was not
that which Asychis himself, or Mycerinus, would have
selected.

I would submit in passing that this explanation of the
relative dimensions of the pyramids of Ghizeh is somewhat
more natural than that given by the pyramid-religionists,
who insist that the great pyramid was built under divine
superintendence (or by divinely inspired architects), and
not intended for a tomb at all, while all the other pyramids,
being meant for tombs, were therefore inferior in size and
construction. Not only is this explanation—the only one
ever attempted of this most significant peculiarity of the
pyramid group—singularly extravagant in itself, and unsatisfactory further as leaving Cheops, the first pyramid builder,
without any pyramid for his tomb, but it gives no explanation whatever of the descent in scale from Chephren's
pyramid to that of Mycerinus, and from this to the pyramid
of Asychis.

Again, however, I have to note that the circumstance
here dwelt upon was not one of those which suggested my
theory, nor was it noticed in the paper in which I first advocated that theory. It is one of those pieces of evidence
which is almost certain to be noticed in favour of a true
theory some time after other evidence has caused such

theory to be adopted. But such things do not happen in the case of untrue theories, save by very rare accident. It will presently be seen that the two characteristics of the pyramids, formerly regarded as perplexing, which find a natural and ready explanation in the astrological theory, are by no means the only ones of which the same may be said.

Among points to which my attention has been specially directed by advocates of the exclusively tombic theory of the pyramids, one of the chief, one which, indeed, I was assured by several persons would convince me of the sufficiency of this theory, was what is called Lepsius's Law of Pyramid Building. It is thus referred to and described by Professor Piazzi Smyth: ' All the Egyptologists of our age, French, English, German, and American, have hailed the advent on their stage of time of the so-called " Lepsius's Law of Pyramid Building ; " they universally declaring that it satisfies absolutely all the observed or known phenomena. And it may do so for every known case of any Egyptian pyramid, *except* the great pyramid ; and there it explains nothing of what *it* chiefly consists in. Taking, however, the cases which it does apply to, viz., the profane Egyptian examples, this alleged " law " pronounces that the sole object of any pyramid was to form a royal tomb—subterranean, as a matter of course—and that operations began by making an inclined descending passage leading down into the rock, and in cutting out an underground chamber at the end of it. The scheme, thus begun below, went on also growing aboveground, every year of the king's reign, by the placing there of a new heap or additional layer of building stones, and piling them, layer above layer, over a central square-based nucleus upon the levelled ground, virtually above the subterranean apartment ; and it was finally (that is, this superincumbent mass of masonry) finished off on that king's death by his successor, who deposited his predecessor's body embalmed and in a grand sarcophagus in the underground chamber, stopping up the passage leading to it, cased in the rude converging sides of the building with bevelled casing

stones, so as to give it a smooth pyramidal form, and left it
in fact a finished Egyptian and Pharaonic pyramid to all
posterity ; and no mean realisation either of prevailing ideas
among some early nations, of burying their monarchs *sub
montibus altis*, in impressive quiet, immovable calm, and
deep in the bosom of mother earth.'

Although Lepsius states that he discovered this solution
of the riddle of pyramidical construction, it was in part
suggested earlier by James Wilde, and is thus described in
the letterpress accompanying Frith's large photographs of
Egypt : 'A rocky site was first chosen, and a space made
smooth, except a slight eminence in the centre to form a peg
upon which the structure should be fixed ' (which is absurd).
' Within the rock, and usually below the level of the future
base, a sepulchral chamber was excavated, with a passage
inclined downwards, leading to it from the north.' After
describing the way in which the work proceeded, the account goes on to say that ' in this manner it was possible
for the building of a pyramid to occupy the lifetime of its
founder, without there being any risk of his leaving it incomplete to any such degree as would afford a valid excuse
for his successor neglecting to perform his very moderate part,
of merely filling up the angles and smoothing off generally.'
This, however, is not precisely the same as Lepsius's law,
and is manifestly less complete and less satisfactory.

But in the first place I am not at all disposed to admit
that Lepsius's law, even though it explains the manner in
which the pyramids may have been built, is either proved by
any evidence cited in its favour, or in turn proves anything
respecting the purpose of any of the pyramids. It agrees
well with the theory that the pyramids, including, of course,
the great one, served as tombs for the several persons to
whom they belonged or were assigned. But no one thinks
of questioning this, so far as all the pyramids, except the
great one, are concerned ; and I apprehend that very few
share Professor Smyth's faith that King Cheops never was
buried, and was never meant to be buried, in the pyramid

which bears his name. None of the difficulties of the exclusively tombic theory seem even touched by Lepsius's theory, whether it be accepted or rejected. The construction of the pyramids by single layers year by year, if proved, and if it prove anything, shows that the use of the pyramids related chiefly to the life of those to whom the pyramids were assigned, not solely to their death and burial.

Lepsius's theory is partly based on a circumstance which no astronomer who attentively considers the matter can fail to interpret in one special manner, bearing very significantly on our ideas respecting the purpose for which the pyramids were constructed.

In all the pyramids of Ghizeh there is a slant passage (in some there are two such passages) leading down into the rock, an under-ground chamber being cut at the end of the passage. Lepsius, of course, like all who regard the astronomical relations fulfilled by the pyramids as of slight importance, pays no special attention to the circumstance that in every case the descending passage passes in a north and south direction at an angle always of about 26 degrees, and has its entrance always on the northern side. Fig. 4 shows the position of the descending passages in the four chief pyramids. But if it were not obvious in other ways that astronomical relations were regarded by the builders of the pyramids as of extreme importance, these slant passages would prove it. They show unmistakably, (1) that the builders proposed to make the pyramids fulfil certain definite astronomical conditions ; and (2) the method in which the builders effected their purpose.

I have shown in my last article on the Great Pyramid how an architect, proposing to set a building in a particular latitude, might use either the sun, when due south, or those stars which circle close round the pole, for that purpose ; that the better the astronomers were in the days of the pyramid-builders, the more likely they were to prefer the latter, or stellar method, to the former, or solar method ; and that, if they adopted the solar method, the building would be set too far north unless correction were made for the refraction of the atmosphere ; while if they adopted the stellar method, the building would be set too far south. Wherefore, as we find the centre of the great pyramid set somewhat south of the latitude 30° north which the builders clearly intended to have it occupy—the error being about a mile and a quarter, while, if refraction were wholly neglected, it would have been about a mile and three-quarters—we may infer that the astronomers who superintended the arrangements for fixing the latitude employed the stellar method ; that they were exceedingly skilful observers, considering they had no telescopic meridian instruments ; and (with less certainty) that they made some correction for atmospheric refraction.

I show also fully in that article that astronomers using the stellar method for that purpose would most certainly employ it to set the sides of the 'pyramid's' square base facing as exactly as possible the four cardinal points. One method would certainly present itself, and only one would be at all suitable for this purpose. They would take their pole-star, whatever it might be, and would note its direction when passing either just above or just below the pole, as of course it does in every sidereal day. The direction of the star at either of these epochs would be due north. But how could they mark this direction on their selected base?

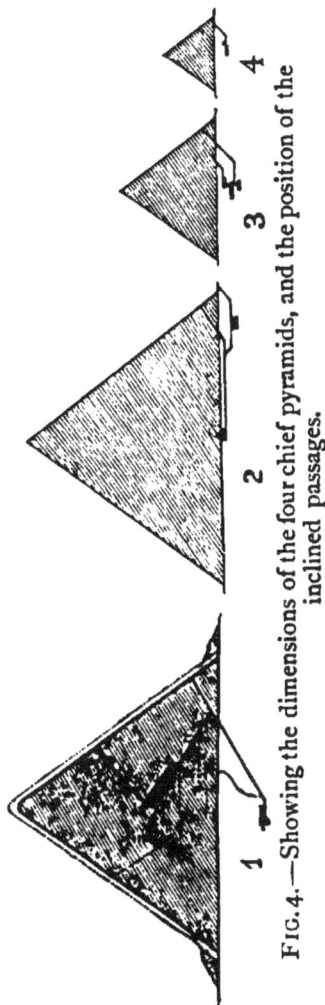

FIG. 4.—Showing the dimensions of the four chief pyramids, and the position of the inclined passages.

They could in the first place set up a pointed upright, as A B
in fig. 5, at the middle of the northern edge of the base, and
another shorter one, C D, so that at one of the epochs, it
would not matter which, an eye placed as at E would see the
points C and E in the same straight line as the pole star S.
Then the line D B would lie north and south.

This would only be a first rough approximation, however. The builders would require a much more satisfactory
north and south line than D B. To obtain this they would
bore a slant passage in the solid rock, as D G, which should

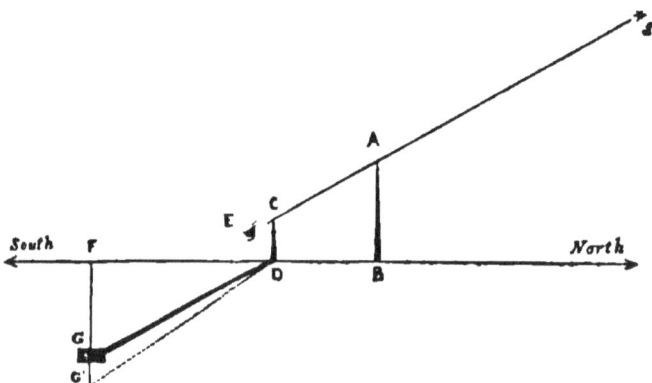

FIG. 5.— Showing how the builders of the pyramid probably
obtained their base.

point directly to the pole-star *s* when due north, starting
their boring by reference to the rough north and south line
D B, but guiding it as they went on, by noticing whether the
pole-star, when due north, remained visible along the
passage. But they would now have to make a selection
between its passage above the pole and its passage below
the pole. In using the uprights D and B, they could take
either the upper or the lower passage; but the underground
boring could have but one direction, and they must choose
whichever of the two passages of the star they preferred.
We cannot doubt they would take the lower passage, not
only as the more convenient passage for observation, but
because the length of their boring D G would be less, for a

given horizontal range F D, if the lower passage of the star
s were taken, than it would be for the upper passage, when
its direction would be as D G'.

When they had bored far enough down to have a sufficient horizontal range F D (the longer this range, of course, the
truer the north and south direction), they would still have to
ascertain the true position of F, the point vertically above G.
For this purpose they would get F first as truly as they could
from the line D B prolonged, and would bore down from F
vertically (guiding the boring, of course with a plumb-line),
until they reached the space opened out at G. The boring
F G might be of very small diameter. Noting where the
plumb-line let down from F to G reached the floor of the
space G, they would ascertain how far F lay to the east or to
the west of its proper position over the *centre* of the floor of
this space. Correcting the position of F accordingly, they
would have F D the true north-and-south line.

This method could give results of considerable accuracy;
and it is the only method in fact which could do so. When,
therefore, we find that the base of the pyramid *is* oriented
with singular accuracy, and secondly that just such a boring
as D G exists beneath the base of the pyramid, *running three
hundred and fifty feet through the solid rock on which the
pyramid is built*, we cannot well refuse to believe that the
slant passage was bored for this purpose, which it was so
well fitted to subserve, and which *has* been so well subserved in some way.

Now, if this opinion is adopted, and for my own part I
cannot see how it can well be questioned, we cannot possibly
accept the opinion that the slant tunnel was bored for
another purpose solely, or even chiefly, unless it can be shown
that that other purpose in the first place was essential to the
plans of the builders, in the second place could be subserved in no other way so well, and in the third place was
manifestly subserved in this way to the knowledge of those
who made the slant borings. Now, it certainly is the case
that, noting the actual position of this slant boring, we can

form a shrewd guess at the date of the great pyramid's erection. In the year 2170 B.C., and again (last before that) in the year 3350 B.C., and also for several years on either side of those dates, a certain bright star *did* look down that boring, or, more precisely, could be seen by any one who looked up that boring, when the star was just below the pole in its circuit round that point. The star was a very important one among the old constellations, though it has since considerably faded in lustre, being no other than the star Alpha of the constellation the Dragon, which formerly was the polar constellation. For hundreds of years before and after the dates 3350 and 2170 B.C., and during the entire interval between those dates, no other star would at all have suited the purposes of the builders of the pyramid ; so that we may be toleraby sure this was the star they employed. Therefore the boring, when first made, must have been directed towards this star. We conclude, then, with considerable confidence, that it was somewhere about one of the two dates 3350 B.C., and 2170 B.C., that the erection of the great pyramid was begun. And from the researches of Egyptologists it has become all but certain that the *earlier* of these dates is very near the correct epoch. But though the boring thus serves the purpose of dating the pyramid, it seems altogether unlikely that the builders of the pyramid intended to record the pyramid's age in this way. They could have done that, if they had wanted to, at once far more easily and far more exactly, by carving a suitable record in one of the inner chambers of the building. But nothing yet known about the pyramid suggests that its builder wanted to tell future ages anything whatever. So far from this, the pyramid was carefully planned to reveal nothing. Only when men had first destroyed the casing, next had found their way into the descending passage, and then had in the roughest and least skilful manner conceivable (even so, too, by an accident) discovered the great ascending gallery, were any of the secrets of this mighty tomb revealed—for a tomb and nothing else it has been ever since Cheops died.

To assert that all these events lay within the view of the architect who *seemed* so carefully to endeavour to render them impossible, is to ask that men should set their reasoning faculties on one side when the pyramid is in question. And lastly, we have not a particle of evidence to show that the builders of the pyramid had any idea that the date of the building *would* be indicated by the position of the great slant passages. They may have noticed that the pole-star was slowly changing its position with respect to the true pole of the heavens; and they may even have recognised the rate and direction in which the pole-star was thus moving. But it is utterly unlikely that they could have detected the fact that the pole of the heavens circles round the pole of the ecliptic in the mighty processional period of 25,920 years;[1] and unless they knew this, they would not know that the position of the slant passage would tell future generations aught about the pyramid's date. On all these accounts, (1) because the builders probably did not care at all about our knowing anything on the subject, (2) because

---

[1] If the architect of the great pyramid knew anything about the great processional period, then—unless such knowledge was miraculously communicated—the astronomers of the pyramid's time must have had evidence which could only have been obtained during many hundreds of years of exact observation, following of course on a long period during which comparatively imperfect astronomical methods were employed. Their astronomy must therefore have had its origin long before the date commonly assigned to the Flood. In passing I may remark that in a paper on the pyramid by Abbé Moigno, that worthy but somewhat credulous ecclesiastic makes a remark which seems to show that the stability and perfection of the great pyramid, and therefore the architectural skill acquired by the Egyptians in the year 2170 B.C. (a date he accepts), proves in some unexplained way the comparative youth of the human race. To most men it would seem that the more perfect men's work at any given date, the longer must have been the preceding interval during which men were acquiring the skill thus displayed. On the contrary, the pyramids, says Abbé Moigno, 'give the most solemn contradiction to those who would of set purpose throw back the origin of man to an indefinite remoteness.' It would have been well if he had explained how the pyramids do this.

if they did they would not have adopted so clumsy a method, and (3) because there is no reason for believing, but every reason for doubting, that they knew the passage *would* tell future ages the date of the pyramid's erection, we must regard as utterly improbable, if not utterly untenable, the proposition that the builders had any such purpose in view in constructing the slant passage.

I am therefore somewhat surprised to find Sir E. Beckett, who does not accept the wild ideas of the pyramid religionists, nevertheless dwelling, not on the manifest value of the slant passages to builders desiring to orient such an edifice as the great pyramid, but on the idea that those builders may have wanted to record a date for the benefit of future ages. After quoting a remark from Mr. Wackerbarth's amusing review of Smyth's book, to the effect that the hypothesis about the slant passage is liable to the objection that, the mouth of the passage being walled up, it is not easy to conceive how a star could be observed through it, Beckett says, 'Certainly not, after it was closed ; but what has that to do with the question whether the builders thought fit to indicate the date to anyone who might in after ages find the passage, by reference to the celestial dial, in which the pole of the earth travels round the pole of the ecliptic in 25,827 years, like the hand of a clock round the dial ? ' But in reality there is no more extravagant supposition among all those ideas of the pyramidalists (which Beckett justly regards as among the wildest illustrations of 'the province of the imagination in science ') than the notion that this motion of the pole of the earth was known to the builders of the pyramid, or that, knowing it, they adopted so preposterous a method of indicating the date of their labours.

Let us return to the purposes which seem to have been actually present in the minds of the pyramid builders.

Having duly laid down the north-and-south line F D, in fig. 5, and being thus ready to cut out from the nearly level face of the solid rock the corner sockets of the square base, they would have to choose what size they would give the base. This would be a question depending partly on the nature of the ground at their disposal, partly on the expense to which King Cheops was prepared to go. The question of expense probably did not influence him much ; but it requires only a brief inspection of the region at his disposal (in the required latitude, and on a firm rock basis) to see that the nature of the ground set definite limits to the base of the building he proposed to erect. As Piazzi Smyth remarks, it is set close to the very verge of the elevated plateau, even dangerously near its edge. Assuming the centre of the base determined by the latitude observations outside, the limit of the size of the base was determined at once. And apart from that, the hill country directly to the south of the great pyramid would not have permitted any considerable extension in that direction, while on the east and west of its present position the plateau does not extend so far north as in the longitude actually occupied by the pyramid.

These considerations probably had quite as much to do with the selection of the dimensions of the base as any that have been hitherto insisted upon. Sir E. Beckett says, after showing that the actual size of the base was in other respects a convenient one (in its numerical relation to previous measures), the great pyramid 'must be some size,' but 'why Cheops wanted his pyramid to be about' its actual size he does not profess to know. Yet, if the latitude of the centre of the base were really determined very carefully, it is clear that the nearest, and in this case the northern, verge of the rock plateau would limit the size of the base ; and we may say that the size selected was the largest which was available, subject to the conditions respecting latitude. True, the latitude is not correctly determined ; but we may fairly assume it was meant to be, and that the actual centre of the base was supposed by the builders to lie exactly in latitude 30 degrees north.

However, we may admit that the dimensions adopted were such as the builders considered convenient also. I fear Sir E. Beckett's explanation on this point, simple and commonplace though it is, is preferable to Professor Smyth's. If, by the way, the latter were right, not only in his views, but in the importance he attaches to them, it would be no mere *façon de parler* to say 'I fear;' for a rather unpleasant fate awaits all who 'shorten the cubit' as Sir E. Beckett does. 'I will not attempt,' says Professor Smyth, 'to say what the ancient Egyptians would have thought' of certain 'whose carriages,' it seems, 'try to stop the way of great pyramid research,' 'for I am horrified to remember the Pharaonic pictures of human souls sent back from heaven to earth, in the bodies of pigs, for far lighter offences than shortening the national cubit.' Sir E. Beckett has sought to shorten the pyramid cubit, with which Smyth is 'the sacred, Hebrew earth-commensurable, anti-Canite cubit,' a far heavier offence probably than merely 'shortening the national cubit.' But after all, it is unfortunately too true, that if the shorter cubit which Beckett holds to have been used by the pyramid builders was not so used, the pyramid does its best to suggest that it was; and if Beckett and those who follow him (as I do in this respect) are wrong, the pyramid and not they must be blamed. For, apart from the trifling detail that the Hebrew cubit of 25 inches is entirely imaginary, 'neither this cubit, nor any multiple of it, is to be found in a single one of all Mr. Smyth's multitude of measurements, except two evidently accidental multiples of it in the diagonals of two of the four corner sockets in the rock ; which are not even square, and could never have been seen again after the pyramid was built, if the superstructure had not been broken up and stolen, which was probably the last thing that Cheops or his architect expected.' But of the other cubit, 'the pyramid and the famous marble "Coffer," in the king's chamber (which was doubtless also Cheops's coffin until his body was "resurrectionised" by the thieves who first broke into the pyramid), do contain clear indications.' The cubit referred to is the working cubit of 20¾ inches, or about a fiftieth of an inch less. For a person of average height, it is equal to about the distance from the elbow to the tip of the middle finger, *plus* a hand's-breadth, the former distance being the natural cubit (for a person of such height). The natural cubit is as nearly as possible half-a-yard, and most probably our yard measure is derived from this shorter cubit. The working cubit may be regarded as a long half-yard, the double working cubit or working Egyptian yard measure, so to speak, being 41½ inches long.

The length of the base-circuit of the great pyramid may be most easily remembered by noticing that it contains as many working cubits as our mile contains yards, viz., 1,760 ; giving 440 cubits as the length of each of the four sides of the base. If Lincoln's Inn Fields were enlarged to a square having its sides equal to the greatest sides of the present Fields, the area of this, the largest 'square' in London, would be almost exactly equal to that of the pyramid's base —or about 13½ acres. The front of Chelsea Hospital has almost the same length as a side of the pyramid's base, so also has the frontage of the British Museum, including the houses on either side to Charlotte Street and Montague Street. The average breadth of the Thames between Chelsea and London Bridge, or, in other words, the average span of the metropolitan bridges, is also not very different from the length of each side of the great pyramid's base. The length measures about 761 feet, or nearly 254 yards. Each side is in fact a furlong of 220 double cubits or Egyptian yards.

The height of the pyramid is equal to seven-elevenths of the side of the base, or to 280 cubits, or about 484 feet. This is about 16 feet higher than the top of Strasburg Cathedral, 24 feet higher than St. Peter's at Rome, and is about 130 feet higher than our St. Paul's.

These are all the dimensions of the pyramid's exterior I here propose to mention. Sir E. Beckett gives a number of others, some of considerable interest, but of course all derivable from the fact that the pyramid has a square base 440 cubits in the side, and has a height of 280 cubits. I may notice, however, in passing, that I quite agree with him in thinking that the special mathematical relation which the pyramid builders intended to embody in the building was this, that the area of each of the four faces should be equal to a square having its sides equal to the height of the pyramid. Herodotus tells us that this was the condition which the builders adopted ; and this condition is fulfilled at least as closely as any of the other more or less fanciful relations which have been recognised by Taylor and his followers.

But what special purpose had the architect in view, as he planned the addition of layer after layer of the pyramidal structure? So far as the mere orienting of the faces of the pyramid was concerned, he had achieved his purpose so soon as he had obtained, by means of the inclined passage, the true direction of the north and south lines. But assuming that his purpose was to provide in some way for astronomical observation, a square base with sides facing the cardinal points would not be of much use. It would clearly give horizontal direction lines, north and south, east and west, north-east and south-west, and north-west and south-east. For if observers were set at the four corners, A, B, C, D, as in fig. 6, with suitable uprights, where dots are shown at these corners, a line of sight from D's upright to A's would be directed towards the south, from the same upright to B's would be directed towards the south-west, and from the same to C's would be directed towards the west. Lines of sight from the other three uprights to each of the remaining ones would give the other directions named, or eight directions in all round the horizon.

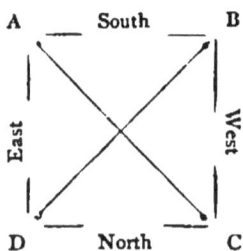

FIG. 6.

But such direction-lines are not very useful in astronomical observation, because the celestial bodies are not always or generally on the horizon. And no one who pays attention for any length of time, or with any degree of care, to the motions of the celestial bodies, will fail soon to recognise that east and west lines are of very little observational use compared with north and south lines, whether taken horizontally or in a direction suitably elevated above the horizon. For whereas every star in the sky comes due south or north (unless it should pass exactly overhead) once in every circuit around the pole (without counting the subpolar northings of those stars which never set), and at the same constant and regular intervals, the sun, moon, and planets also coming south at intervals only slightly varying (because of the motions of these bodies among the stars), the heavenly bodies do not come east and west at the same intervals. The sun does not come east or west at all, for instance, during the winter half of the year, while in the summer half he passes from due east to due west in a time which grows shorter and shorter as the length of the day increases. Without entering further into considerations which I have dealt with more fully in another place, it is manifest that any architect, proposing to erect an edifice for observing the heavenly bodies, would direct his attention specially to the meridian. He would require to observe bodies crossing different parts of the meridian. But he would recognise the fact that the southern half of the meridian was altogether more important than the northern ; for the sun and moon and all the planets cross the meridian towards the south. Again, those regions towards the south which are crossed by these bodies would be the most important of all.   '

What the architect would do then would be this. He would so raise the building, layer by layer, as to leave a suitable narrow opening, directed north and south, and bearing on the part of the southern sky which the sun, moon, and planets traverse.

Now, the grand gallery in the pyramid of Cheops fulfils precisely such a purpose as this. Before the upper part of the pyramid was added, the passage of the sun and moon and every one of the planets across the meridian, except perhaps Mercury (but I am not at all sure that Mercury need be excepted), could be observed through this remarkable slant gallery. Venus, of course, could only be seen in the daytime when due south ; but we know that at her brightest she can be readily seen in the daytime when her place in the sky is known. And through a long narrow passage like the grand gallery of the pyramid of Cheops she could be seen when much nearer the sun's place in the sky. Of course, to observe the sun, moon, or a planet, the astronomer would only be so far down the tunnel as to see the planet crossing the top of the opening. If he went farther down he would lose the observation ; but the farther down he went without losing sight of the body, the more favourable would be the conditions under which the observations would be made. Sometimes he could go to the very lowest part of the gallery. At midwinter, for instance, the sun could be observed from there, just crossing the top of the exceedingly small narrow slice of sky seen from that place.

I am not, however, specially concerned *here* with the question of the manner in which astronomical observations would be made through the great ascending gallery of the great pyramid. That is a subject full of interest, but I have fully discussed it in the preceding essay. What I desire here specially to note is, that the gallery could only be used when the pyramid was incomplete. While as yet all the portion of the pyramid above the gallery was not erected, the heavenly bodies could be observed not only along the great gallery, but also from the level platform forming the upper surface of the pyramid in that stage of its construction. But when the building began to be carried beyond that stage—unless for a while a long strip in front of the gallery was left incomplete—the chief use of the building for purposes of stellar observation must have come to an end. Not only have we no record that an open space was left in this way, and no trace in the building itself of any such peculiarity of construction, but it is tolerably manifest that no such space could have been safely left after the surrounding portions had been carried beyond a certain height.

It is here that I find the strongest argument for the theory I have advanced respecting the purpose for which the pyramids were built. It is certain that, though these buildings were specially constructed for astronomical observations of some sort, while the entire interior construction of the great pyramid adapted it specially for such a purpose, yet, only a short time after the great gallery and the other passages of this mighty structure had been completed, it was treated as no longer of any use or value for astronomical work. It was carried up beyond the platform where the priestly astronomers had made their observations, until the highest and smallest platform was added; and then the casing stones were fitted on, which left the entire surface of the pyramid perfectly smooth and polished, not the minutest crack or crevice marring either the sloping sides, or the pavement which surrounded the pyramid's base.

Now, I do not say that there is nothing surprising in what is known, and especially in the last-mentioned circumstance, when the theory is admitted that the great pyramid was built by Suphis or Cheops in order that astronomical observations might be continued throughout his life, to determine his future, to ascertain what epochs were dangerous or propitious for him, and to note such unusual phenomena among the celestial bodies as seemed to bode him good or evil fortune. It does seem amazing, despite all we know of the fulness of faith reposed by men of old times in the fanciful doctrines of astrology, that any man, no matter how rich or powerful, should devote many years of his life, a large portion of his wealth, and the labours of many myriads of his subjects, to so chimerical a purpose. It *is* strange that a building erected for that purpose should not be capable of subserving a similar purpose for his successors on the throne of Egypt. Strange also that he should have been able to provide in some way for the completion of the building after his death, though that must have been a work of enormous labour, and very expensive, even though all the materials had been prepared during his own lifetime.

But I do assert with considerable confidence that no other theory has been yet suggested (and almost every imaginable theory has been advocated) which gives the slightest answer to these chief difficulties in the pyramid problem. The astrological theory, if accepted, gives indeed an answer which requires us to believe the kingly builder of the great pyramid, and, in less degree, those who with him or after him built the others, to have been utterly selfish, tyrannical, and superstitious—or, in brief, utterly unwise. But unfortunately the study of human nature brings before us so many illustrations of the existence of such folly and superstition in as great or even greater degree, that we need not for such reasons reject the astrological theory. Of other theories it may be said that, while not one of them except the wild theory which attributes the great pyramid to divinely instructed architects, presents the builders more favourably, every one of these theories leaves the most striking features of the great pyramid entirely unexplained.

Lastly, I would note that the pyramids when rightly viewed must be regarded, not as monuments which should excite our admiration, but as stupendous records of the length to which tyranny and selfishness, folly and superstition, lust of power and greed of wealth, will carry man. Regarded as works of skill, and as examples of what men may effect by combined and long-continued labour, they are indeed marvellous, and in a sense admirable. They will remain in all probability, and will be scarcely changed, when every other edifice at this day existing on the surface of the earth has either crumbled into dust or changed out of all knowledge. The museums and libraries, the churches and cathedrals, the observatories, the college buildings and other scholastic edifices of our time, are not for a moment to be compared with the great pyramid of Egypt in all that constitutes material importance, strength, or stability. But while the imperishable monuments of old Egypt are records of tyranny and selfishness, the less durable structures of our own age are, in the main, records of at least the desire to increase the knowledge, to advance the interests, and to ameliorate the condition of the human race. No good whatever has resulted to man from all the labour, misery, and expense involved in raising those mighty structures which seem fitted to endure while the world itself shall last. They are and ever have been splendidly worthless. On the other hand, the less costly works of our own time, while their very construction has involved good instead of misery to the lowlier classes, have increased the knowledge and the well-being of mankind. The goodly seed of the earth, though perishable itself, germinates, fructifies, and bears other seed, which will in turn bring forth yet other and perchance even better fruits ; so the efforts of man to work good to his fellow man instead of evil, although they may lead to perishable material results, will yet germinate, and fructify, and bear seed, over an ever-widening field of time, even to untold generations.

SUN-SPOTS AND FINANCIAL PANICS.

I RECEIVE so many letters relating to the imagined troubles which the movements of the planets are to occasion during the next few years (chiefly through the intervention of the solar spots), that I think many may find interest in the most recent development of the sun-spot mania—Professor Stanley Jevons's theory that there is a close and intimate connection between commercial crises and spots upon the sun. ·My object is not, I need hardly say, to advocate Jevons's theory. Nor do I propose merely to show how slight is the evidence on which the theory is based, and that, in some respects, it is even opposed to those views in whose support it was adduced. I write more with the view of discouraging that flow of unreasonable and altogether unscientific speculation with regard to sun-spots which has recently set in.

About the year 1862, Professor Jevons prepared two statistical diagrams relating to monetary matters, the price of corn, &c. The study of these satisfied him that the commercial troubles of 1815, 1825, 1836–39, 1847, and 1857, exhibited a true but mysterious periodicity. There was no appearance of like periodicity, indeed, during the first fifteen years of the present century, when 'statistical numbers were thrown into confusion by the great wars, the suspension of specie payments, and the frequently extremely high prices of corn.' He admits, moreover, that the statistical diagram, so far as the eighteenth century is concerned, presents no appreciable trace of periodicity.

In 1875, attracted by questions raised respecting solar influences, Professor Jevons discussed the data in Professor Thorold Rogers's ' Agriculture and Prices in England since 1259.' He then believed, he tells us somewhat naively, that 'he had discovered the solar period' in the prices of corn and various agricultural commodities, and he accordingly read a paper to that effect at the British Association at Bristol. Subsequent inquiry, however, *seemed to show that periods of three, five, seven, nine, or even thirteen years, would agree with Professor Rogers's data just as well as a period of eleven years;* in disgust at which result, Professor Jevons withdrew the paper from further publication. He still looks back, however, with some affection on that, his first essay towards ' finding the solar period' in terrestrial relations, and quotes now, with a certain complacency, a passage from the paper he had withdrawn in disgust from the proceedings of the British Association. ' Before concluding,' he says in this passage, ' I will throw out a surmise, which, though it is a mere surmise, seems worth making. It is now pretty generally allowed that the fluctuations of the money market, though often apparently due to exceptional and accidental events, such as wars, panics, and so forth, yet do exhibit a remarkable tendency to recur at intervals approximating to ten or eleven years. Thus, the principal commercial crises have happened in the years 1825, 1836–39, 1847, 1857, 1866, and I was almost adding 1879, so convinced do I feel that there will, within the next few years, be another great crisis. Now, if there should be, in or about the year 1879, a great collapse comparable with those of the years mentioned, there will have been five such occurrences in fifty-four years, giving almost exactly eleven years (10.8) as the average interval, which sufficiently approximates to 11.1 years, the supposed exact length of the sun-spot period, to warrant speculations as to their possible connection.'

However, Professor Jevons, though he had done his best to follow the course laid down for such researches 'by those who are determined, above all things, that some terrestrial

cycles shall be made to synchronise with the sun-spot cycle,'[1]
had been thus far disappointed. 'I was embarrassed,' he
says, 'by the fact that the commercial fluctuations could
with difficulty be reconciled with a period of 11.1 years. If,
indeed, we start from 1825 and add 11.1 years time after
time, we get 1836.1, 1847.2, 1858.3, 1869.4, 1880.5, which
shows a gradually increasing discrepancy from 1837, 1847,
1857, 1866, and now 1878, the true dates of the crises.'
The true cycle-hunter, however, is seldom without an explanation of such discrepancies. 'I went so far,' he says,
and again his *naïveté* is charming, 'as to form the rather
fanciful hypothesis that the commercial world might be a
body so mentally constituted, as Mr. John Mill must hold, as
to be capable of vibrating in a period of ten years, so that it
would every now and then be thrown into oscillation by
physical causes having a period of eleven years.' Unfortunately for the scientific world, which could not have
failed to profit greatly from the elucidation of so ingenious
a theory, even though it had subsequently been found well
to withdraw it, Professor Jevons became acquainted about
this time with some inquiries by Mr. J. A. Broun, tending to
show that the solar period is 10.45 years, not 11.1. This
placed the matter in a very different light and removed all
difficulties. 'Thus, if we take Mr. John Mill's " Synopsis of
Commercial Panics in the Present Century," and rejecting
1866, as an instance of a premature panic' (this is very
ingenious), 'count from 1815 to 1857, we find that four
credit cycles occupy forty-two years, giving an average
duration of 10.5 years, which is a remarkably close approximation to Mr. Broun's solar period.'

Encouraged by the pleasing aspect which the matter had

---

[1] 'The thing to hunt down,' says one of these, 'is a cycle, and if
that is not to be found in the temperate zones, then go to the frigid
zones or to the torrid zone to look for it; and if found, then above all
things and in whatever manner (!) lay hold of, study, and read it, and
see what it means,'—or make a meaning for it, if it has none, he should
have added.

now assumed, Professor Jevons determined to go further afield for evidence. 'It occurred to me at last,' he says, 'to look back into the previous century, where facts of a strongly confirmatory character at once presented themselves. Not only was there a great panic in 1793, as Dr. Hyde Clarke remarked, but there were very distinct events of a similar nature in the years 1783, 1772–3, and 1763. About these dates there can be no question, for they may all be found clearly stated on pp. 627, 628, of the first volume of Mr. Macleod's unfinished " Dictionary of Political Economy." Mr. Macleod gives a concise, but I believe correct account of these events, and as he seems to enter-tain no theory of periodicity, his evidence is perfectly un-biassed.' It is true that neither Wolff's nor Broun's period can be strictly reconciled with the occurrence of four commercial crises, at intervals of exactly ten years ; for three times 11.1 are 33.3, and three times 10.45 are 31.35, whereas the interval from 1763 to 1793 amounts only to 30. However we only have to regard the crisis of 1793 as a 'premature panic' to remove this difficulty. Indeed with premature panics and delayed panics, overhasty sunspot crises and unduly retarded ones, we can get over even more serious difficulties.

This 'beautiful coincidence,' as Professor Jevons called it, led him to look still farther backward, 'and to form the apparently wild notion that the great crisis, generally known as that of the South Sea Bubble, might not be an isolated and casual event, but only an early and remarkable manifes-tation of the commercial cycle.' The South Sea Bubble is usually assigned to the year 1720, and as that would be 43 years before 1763, we should have 10¾ years, instead of 10½ years for the average interval, if three commercial crises occurred between 1720 and 1763. But this difficulty is merely superficial. 'It is perfectly well known to the his-torians of commerce,' says Professor Jevons, 'that the general collapse of trade, which profoundly affected all the more advanced European nations, especially the Dutch,

French, and English, occurred in 1721. Now if we assume
that there have been since 1721, up to 1857, thirteen commercial cycles, the average interval comes out 10.46 years.
Or if we consider that we are in this very month (November,
1878), passing through a normal crisis, then the interval of
157 years, from 1721 to 1878, gives an average cycle of
10.466 years.'

Before this could be accepted, however, three commercial panics had to be found to fill in the space between
1721 and 1763. Professor Jevons felt this keenly. He
spent much time and labour during the summer of 1878, 'in
a most tedious and discouraging search among the pam-
phlets, magazines, and newspapers of the period, with a view
to discover other decennial crises.' He seems to have done
everything he could think of, short of advertising—'Wanted
three crises, fitted to fill a crisisless gap in last century's
commercial history'—but the results were not very satisfactory. 'I am free to confess,' he says, 'that in this search, I
have been thoroughly biassed in favour of a theory, and
that the evidence which I have so far found would have no
weight if standing by itself. It is impossible, in this place,
to state properly the facts which I possess ; I can only
briefly mention what I hope to establish by future more
thorough inquiry.' Even this,—which has yet to be established,—amounts to very little ; but that is the fault of the
facts, not of Professor Jevons.

In the first place it is remarkable, he thinks, that the
South Sea Company, which failed in 1720–21, was founded
in 1711, just ten years before, 'and that on the very page
(312) of Mr. Fox Broun's " Romance of Trade," which mentions this fact, the year 1701 also occurs in connection with
speculation and *stock-jobbing*, as the promotion of companies
was then called. The occurrence of a crisis in the years
1710–11–12, is indeed almost established by the list of
bubble insurance companies formed in those years as collected by Mr. Cornelius Walford.'

If the probability that a commercial crisis occurred in

1710–12 (though the history of trade perversely omits to mention such a crisis,) is not considered sufficient, in company even with the mention of 1701 as a year of stock-jobbing, to prove beyond all possibility of question, that commercial crises occurred in 1731, 1742, and 1752, let the hesitating student observe, that quite obviously 'about ten years after stock-jobbing had been crushed by the crisis of 1721, it reared its head again.' It is remarked in the 'Gentleman's Magazine' of 1732 that 'stock-jobbing is grown almost epidemical. Fraud, corruption and iniquity in great companies as much require speedy and effectual remedies now as in 1720. The scarcity of money and stagnation of trade in all the distant parts of England, is a proof that too much of our current coin is got into the hands of a few persons.' Before 1734 matters had become still worse, for Mr. Walford says that 'gambling in stocks and funds had broken out with considerable fervour again during the few years preceding 1734. It was the first symptom of recovery from the events of 1720.' In 1734, accordingly, we find that an act was passed to check stock-jobbing.

It might still seem, however, to some of those doubting spirits, whom no arguments can satisfy, that the occurrence in 1734, of 'the first symptoms of recovery from the events of 1720,' is not in itself proof positive of the occurence of a commercial crisis in 1732. They might, in their perversity, argue that the next commercial crisis, after that of 1720–21, would presumably have followed the recovery, 1734, from the effects of the South Sea collapse. To satisfy these unbelievers, Professor Jevons points out that, in 1732, a society called the 'Charitable Corporation for Relief of the Industrious Poor' became bankrupt. Many people were ruined by the unexpected deficit thus discovered, and Parliament and the public were asked to assist the sufferers.

The failure of a charitable corporation in 1732 is not perhaps absolutely demonstrative of the occurrence of a commercial crisis in 1732 ; but when considered in connection with the founding of the South Sea Company, in 1711, the occurrence of stock-jobbing in 1701, the revival in 1734 from the events of 1720–21, and especially with the circumstance that Professor Jevons's theory absolutely requires a crisis in 1732, it must in charity be accepted. It would indeed be exceedingly unkind to reject the evidence thus offered for a commercial panic in 1732, because none can be found to show that between 1732 and 1763 'anything approaching to a mania or crisis,' took place. ' My learned and obliging correspondents, at Amsterdam and Leyden,' says Professor Jevons, ' disclaim any knowledge of such events in the trade of Holland at that time, and my own diagram, showing the monthly bankruptcies throughout the interval, displays a flatness of a thoroughly discouraging character.'

This would dishearten perhaps any one but a believer in sun-spot influences. But the rule laid down by the high-priest of their order, to hold on resolutely to any cycle found or imagined, 'above all things *and in whatever manner*, to lay hold of' such a cycle, despite all difficulties and every discouragement, is one which they follow with a zeal worthy of a more scientific and logical system of procedure. Though Professor Jevons could find no evidence whatever of a crisis between the well-imagined one in 1732 and the real crisis in 1763, inquiry leads him to believe, he says, ' that yet there were remarkable variations in the activity of trade and the prices of some staple commodities, such as wool and tin, sufficient to connect the earlier with the later periods.' The evidence is not complete, and as it does not quite agree with the sun-spot theory, it is ' probably misleading.' Any one who can point out to Professor Jevons a series of prices of metals, or other commodities not merely agricultural, before 1782, will, he announces, confer a very great obligation upon him by doing so.

However, though the theory absolutely requires a crisis in 1742 and another in 1752, or thereabouts, let us defer for the present any minuter inquiry on this point. ' I permit myself to assume,' says Professor Jevons, ' that there were, about the years 1742 and 1752, fluctuations of trade which connect the undoubted decennial series of 1711, 1721, and 1732, with that commencing again in the most unquestionable manner in 1763.' There is something very pleasing in this. Our hero permits himself to assume that the strongest possible evidence of steady commercial relations between 1732 and 1763 may be set on one side. He makes a series of undoubted crises out of three dates : of these the first (1711) marking the time when one of the greatest commercial swindles of the last two centuries was started, indicates a season of undue confidence, instead of undue depression ; the second (1721) is not the true date of the event with which it is connected; and the third (1732) was not marked by any commercial event in the remotest degree resembling a general panic or crisis. Having achieved this noteworthy deed of derring-do—running atilt against, and for the time being overthrowing, all the rules of logic (as if in a tourney a knight should overthrow the marshals, instead of his armed opponents)—Professor Jevons is able triumphantly to declare that the whole series of decennial crises may be stated as follows : (1701 ?), 1711, 1721, 1731–32, (1742 ? 1752 ?), 1763, 1772–3, 1783, 1793, (1804–5), 1815, 1825, 1836-39, (1837, in the United States), 1847, 1857, 1866, 1878. A series of this sort, we are told, is not like a chain, as weak as its weakest part ; on the contrary, the strong parts add strength to the weak parts. In spite, therefore, of the doubtful existence of some of the crises, as marked in the list, ' *I can entertain no doubt whatever* ' (the italics are most emphatically mine), ' I can entertain no doubt whatever that the principal commercial crises do fall into a series having the average period of about 10.466 years. Moreover, the almost perfect coincidence of this period with Broun's estimate of the sun-spot period (10.45) is by itself strong evidence that the phenomena are causally connected.' There is evidence of splendid courage in these statements ; it is in this way that, according to the Scotch proverb, a man either ' makes a spoon or spoils a horn.'

Before proceeding to consider the evidence by which the

series of commercial crises is to be connected, or otherwise, with the series of sun-spot changes, let it be permitted to us to separate the actually recorded crises from those which Professor Jevons has either invented (as 1701, 1711, and 1732), or assumed (as 1742, 1752, and 1804-5). There remain the dates 1721, 1763, 1772-3, 1783, 1793, 1815, 1825, 1836-39, 1847, 1857, 1866 and 1878. The corresponding intervals (taking, when an interval instead of a date is given, the date midway between the two named), are as follows : 42 years, 9½ years, 10½ years, 10 years, 22 years, 10 years, 12½ years, 9½ years, 10 years, 9 years, and 12 years. The evidence for the decennial period is not demonstrative, and the logical condition of the mind which, in presence of this evidence, ' can entertain no doubt whatever ' that the true average period is 10.466 years—which, be it noted, is a period given to the thousandth part of a year, or to about 8¾ *hours*—must be enviable to those who possess a much smaller capacity for conviction—that is, a much greater capacity for doubt.

But it may happen, perchance, that the irregularity of the recurrence of crises affords evidence in favour of a connection between commercial panics and the sun-spot period. It is well known that the epochs when the sun is most spotted do not occur at regular intervals, either of 11.1 years, 10.45 years, or any other period. If the irregularities of the sun-spot period should be reflected, so to speak, in the irregularities of the panic period, the evidence would be even more satisfactory than if both periods were quite regular and they synchronised together. For in the latter case there would be only one coincidence,—a coincidence which, though striking, might yet be due to chance ; in the other there would be many coincidences, the co-existence of which could not reasonably be regarded as merely fortuitous.

Only, at the outset it may be as well to determine beforehand what our conclusions ought to be, if no such resemblance should be recognised between the irregularities of the two periods. We must not, perhaps, expect too close a resemblance. We may very well believe that while the normal relationship between two connected sets of phenomena might result either in absolutely simultaneous oscillations, or, at least, in oscillations of perfectly equal period (so that whatever discrepancy might exist between the epochs of the respective maxima or minima should be constantly preserved), yet that a multitude of more or less extraneous disturbing influences might prevent either form of synchronism from being actually observed. For instance, if we supposed that the absence of sun-spots is the cause of commercial depression, we might imagine that, at the time of fewest sun-spots, a commercial crisis would occur unless extraneous causes delayed it ; or we might imagine that, as a regular rule, the crisis would follow the time of fewest sun-spots by a given interval, as a year or two years ; yet we might very well understand that occasionally a crisis might be hastened by a few months, or even a year, or might be in equal degree delayed. Still there are limits to the amount of disturbance which we could thus account for without being forced to abandon altogether the theory that sun-spots influence trade,—despite the antecedent probability (which some consider so great) of a relationship of this kind. For instance, if we found commercial crises occurring in a year of maximum disturbance at one time, while at another they occurred in a year of minimum disturbance, at another, midway between a maximum and the next following minimum, at yet another midway between a minimum and the next following maximum, we should not feel absolutely forced to accept the theory that sun-spots somehow govern trade relations. Nay, I think a logically-minded person would feel that in the presence of such discrepancies nothing could establish the theory—otherwise so extremely probable—of the influence of sunspots on trade.

Professor Jevons has not definitely indicated his own opin ions on this point. Perhaps, if he had, we should have found that he would allow wider latitude to the discrepancies which may exist, than one less attached to the sun-spot theory of trade would consider permissible. We have seen how readily he has been satisfied respecting crises which had to be either invented or assumed.[1] Perhaps a little further evidence on this point may be useful, as showing the extent to which that bias in favour of his theory, which he has so frankly admitted, seems really to have influenced him. We have seen that if crises fail to occur when his theory requires them, he readily constructs or assumes crises to fit into the vacant places. He is equally ready to deal with what others would regard as the equally fatal difficulty, that crises take place when, according to the decennial theory (a wider theory than the solar one, be it noticed), they should not have occurred. ' There is nothing in this theory,' he says, ' inconsistent with the fact that crises and panics arise from other than meteorological causes. There was a great political crisis in 1798, a great commercial collapse in 1810–11, (which will not fall into the decennial series) ; there was a stock-exchange panic in 1859 ; and the great American collapse of 1873–75. There have also been several minor disturbances in the money market, such as those of February, 1861, May and September, 1864, August, 1870, November, 1873 ; but they are probably due to exceptional and disconnected reasons. Moreover, they have seldom, if

---

[1] Professor Roscoe, in a lecture on ' Sun-spots and Commercial Crises' (delivered, strangely enough, as one of a series of science lectures for the people), has raised Professor Jevons's assumed crisis a grade higher in the scale of probability. The dates, 1742, 1752, and 1804-5, when a crisis ought to have occurred, but did not, were given by Professor Roscoe as dates of doubtful crises, by which his audience understood that crises but of comparatively small extent occurred at those dates. Certainly the audience did not understand that, after long and careful search for the crises which should theoretically then have taken place, Professor Jevons had failed to find any trace whatever of their occurrence. By the way, the audience at Manchester would not seem to have been very profoundly impressed by a conviction of the antecedent probability of the theory advocated by the lecturer. At first, Professor Roscoe's statement of the theory was received as a joke. ' Laughter,' ' laughter,' and ' renewed laughter,' followed the enunciation of the theory. Only when the evidence, carefully freed from whatever might suggest doubt or difficulty, was brought forward, did the audience gradually become convinced that the lecturer was in earnest.

ever, the intensity, profundity and wide extension of the true decennial crises.' In other words, if recognisable crises fail to occur when the decennial period requires them, yet we may assume that, at the proper time, some trade disturbances have taken place, only on so small a scale as to escape notice ; but if trade disturbances occur which even attract notice, at times not reconcilable with the decennial theory, then we may overlook them, because a true decennial crisis is intense, profound, and widely extended. It is a case of 'heads I win, tails you lose' with the supporters of the decennial theory. Though even with this free-and-easy method of reasoning, the American crisis in 1873–75 might seem rather awkward to deal with. Americans, at any rate, are not very likely to accept the doctrine that that crisis was not intense, profound, and widely extended.

I may remark in passing that, in jestingly advancing the theory which Professor Jevons has since adopted, I dealt— also jestingly—with this very difficulty in a way which seems to be at least as satisfactory as Professor Jevons's method of treating it. 'The last great monetary panic,' I wrote in 1877, 'occurred in 1866, at a time of minimum solar macu- lation. Have we here a decisive proof that the sun rules the money market, the bank rate of discount rising to a maximum as the sun-spots sink to a minimum, and *vice versâ*? The idea is strengthened,' I pointed out, 'by the fact that the American panic in 1873 occurred when spots were very numerous, and its effects have steadily subsided as the spots have diminished in number ; for this shows that the sun rules the money-market in America on a prin- ciple diametrically opposite to that on which he (manifestly) rules the money-market in England,—precisely as the spots cause drought in Calcutta and plenteous rain-fall at Madras, wet south-westers and dry south-easters at Oxford, and wet south-easters and dry south-westers at St. Petersburg. Surely it would be unreasonable to refuse to recognise the weight of evidence which thus tells on both sides at once.' This was nonsense, and was meant to be taken as nonsense ; but it strikingly resembles some arguments which have been urged, within the last hundred years too, respecting solar influences.

Let us turn, however, to the actual records of sun-spots, and compare them with Professor Jevons's list of commercial crises.

We have no better collection of evidence respecting sun-spots than that formed by Professor Wolff. Broun and Lamont have called in question some of Wolff's conclusions, as will presently be more particularly noticed. But, in the main, Wolff's evidence remains unshaken. Very few astronomers—we may even say no astronomers of repute —have adopted the adverse views which have been thus expressed, and certainly none, even among those who have admitted the possible validity of such views on points of detail, entertain the least doubt respecting the general validity of the conclusions arrived at by Wolff.

After carefully examining all the evidence afforded by observatory records, the note-books of private astronomers, and so forth, Wolff has deduced the following series of dates for the maxima and minima of solar disturbances since the year 1700 :

Intervals in years.	Dates of Maxima.	Possible error in years.	Intervals in years.	Dates of Minima.	Possible error in years.
12.5	1705.0	2.0	11.0	1712 0	1.0
10.0	1717.5	1.0	10.0	1723.0	1.0
11.0	1727.5	1.0	12.0	1733.0	1.5
11.5	1738.5	1.5	10.7	1745.0	1.0
11.5	1750.0	1.0	10.8	1755.7	0.5
8.5	1761.5	0.5	9.3	1766.5	0.5
9.5	1770.0	0.5	9.0	1775.8	0.5
9.0	1779.5	0.5	13.7	1784.8	0.5
15.5	1788.5	0.5	12.0	1798.5	0.5
12.8	1804.0	0.1	12.7	1810.5	0.5
12.7	1816.8	0.5	10.6	1823.2	0.2
7.7	1829.5	0.5	10.2	1833.8	0.2
11.4	1837.2	0.5	12.2	1844.0	0.2
11.6	1848.6	0.5	10.9	1856.2	0.2
10.6	1860.2	0 2	11.4	1867.1	0.1
	1870.8			1878.5	

The dates below the line are not in Wolff's list.

It would be difficult, I conceive, for the most enthusiastic believer in sun-spot influences to recognise any connection between the crises and the variations of solar maculation, whether Professor Jevons's list or the natural crises be considered. To quote from an article in the London 'Times,' which has been attributed to myself (correctly):

Taking 5¼ years as the average interval between the maximum and minimum sun-spot frequency, we should like to find every crisis occurring within a year or so on either side of the minimum; though we should prefer, perhaps, to find the crisis always following the time of fewest sun-spots, as this would more directly show the depressing effect of a spotless sun. No crisis ought to occur within a year or so of maximum solar disturbance; for that, it should seem, would be fatal to the suggested theory. Taking the commercial crises in order, and comparing them with the (approximately) known epochs of maximum and minimum spot frequency, we obtain the following results (we italicise numbers or results unfavourable to the theory): The doubtful [I ought to have written 'assumed'] crisis of 1701 followed a spot minimum by *three* years; the crisis '(imagined)' of 1711 preceded a minimum by one year; that of 1721 preceded a minimum by *two* years; 1731-32 '(imagined crisis)' preceded a minimum by one year; 1742 '(no crisis known)' preceded a minimum by *three* years; 1752 (no crisis) followed a maximum by *two* years; 1763 followed a maximum by a *year and a half;* 1772-73 came *midway* between a maximum and a minimum; 1783 preceded a minimum by *nearly two* years; 1793 came *nearly midway* between a maximum and a minimum; 1804-05 '(no known crisis)' '*coincided* with a maximum; 1815 preceded a maximum by *two years;* 1825 followed a minimum by *two years;* 1836-39 *included* the year 1837, of maximum solar activity (that being the year, also, when a commercial panic occurred in the United States;') 1857 preceded a minimum by one year [this case was, by some inadvertence of mine, omitted from the 'Times' article]; 1866 preceded a minimum by a year; and 1878 follows a minimum by a year. Four favourable cases [it should have been five] out of seventeen [it should have been eighteen] can hardly be considered convincing. If we include cases lying within two years of a minimum, the favourable cases mount up to seven (eight) leaving ten unfavourable cases.

I might have added, at this point, that if a number of dates were scattered absolutely at random over the interval

of 1701–1880, we should expect to find some such proportion between dates falling within two years on either side of
a minimum and those not so falling.

It must be remembered, I added in the 'Times' article,
that a single decidedly unfavourable case, as in 1815 and
1837, 'does more to disprove such a theory than twenty
favourable cases would do towards establishing it.'

To the 'Times' article Professor Jevons replied in a
letter, which scarcely seemed to require an answer. At any
rate, it left entirely undefended the weakest part of his
theory. The agreement between the average period for
commercial crises and Broun's estimate of the average
sun-spot period was insisted upon afresh ; but the circumstance that crises have occurred at every phase of the sun-
spot wave—at the maximum, at the minimum, soon after
either of these phases, just before either and midway
between maximum and minimum, both when spots are
increasing and when they are diminishing in number—was
in no way accounted for. General doubts were thrown,
indeed, on Wolff's accuracy ; but no special error was indicated in his interpretation of the evidence he had collected, and still less was any definite objection taken to
Wolff's spot curve, regarded as a whole.

Soon after, however in the 'Athenæum' Professor Jevons
advanced a more definite defence of his theory. He first
argued in favour of Broun's average period of 10.45 years,
and then commented unfavourably on some definite dates in
Wolff's series.

By the elaborate comparison of magnetic, auroral, and
sun-spot data, he said, ' Mr. Broun appears to show con-
clusively that the solar period is not 11.1 years, but about
10.45, this last estimate confirming the earlier determination
of Dr. Lamont.' It should be mentioned here that the
magnetic and auroral data cannot be regarded as of themselves proving anything respecting the sun-spot period ;
they are as invalid in this respect as some of the evidence
which Hansteen and others have derived from terrestrial

relations respecting the solar rotation. The real fact is that, having shown clearly enough that the average magnetic and auroral period has (at any rate during the last century) been 10.45 years, Broun has endeavoured to invalidate the evidence obtained by Wolff for a sun-spot period of 11.1 years, simply because, if such a period is admitted, the theory of synchronism between magnetic and solar disturbances must of necessity be rejected. For this purpose, Broun has endeavoured to show that Wolff has overlooked a small maximum of sun-spots in 1797. The table given above shows very clearly that, if an extra maximum is to be thrown in anywhere, it must be between the maxima of 1788.5 and 1804.0, the interval between which is 15½ years. Broun has certainly not succeeded in demonstrating that 1797 was a year of many spots, nor could a small maximum then occurring be regarded as affecting the sun-spot curve more than the two small maxima which can be recognised in Wolff's picture of the sun-spot curve at about the years 1793 and 1795. Professor Jevons, however, complacently adopts, as proved, what Mr. Broun has surmised with very little probability. 'The fact is,' he says, 'that Dr. Wolff overlooked a small maximum in 1797, and was thus led to introduce into his curve an interval of seventeen years' (15½ only), 'an interval quite unexampled in any other part of the known solar history.' This again is incorrect : there was precisely such an interval between the maxima of 1639.5 and 1655.0 as between those of 1788.5 and 1804.0 ; while the maximum of 1655.0 was followed by an interval of *twenty* years before another maximum occurred. We have on this point the definite information of Cassini, who, writing in 1671, when spots were beginning to re-appear, said : 'It is now nearly twenty years since astronomers have seen any considerable spots on the sun.' 'Mr. Broun shows, moreover,' proceeds Professor Jevons, 'that the 11.1 period fails to agree with all the earlier portions of Dr. Wolff's own data, which yield a period varying between 10.21 and 10.75 at the utmost. This must relate to the earlier portion of what

Wolff calls the modern series, viz., from 1750 onwards. It would be just as much or as little to the purpose to reply that the six intervals from the first maximum of the present century, 1804.0, to the last, which cannot be set earlier than 1870.6, have an average length of exactly 11.1 years. It is admitted that five or six periods do not afford sufficient evidence to determine the average, and for my own part, I may as well admit that I doubt the stability of the sun-spot period altogether, believing that in one century it may amount to fifteen or twenty years, and in another to seven or eight. But at least the observations of the present century and the mean period of 11.1 years resulting from them are open to no sort of question, whereas the very arguments on which Professor Jevons and Mr. Broun insist in opposing Wolff's conclusions would (if admitted) shake all faith in the evidence he adduces from Wolff's earlier dates of maxima and minima.

The next point insisted on by Professor Jevons seems still less to the purpose, except as bearing on Wolff's general accuracy. 'Almost more serious,' he says, 'as regards the credibility of Dr. Wolff's results is the fact that Mr. Broun gives good reasons for believing that the year 1776 was a year of maximum sun-spots, whereas Dr. Wolff sets that very year down as one of minimum sun-spots.' The following are Broun's own words : 'There are no means of testing the earlier epochs of Dr. Wolff; but no long period given by him will be satisfied by them. If I have already shown good grounds for substituting a maximum in 1776 for Dr. Wolff's minimum, a similar change in some of the epochs of the preceding century and a half may be quite possible.' 'Now, a highly scientific writer in the "Times,"' proceeds Professor Jevons, 'has condemned the theory of decennial crises, because the dates assigned will not agree with those of maximum and minimum sun-spots, taken, no doubt, according to Dr. Wolff's estimates ; and an eminent French statist has rejected the theory on the same ground. I think I am entitled, therefore, to point to the doubts which Mr. Broun's careful inquiries throw upon the accuracy of Dr. Wolff's relative numbers.'

Now, a study of the curve of sun-spots will show how little Dr. Wolff's accuracy is, in reality, impugned by Mr. Broun's attack. We recognise in the curve, which, be it remembered, is Wolff's, a double minimum in the space between the year-ordinates for 1771 and 1781. One corresponds to the year 1773, the other to the last quarter of the year 1775. As the latter appeared from the evidence examined by Wolff to be a more marked minimum, the former he regards as the true minimum for that particular wave of spots. But no one who knows anything about the varying aspects of the sun's disc during the two or three years which include the minimum, will wonder if the study of records, necessarily incomplete (for until Schwabe's time no one thought of keeping the sun constantly under survey), should have left the time of the actual minimum rather doubtful in one or two cases. The wonder is that Wolff should have found sufficient evidence to determine the true minimum in so many cases. This of itself would suffice to show how laborious must have been his researches. In the particular case about which Mr. Broun raises his question, it can be seen from Wolff's curve of spots that after an apparent minimum in 1773, spots began to appear, then grow fewer in number, till they reached a lower minimum in 1775, neither of these minima, however, being such as to correspond to an absolute spotlessness (which is represented by the level of the lowest minima in Wolff's curve). Then they increased rapidly in number, being greater in number in 1777 than they had been at any of the three preceding maxima. That in 1776, when the spots had already become very numerous, there should be records from which Mr. Broun could infer the existence of an actual maximum, is not at all surprising, though no astronomer accepts the inference ; nor if any did, would the inference at all carry with it the weight which Mr. Broun and Professor Jevons seem to recognise in it. Again, it is absolutely certain that there was a maximum

in 1779 ; so that the supposed maximum of 1776 would
involve one more wave, which, with the new wave introduced between 1790 and 1800, would give seventeen complete waves between the maxima of 1705 and 1870, an interval of less than one hundred and sixty-five years. This
would make the average length of the sun-spot period 9.7
years, which would not at all suit the views of Mr. Broun
and M. Lamont.

In passing, I may remark that in the article in the
' Times ' (I am obliged to identify myself with Professor
Jevons's ' highly scientific writer,' simply because I wrote the
article in question) I did not condemn the theory of commercial crises ; I expressed no opinion on that theory. What I
indicated was simply that no possible connection can exist
between that theory and the theory of sun-spots. As a matter
of fact, I do not believe in the decennial theory of crises,
though I perceive that in quite a number of cases commerce
has oscillated through depression, revival and excitement
to the next depression, in about that time. Nor again, do
I believe in the sun-spot theory, though I perceive that
during the last century or two the average sun-spot period has
been about what Dr. Wolff indicates. But I have not attacked,
and certainly I have not condemned, either of these theories.
What I do insist upon very strongly, however, is, that the
oscillations of commercial credit and the variations of the
sun's condition as to maculation have, since the beginning
of the last century, shown no approach to agreement.

' I will even go a step further,' adds Professor Jevons,
' and assert that in a scientific point of view it is a questionable proceeding to dress up a long series of relative numbers
purporting to express the number of sun-spots occurring
during the last century, with the precision of one place of
decimals. As Mr. Broun had pointed out, there were no
regular series of observations then, and results deduced from
the occasional observations of different astronomers cannot
be reduced into one consecutive series without a large
exercise of discretion. As Mr. Broun has pointed out, Dr.

Lamont has criticised some of the epochs which Dr. Wolff considers certain (*sicher*), and has shown that they depend on few observations. He remarks that old observers directed their attention chiefly to large sun-spots, so that Flaugergues (one of the principal observers during the period in question), saw the sun frequently without spots, when many were seen by other observers. The true scientific procedure would have been that which Professor Loomis has pursued in regard to auroras, namely, to place in a table all the reasonable observations, carefully distinguishing those by different observers, so that there should be the least possible admixture of Dr. Wolff's own personal equations.' I have quoted this passage in full—first, because it presents the opinions of those adverse to Professor Wolff in this matter ; secondly, because the remarks about the difficulties of the subject (difficulties, that is, with which Professor Wolff has had to contend, and with which he has contended energetically and skilfully) are in the main just ; but thirdly and chiefly because it affords sound criterions by which to test Professor Jevons's method of procedure. If we should eschew one place of decimals in dealing with the results of observations counted by hundreds, what are we to think of three places of decimals deduced from a few dozen records of commercial matters ? If a sun-spot period derived from determinations of maxima and minima, every one of which is based on real observation, is untrustworthy, what opinion are we to form of a trade period based on crises of which five, or nearly a third of the whole number, are either imagined or assumed ? If, in fine, Dr. Wolff's method is unscientific, what name shall we find for that by which having derived a decennial period from admittedly unsatisfactory evidence, and having rejected the sun-spot period accepted by astronomers for one carefully concocted to fit another theory, Professor Jevons insists on the agreement of this fictitious crisis period and this incorrect sun-spot period, without attempting to show that the admitted variations of one agree with the admitted variations of the other?

For, after all, the strongest evidence against the theory that commercial crises depend on sun-spots, is given by those crises and sun-spot waves about which there is no sort of doubt or question—the crises on the one hand, and the maxima and minima of sun-spots on the other, recorded during the present century. The study of the second half of the table given above will satisfy any unprejudiced person that this is the case, from the crisis of 1804–5 (which never took place, but must be assumed to have taken place, to make up the series for the decennial theory of crises), to the crises of 1866 and 1878, we have crises occurring in every part of a sun-spot wave—on the crest, on the valley, on the ascending slope, and on the descending slope. No theory of association can hold out against such obvious evidence of the absolute independence of the two orders of events.[1]

[1] The matter has been well summed up by a correspondent of the 'Athenæum.' 'Professor Jevons,' he says, 'seems to attach great weight to the length of the average sun-spot period ; but if the average length of the period between commercial crises during a couple of centuries were shown to be identical with, or to differ but slightly from, the average period of sun-spots, this would be but a small step towards proving association between the two phenomena. The separate periods of minima must be shown to correspond with speculative crises, and the curve also must be proved to be of the same character. Professor Jevons does not appear to be aware that Dr. Wolff has in the forty-third volume of the "Memoirs of the Astronomical Society," given a list of the manuscripts and printed authorities from which he derives his data. Similar but fuller information is supplied by Dr. Wolff in the pages of his " Astronomische Mittheilungen." Dr. Wolff does not pretend to equal accuracy for all the periods, but there can be little doubt with regard to the sun-spot periods which have occurred during this century, and according to Professor Jevons, there seem to be serious discrepancies between these and the periods of commercial depression.'

COLD AND WET.

DAY after day throughout May, June, and July, 1879, the same monotonous record continued—'The mean temperature has been considerably below the average.' Taking monthly means, we have to go back as far as October, 1878, for a month which was as warm as the average of former years. The cold of the winter months, though of course far more bitter, attracted less attention—we may even say excited less apprehension—than the cold which prevailed through May, June, and July. · Accompanied by an unusually, though not quite unprecedentedly, heavy rainfall, the average rainfall for the whole year having been exceeded before the end of July, the low temperature, which actually has been unprecedented since trustworthy records of such matters have been kept, excited a feeling of anxiety, if not of alarm. Many are in-quiring whether some change may not have occurred by which the climate itself of this country, and, indeed, of the whole of Europe, has been modified. Perhaps the favourite theory in this direction is that the Gulf Stream has changed its course. But others take a still more melancholy view of matters, imagining that not Europe alone, but the whole earth, has experienced some dismal change. Either the sun has ceased to pour the due amount of heat upon the earth or the planets have combined to destroy our comfort, or else the whole of the solar system, in the course of its well known motion towards the constellation Hercules, has passed into some region where cosmical cold prevails, and suffers accordingly. It happens, unfortunately, that the

dismal weather we have lately had has appeared to correspond in some degree with a series of gloomy vaticinations
respecting the state of the earth during the years 1880–1885,
as though our present troubles were 'the beginning of the
end.' We learned from the Astronomer Royal for Scotland
that in the building which he regards as a sort of stone
Bible the 'Second Coming' is announced for the year 1882,
with several prior years of discomfort, indicated by the 'im-
pending south wall' of the great ascending gallery. The
apocryphal prophecies of Mother Shipton indicate the year
'eighteen hundred and eighty-one,' as that in which, regard-
less of rhyme, she considered that 'this our world to an end
must come ;' and as it happened that among the signs of
the approaching end we were to have the seasons so con-
founded as only to be known by the trees (a state of things
which has certainly prevailed of late, when but for the fresh
green foliage we might have judged from appearances that
we were passing through a late autumn), many begin to
think that, after all, there may be something in the old lady's
predictions. But far more effective than any such prophecies,
because less readily to be understood, have been the warnings
of some American astrologer, who has announced that
between 1880 and 1885 the perihelia of the four giant
planets—Jupiter, Saturn, Uranus, and Neptune—would
coincide (so the statement has reached us, it is not our
fault if as so stated it should appear, as it does, sheer nonsense to the astronomer), wherefore obviously all the inhabitants of earth must during that time be exposed to the most
grievous calamities, of which the bad weather we have experienced affords merely a slight foretaste. And although
these ideas are too absurd to be worth serious refutation,
they find much wider acceptance than those imagine who
suppose that in these days scientific facts are generally
known, even though they may not be very generally understood. In speaking, indeed, of such ideas as absurd we are
obliged to include the teachings of one who is deservedly
regarded as a man of science ; albeit the exact measurements

and observations by which Professor Smyth has determined the proportions of the Great Pyramid, must be carefully distinguished from the wild fancies which have led him to believe that the future of the world was prefigured in stone in that building 4,050 years ago.

It may be well to consider how far the weather we have recently experienced can be regarded as abnormal (unusual it certainly has been), that those who take a rational view of such matters may form an opinion as to the prospect of approaching change, while the fanciful and superstitious may possibly find reason for believing that, after all, the beginning of the end may not yet have commenced.

In the first place, we know from the imperfect records of olden times that long periods of cold and rainy weather have from time to time been experienced in this country and in Europe generally during past centuries. It is interesting to notice that the long-continued cold of the years 1593 and 1594 led many to form views as gloomy respecting the future as those which many ill-informed persons recently entertained. In the middle summer of the latter of those years Shakespeare wrote his *Midsummer Night's Dream.* He describes, in Titania's rebuke of Oberon, the bitter weather which had then prevailed for months in England :—

> The winds, piping to us in vain,
> As in revenge, have suck'd up from the sea
> Contagious fogs; which, falling in the land,
> Have every pelting river made so proud,
> That they have overborne their continents ;
> The ox hath therefore stretch'd his yoke in vain,
> The ploughman lost his sweat ; and the green corn
> Hath rotted ere his youth attain'd a beard ;
> The fold stands empty in the drowned field,
> And crows are fatted with the murrain flock ;
> The nine-men's morris is fill'd up with mud ;
> And the quaint mazes in the wanton green,
> For lack of tread are undistinguishable ;

(which, substituting the agricultural show and our cricket

o

fields for nine-men's morris and the wanton green, accords
closely enough with our recent experience)

> And through this distemperature we see
> The seasons alter ; hoary-headed frosts
> Fall in the fresh lap of the crimson rose ;
> And on old Hyems' chin, and icy crown,
> An odorous chaplet of sweet summer buds
> Is, as in mockery, set ; the spring, the summer,
> The childing autumn, angry winter, change
> Their wonted liveries ; and the 'mazed world,
> By their increase, *now knows not which is which.*

Nor is the interpretation of these troubles thereon advanced
much wilder than are some of the theories now gravely
urged and discussed. 'And this same progeny of evil,'
quoth Titania,

> > > > Comes
> From our debate, from our dissension ;
> We are their parents and original.

The fairies have quite as much to do with our present
weather-troubles as the perihelia of Jupiter, Saturn, Uranus,
and Neptune.

But we have more exact evidence than poetical descrip·
tions such as these with which to compare our recent experience. For 115 years we have a series of records of
monthly mean temperatures in North Britain, and though it
would not be safe to infer from such a series that throughout
the whole of Great Britain the temperature had been below
or above the average when it was below or above respectively on the shores of the Moray Firth and Firth of Forth,
yet it may safely enough be assumed that if we had records
as complete for any other spot in Great Britain, we should
find similarly long periods of low or high temperature.
From the records in question the following table has been
formed, in which all periods of low temperature, lasting
not less than five months, the mean temperature being

more than three degrees below the average, have been included :—

Date of Cold.	Duration in months.	Under mean temperature of the months.
February–November, 1782 . .	10	−5.1
January–August, 1799 . .	7	−3.8
October–March, 1799–1800 .	6	−3.3
November–April, 1807–8 . .	6	−3.5
March–August, 1812 . . .	6	−3.4
October–March, 1813–14 . .	6	−3.6
November–August, 1815–16 .	10	−3.5
January–May, 1838 . . .	5	−4.2
January–May, 1855 . . .	5	−3.5
December–April, 1859–60 . .	5	−3.0

It is noteworthy that during the 18 years preceding the cold interval of 1782, the most intense and, with one exception, the most protracted of the above series, there had been no instance of a temperature more than three degrees below the average and lasting so long as five months. Then came a period of 16 years without such a cold interval. So that the occurrence of long protracted and intense cold does not necessarily render it likely that such falls of temperature will for a while thereafter recur at short intervals. In the 16 years 1800–1816 there were no less than five instances of long-protracted cold ; but in the 63 years since 1816, only three such instances have been recorded besides the period of cold through which we passed in 1878–80. Whether this great difference between the last 64 years and the preceding 16 is due merely to accident or to causes affecting observatories situate near large cities is, as yet, not definitely made out. If the latter view be adopted, the cold of the eight months ending August 31, 1879 will appear the more exceptional. That period of cold exceeded in intensity any of similar length of which we have authentic records. But the period wanted a month of the longest recorded in the above table. When we consider only cases in which the mean temperature of the month has not exceeded the average, we find

yet longer periods of consecutive cold months. The longest
. of these (I am indebted for this information to an interesting
paper in a recent number of *Nature*) is the period of 19
months from September 1798, to March, 1800, during which
the mean temperature was 2.8 deg. below the average ; next
in length comes a period of 17 months from September, 1859,
to January, 1861, when the temperature was 2.2 deg. below
the average ; thirdly, a period of 15 months, from February,
1782, to March, 1783, when the temperature fell 4.4 deg.
below the average of those months. So that quite possibly
—since what has happened more than once already may
happen again (without bringing with it the end of the world)
—such cold weather as that of 1879 may last for a much
longer time.

It will, perhaps, hardly be thought necessary to explain
that the cold and wet weather of the nine months ending
August 31, 1879, was not brought about by planetary influence. It came, indeed, too soon for those astrologers whose
faith had been pinned on the perihelion passages between
1880 and 1881, and it continued too long for those
believers in cycles who promised or threatened drought
in 1879. In passing, the perihelion predictions for the
five years ending 1885, which have actually terrified some
in a remarkable degree—especially farmers, many of whom
are almost as superstitious as sailors, probably because,
like sailors, their well-being depends so much on the
inconstant weather—may be briefly dealt with. Jupiter,
the nearest of the giant planets and far the largest
(two-and-a-half times larger than all the rest together, with
Venus, the Earth, Mars, Mercury, and the Moon thrown in
as make-weights), passed his perihelion on September 5,
1880 ; but as he passes his perihelion once in every 11 5-6th
years, this can hardly be regarded as so exceptional a
phenomenon that the end of the world must inevitably
follow or be hastened by its occurrence. Saturn, which has
been regularly passing his perihelion once every 29½ years
(roughly) since the world began, if not for millions of years

before (according to the development theory), will not pass his perihelion before the autumn of 1885, by which time Jupiter will not be very far from aphelion. In other words, whatever mischief our theorists associate with Saturn's passage of the part of his orbit nearest the Sun ought presumably to be counteracted by Jupiter's approach to the part of his orbit farthest from the Sun. As for Uranus and Neptune which lie respectively twice and three times as far from the Sun as Saturn, while their combined mass is not a third of his, their perihelion passages can hardly produce very terrible results (somehow by the way astrology was as successfully prosecuted before these planets were discovered as now, when they must be considered in every horoscope). However, as a matter of fact, they do pass their perihelia in 1882, at the convenient distances of about 1,700 and about 2,750 millions of miles respectively from our comparatively near neighbour the Sun. Lest this statement should encourage the notion that these two planets thus passing their perihelia in one and the same year (terrible coincidence) are very closely consorted to work mischief, let it be remarked that throughout the whole of the five years during which such terrible troubles are promised, the distance separating Uranus and Neptune will not be less than about 3,500 millions of miles.

The question whether recent inclement weather depends in any way on the Sun's condition with regard to spots is better worth discussing than the nonsense of the astrologers. We may remark in passing, however, that astrological absurdities have been to some degree encouraged by the enunciation of the doctrine that the planets in their courses influence the solar fluid envelopes and thus cause the number of spots to increase or to diminish—a doctrine for which there seemed some evidence so long as the average solar spot period had not been accurately determined and might therefore be supposed to synchronise with the period of 11 5-6th years in which Jupiter completes his circuit. Now that the two periods are found to differ by three-quarters of

a year at least, and if Mr. Broun's estimate is correct by
about a year and five months, the theory of Jupiter's influence
must be regarded as inadmissible, seeing that though for
many years together sun-spots may be most numerous when
Jupiter is near perihelion, for as many years together thereafter they will be most numerous when he is near aphelion.
However, the theory that sun-spots influence terrestrial
phenomena does not, in reality, depend on the theory that the
planets produce the sun-spots. If we inquire whether the
cold and wet weather of 1879–80 was in any way associated
with the paucity of sun-spots during those years, we find
other and more important difficulties than those arising
from the failure of the planetary theory of sun-spot production. In the first place, though Europe suffered from
cold, America suffered rather from excessive heat, while
in the southern hemisphere the average supply of heat
was maintained without being anywhere in any noteworthy
degree exceeded. But as the theory of solar influence
on weather is not incompatible with a diversity of effects
in different parts of the world—nay, admits, or rather
insists, upon the production of absolutely contrary effects in
parts of one and the same country, we must inquire whether
the other cases of long-continued cold cited above have
coincided or not, like the present cold period, with a period
of few sun-spots.

The first and most remarkable of the intervals of cold
tabulated above extended from February to November,
1782 ; the *maximum* of sun-spot frequency had been
reached in about the middle of 1779, and the following
minimum towards the end of 1784 ; thus the middle of
the depression of temperature falling in the middle of
1782 followed a *maximum* by three years and preceded a
minimum by nearly two years and a half. We may say
roughly that the cold period fell midway between a *maximum* and a *minimum*, in the decreasing phase of sun spots.
The next cold interval ran from January to August, 1799,
its middle, therefore, in May, 1799 ; thus following a *mini-*

mum of sun-spots in the middle of 1798 by about one year, and preceding a *maximum* at the beginning of 1804 by four years and a half. It fell then nearer a *minimum* than a *maximum* and in the increasing phase of sun-spots. The next cold interval, from October, 1799, to March, 1800, fell on the same slope of a sun wave, but not so near a *minimum* by half a year. The next, from November, 1807, to April, 1808, fell about midway between the sun-spot *maximum* of 1804.0 and the *minimum* of 1810.5, but rather nearer the *minimum* than the *maximum* and on the decreasing slope. The next—March to August, 1812—occurred during the increasing stage of sun-spots, following a *minimum* by two years and preceding a *maximum* (1816.8) by rather more than four years. The cold interval from October, 1813, to March, 1814, fell on the same increasing slope, but as much nearer to the *maximum* as the former had been nearer to the *minimum*. Then came the long cold interval from November, 1815, to August, 1816. The middle of this interval fell in April, 1816, say 1816.3, or may be said to have coincided with the *maximum* of sun-spots in that year, set at 1816.8. The cold interval of January to May, 1838, followed almost as closely after a *maximum* of sun-spots (1837.2) as the cold interval of 1815-16 preceded one. That of January to May, 1855, preceded a *minimum* of sun-spots (1856.2) by about a year. That of December, 1859, to April, 1860, coincided exactly with the *maximum* of sun-spots in 1860-2. And lastly the present cold period follows only by a few months the *minimum* of sun-spots in 1878.

We thus see that the most remarkable intervals of protracted cold during the last 115 years have occurred in all parts of the sun-spot period indifferently—at the *maximum*, at the *minimum*, midway between a *maximum* and the following *minimum*, midway between a *minimum* and the following *maximum*, soon after a *maximum*, soon after a *minimum*, shortly before a *minimum*, and lastly, shortly after a *minimum*. It will be rather difficult, then, to show that these cold periods depend directly or indirectly on the sun's condition with respect to spots, though when the bare announcement is made that the remarkable cold from which we have suffered in 1879–80 came after the sun had long been almost free from spots, many are ready to believe at once that the cold has been caused by the sun's spotless condition.

On the whole, it may fairly be inferred that as yet, despite our meteorological observations and long-continued statistical researches, we are not able either to foretell seasons of cold or heat, of rain or draught, nor at present can any safe guess be made as to the duration of any cold interval which may be in progress. It may be mentioned in passing for the benefit of those who believe in weather prophecies, that the *Almanach Mathieu*, the favourite oracle of French farmers, promised exceedingly warm weather from the 19th to the 26th of July, 1879, during which interval, in reality, the temperature was considerably below the average.

OUR WINTERS.

WHEN frost and snow prevail, we hear a good deal about old-fashioned winters, seasonable Christmas weather, and so forth, the idea being generally prevalent that some 30 or 40 years ago our winters were much colder than they are now, and that, in particular, December was of yore a month of much frost and snow. Meteorological records give no support to these views, which appear to be based solely on imperfect recollection of bitter winters in the past, winters as exceptional then as such winters are now, but remembered as though they had occurred in successive years and for many years in succession. Forty years ago men spoke of old-fashioned winters much as many of us do now. The belief was just as prevalent then as now that some 30 or 40 years earlier the winters had been much more severe than at the then present time. It is true this does not of itself prove that no such change has occurred as many believe in ; for the winters 80 years ago might have been as much bitterer than the winters 40 years ago as these are supposed to have been bitterer than our present winters. But we should have to believe in a much greater change during the last 80 years than is assumed to have happened in the last 40 years. So that, as we have records of the winter weather 80 years ago, it becomes easier to put the prevalent superstition about the bitterness of past winters to the test. When this is done, we find nothing to suggest that the average winter weather 80 or 100 years ago was severer than that which we now experience,

Before considering some of the evidence relating to past winters, we may as well note that, so far as Christmas weather is concerned, there is a real foundation for the theory that there has been a change, though none whatever for the theory that winter weather has changed. The old-fashioned Christmas weather—not the Christmas weather 30 or 40 years, but a century and a half ago—was, in fact, the weather of a different part of the year. Christmas Day during the first half of last century, instead of occurring as now four or five days after the shortest day or winter solstice, fell more than a fortnight after that epoch. Now the coldest part of the year, on the average, falls about four weeks after the winter solstice ; so that we can very well understand that on the average of many years old Christmas Day and the old Christmas season would be colder than our present Christmas-tide. A study of the meteorological records of the last half century shows very clearly that such a difference exists between the Christmas weather of the New Style and that of the Old Style with its seasonal error of ten days. Thus, compare the weather of the last fortnight in December in which our present Christmas season falls with that of the first fortnight in January to which old Christmas-tide belonged. We find in 50 years seven in which the weather of the last fortnight in December was of a neutral character, mild and cold weather alternating in about equal proportions ; 27 in which the weather of that fortnight was mild, and in the remaining 16 only the weather was severe. On the contrary, while there were eight years of neutral weather during the first fortnight in January, there were 15 only in which the weather of that fortnight was mild, the weather being severe in 27. We can understand, then, why December was depicted by the poets down to the time of the change of style as a colder month than we now find it. It belonged to a colder part of the year, just as Spenser's ' Mery Moneth of May ' belonged to a warmer part of the year than our present May.

Those who quote the accounts which have been handed down of bitter winters in past times have been apt to over-

look the circumstance that those accounts nearly always tend
to disprove, not to establish, the theory of change. Those
records tell us of the exceeding severity of cold which prevailed at such and such a time, but they also tell us that the
cold was altogether exceptional. Sometimes even we find
that while the *maximum* degree of cold recorded has fallen
short of what has been experienced within the last 20 or 30
years, it is described as exceeding aught that even the oldest
persons could remember. Gilbert White speaks of the cold
in December, 1784, as very extraordinary ; but he mentions
one degree below zero as the lowest temperature recorded
out of doors in the shade. In January, 1855, a temperature
of four degrees below zero was recorded in the neighbourhood of London. One circumstance, indeed, which White
mentions, would seem to show that cold such as we had in
January, 1855, was regarded in his day as too improbable to
be worth considering in making thermometers ; for he says
that a thermometer by Martin, a well-known maker of
scientific instruments, was graduated only down to four
degrees above zero, so that the mercury sank quite below
the brass guard of the bulb. Again, in describing the
severe weather of January, 1776, when the Thames was
frozen over, both above and below bridge, White tells us
that during the four coldest nights the thermometer at South
Lambeth fell to 11, seven, six, and six (above zero), and at
Selborne sank on one night exactly to zero ; but he adds
that this was 'a most unusual degree of cold for the south
of England.' It was the long continuance of the frost of
1776, not its intensity, which caused the effects to be so
remarkable. The snow lay 26 days on the houses in the
city, being all that time perfectly dry, so that the snow in
the streets 'crumbled and trod dusty, and, turning gray,
resembled bay salt.' The long continuance of the frost
depended on the long-continued northerly winds. At any
time we might have a similar experience. We have been so
far fortunate that for many years it has never chanced to
blow continuously from northerly quarters for three or four

weeks in January, the coldest month in the year. And we may safely conclude, from long experience that such a continuance of northerly winds at that season is improbable. But there is no reason why it should not happen now as in 1776 and other past years. It was as little anticipated in the first week of 1776 as in the first week of 1879. Their experience was as ours has been. ' The old housekeepers living,' White tells us, ' did not remember ' a frost which had lasted (continuously) so long as that of January, 1776.

Forty or fifty years ago those who believed that a great change had in the course of a generation or so affected winter weather in Great Britain were at a loss to explain the greater mildness of the season. In the United States and Canada, where a similar change was, quite erroneously, believed to have occurred, a cause was imagined in the clearing of forests and the consequent exposure of large tracts of land to the sun's rays. But in Great Britain and in Europe generally there had been no clearing away of many millions of acres of forest timber. So that, as a writer in 1837 admitted, 'If the climate of Great Britain has actually undergone a change, the cause, whatever it may be, must be of a different nature from that generally supposed to affect the climate of North America.' The imagined change in the last 40 years has been attributed to a cause which, perhaps, has some real effect on climatic relations, though certainly no such effect as has been attributed to it —the enormous annual consumption of coal. It is possible that in manufacturing towns and in the larger cities, the mean temperature of the winter months may be slightly increased in this way ; though there is no valid evidence to show that this is the case, and any such increase must be very small. That the climate of the country should be influenced by the consumption of coal is altogether incredible. Only a portion of the heat resulting from the use of coal in this country tends to warm the air, directly or indirectly. Most of it is or ought to be expended in generating various forms of force. But even if all the coals raised annually were used to increase the warmth of our air, the effect would be very slight by comparison with the heat received from the sun. The combustion of four times as many tons of coal as are annually raised in Great Britain would barely suffice to dry the Island after one day's heavy rainfall, if we could imagine it used in that way.

If there had been, as some imagine, a change in the direction of the ocean currents which reach our shores, or in the temperature of the water which they bring to us from distant seas, we could understand that the climate of Great Britain should have been greatly changed. But all the evidence we have tends to show that the Gulf Stream, or the extension of the Gulf Stream to which we incorrectly give that name, occupies the same position and has the same character now as a century ago. And, in reality, not only is the mean temperature for each month the same now (or apparently so) as it was 50 or 100 years ago, but the prevalent weather of special months appears to have undergone no alteration other than that apparent alteration which has resulted from the change of style, an alteration which is observable only in comparing the weather of our present months with that ascribed to the same months by poets and others before the year 1752, when the change of style was effected. We have seen how marked a difference at present exists between the average weather of the last fortnight in December and that of the first fortnight in January, and how we can thus explain the contrast between the ordinary Christmastide weather of our time and that described by poets before the change of style. Many, however, believed that in this respect, at any rate, if not in the mean monthly temperature, there has been a marked change within a much shorter time. Forty or fifty years ago, they say, Christmas weather was nearly always frosty. Confronted by meteorological records which prove the reverse, they still believe that 80 or 90 years ago (when as yet no systematic meteorological records were kept) the old-fashioned Christmas weather prevailed in nine years out of ten. It may be of interest to inquire whether this really was the case or not. The answer comes in no doubtful terms. Gilbert White of Selborne has left a rough record of the weather from the beginning of 1768 to the end of 1792. Of the 25 years thus recorded, we find that three ended with a fortnight of alternate rain and frost, in eight the last fortnight was frosty, and in the remaining 14 that fortnight was mild and rainy, mostly without frost, but in some of the 14 years a few slight frosts occurred. On the other hand, at that time, as now, the first fortnight in January was commonly much colder than the last fortnight in December. The neutral cases were four ; in eight years the first fortnight in January was mild, and in the remaining 13 hard frost prevailed during that fortnight.

ABOUT LOTTERIES.

In an essay which appeared a few years since in the *Cornhill Magazine*, I considered among gambling superstitions some relating indirectly to such ventures as are made when tickets in lotteries are bought, a small certainty being exchanged for the small chance of a large profit. Whether it is that men are so well known to be inconsistent in such matters, that if any one points out the folly of gambling he may be regarded as almost certain to be a gambler himself, or whether the case is a merely casual coincidence, I do not know; but certain it is that during the years which have elapsed since that essay appeared, I have received more invitations to purchase lottery-tickets and to take part in wildly speculative transactions than during any ten preceding years of my life. Not only so, but in some cases invitations have been addressed to me to purchase tickets from persons claiming to be exceptionally lucky in selecting numbers. I have no doubt many of my readers have received such invitations, couched in terms implying that a very special favour was offered which must be quickly accepted lest it should be too late to gain the wealth thus generously proffered. But it struck me as being a singularly cool proceeding in my case, simply because much that I had written bore directly not only on the question whether such hopes as are held out in offers of the sort can possibly be well founded, but also on this other question, Can those who hold out such hopes be by any possibility honest men? Without definitely expressing any opinion on

the second and more delicate of these questions, I propose to consider here a few matters connected with lotteries,
noting some of the systems on which they have been formed.
Probably the reader will not find it very difficult to determine what my answer would be to the question, if a cate-
gorical reply were required from me.

The simplest, and in many respects the best, form of
lottery is that in which a number of articles are taken as
prizes, their retail prices added together, and the total
divided into some large number of parts, the same number
of tickets being issued at the price thus indicated. Suppose,
for instance, the prizes amount in value to 200*l.*, then a
thousand tickets might be sold at 4*s.* each, or 4,000 at 1*s.*
each, or a larger number at a correspondingly reduced price.
In such a case the lottery is strictly fair, supposing the prizes
in good saleable condition. The person who arranges the
lottery gains neither more nor less than he would if he sold
the articles separately. There may be a slight expense in
arranging the lottery, but this is fully compensated by the
quickness of the sale. The arrangement, I say, is fair ;
but I do not say it is desirable, or even that it should be
permissible. Advantage is taken of the love of gambling,
innate in most men, to make a quick sale of goods which
otherwise might have lain long on hand. Encouragement
is given to a tendency which is inherently objectionable if
not absolutely vicious. And so far as the convenience is
concerned of those who collectively buy (in fact) the prizes,
it manifestly cannot be so well suited as though those only
had bought who really wanted the articles, each taking the
special article he required. Those who buy tickets want to
get more than their money's worth. Some of them, if not
all, are believers in their own good luck, and expect to get
more than they pay for. They are willing to get, in this way,
something which very likely they do not want, something
therefore which will be worth less to them in reality than
the price for which it is justly enough valued in the list of
prizes.

Unfortunately those who arrange lotteries of this sort for mere trade purposes (they are not now allowed in this country, but abroad they are common enough, and English people are invited to take part in these foreign swindles) are not careful to estimate the price of each article justly. They put a fancy price on good articles, a full price on damaged articles, and throw in an extra sum for no articles at all. Many of them are not at all particular, if the sale of tickets is quick, about throwing in a few hundred more tickets than they had originally provided for, without in the least considering it necessary to add correspondingly to the list of prizes.

But this is not all. How much those who arrange such lotteries really wrong the purchasers of tickets cannot be known. But we can learn how ready the ticket-buyers are to be wronged, when we note what they will allow. It seems absurd enough that they should let the manager of a lottery act entirely without check or control as to the number of tickets or the plan according to which these are drawn. But at least when a day is appointed for the drawing, and the prizes are publicly exhibited in the first instance, and as publicly distributed eventually, the ticket-buyers know that the lottery has been in some degree *bonâ fide.* What, however, can we think of those who will pay for the right of drawing a ticket from a ' wheel-of-fortune,' without having the least means of determining what is marked on any of the tickets, or whether a single ticket is marked for a prize worth more than the price paid for a chance, or even worth as much ? Yet nothing is more common where such wheels are allowed, and nothing was more common when they were allowed here, than for a shopman to offer for a definite sum, which frequenters of the shop would readily pay, the chance of drawing a prize-ticket out of a wheel-of-fortune, though he merely assured them, without a particle of proof, that some of the tickets would give them prizes worth many times the price they paid. Even when there were such tickets, again, and some one had secured a prize (though the chances were that the prize-drawer was connected with

P

the business), people who had seen this would buy chances as though the removal of one good prize ticket had made no difference whatever in the value of a chance. They would actually be encouraged to buy chances by the very circumstance which should have deterred them. For if a good prize is drawn in such a case, the chances are that no good prize is left.

Although lotteries of this sort are no longer allowed by law, yet are they still to some degree countenanced in connection with charity and the fine arts. Now, setting aside lotteries connected with the fine arts as singularly nondescript in character—though it must not for a moment be supposed that we regard a taste for gambling with a love of the beautiful as forming an agreeable mixture—we note that in lotteries started for charitable purposes there is usually no thought of gain on the part of those who originate the scheme. That is, they have no wish to gain money for themselves, though they may be very anxious to gain money for the special purpose they have in view. This wish may be, and indeed commonly proves to be, inconsistent with strict fairness towards the buyers of tickets. But as these are supposed to be also possessed with the same desire to advance a charitable purpose that actuates the promoters of the scheme, it is not thought unfair to sell them their tickets rather dearly, or to increase the number of tickets beyond what the true value of the prizes would in strict justice permit. It is, however, to be noted that the assumption by which such procedure is supposed to be justified is far from being always accurate. It is certain that a large proportion of those who buy tickets in charitable lotteries take no interest whatever in the object for which such lotteries are started. If lotteries were generally allowed, and therefore fairer lotteries could be formed than the charitable ones —which are as unfair in reality as the dealings of lady stall-keepers at fancy bazaars—the sale of tickets at charitable lotteries would be greatly reduced. It is only because those who are possessed by the gambling spirit can join no other

lotteries that they join those started for charitable purposes.
The managers of these lotteries know this very well, though
they may not be ready to admit very publicly that they do. If
pressed on the subject, they speak of spoiling the Egyptians,
of the end justifying the means, and so forth. But, as a
matter of fact, it remains true that these well-intentioned
folk, often most devout and religious persons, do, in the
pursuit of money for charitable purposes, pander to the
selfishness and greed of the true gambler, encourage the
growth of similar evil qualities in members of their own
community, and set an evil example, moreover, by systematically breaking the law of the country. It would be
harsh, perhaps, to speak strongly against persons whose in-
tentions are excellent, and who are in many cases utterly
free from selfish aims ; but they cannot be acquitted from a
charge of extreme folly, nor can it be denied that, be their
purpose what it may, their deeds are evil in fact and evil in
their consequences. It might be difficult to determine
whether the good worked by the total sum gained from one
of these charitable lotteries was a fair equivalent for the mischief wrought in getting it. But this total is not all gained
by choosing an illegal method of getting the sum required.
The actual gain is only some slight saving of trouble on the
part of the promoters of the charitable scheme, and a
further slight gain to the pockets of the special community
in which the charity is or should be promoted. And it is
certain that these slight gains by no means justify the use of
an illegal and most mischievous way of obtaining money.
It would be difficult to find any justification for the system,
once the immorality of gambling is admitted, which might
not equally well be urged for a scheme by which the proceeds
(say) of one week's run of a common gaming-table should
be devoted to the relief of the sick poor of some religious
community. Nay, if charitable ends can at all justify
immoral means, one might go further still, and allow money
to be obtained for such purposes from the encouragement
of still more objectionable vices. We might in fact recog-

nise quite a new meaning in the saying that 'Charity covers a multitude of sins.'

I have said that a lottery in which all the prizes were goods such as might be sold, retail, at prices amounting to the total cost of all the tickets sold would be strictly fair. I do not know whether a lottery ever has been understood in that way. But certainly it seems conceivable that such a thing might have happened ; and in that case, despite the objections which, as we have shown, exist against such an arrangement, there would have been a perfectly fair lottery. Adam Smith, in his *Wealth of Nations*, seems to have omitted the consideration of lotteries of this kind, when he said that 'the world neither ever saw, nor ever will see, a perfectly fair lottery, or one in which the whole gain compensated the whole loss ; because the undertaker could gain nothing by it.' Indeed, it has certainly happened in several cases that there have been lotteries in which the total price of the tickets fell short of the total value of the prizes—these being presents made for a charitable purpose, and the tickets purposely sold at very low prices. It is well known, too, that in ancient Rome, where lotteries are said to have been invented, chances in lotteries were often, if not always, distributed gratuitously.

But assuredly Adam Smith is justified in his remark if it be regarded as relating solely to lotteries in which the prizes have been sums of money, and gain has been the sole object of the promoters. 'In the State lotteries,' as he justly says, ' the tickets are really not worth the price which is paid by the original subscribers,' though from his sequent remarks it appears that he had very imperfect information respecting some of the more monstrous cases of robbery (no other word meets the case) by promoters of some of these State swindles.

The first idea in State lotteries seems to have been to adopt the simple arrangement by which a certain sum is paid for each of a given number of tickets, a series of prizes being provided less in total value than the sum thus obtained.

It was soon found, however, that people are so easily gulled in matters of chance, that the State could safely assume a very disinterested attitude. Having provided prizes of definite value, and arranged the number of tickets, it simply offered these for sale to contractors. The profit to the State consisted in the excess of the sum which the contractors willingly offered above the just value (usually 10*l*.) of each ticket. This sum varied with circumstances, but generally was about 6*l*. or 7*l*. per ticket beyond the proper price. That is, the contractors paid about 16*l*. or 17*l*. for tickets really worth 10*l*. They were allowed to divide the tickets into shares,—halves, quarters, eighths, and sixteenths. When a contractor sold a full ticket he usually got about from 21*l*. to 22*l*. for it ; but when he sold a ticket in shares his gain per ticket was considerably greater. The object in limiting the subdivision to one-sixteenth was to prevent labouring men from risking their earnings. It is hardly necessary to say, however, that the provision was constantly and easily evaded, or that the means used for evading the limitation only aggravated the evil. At illegal offices, commonly known as 'little goes,' any sum, however small, could be risked, and to cover the chance of detection and punishment these offices required greater profits than the legal lottery-offices. 'All the efforts of the police,' we read, 'were ineffectual for the suppression of these illegal proceedings, and for many years a great and growing repugnance was manifested in Parliament to this method of raising any part of the public revenue. At length, in 1823, the last Act that was sanctioned by Parliament for the sale of lottery-tickets contained provisions for putting down all private lotteries, and for rendering illegal the sale, in this kingdom, of all tickets or shares of tickets in any foreign lottery,' which latter provision is to this day extensively evaded.

The earliest English lottery on record is that of the year 1569, when 40,000 chances were sold at 10*s*. each, the prizes being articles of plate, and the profit used in the repair of certain harbours. The gambling spirit seems to have developed greatly during the next century ; for, early in the reign of Queen Anne, it was found necessary to suppress private lotteries 'as public nuisances,' a description far better applicable (in more senses than one) to public lotteries. ' In the early period of the history of the National Debt,' says a writer (De Morgan, we believe) in the *Penny Cyclopædia*, ' it was usual to pay the prizes in the State lotteries in the form of terminable annuities. In 1694 a loan of a million was raised by the sale of lottery-tickets at 10*l.* per ticket, the prizes in which were funded at the rate of 14 per cent. for sixteen years certain. In 1746 a loan of three millions was raised on 4 per cent. annuities, and a lottery of 50,000 tickets of 10*l.* each ; and in the following year one million was raised by the sale of 100,000 tickets, the prizes in which were funded in perpetual annuities at the rate of 4 per cent. per annum. Probably the last occasion on which the taste for gambling was thus made use of occurred in 1780, when every subscriber of 1,000*l.* towards a loan of twelve millions, at 4 per cent., received a bonus of four lottery-tickets, the intrinsic value of each of which was 10*l.*' About this time the spirit of gambling had been still more remarkably developed than in Anne's reign, despite the laws passed to suppress private lotteries. In 1778 an Act was passed by which every person keeping a lottery-office was obliged to take out a yearly license costing 50*l.* This measure reduced the number of such offices from 400 to 51. In France the demoralisation of the people resulting from the immorality of the Government in encouraging by lotteries the gambling spirit, was greater even than in England.

The fairest system for such lotteries as we have hitherto considered was that adopted in the Hamburg lotteries. The whole money for which tickets were sold was distributed in the form of prizes, except a deduction of 10 per cent. made from the amount of each prize at the time of payment.

Before pausing to consider the grossly unfair systems which have been, and still are, adopted in certain foreign lotteries, it may be well to notice that the immorality of lotteries was not recognised a century ago so clearly as it is now ; and therefore, in effect, those who arranged them were not so blameworthy as men are who, in our own time, arrange lotteries, whether openly or surreptitiously. Even so late as half a century ago an American lawyer, of high character, was not ashamed openly to defend lotteries in these terms. ' I am no friend,' he said, ' to lotteries, but I cannot admit that they are *per se* criminal or immoral when authorised by law. If they were nuisances, it was in the manner in which they were managed. In England, if not in France ' (how strange this sounds), ' there were lotteries annually instituted by Government, and it was considered a fair way to reach the pockets of misers and persons disposed to dissipate their funds. The American Congress of 1776 instituted a national lottery, and perhaps no body of men ever surpassed them in intelligence and virtue.' De Morgan, remarking on this expression of opinion, says, that it shows what a man of high character for integrity and knowledge thought of lotteries twenty years ago (he wrote in 1839). ' The opinions which he expressed were at that time,' continues De Morgan, ' shared, we venture to say, by a great number.'

The experience of those who arranged these earlier State lotteries showed that from men in general, especially the ignorant (forming the great bulk of the population who place such reliance on their luck), almost any price may be asked for the chance of making a large fortune at one lucky stroke. Albeit, it was seen that the nature of the fraud practised should preferably be such that not one man in a thousand would be able to point out where the wrong really lay. Again, it was perceived that if the prizes in a lottery were reduced too greatly in number but increased in size, the smallness of the chance of winning one of the few prizes left would become too obvious. A system was required by which the number of prizes might seem unlimited and their possible value very great, while also there should be a possibility of the founders of the lottery not getting back all they ventured. So long as it was absolutely certain that, let the event be what it might, the managers of the lottery would gain, some might be deterred from risking their money by the simple statement of this fact. Moreover, under such conditions, it was always possible that at some time the wrath of losers (who would form a large part of the community if lottery operations were successful) might be roused in a dangerous way, unless it could be shown that the managers of public lotteries ran some chance, though it might be only a small chance, of losing, and even some chance of ruin as absolute as that which might befall individual gamblers.

It was to meet such difficulties as these that lottery systems like that sometimes called the Geneva system were invented. This system we propose now to describe, as illustrating these more speculative ventures, showing in particular how the buyers of chances were defrauded in the favourite methods of venturing.

In the Geneva lottery there are ninety numbers. At each drawing five are taken. The simplest venture is made on a single number. A sum is hazarded on a named number, and if this number is one of the five drawn, the speculator receives fifteen times the value of his stake. Such a venture is called a *simple drawing*. It is easy to see that in the long run the lottery-keeper must gain by this system. The chance that the number selected out of ninety will appear among five numbers drawn, is the same that a selected number out of eighteen would appear at a single drawing. It is one chance in eighteen. Now if a person bought a single ticket out of eighteen, each costing (say) 1*l.*, his fair prize if he drew the winning ticket should be 18*l.* This is what he would have to pay to buy up all the eighteen tickets (so making sure of the prize). The position of the speculator who buys one number at 1*l.*, in the Geneva lottery, is precisely that of a purchaser of such a ticket, only that instead of a prize being 18*l.*, if he wins, it is only 15*l.*

The lottery-keeper's position on a single venture is not precisely that of one who should have sold eighteen tickets at 1*l.* each for a lottery having one prize only ; for the latter would be certain to gain money if the prize were any sum short of 18*l.*, whereas the Geneva lottery-keeper will lose on a single venture, supposing the winning number is drawn, though the prize is 15*l.* instead of 18*l.* But in the long run the Geneva lottery-keeper is certain to win at these odds. He is in the position of a man who continually wagers odds of 14 to 1 against the occurrence of an event the real odds against which are 17 to 1. Or his position may be compared to that of a player who takes seventeen chances out of eighteen at (say) their just value, 1*l.* each, or 17*l.* in all, his opponent taking the remaining chance at its value, 1*l.*, but instead of the total stakes, 18*l.*, being left in the pool, the purchaser of the larger number abstracts 3*l.* from the pool at each venture.

That men can be found to agree to such an arrangement as this shows that their confidence in their own good fortune makes them willing to pay, for the chance of getting fifteen times their stake, what they ought to pay for the chance of getting eighteen times its value. The amount of which they are in reality defrauded at each venture is easily calculated. Suppose the speculator to venture 1*l.* Now the actual value of one chance in eighteen of any prize is one-eighteenth of that prize, which in this case should therefore be 18*l.* If, then, the prize really played for has but fifteen-eighteenths of its true value, or is in this case 15*l.*, the value of a single chance amounts only to one eighteenth of 15*l.*, or to 16*s.* 8*d.* Thus at each venture of 1*l.* the speculator is cheated out of 3*s.* 4*d.*, or one-sixth of his stake.

This, however, is a mere trifle. In the old-fashioned English system of lotteries, the purchaser of a 10*l.* ticket often paid more than 20*l.*, so that he was defrauded by more than half his stake ; and though less than half the robbery went into the hands of the contractor who actually sold the ticket, the rest of the robbery went to the State. In other ventures, by the Geneva system, the old-fashioned English system of robbery was far surpassed.

Instead of naming one number for a drawing (in which five numbers are taken) the speculator may say in what position among the five his number is to come. If he is successful, he receives seventy times his stake. This is, in effect, exactly the same as though but one number was drawn. The speculator has only one chance out of ninety instead of one chance out of five. He ought then, in strict justice, to receive ninety times his stake, if he wins. Supposing his venture $1l.$, the prize for success should be $90l.$ By reducing it to $70l.$ the lottery-keeper reduces the real value of the ticket from $1l.$ to one-nineteenth part of $70l.$, or to $15s$ $6\frac{2}{3}d.$, defrauding the speculator of two-ninths of his stake. Such a venture as this is called a *determinate drawing.*

The next venture allowed in the Geneva system is called *simple ambe.* Two numbers are chosen. If both these appear among the five drawn, the prize is 270 times the stake. Now among the 90 numbers the player can select two, in $8,010$ different ways; for he can first take any one of the 90 numbers, and then he can take for his second number any one of the 89 numbers left; that is, he may make 90 different first selections, each leaving him a choice of 89 different second selections; so that there are 90 times 89 (or $8,010$) possible selections in all. But in any set of five numbers there are, treating them in the same way, only 20 (or 5 times 4) different arrangements of two numbers. So that out of $8,010$ possible selections only 20 appear in each drawing of five numbers. The speculator's chance then is only 20 in $8,010$, or 2 in 801; and he ought, if he wins, to have for prize his stake increased in the ratio of 801 to 2, or $400\frac{1}{2}$ times. Instead of this it is increased only 270 times. At each venture he receives in return for his stake a chance worth less than his stake, in the same degree that 270 is less than $400\frac{1}{2}$, or is, in fact, defrauded of nearly one-third the value of his stake.

The next venture is called *determinate ambe.* Here the

speculator names the order in which two selected numbers will appear. Instead of 20 chances at any drawing of five numbers, he has only one chance—one chance in 8,010. He ought then to receive 8,010 times his stake, if he wins. As a matter of fact he receives only 5,100 times his stake. From this it follows that he is defrauded of 2,910 parts out of 8,010 of his stake, or very nearly three-eighths of the stake's value.

But more speculative ventures remain. The speculator can name three numbers. Now there are 704,880 possible selections of three numbers out of 90. (There are 8,010 possible selections of two numbers, as already shown, and with each of these any one of the remaining 88 numbers can be taken to make the third number ; thus we have 88 times 8,010, or 704,880 sets of three numbers in all.) These can appear among the five drawn numbers in 60 different ways (5 times 4 times 3). Thus the speculator has 60 chances out of 704,880, or one chance in 11,748. He ought then to receive 11,748 times his stake, if he wins ; but in reality he receives only 5,500 times his stake in this event. Thus the lottery-keeper robs him of more than half of his just winnings, if successful, and of more than half the mathematical value of his stake at the outset. The venture in this case is called *simple terne. Determinate terne* is not allowed. If it were, the prize of a successful guess should be 704,880 times the stake.

Quaterne involves the selection of four numbers. With 90 numbers, 61,334,560 (704,880 times 87) different selections of four numbers can be made. Among the five drawn numbers there can only be found 120 arrangements of four numbers. Thus the speculator has only 120 chances out of 61,334,560, or one chance out of 511,038. He ought therefore if he wins to receive 511,038 times his stake. The prize is only 75,000 times the stake. The lottery keeper deducts in fact, six-sevenths of the value of the stake at each venture. *Determinate quaterne* is, of course, not admitted.

Simple *quaterne* is, at present, the most speculative

venture adopted. Formerly *quine* was allowed, the speculator having five numbers, and, if all five were drawn, receiving a million times the value of his stake. He should
have received 43,949,268 times its value; so that, in effect,
he was deprived of more than 42 forty-thirds of the true
value of his venture.

The following table shows the amount by which the
terms of the Geneva system reduce the value of the stake
in these different cases, the stake being set at 1*l.* for convenience :—

	Actual Worth of 1*l.* Stake.		Robbery per 1*l.* Stake.	
	s.	*d.*	*s.*	*d.*
Simple drawing . . .	16	8	3	4
Determinate drawing . .	15	$6\frac{3}{4}$	4	$5\frac{1}{4}$
Simple Ambe . . .	13	6	6	6
Determinate Ambe . .	12	9	7	3
Terne	9	$4\frac{1}{2}$	10	$7\frac{1}{2}$
Quaterne	2	$11\frac{1}{4}$	17	$0\frac{3}{4}$

It may be thought, perhaps, that such speculative ventures
as terne and quaterne would very seldom be made. But the
reverse was the case. These were the favourite ventures;
and that they were made very often is proved to every one
acquainted with the laws of chance by the circumstance that
they not unfrequently proved successful. For every time
such a venture as a simple quaterne was won, it must have
been lost some half a million times.

It appears that in France the Geneva system was adopted
without any of the limitations we have mentioned, and with
some additional chances for those who liked fanciful ventures.
Professor De Morgan, in his *Budget of Paradoxes*, says :—
' In the French lottery five numbers out of ninety were
drawn at a time : any person, in any part of the country,
might stake any sum upon any event he pleased, as that 27
should be drawn ; that 42 and 81 should be drawn ; that
42 and 81 should be drawn, and 42 first ; and so on up to a
quine déterminé, if he chose, which is betting on five given

numbers in a given order.' The chance of a successful guess, in this last case, is 1 in 5,274,772,160. Yet if every grown person in Europe made one guess a day venturing a penny on the guess, and receiving the just prize, or say 4,800,000,000 times his stake, on winning, it would be practically certain that in less than a year some one would win 20,000,000*l.* for a penny ! It would be equally certain that though this were repeated dozens of times, the lottery-keepers would gain by the arrangement, even at the rate above stated. Nay, the oftener they had to pay over 20,000,000*l.* for a penny the greater their gains would be. As the actual prize in such a case would be 10 million instead of merely 5,275 million times the stake, their real gains, if they had to pay such prizes often, would be enormous. For, in the long run, every prize of half a million pounds for a shilling stake would represent a clear profit of 250 million pounds. The successful ventures would be only 1 in about 5,000 millions of unsuccessful ones, while paid for only at the rate of 10 million stakes.

No instances are on record of a *quine déterminé* being won, but a simple *quine*, the odds against which, be it remembered, are nearly 44 millions to 1, has been won ; and simple *quaternes*, against which the odds are more than half a million to 1, have often been won. In July 1821 a strange circumstance occurred. A gambler had selected the five numbers 8, 13, 16, 46, and 64, and for the same drawing another had selected the four numbers 8, 16, 46, and 64. The numbers actually drawn were

8   46   16   64   13

so that both gamblers won. Their stakes were small, unfortunately for them and fortunately for the bank, and their actual winnings were only 131,350 francs and 20,852 francs respectively. If each had ventured 1*l.* only, their respective winnings would have been 1,000,000*l.*, and 75,000*l.* The coincidence was so remarkable (the antecedent probability against two gamblers winning on a simple drawing or

simple *quine* and a simple *quaterne* being about 22 billions
to 1), that one can understand a suspicion arising that a hint
had been given from some one employed at the lottery-office.
M. Menut insinuates this, and a recent occurrence at Naples
suggests at least the possibility of collusion between gamblers
and the drawers of lottery numbers.   But in the case above
cited the smallness of the stakes warrants the belief that the
result was purely accidental.   Certainly the gamblers would
have staked more had they known what was to be the actual
result of the drawing.   The larger winner seems to have
staked two sous only, the prize being I suppose, 1,313,500
times the stake, instead of 1,000,000 as on a similar venture
in the Geneva lottery.   Possibly the stake was a foreign
coin, and hence the actual value of the prize was not a round
number of francs.   The smaller winner probably staked five
sous or thereabouts in foreign coin.

Simple *quaternes*, as we have said, occurred frequently in
France.   De Morgan remarks that the enormous number of
those who gambled ' is proved to all who have studied
chances arithmetically by the numbers of simple *quaternes*
which were gained : in 1822, fourteen; in 1823, six; in 1824,
sixteen ; in 1825, nine, &c.'   He does not, however, state
the arithmetical proportion involved.   If we take the average
number at ten per annum, it would follow that about five
million persons per annum staked money on this special
venture—the simple *quaterne*—alone.   Quetelet states that
in the five years 1816–1820, the total sums hazarded on all
forms of venture in the Paris lottery amounted to 126,944,000
francs,—say 5,000,000*l*.   The total winnings of the speculators amounted to 94,750,000 francs,—say about 3,790,000*l*.
The total amount returned to the treasury was 32,194,000
francs, or about 1,288,000*l*., a clear average profit of 257,600*l*.
per annum.   Thus the treasury received rather more than a
fourth of the sum hazarded.   The return to the speculators
corresponded nearly to that which would have been received if all the ventures made had been on a determinate
single number.

In all these methods, the greater the number of spec.u lators the greater the gains of those who keep the lottery. The most fortunate thing which can happen to the lottery-keepers is that some remarkably lucky hit should be made by a speculator, or a series of such. For then they can advertise the great gains made by a few lucky speculators, saying nothing of the multitudes who have lost, with the result that millions are tempted to become speculators. There is this great advantage in the Geneva system : that the total number of losers can never be known except to the lottery-keepers. In the old-fashioned English system the number of losers was as well known as the number of winners and their respective gains. But the keepers of the Paris and Geneva lotteries, as of those which have since been established on the same system, could publish the lists of winners without any fear that newspaper writers or essayists would remind the general public of the actual number of losers. The student of probabilities might readily calculate the probable number of losers, and would be absolutely certain that the real number could not differ greatly from that calculated ; but he could not definitely assert that so many had lost, or that the total losses amounted to so much.

It occurred to the Russian Government, which has at all times been notably ready to take advantage of scientific discoveries, that a method might be devised for despoiling the public more effectually than by the Geneva method. A plan had been invented by those who wanted the public money, and mathematicians were simply asked to indicate the just price for tickets, so that the Government, by asking twice that price, or more, might make money safely and quickly. The plan turned out to be wholly impracticable ; but the idea and the result of its investigation are so full of interest and instruction that I shall venture to give a full account of them here, noting that the reader who can catch the true bearing of the problem involved may consider himself quite safe from any chance of being taken in by

the commoner fallacies belonging to the subject of probabilities.

The idea was this. Instead of the drawing of numbers,
the tossing of a coin was to decide the prize to be paid, and
there were to be no blanks. If 'head' was tossed at a first
trial the speculator was to receive a definite sum—2*l*. we
take for convenience, and also because this seems to have
been nearly the sum originally suggested in Russian money.
If 'head' did not appear till the second trial the speculator
was to receive 4*l*.; if 'head' did not appear till the third
trial, he received 8*l*.; if not till the fourth, he received 16*l*.;
if not till the fifth, 32*l*.; till the sixth, 64*l*.; the seventh, 128*l*.;
the eighth, 256*l*., and so on ; the prize being doubled for
each additional tossing before 'head' appeared. It will be
observed that the number of pounds in the prize is 2 raised
to the power corresponding to the number of the tossing at
which 'head' first appears. If it appears first, for instance,
at the tenth trial, then we raise 2 to the 10th power, getting
1,024, and the prize is 1,024*l*.; if 'head' appears first at the
twelfth trial, we raise 2 to the 12th power, getting 4,048, and
the prize is 4,048*l*.

Doubtless the origin of this idea was the observed
circumstance that the more speculative ventures had a great
charm for the common mind. Despite the enormous deduction made from the just value of the prize, when *ternes*,
quaternes, and other such ventures were made, the public in
France, Switzerland, and Italy bought these ventures by
millions, as was shown by the fact that several times in each
year even *quaternes* were won. Now in the Petersburg plan
there was a chance, however small, of enormous winnings.
Head might not appear till the tenth, twelfth, or even the
twentieth tossing; and then the prize would be 1,024*l*.,
4,048*l*., or 1,048,576*l*., respectively. It was felt that tens of
millions would be tempted by the chance of such enormous
gains ; and it was thought that the gains of Government
would be proportionately heavy. All that was necessary
was that the just value of a chance in this lottery should be

ascertained by mathematicians, and the price properly raised.

Mathematicians very readily solved the problem, though one or two of the most distinguished (D'Alembert, for instance) rejected the solution as incomprehensible and paradoxical. Let the reader who takes interest enough in such matters pause for a moment here to inquire what would be a natural and probable value for a chance in the suggested lottery. Few, we believe, would give 10*l.* for a chance. No one, we are sure—not even one who thoroughly recognised the validity of the mathematical solution of the problem—would offer 100*l.* Yet the just value of a chance is greater that ·10*l.*, greater than 100*l.*, greater than any sum which can be named. A Government, indeed, which would offer to sell these chances at say 50*l.* would most probably gain, even if many accepted the risk and bought chances, which would be very unlikely, however. The fewer bought chances the greater would be the Government's chance of gain, or rather their chance of escaping loss. But this of course is precisely the contrary to what is required in a lottery system. What is wanted is that many should be encouraged to buy chances, and that the more chances are bought the greater should be the security of those keeping the lottery. In the Petersburg plan, a high and practically prohibitory price must first be set on each chance, and even then the lottery-keepers could only escape loss by restricting the number of purchases. The scheme was therefore abandoned.

The result of the mathematical inquiry seems on the face of it absurd. It seems altogether monstrous, as De Morgan admits, to say that an infinite amount of money should in reality be given for each chance, to cover its true mathematical value. And to all intents and purposes any very great value would far exceed the probable average value of any possible number of ventures. If a million million ventures were made, first and last, 50*l.* per venture would probably bring in several millions of millions of pounds clear profit to the lottery-keepers ; while 30*l.* per venture

Q

would as probably involve them in correspondingly heavy losses. 40*l.* per venture would probably bring them safe, though without any great percentage of profit. If a thousand million ventures were made, 30*l.* per venture would probably make the lottery safe, while 35*l.* would bring great gain in all probability, and 25*l.* would as probably involve serious loss. If all the human beings who have ever lived on this earth, during every day in their lives had been taking chances in such a lottery, the average price of all the sums gained would be quite unlikely to approach 100*l.* Yet still the mathematical proposition is sound, that if the number of speculators in the Petersburg lottery were absolutely un-limited, no sum, however great, would fairly represent the price of a chance. And while that unpractical result (for the number of speculators would not be unlimited) is true, the practical result is easily proved, that the larger the number of venturers the greater should be the price for each chance —a relation which absolutely forbids the employment of this method of keeping lotteries.

Let us see how this can be shown. De Morgan has given a demonstration, but it is not one to be very readily understood by those not versed in mathematical methods of reasoning. I believe, however, that the following proof will be found easy to understand, while at the same time satisfactory and convincing.

Suppose that eight ventures only are made, and that among the eight, four, or exactly half, toss head the first time ; of the remaining four, two half-toss head at the second trial ; of the remaining two, one tosses head at the third trial ; while the other tosses head at the fourth trial. This may be regarded as representing what might on the average be expected from eight trials, though in reality it does not ; for of course, if it did, the average price per chance, inferred from eight such trials, would be the true average for eight million trials, or for eight million times eight million. Still it fairly represents all that could be hoped for from a single set of eight ventures. Now we see that the sums paid in prizes, in this case, would be four times 2*l*. for those who tossed 'head' at the first trial; twice 4*l*. for those who tossed 'head' at the second trial; 8*l*. for him who tossed 'head' at the third trial; and 16*l*. for the last and most fortunate of the eight; or 40*l*. in all. This gives an average of 5*l*. for each chance.

Now suppose there are sixteen ventures, and treat this number in the same way. We get eight who receive 2*l*. each; four who receive 4*l*. each; two who receive 8*l*. each; one who receives 16*l*.; and one who receives 32*l*. The total, then, is 96*l*., giving an average of 6*l*. for each chance.

Next take thirty-two ventures. Sixteen receive 2*l*. each; eight 4*l*. each; four 8*l*. each; two 16*l*. each; one 32*l*.; and one 64*l*.; a total of 224*l*., giving an average of 7*l*. for each venture.

It will be noticed that the average price per venture has risen 1*l*. at each doubling of the total number of speculators. Nor is it difficult to perceive that this increase will proceed systematically. To show this we take a larger number, 1,024, which is 2 doubled ten times, or technically 2 raised to the 10th power. Treating this like our other numbers, we find that 512 speculators are to receive 2*l*. each, making 1,024*l*. in all; thus we get as many pounds as there are ventures for this first halving. Next, 256 receive 4*l*. each, or 1,024*l*. in all; that is, again we get as many pounds as there are ventures, for this second halving. Next, 128 receive 8*l*., or 1,024*l*. in all; or again, we get as many pounds as there are ventures, for this third halving. This goes on ten times, the tenth halving giving us one speculator who receives 1,024*l*., and still leaving one who has not yet tossed 'head.' Since each halving gives us 1,024*l*., we now have ten times 1,024*l*. The last speculator tosses 'head' at the next trial and wins 2,048*l*.; making a grand total of twelve times 1,024*l*., or twelve times as many pounds as there are speculators. The average, therefore, amounts to 12*l*. per chance; and we see, by the way in which the result has been obtained that in every such case the chance will be worth 2*l*. more than as many pounds as there are halvings. Of course the number of halvings is the number representing the power to which 2 is raised to give the number of speculators. The number of speculators need not necessarily be a power of 2. We have only supposed it so for simplicity of calculation. But the application of the method of halving can be almost as readily made with any number of speculators. It is only when we get down to small numbers, as 9, 7, 5, or 3, that any difficulty arises from fractional or half men ; but the result is not materially affected where the original number is large, by taking 4 or 3 as the next halving after either 7 or 9 (for example), or 2 as the next halving after 3. But practically we need not carry out these halvings, after we have once satisfied ourselves of the validity of the general rule. Thus suppose we require to ascertain a fair value for a million chances. We find that the nearest power of 2 to the number one million is the 20th : 22*l.*, then, is a fair value.

But of course, the whole train of our reasoning proves that while probably 22*l.* would be a fair value for a million ventures, it could not be the mathematically just value. For who is to assure the lottery-keeper that after the million ventures, another million will not be taken ? Now for two million ventures the probable value according to our method would be 23*l.*, since two millions is nearly equal to 2 raised to the 21st power. There might be a million million ventures ; and if 22*l.* were really the true price for one million, it would be the true price for each of the million ventures. But since a million million are roughly equal to 2 raised to the 40th power, the price according to our method would be about 42*l.* per chance.

All that can be said is that among any definite number of trials it is not antecedently probable that there will be any of those very long runs of 'trials' which are practically certain to occur when many times that number of trials (whatever it may be) are made.

The experiment has been actually tried, though it was not necessary to establish the principle. So far as the relatively small average value of the chance, when a few ventures only are made, the reader can readily try the experiment for himself. Let him make, for instance, eight trials, each trial ending when he has tossed head ; and according as head comes at the first, second, or third tossing in any trial, let him write down 2*l.*, 4*l.*, 8*l.*, &c., respectively. The total divided by eight will give the average value of each trial. Buffon and each of three correspondents of De Morgan's made 2,048 trials—an experiment which even the most enthusiastic student of chances will not greatly care to repeat. Buffon's results, the only set we shall separately quote, were as follows. In 1,061 trials, 'head' showed at the first tossing; in 494, at the second ; in 232, at the third ; in 137, at the fourth ; in 56, at the fifth ; in 29, at the sixth ; in 25, at the seventh ; in 8, at the eighth ; in 6, at the ninth. The 2,048 trials, estimated according to the Petersburg system, would have given 20,114*l.* in all, or nearly 10*l.* per game. According to our method, since 2,048 is the eleventh power of 2*l.*, the average value of each chance would be 13*l.* ; [1]

[1] We note that De Morgan obtains the value 11*l.* instead of 13*l.* But he strangely omits one of the last pair of trials altogether. Thus, he says, 'in the long run, and on 2,048 trials, we might expect two sets in which "heads" should not appear till the tenth throw,' which is right, 'and one in which no such thing should take place till the eleventh,' which is also right. But it is because there will probably be four trials of which two only will probably give 'heads,' that we may expect two to give 'tails' yet once more. The two which gave 'heads' are the two first mentioned by De Morgan, in which 'heads' appear at the tenth throw. Of the two remaining we expect one to give 'head,' the other 'tail.' The former is the 'one' next mentioned by De Morgan, in which 'head' appears at the eleventh throw. The other in which 'tail' may be expected to appear is the most valuable of all. Even if 'head' appears at the next or twelfth tossing, this trial brings a prize worth twice as many pounds as the total number of trials—and therefore adds 2*l.* to the average value of each trial. It is quite true that Buffon's experiment chances to give a result even less than De Morgan's value, and still further therefore from mine. But as will be seen, the other experiment gave an average result above his estimate, and even above mine. It cannot possibly be correct to omit all consideration of the most profitable trial of all,

and Buffon's result is quite as near as could be expected in a single experiment on 2,048 trials.

But when we take the four experiments collectively, getting in this way the results of 8,192 trials (which De Morgan, strangely enough, does not seem to have thought of), we find the average value of each chance greatly increased, as theory requires, and, as it happens, increased even beyond the value which theory assigns as probable for this number of trials. Among them there was only one in which head appeared after tail had been tossed 11 times, whereas we might expect that there would be four such cases ; but there was one case in which head only appeared after tail had been tossed 13 times, and there were two cases in which head only appeared after tail had been tossed 15 times. Of course this was purely accidental. We may always be tolerably sure that in a large number of tossings, about one half will be head and about one half tail. But when only a few tossings are to be made, this proportion can no longer be looked for with the same high degree of probability. When, again, only four or five chances are left, we may find these all dropping off at once, on the one hand, or one or two of them may run on with five or six more successful tossings ; and as at each tossing the prize, already amounting for the last trial to as many pounds as there were originally chances, is doubled, we may find the average price of each chance increased by 1*l.*, 2*l.*, 4*l.*, 8*l.*, 16*l.*, or more, by the continued success of the longest lasting trial, or perhaps of two or three lasting equally long. This happened in the 8,192 trials whose results are recorded by De Morgan. I find that the total amount which would have been due in prizes, according to the Petersburg plan, would have been 150,830*l.*, an average of 18*l.* 8*s.* 2½*d.* (almost exactly) per trial ; whereas the theoretical average for 8,192 trials would be only 15*l.*

It is manifest that, though in a million trials by this method some such sum as 30*l.* per trial would probably cover all the prizes gained, it would be unsafe to put any definite price on each venture, where the number of venturers would of necessity be unlimited. And since even a price which would barely cover the probable expenses would be far more than speculators would care to give, the plan is utterly unsuited for a public lottery. It may be well to note how large a proportion of the speculators would lose by their venture, even in a case where the total ventured was just covered by the prizes. Suppose there were rather more than a million speculators (more exactly, that the numbers were the 20th power of 2, or 1,048,576), and that the average result followed, the price per venture being 22*l.* Then 524,288 persons would receive only 2*l.* and lose 20*l.* each; 262,144 would receive only 4*l.*, and lose 18*l.* each; 131,072 would receive 8*l.* and lose 14*l.* each; 65,536 would receive 16*l.* and lose 6*l.* each. All the rest would gain; 32,768 would receive 32*l.* and gain 10*l.* each; 16,384 would receive 64*l.* and gain 42*l.* each; and so on; 8,192 would receive 128*l.* each; 4,096 would receive 256*l.* each; 2,048 each 512*l.*; 1,024 each 1,024*l.*; 512 each 2,048*l.*; 256 each 4,096*l.*; 138 each 8,192*l.*; 64 each 16,384*l.*; 32 each 32,768*l.*; 16 each 65,536*l.*; 8 each 131,072*l.*; 4 each 262,144*l.*; 2 each 524,288*l.*; 1 would receive 1,048,572*l.*; and lastly, one would receive 2,097,952*l.* But there would be only 65,536 out of 1,048,576 speculators who would gain, or only 1 in 16.

It is singular that whereas it would be almost impossible to persuade even one person to venture 22*l.* in such a lottery as we have described, almost any number of persons could be persuaded to join again and again in a lottery where the prizes and blanks were arranged as in the way described in the preceding paragraph as the average outcome of 1,048,576 ventures. In other words, no one puts so much faith in his luck as to venture a sum on the chance of gaining a little if he tosses 'tail' four times running (losing if 'head' appears sooner), and of gaining more and more the oftener 'tail' is tossed, until, should he toss tail 20 times running, he will receive more than two million pounds. But almost every person who is willing to gamble at all will be ready to venture the same sum on the practically equivalent chance of winning in a lottery where there are rather more than a million tickets, and the same prizes as in the other case. Whatever advantage there is, speaking mathematically, is in favour of the tossing risk ; for the purchaser of a trial has not only the chance of winning such prizes as in a common lottery arranged to give, with prizes corresponding to the above-described average case, but he has a chance, though a small one, of winning four, eight, sixteen, or more millions of pounds for his venture of 22*l.* We see, then, that the gamblers are very poor judges of chances, rejecting *absolutely* risks of one kind, while accepting *systematically* those of another kind, though of equal mathematical value, or even greater.

In passing, we may note that the possibility of winning abnormally valuable prizes in the Petersburg lottery affords another explanation of the apparent paradox involved in the assertion that no sum, however large, fairly represents the mathematical value of each trial. To obtain the just price of a lottery-ticket, we must multiply each prize by the chance of getting it, and add the results together; this is the mathematical value of one chance or ticket. Now in the Petersburg lottery the possible prizes are 2*l.*, 4*l.*, 8*l.*, 16*l.*, and so on, doubling to infinity ; the chances of getting each are, respectively, one-half, one-fourth, one-eighth, one-sixteenth, and so on. The value of a chance, then, is the half of 2*l.*, added to the quarter of 4*l.*, to the eighth of 8*l.*, and so on to infinity, each term of the infinite series being 1*l.* Hence the mathematical value of a single chance is infinite. The result appears paradoxical ; but it really means only that the oftener the trial is made, the greater will be the probable average value of the prizes obtained. Or, as in fact the solution is that if the number of trials were infinite the value of each would be infinite, we only obtain a paradoxical result in an impossible case. Note also that the two kinds of infinity involved in the number of trials and in the just mathematical price of each are different. If the number of trials were 2 raised to an infinitely high power, the probable average value of each trial would be the infinitely high number representing that power. But 2 raised to that power would give an infinitely higher number. To take very large numbers instead of infinite numbers, which simply elude us :—Suppose the number of trials could be 2 raised to the millionth power ; then the probable average value of each would be 1,000,002*l*., which is a large number of pounds ; but the number is a mere nothing compared with the number of trials, a number containing 301,031 *digits* ! If the smallest atom, according to the estimate made by physicists, were divided into a million millions of parts, the entire volume of a sphere exceeding a million million times in radius the distance of the remotest star brought into view by Lord Rosse's mighty telescope, would not contain a million millionth of that number of these indefinitely minute subdivisions of the atom. Nay, we might write trillions or quadrillions where we have just written millions in the preceding lines, and yet not have a number reaching a quadrillionth part of the way to the inconceivable number obtained by raising 2 to the millionth power. Yet for this tremendous number of trials the average mathematical value of each would amount but to a poor million—absolutely nothing by comparison.

BETTING ON RACES.

ABOUT ten years ago, in an article called 'The State of the Odds,' subsequently reprinted in the first series of my 'Light Science for Leisure Hours,' I described the meaning of those mysterious columns in the daily papers which indicate the opinion of the betting world as to the probable results of horse races and other contests. I do not propose to go over the same ground at present, though, in order to leave no occasion to refer my readers to that essay, I shall explain, as occasion requires, such technical expressions as might otherwise cause perplexity. My present object is to consider betting in a scientific yet common-sense aspect, pointing out in particular the fraudulent nature of many transactions which are regarded by many as altogether permissible. I do not wish it to be understood that I consider any sort of betting or gambling unobjectionable. Indeed, I shall take occasion to indicate not merely the objections which exist against gambling on the score of the injury to the gambler, but the objection which has been justly described by Herbert Spencer as the fundamental reason for condemning the practice. There is, however, a marked distinction between fair and unfair betting, and I propose specially to consider here unfair or other fraudulent betting. The subject includes, indeed, nearly all the betting transactions in the so-called sporting world ; though many persons of fair and honourable dispositions take part in such transactions without apparently noticing the fundamentally fraudulent nature of many of their proceedings.

It is well to have some convenient standard of reference, not only as respects the fairness or unfairness of betting transactions, but as to the true nature of the chances involved or supposed to be involved. Many men bet on horse races without any clear idea of the chances they are really running. To see that this is so, it is only necessary to notice the preposterous way in which many bettors combine their bets. Leech's sketch, called, I think, 'Signs of the Commission,' by no means exaggerated the fatuity of inexperienced bettors, that is, of about nine out of ten among all who offer and accept wagers. ' The odds are 2 to 1 against So-and-So,' says one, 'and 4 to 1 against such another ; what's the betting about the pair?' ' Don't know, I'm suah,' says the other ; ' but I'll give you 6 to 1.' I do not say that many, even among the idiots who wager on horses they know nothing about, would lay heavier odds against the winning of a race by one of two horses than he would lay against the chance of either horse separately ; but it is quite certain that not one bettor in a hundred knows either how to combine the odds against two, three or more horses, so as to get the odds about the lot, or how to calculate the chance of double, triple, or multiple events. Yet these are the very first principles of betting ; and a man who bets without knowing anything about such matters runs as good a chance of ultimate success, as a man who, without knowing the country, should take a straight line in the hunting field.

Now, apart from what may be called roguery in horse-racing, every bet in a race may be brought into direct comparison with the simple and easily understood chance of success in a lottery where there is a single prize, and therefore only one prize ticket : and the chance of the winner of a race, where several horses run, being one particular horse, or one of any two, three, or more horses, can always be compared with the easily understood chance of drawing a ball of one colour out of a vase containing so many balls of that colour and so many of another. So also can the chance of a double or triple event be compared with a chance of the second kind.

Let us first, then, take the case of a simple lottery, and distinguish between a fair lottery and an unfair one. Every actual lottery, I remark in passing, is an unfair one ; at least, I have never yet heard of a fair one, and I can imagine no possible case in which it would be worth anyone's while to start a fair lottery.

Suppose ten persons each contribute a sovereign to form a prize of 10*l.* ; and that each of the ten is allowed to draw one ticket from among ten, one marked ticket giving the drawer the prize. That is a fair lottery ; each person has paid the right price for his chance. The proof is, that if anyone buys up all the chances at the price, thus securing the certainty of drawing the marked ticket, he obtains as a prize precisely the sum he has expended.

This, I may remark, is the essential condition for a fair lottery, whatever the number of prizes ; though we have no occasion to consider here any case except the very simple case of a one-prize lottery. Where there are several prizes, whether equal or unequal in value, we have only to add their value together : the price for all the tickets together must equal the sum we thus obtain. For instance, if the ten persons in our illustrative case, instead of marking one ticket, marked three, for prizes worth 5*l.*, 3*l.*, and 2*l.*, the lottery would be equally fair. Anyone, by buying up all the ten tickets, would be sure of all three prizes, that is, he would pay ten pounds and get ten pounds—a fair bargain.

But suppose, reverting to one-prize lotteries, that the drawer of the marked ticket was to receive only 8*l.* instead of 10*l.* as a prize. Then clearly the lottery would be unfair. The test is, that a man must pay 10*l.* to insure the certainty of winning the prize of 8*l.*, and will then be 2*l.* out of pocket. So of all such cases. When the prize, if there is but one, or the sum of all the prizes together if there are several, falls short of the price of all the tickets together, the lottery is an unfair one. The sale of each ticket is a swindle ; the

total amount of which the ticket-purchasers are swindled
being the sum by which the value of the prize or prizes fall
short of the price of the tickets.

We see at once that a number of persons in a room together would never allow an unfair lottery of this sort. If
each of the ten persons put a sovereign into the pool, each
having a ticket, the drawer of the prize ticket would be
clearly entitled to the pool. If one of the ten started the
lottery, and if when the 10*l.*, including his own, has been
paid in to the pool, he proposed to take charge of the pool,
and to pay 8*l.* to the drawer of the marked ticket, it would
be rather too obvious that he was putting 2*l.* in his pocket.
But lotteries are not conducted in this simple way, or so
that the swindle becomes obvious to all engaged. As a
matter of fact, all lotteries are so arranged that the manager
or managers of the lottery put a portion of the proceeds
(or pool) into their pockets. Otherwise it would not be
worth while to start a lottery. Whether a lottery is started
by a nation or for a cause, or for personal profit, it always
is intended for profit ; and profit is always secured, and,
indeed, can only be secured by making the total value of the
prizes fall short of the sum received for the tickets.

I would not be understood to say that I regard all unfair
lotteries as swindles. In the case of lotteries for a charitable
purpose I suppose the object is to add gambling excitement
to the satisfaction derived from the exercise of charity. The
unfairness is understood and permitted, just as, at a fancy
fair, excessive prices are charged, change is not returned,
and other pleasantries are permitted which would be
swindles if practised in real trading. But in passing I may
note that even lotteries of this kind are objectionable.
Those who arrange them have no wish to gain money for
themselves ; and many who buy tickets have no wish to
win prizes, and would probably either return any prize they
might gain or pay its full value. But it is not so with all
who buy tickets ; and even a charitable purpose will not
justify the mischief done by the encouragement of the

gambling spirit of such persons. In nearly all cases the money gained by such lotteries might, with a little more trouble, but at less real cost, be obtained directly from the charitably minded members of the community.

To return, however, to my subject.

I have supposed the case of ten persons gambling fairly in such a way that each venture made by the ten results in a single-prize lottery. But as we know, a betting transaction is nearly always arranged between two persons only. I will therefore now suppose only two persons to arrange such a lottery, in this way :—The prize is 10*l.*, as before, and there are ten tickets ; one of the players, A, puts, say, 3*l.* in the pool while the other, B, puts 7*l.* ; three tickets are marked as winning tickets ; A then draws at random once only ; if he draws a marked ticket, he wins the pool ; if he draws an unmarked ticket, B takes the pool. This is clearly fair ; in fact, it is only a modification of the preceding case. A takes the chances of three of the former players, while B takes the chances of the remaining seven. True, there seems to be a distinction. If we divided the former ten players into two sets, one of three, the other of seven, there would not be a single drawing to determine whether the prize should go to the three or to the seven : each of the ten would draw a ticket, all the tickets being thus drawn. Yet in reality the methods are in principle precisely the same. When the ten men have drawn their tickets in the former method, three tickets have been assigned at random to the three men and seven tickets to the other seven ; and the chance that the three have won is the chance that one of the three tickets is the marked one. In the latter method there are ten tickets, of which three are marked ; and the chance that A wins the prize is the chance that at his single drawing he takes one of the three marked tickets. But obviously the chance that a certain marked ticket in ten is one of the three taken at random must be exactly the same as the chance that a certain ticket taken at random from among the ten is one of three marked tickets ; for each of these chances is clearly three times as good as the chance of drawing, at a single trial, one particular ticket out of ten.

It will be found that we can now test any wager, not merely determining whether it is fair or unfair, but the extent to which it is so, if only the actual chance of the horse or horses concerned is supposed to be known. Unfortunately, in the great majority of cases bets are unfair in another way than that which we are for the moment considering, the odds not only differing from those fairly representing the chances of the horse or horses concerned, but one party to the wager having better knowledge than the other what those chances are. Cases of this kind will be considered further on.

Suppose that the just odds against a horse in a race are 9 to 1. By this I mean that so far as the two bettors are concerned, (that is, from all that they know about the chances of the horse,) it is nine times more likely that the horse will not win the race than that he will. Now, it is nine times more likely that a particular ticket among ten will not be drawn at a single trial than that it will. So the chance of this horse is correctly represented by the chance of the prize ticket being drawn in a lottery where there are ten tickets in all. If two persons arrange such a lottery, and A pays in 1*l.* to the pool, while the other, B, pays in 9*l.*, making 10*l.* in all, A gets a fair return for his money in a single drawing, one ticket out of the ten being marked for the prize. A represents, then, the backer of the horse who risks 1*l.*; B the layer of the odds who risks 9*l.* The sum of the stakes is the prize, or 10*l.* If A risks less than 1*l.*, while B risks 9*l.*, the total prize is diminished; or if, while A risks 1*l.*, B risks less than 9*l.*, the total is diminished. In either case the wrong done to the other bettor amounts precisely to the amount by which the total is diminished. If, for instance, A only wagered 18*s.* against B's 9*l.*, the case is exactly the same as though A and B having severally contributed 1*l.* and 9*l.* to a pool, one ticket out of ten having been marked, A to have one chance only of drawing it (which we have just seen would be strictly fair), A abstracted two shillings from the pool. If B only wagered 7*l.* instead of 9*l.*, against A's 1*l.*, the case would be just the same as though, after the pool had been made up as just described, B had abstracted 2*l.*

Take another case. The odds are 7 to 3 against a horse. The chance of its winning is the same as that of drawing a marked ticket out of a bag containing ten, when three are marked and seven are unmarked. We know that in this case two players, A and B, forming the lottery, must severally contribute 3*l.* and 7*l.* to the pool, and if on a single drawing one of the three marked tickets appears, then A wins the pool, or 10*l.*, whereas B takes it if one of the seven unmarked tickets is drawn. If the backer of the horse, instead of wagering 3*l.*, wagered only 2*l.* against 7*l.*, he would be precisely in the position of a player A, who, having paid in his 3*l.* to the pool of 10*l.* in all, should abstract a pound therefrom. If the layer of the odds wagered only 5*l.* against 3*l.*, he would be in the position of a player B, who, having paid in his 7*l.* to the pool of 10*l.* in all, should abstract 2*l.* therefrom.

Or, if any difficulty should arise in the reader's mind from this way of presenting matters, let him put the case thus :—Suppose the sum of the stakes 10*l.*; then the odds being 7 to 3 against, the case is as though three tickets were marked for the prize and seven unmarked ; and the two players ought therefore to contribute severally 3*l.* and 7*l.* to make up the 10*l.* If the 10*l.* is made up in any other way, there is unfairness ; one player puts in too much, the other puts in too little. If one puts in 2*l.* 10*s.* instead of 3*l.*, the other puts in 7*l.* 10*s.* instead of 7*l.*, and manifestly the former has wronged the latter to the extent of 1*l.*, having failed to put in 10*s.* which he ought to have put in, and having got the other to put in 10*s.* which ought not to have been put in. This seems clearer, I find, to some than the other way of presenting the matter. But as, in reality, bets are not made in this way, the other way, which in principle is the

sáme, is more convenient. Bettors do not take a certain
sum of money for the total of their stakes, and agree how
much each shall stake towards that sum ; but they bet a certain sum against some other sum. It is easy to take either of
these to find out how much *ought* to be staked against it,
and thus to ascertain to what extent the proper total of the
stakes has been affected either in excess or defect. And we
can get rid of any difficulty arising from the fact that according to the side we begin from we get either an excess or
a defect, by beginning always from the side of the one who
wagers not less than he should do, at the proper odds, whatever they may be.

As a general rule, indeed, the matter is a good deal
simplified by the circumstance that fraudulent bettors nearly
always lay the odds. It is easy to see why. In fact, one of
the illustrative cases above considered has already probably
suggested the reason to the reader. I showed that when
the odds are 9 to 1 and only 7 to 1 is laid, in pounds, the
fraud is the same as removing 2*l.* from a pool of 10*l.*; whereas with the same odds, backing the horse by 18*s.* instead of
1*l.*, corresponded to removing two shillings from such a pool.
Now, if a fraudulent gambler had a ready hand in abstracting
coins from a pool, and were playing with some one who did
not count the money handed over to him when he won, it
would clearly be the same thing to him whether he contributed the larger or smaller sum to the pool, for he would
abstract as many coins as he could, and it would be so much
clear gain. But if he could not get at the pool, and therefore could only cheat by omitting to contribute his fair share,
it would manifestly be far better for him to be the buyer of
the larger share of the chances. If he bought nine tickets
out of ten, he might put in 7*l.* pretending to put in 9*l.*, and
pocket 2*l.*; whereas if he only bought one ticket, he could
only defraud his companion by a few shillings out of the
price of that ticket. Now, this is the hardship under which
the fraudulent bettor labours. He cannot, at least he cannot

R

generally, get at the stakes themselves ; or, which comes to the same thing, he must pay up in full when he loses, otherwise he has soon to give up his profitable trade. Of course he may levant without paying, but this is only to be adopted as a last resource; and fraudulent betting is too steadily remunerative to be given up for the value of a single robbery of the simpler kind. Thus the bettor naturally prefers laying the odds. He can keep so much more out of the larger sum which ought to be laid against a horse than he could out of the smaller sum with which the horse would be backed.

Then there is another circumstance which still more strongly encourages the fraudulent bettor to lay the odds. It is much easier for him to get his victims to back a horse than to bet against one. In the first place, the foolish folk who expect to make a fortune by betting, take fancies for a particular horse, while they are not so apt to take fancies against any particular horse. But secondly, and this is the chief reason of their mode of betting, they want to make a great and sudden gain at a small risk. They have not time, for the most part, to make many wagers on any given race ; and to wager large sums against two or three horses would involve a great risk for a small profit. This, then, they do not care to do ; preferring to back some particular horse, or perhaps two or three, by which they risk a comparatively small sum, and may win a large one. As Mr. Plyant truly remarks in Hawley Smart's ' Bound to Win,' ' The public is dramatic in its fancies ; the public has always a dream of winning a thousand to ten if it can raise the tenner. The public, Mr. Laceby, knows nothing about racing, but as a rule is wonderfully up in the story of Theodore's winning the Leger, after a hundred pounds to a walking-stick had been laid against him. The public is always putting down its walking-stick and taking to crutches in consequence. . . . What the public will back at the lists the last few days before the Derby would astonish you ; they've dreams, and tips, and fancies about the fifty to one lot you couldn't

imagine.' Is it to be wondered at that the public finds its
tastes in this respect humoured by the bookmakers, when
we remember that it is from just such wagers as the public
like to make that the bookmaker can most readily obtain
the largest slice of profit?

But we must not fall into the mistake of supposing that
all the foolish folk who back horses at long odds necessarily
lose. On the contrary, many of them win money—unfortunately for others, and often for themselves. It would be a
very foolish thing to pay 1*l.* for one of ten tickets in a lottery
where the single prize was only worth 9*l.* Yet some one of
the foolish fellows who did this must win the prize, gaining
8*l.* by the venture. If many others were encouraged to
repeat such a venture, or if he repeated it himself (inferring
from his success that he was born under a lucky star), they
and he would have reason to repent. He might, indeed,
be lucky yet again; and perhaps more than once. But
the more he won in that way, the more he would trust in
his good luck; and in the long run he would be sure to
lose, if all his ventures were of the same foolish kind as the
first.

We see, however, that the foolish bettor in any given
case is by no means certain to lose. Nor is the crafty
bettor who takes advantage of him at all sure to win. A
man might steal 2*l.* or 3*l.* from the pool, after making up 9*l.*
out of the 10*l.*, in the case I have imagined, and yet lose,
because his opponent might be fortunate enough to draw
the single marked ticket, and so win the 7*l.* or 8*l.* left in the
pool.

In reality, however, though quite possibly some among
the foolish bettors not only win money but even keep
what they win, refraining from trying their luck afresh, it
must not be supposed that the fraudulent bettor exposes
himself to the risk of loss in the long run. He plays a safe
game. Every one of his bets is a partial swindle; yet in
each he runs the risk of loss. His entire series of bets is a
complete swindle, in which he runs no risk whatever of loss,

but ensures a certain gain. Let us see how this is to be done.

Suppose there are two horses in a race, A and B, and that the betting is 3 to 1 against B. In other words, the chance of A winning is as the chance of drawing a marked ticket out of a bag containing four tickets of which three are marked, while B's chance of winning is as that of drawing the single unmarked ticket. In this case, as the odds are in favour of one horse, our bookmaker will have to do a little backing, which, preferably, he would avoid. In fact, a race such as this, that is, a match between two horses, is not altogether to the bookmaker's taste ; and what he would probably do in this case would be to obtain special information in some underhand way about the horses, and bet accordingly. Supposing, however, that he cannot do this, poor fellow, let us see how he is to proceed to insure profit. The first thing is to decide on some amount which shall be staked over each horse ; and the theoretically exact way— the mathematical manner—of swindling would be as follows :—Suppose that with some person a wager were made at the just odds in favour of A, in such sort that the stakes on both sides amounted, let us say, to 1,200*l.* ; the fair wager would be 900*l.* to 300*l.* that A will win ; our swindler, however, having found some greenhorn X, whom he can persuade to take smaller odds, takes his book and writes down quickly 800*l.* to 300*l.* in favour of A. He now finds some other greenhorn, Y, who is very anxious to back A, and having duly bewailed his misfortune in having no choice but to lay against a horse who is—so he says— almost certain to win, he asks and obtains the odds of 900*l.* to 200*l.* in favour of A ; that is to say, he wagers 200*l.* to 900*l.* against A. Let us see how his book stands. He has wagered—

> 800. to 300*l.* with X, that A wins ;
> 200*l.* to 900*l.* with Y, that B wins.

If A wins, he receives 300*l.* from X, and pays 200*l.* to Y, pocketing a balance of 100*l.* If B wins, he pays 800*l.* to X and receives 900*l.* from Y, pocketing equally 100*l.*

Take now a case in which there are five horses, A, B, C, D, and E ; and let the just odds about these five horses be—

2 to 1 against A

3 to 1 against B

5 to 1 against C

5 to 1 against D

11 to 1 against E

(the odds against E are determined from the odds against the other four, in the manner explained in my article above referred to on the 'State of the Odds '; it will readily be found that A's chance, B's chance, and the chance of either C or D, are the same as that of drawing one of 4 balls, one of 3 balls, and one of 2 balls out of a bag containing 12 in all ; and adding 4, 3, 2, and 2, we get 11 ; whence the chance of E is equal to that of drawing one ball out of a bag of twelve, or the odds are 11 to 1 against E.)

Now assign for the sum which at these odds should be wagered over each horse, that is, the total stakes in each case 12,000*l.* Then our bookmaker, laying the odds against all five horses, *ought* to lay 8,000*l.* to 4,000*l.* against A, 9,000*l* to 3,000*l.* against B, 10,000*l.* to 2,000*l.* against each of the two C and D, and lastly 11,000*l.* to 1,000*l.* against E. Each wager would be perfectly fair, and owing to the special manner in which the sums are arranged (the sum of the stakes on each horse being the same), not only is each wager fair, but whichever horse might win, the bookmaker would be neither a penny the better nor a penny the worse for his wagering—a result which would by no means suit his book (observe how betting phraseology has become a part of our language, just as betting rascality threatens to affect the character of our nation). All that the bookmaker then has to do is to find a number of foolish folk and to wager with them (collectively or severally, it matters not which) something considerably short of the sums just named against each horse. Say that he wagers—

> 7,000*l.* to 4,000*l.* against A
> 7,500*l.* to 3,000*l.* against B
> 8,000*l.* to 2,000*l.* against C
> 8,000*l.* to 2,000*l.* against D
> 8,000*l.* to 1,000*l.* against E

If A wins, he pays 7,000*l.*, and gets 3,000*l.*, 2,000*l.*, 2,000*l.*, and 1,000*l.*, or 8,000*l.* in all ; pocketing 1,000*l.* If B wins, he pays 7,500*l.*, and gets 4,000*l.*, 2,000*l.*, 2,000*l.*, 1,000*l.*, or 9,000*l.* in all, pocketing 1,500*l.* If either C or D wins, he pays 8,000*l.*, and gets 4,000*l.*, 3,000*l.*, 2,000*l*, and 1,000*l.*, or 10,000*l.* in all ; pocketing 2,000*l.* And lastly, if E wins, he pays 8,000*l.*, and gets 4,000*l.*, 3,000*l.*, 2,000*l.*, and 2,000*l.*, or 11,000*l.*, in all ; pocketing 3,000*l.*

It is easy to see why the bookmaker can get more when a non-favourite than when a favourite wins. He finds it easy enough to lay 8,000*l.* to 1,000*l.* instead of 11,000*l.* to 1,000*l.*, but not so easy to reduce the proper wager of 8,000*l.* to 4,000*l.* (whether made up of many separate wagers or few) against the favourite, by anything like the same amount. In other words, he could not well offer 5 to 4 instead of 2 to 1 about the favourite, whereas he finds it easy to get the offer of 8 to 1 instead of 11 to 1, about the outsider E, accepted to the required amount.

We can understand, then, why the success of a favourite is called in the papers a blow for the bookmakers. It is not that they lose ; but that they do not gain so much as when an outsider wins. Besides, in the latter case, some remarkably lucky hits must have been made by the backers of horses, and this encourages the gambling spirit. If a favourite wins, backers of the favourite win, but not very largely compared with what they risked ; whereas when an outsider wins, those who have backed him gain a goodly sum. Their good luck is spread abroad, and the news of it induces many more to try their luck.

The bookmaker's path to success, then, so far as it depends on the true chances of the various horses engaged in a race, is at once simple and sure. He has only to arrange matters so that the total stakes on each horse (that is, the sum of the money he and his opponents stake on each horse) would be alike if the just odds were followed; but for each wager of his he must deduct from the correct sum as much as he can persuade his opponent to allow. If he does this, he is sure to win. It does not matter whether he gives or takes the odds, so long as he brings up the total stakes about each horse to the correct amount, when to his own stake had been added what he has deducted for profit. The only disadvantage of taking the odds is, that he can get less out of it, as already shown. So the bookmaker lays the odds, and, as a rule, finds very little trouble in doing so to any amount he may require.

It will be seen that this system has great advantages over the plan formerly adopted at public gaming-houses, and probably adopted still, though less publicly. At the gaming-house the bankers did run some little risk. They were bound to win in the long run ; but they might lose for a night or two, or might even have a tolerably long run of bad luck. But a judicious bookmaker can make sure of winning money on every great race. Of course, if the bookmakers like a little excitement—and they are men, after all, though they do make their own providence—they can venture a little more than the nothing they usually venture. For instance, instead of laying the odds against all the horses, they can lay against all but one, and back that one heavily. Then, if that horse wins, they 'skin the lamb,' in the pleasing language of their tribe. But the true path to success is that which I have indicated above, and they know it (or I would assuredly not have indicated it).

Still, in every depth there is a deeper still. In the cases hitherto considered I have supposed that the chances of a horse really are what the public odds indicate. If they are not, it might be supposed that only the owner of the horse and a few friends, besides the trainer, jockey, and one or two other *employés*, would know of this. But, as a matter of fact, the bookmakers generally find out tolerably soon if anything is wrong with a horse, or if he has had a very good trial and has a better chance of winning than had before been supposed. Before very long this knowledge produces its effect in bringing the horse to its true price, or near it. In the former case the horse is very diligently ' pencilled ' by the bookmakers, and recedes step by step in the betting, till he is either at long odds or is no longer backed at any price. In the latter, the horse is as diligently backed, till he has reached short odds, taking his place among the favourites, or perhaps as first favourite.

But in either process—that of driving a horse to long odds, or that of installing him in a position among the favourites, according to the circumstances—a great deal of money is made and lost—made by those who know what has really happened, lost by those who do not. We may be tolerably sure it is not ' the public ' which gains. It is to ' the professional,' naturally, that the information comes first, and he makes a handsome profit out of it, before the change in the betting shows the public what has happened.

Now here, unfortunately, we touch on a part of our subject which affects men who are not, in a proper sense of the word, ' bookmakers.' It is a singular circumstance—or rather it is not at all singular, but accords with multiplied experiences, showing how the moral nature becomes seared by gambling transactions—that men who are regarded by the world, and regard themselves, as gentlemen, seem to recognise nothing dishonourable in laying wagers which they *know* not to accord with the real chances of a horse. A man who would scorn to note the accidental marks on the backs of playing cards, and still more to make such marks, will yet avail himself of knowledge just as unfair in horse-racing as a knowledge of the backs of certain cards would be in whist or écarté.

In one of the daily papers I cited as an illustration the

use which Hawley Smart, in one of his novels ('Bound to Win'), makes of this characteristic of sporting men. It has been objected, somewhat inconsistently, that in the first place the novelist's picture is inaccurate, and in the second the use which the hero of that story makes of knowledge about his own horses was perfectly legitimate. As to the first point, I may remark that I do not need to read Hawley Smart's novels, or any novels, to be well assured that the picture is perfectly accurate, and that sporting men do make use of special knowledge about a horse's chances to make profitable wagers. As to the second point, I note that it well illustrates my own position, that gambling has the effect of darkening men's sense of right and wrong. Many sporting men regard as legitimate what is manifestly unfair.

Not to go over ground already trodden, I turn to another of Hawley Smart's lively tales, the hero of which is a much more attractive man than Harold Luxmore in 'Bound to Win'—Grenville Rose in 'A Race for a Wife.' He is not, for a wonder, a sporting hero ; in everything but the racing arrangements, which he allows to be made in his name, he behaves much as a gentleman should, and manifestly he is intended to represent an English gentleman. He comes across information which shows that, by the action of an old form of tenure called 'right of heriot,' a certain horse which is the leading favourite for the Two Thousand can be claimed and so prevented from running. Of the direct use of this information, to free the heroine from a rascally sporting lawyer, nothing need be said but 'serve the fellow right.' Another use is, however, made of the knowledge thus obtained, and it is from this use that the novel derives its name. To a racing friend of his, a lawyer (like himself, and the villain of the story), the hero communicates the secret. To him the racing friend addresses this impressive response : 'Look here, old fellow. Racing is business with me ; if you're not in for a regular mare's nest, there's heaps of money to be made out of this . . . . don't whisper it to your carpet-bag till you've seen me again. I say this honestly, (!) with a view to doing my best for you.' What this best is presently appears. I need not follow the workings of the plot, nor tell the end of the story. All that answers my present purpose is to indicate the nature of the ' book ' which the gentlemanly Dallison, Silky Dallison as his friends call him, succeeds in making for himself and his equally gentlemanly friend on the strength of the 'tip' given by the latter. 'We now stand to win between us 10,170*l.* if Coriander wins the Two Thousand, and just quits if he loses ; not a bad book, Grenville !' To which Grenville, nothing loth, responds, ' By Jove ! no.' Yet every wager by which this result has been obtained, if rightly considered, was as certainly a fraud as a wager laid upon a throw with cogged dice. For, what makes wagers on such throws unfair, except the knowledge that with such dice a certain result is more likely than any other ? and what essential difference is there between such knowledge about dice and special knowledge about a horse's chance in a race ? The doctrine may not be pleasant to sporting gentlemen who have not considered the matter, but once duly considered there cannot be a doubt as to its truth : a wager made with an opponent who does not possess equally accurate information about the chances involved, is not a fair wager but a fraud. It is a fraud the same in kind as that committed by a man who wagers after the race, knowing what the event of the race has been ; and it only differs from such a fraud in degree in the same sense that robbing a till differs from robbing a bank.

It may be argued that by the same reasoning good whist players defraud inferior players who play with them for equal stakes. But the cases are altogether different. Good whist players do not conceal their strength. Their skill is known ; and if inferior players choose to play on equal terms, trusting in good luck to befriend them, they do it at their own risk. If a parallel is to be sought from the whist-table, it would be rather derived from the case of two players who had privately arranged a system of signalling ;

for in such a case there is knowledge on one side which is not only wanting on the other side, but of the possession of which the other side have no suspicion. No one would hesitate to call that swindling. Now take the case of one who knows that, as the result of a certain trial, a horse which is the favourite in a great race will take part in it, indeed, but will only do so to make running for a better horse. Until the time when the owner of the horses declares to win with the latter, such knowledge enables its possessor to accept safely all wagers in favour of the horse ; and he knows perfectly well, of course, that not one such wager is offered him except by persons ignorant of the true state of the case. Even if such offers are made by bookmakers, whose profession is swindling, and though we may not have a particle of sympathy with such men when they lose in this way, the acceptance of such wagers is in no sense justified. Two wrongs do not, in this case more than in any other, make a right.

I have said that in every depth there is a deeper still. In the subject I am dealing with there is a deepest depth of all. I will not, however, sully these pages with the consideration of the foulest of the rascalities to which horse-racing has led. Simply to show those who bet on horse races how many risks of loss they expose themselves to, I mention that some owners of horses have been known to bring about the defeat of their own horse, on which the foolish betting public had wagered large sums, portions of which find their way into the pockets of the dishonest owners aforementioned. I may add that, according to an old proverb, there are more ways of killing a cat than by choking it with cream. A horse may be most effectually prevented from winning without any such vulgar devices as pulling, roping, and so forth. So also a horse, whose owner is honest, may be 'got at' after other fashions than have been noted yet, either in the police courts or in sporting novels.

Let us turn, however, from these unsavoury details, and consider briefly the objections which exist against gambling, even in the case of cash transactions so conducted that no unfair advantage is taken on either side.

The object of all gambling transactions is to win without the trouble of earning. I apprehend that nearly every one who wagers money on a horse race has, for some reason or other, faith in his own good fortune. It is a somewhat delicate question to determine how far such faith makes gambling unfair. For if, on the one hand, we must admit that a really lucky man could not fairly gamble against others not so lucky, yet, as it is absolutely certain in the scientific sense that no such thing as *luck which may be depended upon* exists, it is difficult to say how far faith in a non-existent quality can be held to make that fraudulent which would certainly be fraudulent did the quality exist. Possibly if a man, A, before laying a wager with another, B, were to say, ' I have won nearly every bet I have made,' B might decline to encounter A in any wager. In the case of a man who had been so lucky as A, it is quite probable that, supposing a wager made with B and won by A, B would think he had been wronged if A afterwards told him of former successes. B might say, ' You should have told me that before I wagered with you ; it is not fair to offer wagers where you know you have a better chance of winning than your opponents.' And though B would, strictly speaking, be altogether wrong, he would be reasoning correctly from his incorrect assumption, and A would be unable to contradict him.

If we were to assume that every man who wagered because he had faith in his own good luck, was guilty of a moral though not of a logical or legal wrong, we should have to regard ninety-nine gamblers out of a hundred as wrong-doers. Let it suffice to point out that, whether believing in his luck or not, the gambler is blameworthy, since his desire is to obtain the property of another without giving an equivalent. The interchange of property is of advantage to society ; because, if the interchange is a fair one, both parties to the transaction are gainers. Each exchanges something which is of less use to him for something which is of more use. This is equally the case whether there is a direct exchange of objects of value, or one of the parties to the exchange gives the other the benefit of his labour or of his skill acquired by labour. But in gambling, as where one man robs another, the case is otherwise. One person has lost what he can perhaps ill spare, while the other has obtained what he has, strictly speaking, no right to, and what is almost certainly of less value to him than to the person who has lost it. Or, as Herbert Spencer concisely presents the case :—' Benefit received does not imply effort put forth, and the happiness of the winner involves the misery of the loser : this kind of action is therefore essentially anti-social ; it sears the sympathies, cultivates a hard egoism, and so produces a general deterioration of character and conduct.'

A GAMBLING SUPERSTITION.

THERE are few more mistaken, yet few more persistent superstitions, than the belief in systems by which, so to speak, chance may be cheated, and success made a certainty, in gambling.   In an article which I wrote some years since for the *Cornhill Magazine*, on the subject of Gambling Superstitions, I described one system, which its inventor supposed to be a certain way to fortune.   It so chanced that on its first trial it succeeded well ; and he was so persuaded that this was only the beginning of a long series of successes, that he forthwith opened a new banking account, which he proposed to increase daily by the proceeds of his system.   But he very soon found that the system was utterly untrustworthy ; his daily banking operations consisted in drawing money to meet losses, not in paying fresh sums to his credit.   For particulars I refer the reader to the article above mentioned, which has since been republished in my ' Borderland of Science.'   Here I propose to describe another system, which has been far more generally adopted, and seems at first exceedingly plausible.   But perhaps a few words on the other system, and a comparison between the two, will serve to strengthen the lesson which I wish now to convey—this, namely, that there is absolutely no method, and that there can be none, by which gambling may be made safe, except the one sure plan of swindling (with many modifications of method) by which proprietors of gambling houses were formerly allowed in this country, and are still allowed elsewhere, to bring thousands to ruin. The general lesson against gambling, not on account of its innate immorality, but on the lower ground of its folly, is quite as much needed here now, when gambling houses are forbidden, as in the old times when Crockford's doors were open to the fools of quality, and hundreds of less splendid, but not less mischievous 'hells,' for fools of the middle and lower classes.

The plan I before described was based on the belief that after a series of events of one kind, in games of pure chance, a series of the opposite kind, or at any rate a change, may be expected. The inventor of the system would wait until, in *rouge-et-noir*, for example, there had been a run of six or seven on one colour, and would then begin to back the other colour. He supposed the chances were then more in his favour than if he had simply played on black or red at random. He took a very sound principle of probabilities as the supposed basis of his system, though in reality he entirely mistook the nature of the principle. That principle is, that where the chances for one or another of two results are equal for each trial, and many trials are made, the number of events of one kind will bear to those of the other kind a very nearly equal ratio : the greater the number of events, the more nearly will the ratio tend to equality. This is perfectly true ; and nothing could be safer than to wager on this principle. Let a man toss a coin for an hour, and I would wager confidently that neither will 'heads' exceed 'tails,' or 'tails' exceed 'heads' in a greater ratio than that of 21 to 20. Let him toss for a day, and I would wager as confidently that the inequality will not be greater than that represented by the ratio of 101 to 100. Let the tossing be repeated day after day for a year, and I would wager my life that the disproportion will be less than that represented by the ratio of 1,001 to 1,000. Yet so little does this principle bear the interpretation placed upon it by the inventor of the system above described, that if on any occasion during this long-continued process of tossings 'head' had been tossed (as it certainly would often be) no less than twenty times in succession, I would not wager a sixpence on the next tossing giving 'tail,' or trust a sixpence to the chance of 'tail' appearing oftener than 'head' in the next five, ten, or twenty tossings. Not only should reason show the utter absurdity of supposing that a tossing, or a set of five, ten, or twenty tossings, can be affected one way or the other by past tossings, whether proximate or remote ; but the experiment has been tried, and it has appeared (as might have been known beforehand) that after any number of cases in which 'heads' (say) have appeared such and such a number of times in succession, the next tossing has given 'heads' as often as it has given 'tails.' Thus, in 124 cases, Buffon, in his famous tossing trial, tossed 'tails' four times running. On the next trial, in these 124 cases, 'head' came 56 times and 'tail' 68 times. So, most certainly, the tossing of 'tail' four times running had not diminished the tendency towards 'tail' being tossed. Among the 68 cases which had thus given 'tail' five times running, 29 failed to give another 'tail,' while the remaining 39 gave another, that is, a sixth 'tail.' Of these 39, 25 failed to give another 'tail,' while 14 gave a seventh 'tail ;' and here it might seem we have evidence of the effect of preceding tosses. The disproportion is considerable, and even to the mathematician the case is certainly curious ; but in so many trials such curiosities may always be noticed. That it will not bear the interpretation put upon it is shown by the next steps. Of the 14 cases, 8 failed to give another 'tail,' while the remaining six gave another, that is, an eighth 'tail ;' and these numbers eight and six are more nearly equal than the preceding numbers 25 and 14 ; so that the tendency to change had certainly not increased at this step. However, the numbers are too small in this part of the experiment to give results which can be relied upon. The cases in which the numbers were large prove unmistakably, what reason ought to have made self-evident, that past events of pure chance cannot in the slightest degree affect the result of sequent trials.

To suppose otherwise is, indeed, utterly to ignore the relation between cause and event. When anyone asserts that because such and such things have happened, therefore such and such other events will happen, he ought at least to be able to show that the past events have some direct influence on those which are thus said to be affected by them. But if I am going to toss a coin perfectly at random, in what possible way can the result of the experiment be affected by the circumstance that during ten or twelve minutes before I tossed ' head ' only or ' tail ' only ?

The system of which I now propose to speak is more plausible, less readily put to the full test, and consequently far more dangerous than the one just described. In it, as in the other, reliance is placed on a ' change ' after a ' run ' of any kind, but not in the same way.

Everyone is familiar with the method of renewing wagers on the terms ' double ' or ' quits.' It is a very convenient way of getting rid of money which has been won on a wager by one who does not care for wagering, and, not being to the manner born, does not feel comfortable in pocketing money won in this way. You have rashly backed some favourite oarsman, let us say, or your college boat, or the like, for a level sovereign, not caring to win, but accepting a challenge to so wager rather than seem to want faith in your friend, college, or university. You thus find yourself suddenly the recipient of a coin to which you feel you are about as much entitled as though you had abstracted it from the other bettor's pocket. You offer him ' double or quits,' tossing the coin. Perhaps he loses, when you would be entitled to two sovereigns. You repeat the offer, and if he again loses (when you are entitled to four sovereigns), you again repeat it, until at last he wins the toss. Then you are ' quits,' and can be happy again.

The system of winning money corresponds to this safe system of getting rid of money which has been uncom-

fortably won.   Observe that if you only go on long enough
with the double-or-quits method, as above, you are sure to
get rid of your sovereign; for your friend cannot go on
losing for ever.   He might, indeed, lose nine or ten times
running, when he would owe you 512*l.* or 1,024*l.* ; and if he
then lost heart, while yet he regarded his loss, like his first
wager, as a debt of honour from which you could not release
him, matters would be rather awkward.   If he lost twenty
times, he would owe you a million, which would be more
awkward still ; except that, having gone so far, he could not
make matters worse by going a little farther ; and in a few
more tossings you would get rid of your millions as completely as of the sovereign first won.   Still, speaking generally, this double-or-quits method is a sure and easy way of
clearing such scores.   But it may be reversed, and become
a pretty sure and easy way of making money.

Suppose a man, whom we will call A, to wager with another,
B, one sovereign on a tossing (say).   If he wins, he gains a
sovereign.   Suppose, however, he loses his sovereign.   Then
let him make a new wager of two sovereigns.   If he wins,
he is the gainer of one sovereign in all : if he loses, he has
lost three in all.   In the latter case let him make a new
wager, of four sovereigns.   If he wins, he gains one sovereign ; if he loses, he has lost seven in all.   In this last case
let him wager eight sovereigns.   Then, if he wins, he has
gained one sovereign, and if he loses he has lost fifteen.
Wagering sixteen sovereigns in the latter case, he gains one
in all if he wins, and has lost 31 in all if he loses.   So he goes
on (supposing him to lose each time) doubling his wager
continually, until at last he wins.   Then he has gained one
sovereign.   He can now repeat the process, gaining each
time a sovereign whenever he wins a tossing.   And manifestly in this way A can most surely and safely win every
sovereign B has.   Yet every wager has been a perfectly fair
one.   We seem, then, to see our way to a safe way of making
any quantity of money.   B, of course, would not allow this
sort of wagering to go on very long.   But the bankers of a gam-

bling establishment undertake to accept any wagers which may be offered, on the system of their game, whether *rouge-et-noir*, roulette, or what not, between certain limits of value in the stakes. Say these limits are from five shillings to 100*l.*, as I am told is not uncommonly the case. A man may wager five shillings on this plan, and double eight times before his doublings carry the stake above 100*l.* Or with more advantage he may let the successive stakes be such that the eighth doubling will make the maximum sum, or 100*l.* ; so that the stakes in inverse order will be 100*l.*, 50*l.*, 25*l.*, 12*l.* 10*s.*, 6*l.* 5*s.*, 3*l.* 2*s.* 6*d.*, 1*l.* 11*s.* 3*d.*, 15*s.* 7*d.* (fractions of a penny not being allowed, I suppose[1]), and, lastly, 7*s.* 9*d.* ; nine stakes, or eight doublings in all. It is so utterly unlikely, says the believer in this system, that where the chances are practically equal on two events, the same event will be repeated nine times running, that I may safely apply this method, gaining at each venture ('though really there is no risk at all') 7*s.* 9*d.*, until at last I shall accumulate in this way a small fortune, which in time will become a large fortune.

The proprietors of gambling houses naturally encourage this pleasing delusion. They call this power of varying the stakes a very important advantage possessed by the player at such tables. They say, truly enough, a single player would not wager if the stakes could be varied in this manner (he possessing no power of refusing any offer between such limits). And since a single player would refuse to allow this arrangement, it is manifest the arrangement is a privilege. Being a privilege, it is worth paying for. It is on this account that we poor 'bankers,' who oblige those possessed of gambling perpensities by allowing them to exercise their tastes that way, must have a certain small percentage of odds in our favour. Thus at *rouge-et-noir* we really must have one of the 'refaits' allowed us, say the first, the *trente-et-un*, though any other would suit us equally

---

[1] Possibly pence are not allowed, in which case the successive stakes would be 7*s.*, 14*s.*, 1*l.* 8*s.*, 2*l.* 16*s.*, 5*l.* 12*s.*, 11*l.* 4*s.*, 22*l.* 8*s.*, 44*l.* 16*s.*, and lastly, 89*l.* 12*s.*

well : but even then we do not win what is on the table ; the *refait* may go against us, when the players save their stakes, and if we win we only win what has been staked on one colour, and so forth.

Those who like gambling, too, and so like to believe that the bankers are strictly fair, adopt this argument. Thus the editor of *The Westminster Paper* says : ' the Table at all games has an extra chance, a chance varying from one zero at one table to two at another ; that is a chance every player understands when he sits down to play, *and it is perfectly fair and honest* (! !) That this advantage over a long series must tell is as certain as that two and two make four. But . . . . the bank does not always win ; on the contrary,' we often 'hear of the bank being broken and closed until more cash is forthcoming. The number of times the bank loses, and nothing is said about it, would amount to a considerable number of times in the course of a year. A small percentage on one side or the other, extended over a long enough series, will tell ; but on a single event the difference in the gambler's eyes ' (yes, truly, in *his* eyes) 'is small. For that percentage the punter is enabled to vary his stakes from 5*s.* say, to 100*l.* Without some such advantage, no one would permit his adversaries thus to vary the stakes. The punter' (poor moth !) 'is willing to pay for this advantage.'

And all the while the truth is that the supposed advantage is no advantage at all—at least, to the player. It is of immense advantage to the bankers, because it encourages so many to play who otherwise might refrain. But in reality the bankers would make the same winnings if every stake were of a fixed amount, say 10*l.*, as when the stakes can be varied—always assuming that as many players would come to them, and play as freely, as on the present more attractive system.

Let us consider the actual state of the case, when a player at a table doubles his stakes till he wins—repeating the process from the lowest stakes after each success.

But first—or rather, as a part of this inquiry--let us consider why our imaginary player B would decline to allow A to double wagers in the manner described. In reality, of course, A's power of doubling is limited by the amount of A's money, or of his available money for gambling. He cannot go on doubling the stakes when he has paid away more than half his money. Suppose, for instance, he has 1,000*l.* in notes and 30*l.* or so in sovereigns. He can wager successively (if he loses so often) 1*l.*, 2*l.*, 4*l.*, 8*l.*, 16*l.*, 32*l.*, 64*l.*, 128*l.*, 256*l.*, 512*l.*, or ten times. But if he loses his last wager he will have paid away 1,023*l.*, and must stop for the time, leaving B the gainer of that sum. This is a very unlikely result for a single trial. It would not be likely to happen in a hundred or in two hundred trials, thought it might happen at the first trial, or at a very early one. Even if it happened after five hundred trials, A would only have won 500*l.* in those, and B winning 1,023*l.* at the last, would have much the better of the encounter.

Why, then, would not B be willing to wager on these terms? For precisely the same reason (if he actually reasoned the matter out) that he would be unwilling to pay 1*l.* for one ticket out of 1,024 where the price was 1,024*l.* Each ticket would be fairly worth that sum. And many foolish persons, as we know, are willing to pay in that way for a ticket in a lottery, even paying more than the correct value. But no one of any sense would throw away a sovereign for the chance (even truly valued at a sovereign) of winning a thousand pounds. That, really, is what B declines to do. Every venture he makes with A (supposing A to have about 1,000*l.* at starting, and so to be able to keep on doubling up to 512*l.*) is a wager on just such terms. B wins nothing unless he wins 1,024*l.* ; he loses at each failure 1*l.* His chance of winning, too, is the same, at each venture, as that of drawing a single marked ticket from a bag containing 1,024 tickets. Each venture, though it may be decided at the first or second tossing, is a venture of ten tossings. Now, with ten tossings there are 1,024 possible results, any one of which is as likely as any other. One of these, and one only, is favourable to B., viz. the case of ten 'heads,' if he is backing 'heads,' or ten 'tails,' if he is backing 'tails.' Thus he pays, in effect, one pound for one chance in 1,024 of winning 1,024*l.*, though, in reality, he does not pay the pound until the venture is decided against him ; so that, if he wins, he receives 1,023*l.*, corresponding (with the 1*l.*) to the total just named.

Now, to wager a pound in this way, for the chance of winning 1,024*l.*, would be very foolish ; and though continually repeating the experiment would in the long run make the number of successes bear the right proportion to the number of failures, yet B might be ruined long before this happened, though quite as probably A would be ruined. B's ruin, if effected, would be brought about by steadily continued small losses, A's by a casual but overwhelming loss. The richer B and A were, the longer it would be before one or other was ruined, though the eventual ruin of one or other would be certain. If one was much richer than the other, his chance of escaping ruin would be so much the greater, and so much greater, therefore, the risk of the poorer. In other words, the odds would be great in favour of the richer of the two, whether A or B, absorbing the whole property of the other, if wagering on this plan were continued steadily for a long time.

Now, if we extend such considerations as these to the case in which an individual player contends against a bank, we shall see that, even without any percentage on the chances, the odds would be largely in favour of the bank. If the player is persistent in applying his system, he is practically certain to be ruined. For it is to be noticed that in such a system the player is exposed to that which he can least afford, namely, sudden and great loss ; it is by such losses that his ruin will be brought about if at all. On the other hand, the bank, which can best afford such losses, has to meet only a steady slow drain upon its resources, until the inevitable *coups* come which restore all that had been thus drained out, and more along with it. If the player were even to carry on his system in the manner which my reasoning has really implied ; if, as he made his small gain at each venture, he set it by to form a reserve fund—even then his ruin would be inevitable in the long run. But every one knows that gamblers do nothing of the sort. 'Lightly come, lightly go,' is their rule, so far as their gains are concerned. [In another sense, their rule is, lightly come (to the gaming table) and heavily go when the last pound has been staked and lost.] Thus they run a risk which, in their way of playing, amounts almost to a certainty of ruining themselves, and they do not even take the precaution which would alone give them their one small, almost evanescent, chance of escape. On the other hand, the bankers, who are really playing an almost perfectly safe game, leave nothing to chance. The bulk of the money gained by them is reserved to maintain the balance necessary for safety. Only the actual profits of their system—the percentage of gain due to their percentage on the chances—is dealt with as income ; that is, as money to be spent.

It is true that in one sense the case between the bankers and the public resembles that of a player with a small capital against a player with a large capital. The bankers have indeed a large capital, but it is small compared with that of the public at large who frequent the gaming tables. But, in the first place, this does not at all help any single player. It is all but certain that the public (meaning always the special gaming public) will not be ruined as a whole, just as it is all but certain that the whole of an army engaged in a campaign, even under the most unfavourable circumstances, will not be destroyed if recruits are always available at short notice. Now, if the circumstances of a campaign are such that each individual soldier runs exceeding risk of being killed, it will not improve the chances of any single soldier that the army as a whole will not be destroyed ; and in like manner those who gamble persistently are not helped in their ruin by the circumstance that, as one is ' pushed from the board, others ever succeed.' Even the chance of the bank being ruined, however, is not favourable to the gambler who follows such a system as I am dealing with, but positively adds to his risks. In the illustrative case of A playing B, the ruin of B meant that A had gained all B's money. But in the case of a gambler playing on the doubling system at a gaming table, the ruin of the bank would be one of the chances against him that such a gambler would have to take into account. It might happen when he was far on in a long process of doubling, and would be almost certain to happen when he had to some degree entered on such a process. He would then be certainly a loser on that particular venture. If a winner on the event actually decided when the bank broke (only one, be it remembered, of the series forming his venture), he would perhaps receive a share, but a share only, of the available assets. The rules of the table may be such that these will always cover the stakes, and in that case the player, supposing he had won on the last event decided, would sustain no loss. Should he have lost on that event, however, which ordinarily would at least not interfere with the opera- tion of his system, he is prevented from pursuing the system till he has recouped his loss. This can never happen in play between two gamblers on this system. For the very circum- stance that A has lost an event involves of necessity the possession by B of enough money to continue the system. B's stake after winning is always double the last stake, but after winning the amount just staked of course he must possess double that amount—since he has his winnings and also a sum at least equal, which he must have had when he wagered an equal stake. But when a player at the gaming tables loses an event in one of his ventures, it by no means follows equally that the bank can continue to double (assuming the highest value allowed to have not been reached). Losses against other players may compel the bank to close when the system player has just lost a tolerably heavy *coup*. His system then is defeated, and he sustains a loss distinct in character from those which his system normally involves. In other words, the chances against him are increased ; and, on the other hand, the bankers' chance of ruin would be small, even if they had no advantage in the odds, simply because the sum staked bears a much smaller proportion to their capital than the wagers of the individual player bear to his property.

Yet the reader must not fall into the mistake of supposing that because the individual player would have enormous risks against him, even if the bankers took no percentage on the chances, the bank would then in the long run make enormous gains. That would be a paradoxical result, though at first sight it seems equally paradoxical to say that, while every single player would be almost certain to be ruined, the bank would not gain in the long run. This, however, is perfectly true. The fact is, that, among the few who escaped ruin, some would be enormous gainers. It would be because of some marvellous runs of luck, and consequent enormous gains, that they would be saved from ruin ; and the chances would be that some among these would be very heavy gainers. They would be few ; and the action of a man who gambled heavily on the chance of being one of these few, would be like that of a man who bought half-a-dozen tickets, at a price of 1,000*l.* each (his whole property being thus expended), among millions of tickets in a lottery, in which were a few prizes of 1,000,000*l.* each. But though the smallness of the chance of being one among the few very great gainers at the gambling table, makes it absurd for a man to run the enormous risk of ruin involved in persistent play, yet, so far as the bankers would be concerned, the great losses on the few winners would in the long run equalise the moderate gains on the great majority of their customers. They would neither gain nor lose a sum bearing any considerable proportion to their ventures, and would run some risk, though only a small one, of being swamped by a long-continued run of bad luck.

But the bankers do not in this way leave matters to chance. They take a percentage on the chances. The percentage they take is often not very large in itself, though it is nearly always larger than it appears, even when regarded properly as a percentage on the chances. But what is usually overlooked by those who deal with this matter, and especially by those who, being gamblers themselves, *want* to think that gaming houses give them very fair chances, is that a very small percentage on the chances may mean, and necessarily does mean, an enormous percentage of profits.

Let us take, as illustrating both the seeming smallness of the percentage on the chances, and the enormous probable percentage of profits, the game of *rouge-et-noir*, so far as it can be understood from the accounts given in the books.[1] I follow De Morgan's rendering of these confused and im-

[1] De Morgan remarks on the incomplete and unintelligible way in which this game is described in the later editions of Hoyle. It is singular how seldom a complete and clear account of any game can be found in books, though written by the best card-players. I have never yet seen a description of cribbage, for example, from which anyone who knew nothing of the game, and could find no one to explain it practically to him, could form a correct idea of its nature. In half-a-dozen lines from the beginning of a description, technical terms are used which have not been explained, remarks are made which imply a knowledge on the reader's part of the general object of the game of which he should be supposed to know nothing, and many matters absolutely essential to a right apprehension of the nature of the game are not touched on from beginning to end, or are so insufficiently described that they might as well have been left altogether unnoticed. It is the same with verbal descriptions. Not one person in a hundred can explain a game of cards respectably, and not one in a thousand can explain a game well. A beginner can pick up a game after awhile, by combining with the imperfect explanations given him the practical illustrations which the cards themselves afford. But there is no reason in the nature of things why a written or a verbal description of such a game as whist or cribbage should not suffice to make an attentive reader or hearer perfectly understand the nature of the game. From what I have noticed in this matter, I would assert with some confidence that anyone who can explain clearly, yet succinctly, a game at cards, must have the explanatory gift so exceptionally developed that he could most usefully employ it in the explanation of such scientific subjects as he might himself be able to master. I believe, too, that the student of science who desires to explain his subject to the general public, can

perfect accounts. It seems to be correct, for his computation of the odds for and against the player leads to the same result as Poisson obtained, who knew the game, though he nowhere gives a description of it.

A number of packs is taken (six, Hoyle says), 'and the cards are well mixed. Each common card counts for the number of spots on it, and the court cards are each reckoned as ten. A table is divided into two compartments, one called *rouge*, the other *noir*, and a player stakes his money in which he pleases. The proprietor of the bank, who risks against all comers, then lays down cards in one compartment until the number of spots exceeds thirty ; as soon as this has happened, he proceeds in the same way with the other compartment.' The number of spots in each compartment is thus necessarily between 31 and 40, both inclusive. The compartment in which the total number of spots is least is the winning one. Thus, if there are 35 card spots on the cards in the *rouge*, and 32 on the cards in the *noir*, *noir* wins, and all players who staked upon *noir* receive from the bank sums equal to their stakes. The process is then repeated. So far, it will be observed, the chances are equal for the players and for the bankers. It will also be observed that the arrangement is one which strongly favours the idea (always encouraged by the proprietors of gaming houses) that the bankers have little interest in the result. For the bank does not back either colour. The players have all the backing to themselves. If they choose to stake more in all on the red than on the black, it becomes the bank's interest that black should win ; but it was by the players' own acts that black became for the time the bank's colour. And not only does this suggest to the players the incorrect idea that the bank has little real interest in the game, but it encourages the correct idea, which it is the manifest interest of the bankers to put very clearly

find no better exercise, and few better tests, than the explanation of some simple game—the explanation to be sufficient for persons knowing nothing of the game.

before the players, that everything is fairly managed. If the
bank chose a colour, some might think that the cards, however seemingly shuffled, were in reality arranged, or else
were so manipulated as to make the bank's colour win
oftener than it should do.   But since the players themselves
settle which shall be the bank's colour at each trial, there
cannot be suspicion of foul play of this sort.

We now come to the bank's advantage on the chances.
The number of spots in the black and red compartments
may be equal.   In this case (called by Hoyle a *refait*) the
game is drawn; and the players may either withdraw, increase, or diminish their stakes, as they please, for a new
game, if the number of spots in each compartment is any
except 31.   But if the number in each be 31 (a case called
by Hoyle a *refait trente-et-un*), then the players are not
allowed to withdraw their stakes.   And not only must the
stakes remain for a new game, but, whatever happens on
this new trial, the players will receive nothing.   Their stakes
are for the moment impounded (or technically, according to
Hoyle, *en prison*).   The new game (called an *après*), unless
it chances to give another *refait*, will end in favour of either
rouge or *noir*.   Whichever compartment wins, the players in
that compartment save their stakes, but receive nothing
from the bank ; the players who have put their stakes in the
other compartment lose them.   De Morgan says here, not
quite correctly, 'should the bank win it takes the stakes,
should the bank lose the player recovers his stakes.'   This
is incorrect, because it at least suggests the incorrect idea
that the bank may either win or the stakes go clear ; whereas
in reality, except in the improbable event of all the players
backing one colour, the bank is sure to win something, viz.,
either the stakes in the red or those in the black compartment, and the only point to be settled is whether the larger
or the smaller of these probably unequal sums shall pass to
the bank's exchequer.   If the *après* gives a second *refait*,
the stakes still remain impounded, and another game is
played, and no stakes are released until either *rouge* or *noir*

has won. But in the mean time new stakes may be put down, before the fate of the impounded stakes has been decided.

Thus, whereas, with regard to games decided at the first trial, the bank has in the long run no interest one way or the other, the bank has an exceptional interest in *refaits*. A *refait trente-et-un* at once gives the bank a certainty of winning the least sum staked in the two compartments, and an equal chance of winning the larger sum instead. Any *refait* gives the bank the chance that on a new trial a *refait trente-et-un* may be made ; and though this chance (that is, the chance that there will first be a common *refait trente-et-un* and then a *refait*) is small, it tells in the long run and must be added to the advantage obtained from the chance of a *refait trente-et-un* at once.

Now it may seem as though the bank would gain very little from so small an advantage. A *refait* may occur tolerably often in any long series of trials, but a *refait trente-et-un* only at long intervals. It is only one out of ten different *refaits*, which to the uninitiated seem all equally likely to occur ; so that he supposes the chance of a *refait trente-et-un* to be only one-tenth of the chance itself small at each trial, that there will be a *refait* of some sort. But, to begin with, this supposition is incorrect. Calculation shows that the chance of a *refait* of some sort occurring is 1,097 in 10,000, or nearly one in nine. The chance of a *refait trente-et-un* is not one-tenth of this, or about 110 in 10,000, but 219, in 10,000, or twice as great as the uninitiated imagine. Thus in very nearly two games in 91, instead of one game in 91, a *refait trente-et-un* occurs. It follows from this, combined with the circumstance that on the average the bank wins half its stakes only in the case of one of these *refaits* (and account being also taken of the slight subordinate chance above mentioned), that the mathematical advantage of the bank is very nearly one-ninetieth of all the sums deposited. The actual percentage is $1\frac{1}{10}$ *per deposit* ; and in passing it may be noticed as affording good illustration of the mistakes the uninitiated are apt to make in such matters, that if instead of the *refait trente-et-un* the bankers took to themselves the *refait quarante,* instead of this percentage per deposit the percentage would be only $\frac{3}{20}$, or 3*s.* per 100*l.*

But even an average advantage of 1*l.* 2*s.* per 100*l.* on each deposit made by the bank is thought by the frequenters of the table to be very slight. It makes the odds against the players about 913 to 892 on each trial, and the difference seems trifling. On considering the probable results of a year's play, however, we find that the bankers could obtain tremendous interest for a capital which would make them far safer against ruin than is thought necessary in any ordinary mercantile business. Suppose play went on upon only 100 evenings in each year; that each evening 100 games were played; and that on each game the total sum risked on both *rouge* and *noir* was 50*l.* Then the total sum deposited by the bank (very much exceeding the total sum *risked,* which on each game is only the difference between the sums staked on *rouge* and on *noir*) would be 500,000*l.*; and $1\frac{1}{10}$ per cent. on this sum would be 5,500*l.* I follow De Morgan in taking these numbers, which seem far below what would generally be deposited in 100 evenings of play. Now, it can be shown that, if the bankers started with such a sum as 5,500*l.,* they would be practically safe from all chance of ruin. So that in 100 playing nights they would probably make cent. per cent. on their capital. In places where gambling is encouraged they could readily in a year make 300 per cent. on their capital at the beginning of the year.

De Morgan points out that, though the editor of Hoyle does not correctly estimate the chances in this game, underrating the bank's advantage; yet, even with this erroneous estimate, the gains per annum on a capital of 5,500*l.* would be 12,000*l.* (instead of 16,500*l.* as when properly calculated). As he justly says, 'the preceding results, or either of them, being admitted, it might be supposed hardly necessary to dwell upon the ruin which must necessarily result to individual players against a bank which has so strong a chance of success against its united antagonists.' 'But,' he adds, 'so strangely are opinions formed upon this subject, that it is not uncommon to find persons who think they are in possession of a specific by which they must infallibly win.' If both the banker and the player staked on each game 1-160th part of their respective funds, and the play was to continue till one or other side was ruined, the bank would have 49 chances to 1 in its favour against that one player. But if, as more commonly is the case, the player's stake formed a far larger proportion of his property, these odds would be immensely increased. If a player staked one-tenth of his money on each game against the same sum, supposed to be 1-160th of the bank's money, the chances would be 223 to 1 that he would be ruined, if he persisted long enough. In other words, his chance of escaping ruin would be the same as that of drawing one single marked ball out of a bag containing 224.

Other games played at the gaming tables, however different in character they may be from *rouge-et-noir,* give no better chances to the players. Indeed, some games give far inferior chances. There is not one of them at which any system of play can be safe in the long run. If the system is such that the risk on each venture is small, then the gains on each venture will be correspondingly small. Many ventures, therefore, must be made in order to secure any considerable gains ; and when once the number of ventures is largely increased, the small risk on each becomes a large risk, and, if the ventures be very numerous, becomes practically a certainty of loss. On the other hand, there are modes of venturing which, if successful once only, bring in a large profit ; but they involve a larger immediate risk.

In point of fact, the supposition that any system can be devised by which success in games of chance may be made certain, is as utterly unphilosophical as faith in the invention of perpetual motion. That the supposition has been entertained by many who have passed all their lives in gambling proves only—what might also be safely inferred from the very fact of their being gamblers—that they know nothing of the laws of probability.   Many men who have passed all their lives among machinery believe confidently in the possibility of perpetual motion.   They are familiar with machinery, but utterly ignorant of mechanics.   So the life-long gambler is familiar with games of chance, but utterly ignorant of the laws of chance.

Yet fortunes can be made at the gambling table.   Fortunes have been so made.   From the preceding pages the method of making such fortunes can be learned.   It is all contained in one precept :—Take advantage of the innate propensity of immense numbers of men to gamble, and swindle them so deftly that they shall not see where or how much they are wronged.

THE FIFTEEN PUZZLE.

TAKING up, the other day, in a Tasmanian hotel, a copy of a Sydney weekly newspaper, I came across an extract from the *Illustrated London News*—a passage in which Mr. Sala comments humorously on the now celebrated, or perhaps one should rather say the now notorious, Fifteen Puzzle. He therein suggests that a short Act of Parliament should be passed 'prohibiting, under penalty of heavy fine and long imprisonment, all and sundry of her Majesty's subjects from playing a dreadful game called " Fifteen," and known in the United States as the "Great Boss Puzzle." ' 'You have a box,' he says, 'containing sixteen numbered blocks or counters You take out the number ' 16 '; you mix up the counters in the box so that they will run irregularly ; and then your task —your fearful task—is, without lifting the tablets from the box, to push them horizontally into a regular sequence ol from 1 to 15.' (The description is not quite correct, by-the· by ; however, every one knows what the puzzle really is, and a scientifically exact account of it is not required in a humorous description.) ' " That way madness lies," ' pro- ceeds Sala ; 'but, pshaw ! what need have I to describe the fearsome game ? Even as I write, thousands of my readers, old and young, may be playing it. If time be indeed money, that Great Boss puzzle must have cost me at least a thousand dollars between January and June last. I played it at Omaha ; I played it at Chicago ; I played it at Great Salt Lake City ; I played it on board the *Hecla* coming home ; and, upon my word, so soon as I have finished writing the

T

" Echoes," I shall be at the great Boss Puzzle again. Why was it not stopped at the Custom House? Why was it not brought under the provisions of dangerous explosives or cattle-plague laws? There would be no use in proceeding against the persons who have naturalised this appalling apparatus in England. Our old friend, "the merest schoolboy," can make a game of Fifteen for himself from so many buttons or draught-counters. It is the players who, in the interest of precious time, should be punished.'

I myself took some part, sad to say, in naturalising the fearsome game in England. For about the time when the Boss Puzzle was most popular—I should say, most mischievous—in America, I sent a description of it to the *Newcastle Weekly Chronicle*. I accompanied that description, however, with a statement that the problem can be proved to be soluble in certain positions, and insoluble in others. In fact, from any one of more than ten million positions the problem can be solved, while from precisely the same number of positions it cannot. Unfortunately, I went on to say that if any one were to assert that he had brought the blocks to their right position from one of the positions of the insoluble class, or had seen the feat achieved, he must either be mistaken or else tell an untruth. This remark, perfectly true and altogether innocent of offence, seeing that I knew of no readers of the *Newcastle Weekly Chronicle* who had asserted or were prepared to assert any such thing, excited the wrath of many who, as they doubtless supposed, had succeeded in solving the problem from all possible positions.

As the proof referred to in the *Newcastle Weekly Chronicle*—as far back, I think, as last March (I wrote my remarks on the puzzle at Chicago last February)—is exceedingly simple, and may prevent many (or theoretically should certainly prevent all) from wasting their time over insoluble positions of the Fifteen Puzzle, I think many readers of these papers may be interested if I indicate briefly and simply how the demonstration runs. It occurred to me a few hours after I had seen the puzzle, and seems so simple and obvious, that I can scarcely imagine others have failed to notice it. Yet it has not, to my knowledge, been given elsewhere. Moreover, I have seen several attempts to analyse the puzzle, some by mathematicians of repute and even of eminence, in which incorrect reasons have been assigned for the insolubility of the problem from certain positions, and incorrect rules laid down for distinguishing soluble from insoluble positions. The rule resulting from the following analysis is, I believe, the only correct one, though it is quite possible there may be others, apparently independent, which are, however, in reality deducible from it.

First, let us consider what the puzzle really is, because it has been through mistaken ideas on this point that many had been led to suppose they had solved the problem from insoluble positions, when, in reality, they had done nothing of the kind.

We have a square box containing sixteen square blocks numbered in order from 1 to 16 The sixteenth block is removed, so that the position of the blocks is that shown in Fig 6. This is called the *won position*, viz. that in which the blocks *read in succession as we read printed matter* (that is, each line from left to right, and line after line in numerical order, run

1	2	3	4
5	6	7	8
9	10	11	12
13	14	15	

FIG. 6.

in the order of the numbers from 1 to 15, *the vacant square being on the fourth or last line.*)

The blocks are next arranged in any random order (which must not be done *solely* by shifting the blocks one by one from the won position without taking any out). The problem is then to bring the numbers into the 'won position' without removing any, that is, by simply shifting them one by one into places successively vacated. It is to be noted that the 'won position' must be obtained precisely as pictured in Fig. 6, or as defined above. Many seem to imagine that the problem is solved if either such a position as that shown in Fig. 7 or that shown in Fig 8 is attained. But this is not the case. In fact both these positions belong to the insoluble class. They not only are not won positions, but the true won position cannot possibly be obtained from either of them. It ought, perhaps, to be unnecessary to add that the problem cannot be fairly solved by taking the 6 and 9 and replacing them each in their own space, but inverted so that they read as 9 and 6 respectively (a change which also alters a position from the insoluble to the soluble class, and *vice versâ*); but, as some seem to imagine the change permissible, it may be as well to mention that it is not. *In fine, the problem is, from any random position of the fifteen numbers to obtain the precise position shown in Fig. 6 without removing any one of the*

1	2	3	
4	5	6	7
8	9	10	11
12	13	14	15

FIG. 7.

4	8	12	
3	7	11	15
2	6	10	14
1	5	9	13

FIG. 8.

blocks otherwise than by sliding it into a neighbouring vacant square.

Before proceeding to discuss the puzzle, it may be well to inquire whether time given to such matters is not altogether wasted. I believe that any problems requiring for their solution the exercise of patience and ingenuity serve a useful purpose; but it must be admitted that some are much less useful than others, while some require so much time, and call into action faculties of such small value, that their use as exercises in patience affords but a small compensation for the time devoted to them. Nine-tenths of the puzzles, charades, rebuses, acrostics and so forth, in periodical literature, are unfortunately of this kind. But problems like the Fifteen Puzzle, Chinese puzzles, and others serve as a means of mental training almost as well as problems in mathematics. That is, they do so if dealt with in the right way. For there is a right way and a wrong way, even in dealing with the simplest puzzles. The wrong way is to set to work in haphazard fashion, trusting to the chapter of accidents for the solution. The right way is to reason the matter out step by step, from the known to the unknown, in the simplest puzzle, precisely as the student of science strives to pass from the known to the unknown in dealing with some great problem of nature.

Now, suppose we examine first the won position; passing from it to others, by simply shifting blocks in the manner allowed when dealing with any ordinary or random presentation of the puzzle. It is clear that any position attained by shifting the blocks thus from the places shown in Fig. 6 *must* be a winning position, since we have only to retrace the steps by which such a position has been obtained to come again into the won position.

We can push block 15 to the vacant corner square, and 14 next to 15, and 13 next to 14. By these changes we do not alter the sequence of the numbers, reading them in the same way as we read printed matter. Nor do we alter the number of the row on which the vacant square lies, counting the horizontal lines as we count the lines of printed matter. We alter only the position of the vacant square in its horizontal line, or the position of the *column* containing the vacant square. But we begin already to see that this change is of far less importance than a change in the number of the *line* containing the vacant square. For the numerical sequence, the arrangement of which is the main aim of any movements for solving the problem from a random position, is not affected at all by shifting a block horizontally.

Replace the shifted blocks as at first, and try the effect of shifting them vertically.

Bring block 12 to the vacant square. By this change *three* blocks, viz. 13, 14, and 15, are thrown out of their proper position ; all the rest, from 1 to 11, should precede 12, and do so ; but these three which now follow should precede 12. There are then *three* displacements, and the vacant square has been shifted from the fourth to the *third line*. Push down next the 8 block. Then there are *six* displacements (9, 10, 11 preceding instead of following 8, and 13, 14, 15 preceding instead of following 12). The vacant square has been shifted to the *second* line. Shifting down the 4 block, there are *nine* displacements, and the vacant square has been shifted to the *first* line. In all three cases, the vacant square is in the fourth column.

Push back the shifted blocks, resuming the won position ; and having shifted 15 to the corner square, push down successively 11, 7, and 3.

When 11 is pushed down, there are *three* displacements (12, 13, and 14 preceding instead of following 11), and the vacant square is on the *third* line ; when 7 is pushed down there are *six* displacements, and the vacant square is on the *second* line ; and, lastly, when 3 is pushed down there are *nine* displacements, and the vacant square is on the *first* line. In all three cases the vacant square is in the *third* column.

These results are the same as when the blocks 12, 8, and 4 were pushed successively down in the fourth column ; and we get the same results if, after resuming the won position, we push both 14 and 15 to the right, bringing the vacant square to the second column, and then push successively 10, 6, and 2 down ; or if we push 13, 14, and 15 down, bringing the vacant square to the first column, and then push down successively 9, 5, and 1.

Let us now arrange the twelve cases just considered, and inquire if any law begins to appear among these twelve winning positions. The cases run thus :—

Case.	No. of Displacements.	No. of Vacant Line.	No. of Vacant Column.
1st	3	3	4
2nd	6	2	4
3rd	9	1	4
4th	3	3	3
5th	6	2	3
6th	9	1	3
7th	3	3	2
8th	6	2	2
9th	9	1	2
10th	3	3	1
11th	6	2	1
12th	9	1	1

It is obvious from this table that if we are seeking in the right direction for some law by which to distinguish winning positions from losing ones, assuming (as at this stage of the inquiry we can but do) that such a law exists, we need pay no further attention to the number of the column on which lies the vacant square. We see that when the number of displacements is even, the number of the partially vacant line is also even ; while where the number of the displacements is odd, the number of the partially vacant line is also odd ; but the number of the partially vacant column varies from odd to even, and from even to odd, independently of any change in the other tabulated relations.

To make one further trial of known winning positions before examining a random position, push down the 12, 11 to the right, and then 15 up, getting the position shown in Fig. 9. Here there are *six* displacements, 15 coming before 11, 13, 14, and 12, instead of coming after those four numbers, and 13 and 14 each coming before instead of after 12. The vacant square is on the *fourth* line. Thus the number of displacements and the number of the partially vacant line are both even. Bring down the 15 again (I take no special notice of the position thus attained, because it is the

1	2	3	4
5	6	7	8
9	10	15	11
13	14		12

FIG. 9.

same as case 1 of the above table, except as to the number of the partially vacant column, which we have seen to have no significance whatever). Push down the 7 into the vacant square, getting the position of Fig. 10. In this position there

1	2	3	4
5	6		8
9	10	7	11
13	14	15	12

Fig. 10.

are *six* displacements (8, 9, 10 before 7, and 13, 14, 15 before 12), and the vacant square is on the *second* row ; or, again, the law that the number of displacements and the number of the partially vacant line are either both even or both odd is fulfilled. So also it is fulfilled if from the position of Fig. 10 we push down the 3 ; for then it will be found that there are *nine* displacements, while the partially vacant line is the *first*.

This, then, seems likely enough to be a law for *all* winning positions : that the total number of displacements as regards numerical sequence, and the number of the partially vacant line, are either both even or both odd.

I might, indeed, go on in this way—that is, starting from the won position—and establish the law just indicated without further ado. But I prefer to attack the puzzle now from the other end—that is, starting from a random position— taking the hint thus obtained for our guidance. I do this, first, because it was in this way that I actually analysed the Fifteen Puzzle ; and secondly, because I believe that non-mathematical readers will find their *aperçu* of the subject clearer after a second review of the primary considerations on which the analysis depends.

9	14	12	4
5	1		8
3	7	15	2
13	10	6	11

Fig. 11.

I take, then, the random position shown in Fig. 11, already employed in analysing the Fifteen Puzzle for the *Australasian*, to which weekly journal I sent an account of the puzzle early in the year.

Guided by what we have already seen, we first count the number of displacements in the arrangement of Fig. 11. (For convenience, I shall hereafter call the number of displacements in any given case the ' total displacement ' ; and instead of saying the number of the partially vacant line is odd or even, as the case may be, I shall say simply the vacant line is odd or even.) We may count the displacements thus, our examination running along the numbers in the order of the lines, as in reading :—

				Displacements.
12	which follows should precede	14	1
4	,,	,,	9, 14, 12	3
5	,,	,,	9, 14, 12	3
1	,,	,,	9, 14, 12, 4, 5 . . .	5
8	,,	,,	9, 14, 12	3
3	,,	,,	9, 14, 12, 4, 5, 8 . .	6
7	,,	,,	9, 14, 12, 8 . . .	4
2	,,	,,	9, 14, 12, 4, 5, 8, 3, 7, 15.	9
13	,,	,,	14, 15	2
10	,,	,,	14, 12, 15, 13 . . .	4
6	,,	,,	9, 14, 12, 8, 7, 15, 13, 10.	8
11	,,	,,	14, 12, 15, 13 . . .	4
		Total displacement	. . .	52

Thus the total displacement is *even*, and the vacant line is also *even* : so that, if our suggested law is correct, the position should be a winning one.

Let us now consider the effect of any change in the position of the blocks from the arrangement shown in Fig. 11. What we want to ascertain is whether, when any such change has been made, by sliding without removing blocks, the position retains the characteristics which we have been led to regard as indicative of a winning position.

It is clear that, whether we push the 1 or the 8 into the vacant place, the ' total displacement ' remains unchanged. If, however, we shift the 12 to the vacant position, the total displacement is altered ; for the numbers 4, 5, and 1, which should precede 12, but did not in the original position, are now made to do so. The ' total displacement ' is reduced from 52 to 49, the vacant line from the second to the first. Thus, the law we are inquiring into still seems to hold good, for now both the total displacement and the vacant line are odd. So also it holds if, instead of pushing down the 12, we push up the 15. For in this case the numbers 3, 7, and 8, which should precede 15, and did precede 15 in the original position, are made to follow 15, the 'total displacement' being thus increased from 52, an even number, to 55, an *odd* number, while the vacant line is also changed from even to *odd*. In all the cases thus far considered the total displacement has either been increased or diminished by three, when a block has been pushed up or down. But if after pushing 15 (Fig. 11) up, we push 6 up, we only change the displacement (55) by *one*; for 6, which had followed and should follow 2, is made to precede 2, increasing the total displacement by one, while 13 and 10, which had not followed 6 as they should, are made to do so, decreasing the total displacement by two, the actual reduction being therefore only *one*. Thus, after this change the total displacement is 54, an *even* number; the vacant line is the fourth, or also *even*; and the law we are considering seems to be fulfilled after this change as after the others.

But we begin now to see that *every* vertical displacement of one block must increase or diminish the total displacement, either by the odd number *three* or by the odd number *one*. An upward displacement puts a number before three others which had been after those numbers. Now, either the displaced number is greater than all those three or greater than two of them, and less than one, or greater than one of them only and less than two, or less than all three of them. In the first case, the total displacement is increased by *three*; in the second, it is increased by two and reduced by one, or increased on the whole by *one*; in the third it is increased by one and reduced by two, or reduced on the whole by *one*; in the fourth case, the total displacement is reduced by *three*. And obviously, pushing down a block must exactly reverse these effects in the respective cases considered; either reducing the total displacement by *three* or by *one*, or increasing it by *one* or by *three*.

Since, then, each vertical change increases or diminishes the total displacement by an odd number (3 or 1), successive changes of this sort cause the total displacement to be alternately odd and even. They also, of course, cause the vacant line to be alternately odd or even. So that, if the total displacement and the vacant line are both odd or both even for any given position, they are both even or both odd after a vertical displacement, both odd or both even after the next vertical displacement, both even or both odd after the next; and so on continually, that is (since horizontal displacements produce no change at all in them), they remain always alike, both even or both odd, whatever changes are made. On the other hand, it is equally clear that if for any given position the 'total displacement' is odd and the vacant line even, the former will be even and the latter odd after a vertical displacement; one odd, the other even, after the next vertical displacement; and so on continually; that is, (since horizontal displacements produce no change at all in them), they remain always unlike—one odd, the other even—whatever changes are made.

Since, then, in the won position the total displacement (o) is even, and the vacant line (4th) is also even, in every position deducible from the won position or reducible to the won position, the total displacement and the vacant line are either both even or both odd. And therefore no position in which the total displacement is even and the vacant line odd, or *vice versâ*, can possibly be a winning position.

We have established a law which at any rate proves the hopelessness of attempting to pass from the position shown in Fig. 12, or from any position

1	2	3	4
5	6	7	8
9	10	11	12
13	15	14	

FIG. 12.

deducible from or reducible to this arrangement, to the won position shown in Fig. 6. For in Fig. 12, the displacement is *one* or odd, and the vacant line even. This, with many, will be regarded as a sufficient analysis of the Fifteen Puzzle, since every one who has ever tried it knows well that we can always reduce any given position in a few minutes, either to the position shown in Fig. 6 (the won position), or to that shown in Fig. 12, which may conveniently be called the lost position.

But in reality something more is required for the complete analysis of the puzzle. We have proved that from none of the multitudinous positions (one-half of the total number) in which the total displacement is odd and the vacant line even, or *vice versâ*, can any position be obtained in which the total displacement and the vacant line are either both even or both odd ; also, that from not one of the multitudinous positions of the latter kind (say the *winning* kind) can one of the former kind (say the *losing* kind) be obtained. But we have not yet proved that from any position of the winning sort any other position of the winning sort, including the won position, can be obtained ; or that from any position of the losing sort any other position of the same sort, including the lost position.

We cannot possibly prove either of these relations experimentally, for the simple reason that there are more than ten millions of millions of positions of the winning sort, and as many of the losing sort.[1]

[1] There are in each position fifteen occupied squares and one square unoccupied, which square we may always suppose to be occupied by the number 16. The total possible number of arrangements, therefore, is the same as the number of permutations of 16 things (all appearing in each arrangement, which is, indeed, understood usually by mathematicians when they use the word permutation as distinguished from combination). This number, it is well known, is that obtained by multiplying together the number, 1, 2, 3, 4, &c., up to 16, or 20,922,789,888,000. Of these, one-half, or 10,461,394,944,000, are winning and as many are losing positions.

I venture to quote here, in passing, some remarks which I made in my article on the Fifteen Puzzle in the *Australasian*—remarks not, of course, intended to be taken *au grand sérieux*, but which were unfortunately so taken by a few whom I must consider rather dull-brained readers. ' Professor Piazzi Smythe, and other believers in the Great Pyramid, may find in the above numbers proof positive that the archi-

Yet it is not difficult to prove that from any winning position any other winning position, and from any losing any other losing position, may be obtained. The demonstration may be arranged as follows :—

When we take a square of four small squares only, and have three numbered blocks (say 1, 2, 3) and one vacant square, we can shift these round from any given position into twelve positions, as thus :—

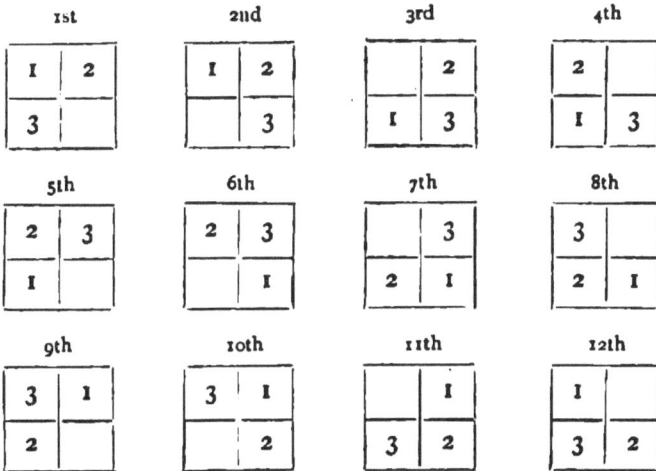

FIG. 13.

These are only half the possible positions of the numbers 1, 2, 3, in a square of four quarter-squares. The other half will be obtained by starting from the position and carrying the vacant square round in the way above shown, for the series of 12 positions from the initial position.

In this, the simplest case, we see that starting from any given position, half the possible arrangements of three numbers in a square of four square spaces, one vacant,

tects of that building at once anticipated the celebrity of the Great Boss Puzzle, and were acquainted with the distance of the star Alpha Centauri, the nearest of all the stars. The proof runs thus : The base of the pyramid is square, like the Fifteen Puzzle box, and has four sides, suggesting manifestly the division of each side into four equal can be obtained, and half only ; but if the sequence of the numbers (going round the square) be altered from 1, 2, 3 to 1, 3, 2, or *vice versâ*,[1] all the remaining positions can be obtained. The movements by which such positions are obtained may be regarded as a turning movement around the central point of the square ; and in this case there is but one point around which such turning movement can be made. Moreover, notice that it matters nothing which way the turning takes place. The successive positions shown in Fig. 13 form a complete re-entering series, and according as we consider this series in the order there shown, or in the reverse order, the turning is supposed to have taken place in the same direction as the hands of a watch or in the reverse direction.

Now, it is to be noticed that in the complete puzzle, or in a similar puzzle with a smaller or greater number of parts, and, by cross lines through these, the division of the square into sixteen squares. But the pyramid has only one apex ; hence is at once suggested the removal of one of the sixteen squares, leaving the magic Fifteen. Then the Fifteen Problem admits of 20,922,789,888,000 distinct positions. Now, all the best measurements of the distance of Alpha Centauri indicate rather more than 20 billions of miles. Un-questionably the true distance must be just 20,922,789,888,000 miles; and this the pyramid architects manifestly knew. But they could not have learned this by any observations possible in their time. Hence we have further evidence of supernaturally imparted knowledge. *Quod erat demonstrandum.'*

[1] There are only two possible arrangements, 1, 2, 3, 1, 2, 3, 1, 2, 3, &c., and 1, 3, 2, 1, 3, 2, 1, 3, 2, &c., so far as sequence round the square is concerned. Further, in each arrangement the numbers run in numerical order, either in one direction or in another. It was from failing to notice this law in the sequence of three numbers that Hum-boldt was led to imagine that there is some significance in the cir-cumstance that the three promontories terminating the continents of America, Africa, and Australia, in the southern seas, approach suc-cessively nearer to the South Pole. As there are only three, they could not but do so, either as we take them in order from east to west, or else as we take them in order from west to east. The point is con-sidered more at length in my essay on equal-surface projections of the globe in 'Essays on Astronomy.'

rectangles (as a 9 square, or a 25 square, or a 3 by 4 rect-angle, or a 5 by 6 rectangle, and so forth), every point of intersection of the cross lines forming the squares is a centre round which, by bringing the vacant square next to any such point, the three blocks left around it can be turned, as in the above case we turned the numbers 1, 2, 3. But we can also turn the numbers round any *line* between such points of intersection. Thus, in the won position of Fig. 6, the blocks 15, 14, 10, 11, 12, can be turned round the line between the blocks 11 and 15, retaining the same sequence round the rectangle of six squares in which these blocks and the vacant square lie; and similarly with any other such line between two squares. Again, the blocks 15, 14, 13, 9, 10, 11, and 12 in the same figure can be turned round the line between the blocks 14, 11, and 14, 15. Next, the blocks round any one of the middle squares can be moved round such squares (after the vacant square has been brought next to it). Thus the blocks 15, 14, 10, 6, 7, 8, and 12, Fig. 6 can be moved round the block 11. So the blocks round any adjacent pair of the blocks now occupied by the number, 6, 7, 10, and 11, in Fig. 6, can be turned round that pair (as, 12, 8, 7, 6, 5, 9, 13, 14, 15 round the pair 10, 11). And lastly, the border squares can be turned round the central set of four squares occupied in Fig. 6 by the numbers 6, 7, 10, 11.

In all, in the complete puzzle, there are thirty-six kinds of turning motion, namely : round nine points of intersec-tion, round twelve lines between squares, round six lines between pairs of squares, round four squares, round four pairs of squares, and round one square of four square.

In what follows, I propose, for the convenience of descrip-tion and explanation, to regard rotations such as are above described as always taking place in one direction, viz. in the direction contrary to that in which the hands of a watch move (this being what mathematicians call the positive direction of rotation); and when I speak of rotation round a rectangle or square of blocks, whether the whole set or

part of a set shown in a figure, I mean that the border
squares in that rectangle are to be rotated round ; also when
I speak of rotation by so many squares I mean that the
vacant square is to be carried round in the forward direction
of rotation so many squares.   At first sight it might appear,
in studying Fig. 13, that the vacant square was carried the
other way round—and, indeed, this is the case if we consider the blocks as moved separately.   But in what follows
we suppose, unless the contrary is specified, that the set of
blocks to be rotated are carried round together.   For instance, we consider there has been a rotation of one square
in moving from position 1 to position 4, of another square in
moving to position 7, of another in moving to position 10,
and of a fourth in moving onwards to the original position 1.

So much premised, I proceed to show, step by step, that
in rectangles and squares six, eight, nine, twelve, and finally
of sixteen blocks, we can always pass from any position to
another of the same kind.

In Fig. 14 we have the won position for five blocks in a
six-block rectangle. Let it be required
to get any three blocks in given order
in the upper row, which is equivalent
to getting any given or possible arrangement
of the five blocks. The two blocks which
are to be where 2 and 3 are now must
either be next to each other (in order of
sequence round the rectangle) or not. If they are not, bring
the one which is to occupy square 3 to that square by rotating round rectangle A B, then the corner vacant in figure will
be occupied with some other block than the one required
to be in square 2.   Rotate round A C till this block comes
to square 2. Now bring these two squares by rotation
round A B to the right-hand column ; and rotate the other
round A C till the one which is to be in square 1 is in square
2. Then a forward rotation by one square round A B
brings the three numbers into the required position. If the

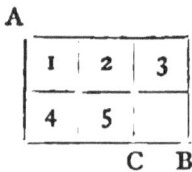

A

1	2	3
4	5	

C   B

FIG. 14.

two numbers to occupy squares 2 and 3 were originally adjacent and in wrong order, we must separate them by rotating round A B till either the top or bottom row are occupied by the two numbers and a vacant square between them, into which vacant square we put the middle block of the bottom or top row, as the case may be. After this the above method can be applied.

So that in every case the top row, or any three squares in sequence round A B, may be occupied by any three blocks we please in any order.

We cannot do more that this, for only two blocks remain, and it may be shown for such a rectangle as A B, precisely as for the original puzzle, that one-half the possible arrangements, though interchangeable *inter se*, are not interchangeable with arrangements belonging to the other half.[1]

Next take the case of a rectangle of eight squares, as A B, Fig. 15, where the won position for such a rectangle is shown. What we have to do in this case is to get a given set of five blocks in assigned order, into the squares 1, 2, 3, 4, and 5. First, as in the last case, we get the two blocks which are to occupy

A	C		
1	2	3	4
5	6	7	

D   B

FIG. 15.

the squares 3 and 4 into these squares, and by rotating backwards round C B, we bring them into the right-hand column. The remaining blocks of the five belong to the last case, since they are in a rectangle (A D) of six squares. We bring them into proper sequence, but in the squares 1, 2, 3 (instead of 5, 1, 2, which they are eventually to occupy). Then all the five blocks are in proper sequence, and a rotation of one square round A B brings them into the proper squares 1, 2, 3, 4, 5.

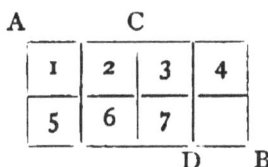

Next take a square of nine squares, as A B, where the won position for such a square is shown. What we have to show

---

[1] The total displacement and the vacant line in all positions reducible to that shown in fig. 14 are either both even or both odd; in all other positions one is even, the other odd.

in this case is that a given set of six blocks can be brought, in a given order, into the squares 1, 2, 3, 4, 5 and 6. Now, of the blocks to occupy squares 1, 2, 3, two, at least, must be in one or other of the rectangles C B, D B. According as two such are in C B or B D, bring them to position, 2, 3, or 4, 7, in their right order of sequence as around A B. In each case, shift them by rotating them round 5 to the position 3, 6, and the vacant square to the corner B. Then, if the third block is at 2, 5, or 8, the case belongs to that first dealt with, the three blocks to be placed being in a rectangle (C B) of six squares, one vacant. Bring them in right sequence (as around 5) to the squares 2, 3, 6, and by a rotation of one square to the position 1, 2, 3. If, however, the third block is at 1 or at 4, shift the block in 5, 8, bringing 8 to the corner B, and then A E is a six-squared rectangle containing the three given blocks and one vacant square, and the three blocks can be brought in the required order to the squares 1, 2, 3. Lastly, if the third block is at 7, rotate 3, 6, and the vacant square round C B to the positions 8, 5, 2, and again the three given blocks are in a six-squared rectangle (A F), and can be brought to the required order in squares 7, 4, 1, and thence rotated round A B to squares 1, 2, 3. These are all possible cases ; and as, after thus correctly filling the squares 1, 2, 3, the remaining five blocks are in a six-square rectangle D B, we can arrange them in any order we please except as regards the two which, in the final position, occupy squares 7 and 8.

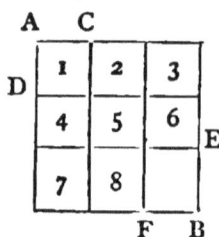

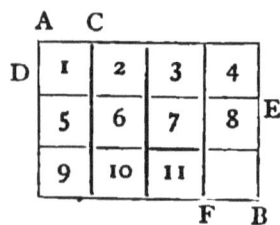

FIG. 16.

FIG. 17.

Next take a rectangle of four squares by three as A B, Fig. 17, where the won position for such a rectangle is shown. Here we have to show that a given set of nine blocks can be brought, in a given order, into the squares of 1, 2, 3, 4, 5, 6, 7, 8, and 9. It will be most convenient in this case to begin by getting into the squares 1, 5, 9, the proper blocks for those squares. (It will be seen at once from what follows, that if the rectangle were three squares broad and four high, instead of three high and four broad, we should begin by the top row of three, the same method applying in all other respects to each case.) Now, of the three blocks for the left-hand column, two must be either in the square C B or in the rectangle D B. In the former case they can be brought at once to the squares 4, 8, in the latter they can be brought to 5, 9, and rotated round A B to the squares 4, 8. Let the vacant square be then brought to the corner B, if not already there. Then, if the third block of the three is in the square C B, the last case enables us at once to bring the three in the right sequence to the squares 2, 3, 4, whence they can be rotated round A B to the required squares 1, 5, 9. If the third block is at 1 or 5, shift the blocks 6, 10, and 11 (11 to corner square). This frees the square 5, and the second case enables us to bring the three blocks to squares 1, 2, 3, in the rectangle A E, whence we rotate them to 1, 5, 9. If the third block is at 9, rotate 4, 8, and the vacant square to the positions 11, 7, 3, and then the three blocks are in a square of nine squares (A F), and can be brought at once in the required order to the squares 1, 5, 9. Then the rest of the rectangle, namely, the square C B, can be arranged, as shown in the last case, so that all the blocks, except those for the squares 10, 11, are in assigned positions.

Note, also, that in this case we might have begun by getting into the right position the four blocks intended to occupy the squares 1, 2, 3, 4. Thus, having first got the blocks for the squares 2, 3, 4, into the squares 9, 5, 1, in the way already shown for *any* three blocks, we bring to the square 10 the block intended for square 1, doing this by rotation around C B or C F, as the case may require, without touching the blocks in 1, 5, 9 ; then rotation around A B brings the four blocks into the required squares, 1, 2, 3, 4, in the assigned order.

U 2

Lastly, we reach the case of the Fifteen Puzzle itself shown in the won position in Fig. 6, and again in Fig. 18. We have to show that a given set of 13 of these blocks can be brought to the squares 1, 2, 3, 4, 5, 6, 7, 8, 9, 10, 11, 12, 13, in an assigned order. Here the reasoning is of precisely the same kind as in the two preceding paragraphs. Three of the four blocks meant for squares 1, 2, 3, 4, must be either in the rectangle C B or in the rectangle D B. In either case we can bring them (directly in one case, by rotation around D B in the other) to the squares 4, 8, 12. If the remaining block is in the oblong C F, we get the four into right order, down the right hand column of the oblong C B by the last case, and rotate to the required squares 1, 2, 3, 4. If the fourth block is in one of the squares 1, 5, 9, rotate the blocks in 11, 15 (bringing the one in 15 to corner B), and then the four blocks lie in the oblong A E, and can be brought to the squares 1, 2, 3, 4, as in last case. Lastly, if the fourth block is at 13, push down the blocks in 4, 8, 12, rotate those in 7, 3, bringing the one in 3 to corner square 4, and then the four blocks are in the oblong D B, and can be brought into the lowest row in the required order, as in the last case, and thence rotated to the squares 1, 2, 3, 4. After this, the rest of the square, namely, the oblong D B, can be arranged, as shown in the last case, so that all the blocks, except those in the squares 14, 15, are in assigned positions.

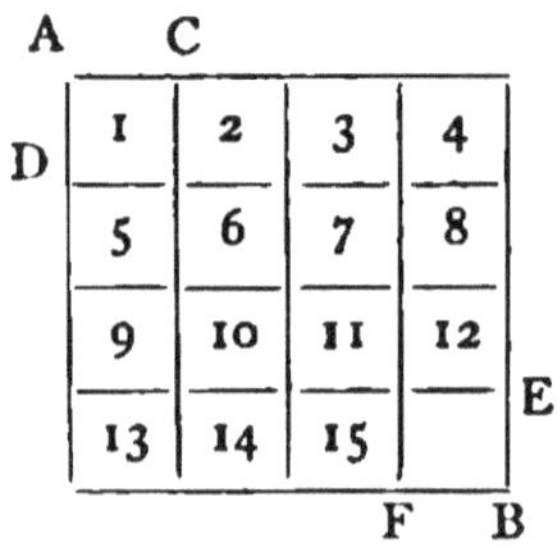

FIG. 18.

I might here go on to show that in any square or oblong whatever, no matter how great the number of blocks in the length and breadth, all except the last two can be brought into any assigned order. To do this, all that would be necessary would be to show that, if in an oblong or square of given numbers of blocks in length and breadth the blocks can so be arranged, they can also be arranged in an oblong or square having one more row added either to its length or breadth. For then, having already shown that we can so arrange an oblong of two by three, an oblong of two by four, a square of three by three, an oblong of three by four, and a square of four by four, it follows that we can similarly arrange an oblong of three by five and of four by five, a square of five by five: and so on, without limit. But I leave this as an exercise for the reader, noting only that the method is precisely similar to that by which the last case above dealt with was obtained from the last but one, that from the preceding, and so forth.

In a paper which appeared in the *Australasian* for August 21, 1880, I have proved the above relations, and also the general case, in another way, not quite so simple but more concise ; showing that from any given position a certain number of positions must always be obtainable, and that number being (with the given position) exactly one-half of the total number of possible arrangements, must include all the cases of its own kind, that is, either winning or losing as the case may be.

I have there also established the following rules for distinguishing winning from losing positions in an oblong or rectangle of any number of squares in the length and breadth.

First, if the number both of horizontal and vertical rows be even (as in the Fifteen Puzzle), the won position, in which the blocks succeed each other in numerical sequence, following the lines as in reading, and leaving the last square vacant, can be obtained from any position in which the ' total displacement ' and the number of the partly vacant square are either both even or both odd ; but if the 'total displacement' is even and the number of the partly vacant line odd, or *vice versâ*, the won position cannot be obtained.

Secondly, if the number of horizontal rows be odd, and the number of vertical rows even, then the won position can be obtained if the 'total displacement' is even and the number of the partly vacant line odd, or *vice versâ*. But if the 'total displacement' and the number of the incomplete line are either both odd or both even, the won position cannot be obtained.

Thirdly and Fourthly. If the number of vertical rows be odd, then, whether the number of horizontal lines be (iii) even or (iv) odd, the won position can be obtained if the 'total displacement' is even, and cannot be obtained if the 'total displacement' is odd.

These four laws include all possible cases.

Let me add in conclusion, that the total number of possible arrangements in a square of ten blocks in the side is so great, that if we imagine each case represented by a tiny globe one millionth of an inch in diameter, and these globes gathered in the form of a great sphere, the extent of that sphere would be greater than that of the entire region of space over which the mightiest telescope yet made by man extends his survey, though, from the remotest star reached by such a telescope, light, with its stupendous velocity of 187,000 miles a second, takes thousands of years in reaching this earth.

It may be noticed, in conclusion, that the above study of the ways of solving the puzzle for six-block and eight-block rectangles will be found to indicate the proper way of dealing with the only cases of difficulty which ever arise in dealing with the Fifteen Puzzle. I wrote the whole of this paper, for instance, without having before me any actual set of blocks, simply drawing mental pictures of the various cases before writing the paragraphs respectively relating to them. Yet, on the first trial with the actual puzzle, I found that four or five minutes sufficed to resolve any position into the final (won or lost) position of its own kind ; and after half-an-hour's practice (based on the principles above explained) I found the solutions averaged only two minutes.

ETNA.

THERE is a marked contrast between the circumstances of the eruption of Etna in the summer of 1879, and those of the last preceding eruption. For many years the great South European volcanic system had shown but few signs of disturbance, and those only slight. Vesuvius had occasionally threatened an outbreak. The crater of that mountain had filled several times to the brim, and had once or twice overflowed ; but there had been no great eruption of Vesuvius. Etna had been almost entirely quiescent for the preceding ten years. The other less important outlets of the South European volcanic system had been equally free from disturbance.

It was otherwise when in November 1868 Etna burst into eruption. During thirteen months the volcanic system of Southern Europe had been disturbed by subterranean movements. Scarcely a single portion of the wide area included under that name had been free from occasional shocks of earthquake. There had been shocks at Constantinople, at Bucharest, at Malta, and at Gibraltar. Mount Vesuvius, the most active though not in all respects the most important of the outlets by which that system finds relief, had been in a state of activity during the whole of the. preceding year, and three several times in actual eruption. But it had seemed as though Vesuvius—owing perhaps to changes which had taken place in its subterranean ducts and conduits—had been unable to give complete relief to the forces then at work beneath the southern parts of

Europe. Whenever Vesuvius had been quiescent for a
while during 1868, earthquakes occurring at far distant
places not only showed the connection which exists between
the action of Vesuvius and the condition of regions far
remote from Vesuvius, but that the great Neapolitan outlet
was not able to relieve as usual the remote parts of that
wide volcanic region. Even in England and Ireland there
were earthquakes, at times corresponding significantly with
the temporary quiescence of Vesuvius. In fact, scarcely
ten days had passed after the occurrence of an earthquake
which alarmed the inhabitants of Western Europe, before a
great eruption of Vesuvius began. A vast cone was thrown
up, from which the imprisoned fires burst forth in rivers of
molten lava ; and round the base of this cone other smaller
ones formed themselves which added their efforts to that of
the central crater and wrought more mischief than in any
eruption of Vesuvius since that of 1797.

But, enormous as was the quantity of lava which those
cones poured forth, it would seem that Vesuvius was still
unable to give perfect relief to the imprisoned gases and
fluids which had long disturbed the South of Europe. All
that Vesuvius could do had been done ; the smaller cones
had discharged the lava which communicated directly with
them, and had then sunk to rest ; the great cone alone continued—but with diminished energy—to pour forth masses
of burning rock and streams of liquid lava. That the imprisoned subterranean fires had not fully found relief was
shown by the occurrence of an earthquake at Bucharest,
late on the evening of November 27, which was only a day
after the partial cessation of the eruption of Vesuvius. Probably the masses of liquid fire which had been flowing
towards Vesuvius had collected beneath the whole of that
wide district which underlies Etna, Stromboli, and the
Neapolitan vents. Be this as it may, it is certain that but a
few hours after the occurrence of the earthquake in Walla-
chia, Mount Etna began to show signs of activity, and by
the evening of November 28, 1868, was in violent eruption.

When we consider these circumstances in connection with the recognised fact that Etna is an outlet of the same volcanic system, we can hardly be surprised that the ineffectual efforts of Vesuvius should have been followed by an eruption of the great Sicilian volcano. We can imagine that the lakes of fire which · underlie the Neapolitan vent should have been inundated, so to speak, by the continual inrush of fresh matter, and that thus an overflow should have taken place into the vast caverns beneath the dome of Etna which had been partially cleared when the Sicilian mountain was in eruption in 1865. During a whole year some such process had probably been going on, until at length the forces which had been silently gathering themselves were able to overcome the resistance of the matter which stopped up the outlets of Etna, and the mountain was forced into violent and remarkably sudden action.

Unlike Vesuvius, Etna has always, within historic times, been recognised as an active volcano. Diodorus Siculus speaks of an eruption which took place before the Trojan war, and was so terrible in character as to drive away the Sicani who had peopled a neighbouring district. We learn also from Thucydides that in the sixth year of the Peloponnesian war a lava-stream destroyed the suburbs of Catania. This eruption, says the historian, was the third which had taken place since the island had been colonised by the Greeks. Classical readers will scarcely need to be reminded of Pindar's graphic description of the eruption which took place fifty years before the one referred to by Thucydides. Although the poet only alludes to the mountain in passing, he has yet succeeded in presenting with a few skilful strokes the solemn grandeur of ancient Etna, the scene of the struggles of the buried giant Typhœus. He portrays the snowy mountain as 'the pillar of the heavens, the nurse of eternal snows, hiding within deep caverns the fountains of unapproachable fire ; by day a column of eddying smoke, by night a bright and ruddy flame ; while masses of burning rock roll ever with loud uproar into the sea.'

The cone of Etna rises to more than twice the height of Mount Vesuvius. Of old, indeed, the Sicilians assigned to their mountain a height not falling very far short of that of the grandest of the Alpine mountains. But in 1815, Captain (the late Admiral) Smyth ascertained by a careful series of trigonometrical observations that the true height of the mountain is 10,874 feet. The Catanians were indignant that a young, and at that time undistinguished, Englishman should have ventured to deprive their mountain of nearly 2,000 feet of the height which had been assigned to it by their own observer Recupero, and they refused to accept the new measurement. Nine years later, however, Sir John Herschel from barometrical observations estimated the mountain's height at 10,872½ feet. The close agreement between the two results was spoken of by Herschel—Lyell tells us—as a 'happy accident;' but, as Dr. Wollaston re-marked, 'it was one of those accidents which would not have happened to two fools.'

The figure of Etna is a somewhat flattened cone, which would be very symmetrical were it not that on the eastern side it is broken by a deep valley called the Val del Bove, which runs nearly to the summit of the mountain, and descending half-way down its banks is connected with a second and narrower valley, called the Val di Colonna. The cone is divided into three regions called the desert, the woody, and the fertile regions. The first of these is a waste of lava and scoriæ, from the centre of which uprises the great cone. The woody region encircles the desert land to a width of six or seven miles. Over this region oaks, pines, and chestnut-trees grow luxuriantly; while here and there are to be seen groves of cork and beech. Surrounding the woody region is a delightful and well-cultivated country lying upon the outskirts of the mountain and forming the fertile region. This part of Etna is well inhabited, and thickly covered with olives, vines, and fruit-trees. One of the most singular peculiarities of the mountain is the preva-lence over its flanks of a multitude of minor cones, nearly a hundred of which are to be seen in various parts of the woody and fertile regions. Of these, Sir Charles Lyell remarks, that 'although they appear but trifling irregularities when viewed from a distance as subordinate parts of so imposing and colossal a mountain, they would, nevertheless, be deemed hills of considerable magnitude in almost any other region.'

It has been calculated that the circumference of the cone is fully eighty-seven English miles; but that the whole district over which the lava extends has nearly twice that circuit.

Of the earlier eruptions of Mount Etna we have not received very full or satisfactory records. It is related that in 1537 the principal cone, which had been 320 feet high, was swallowed up within the hollow depths of the mountain. And again, in 1693, during the course of an earthquake which shook the whole of Sicily and destroyed no fewer than 60,000 persons, the mountain lost a large portion of its height, insomuch that, according to Boccone, it could not be seen from several parts of the Valdemone whence it had before been clearly visible. Minor cones upon the flanks of the mountain were diminished in height during other outbursts in a different manner. Thus in the great eruption of 1444, Monte Peluso was reduced to two-thirds of its former height, by a vast lava-stream which encircled it on every side. Yet, though another current has recently taken the same course, the height of this minor mountain is still three or four hundred feet. There is also, says Sir Charles Lyell, 'a cone called Monte Nucilla, near Nicolosi, round the base of which successive currents have flowed, and showers of ashes have fallen, since the time of history, till at last, during an eruption in 1536, the surrounding plain was so raised, that the top of the cone alone was left projecting above the general level.'

But the first eruption of which we have complete and authentic records is the one which occurred in the year 1669. An earthquake had taken place by which Nicolosi, a town situated about twenty miles from the summit of Etna, was levelled to the ground. Near the site of the destroyed town two gulfs opened soon after, and from these gulfs such enormous quantities of sand and scoriæ were thrown out that a mountain having a double peak was formed in less than four months. But, remarkable as was the evidence thus afforded of the energy of the volcanic action which was at work beneath the flames of the mountain, a yet more striking event presently attracted the attention of the alarmed inhabitants of the neighbouring country. On a sudden, and with a crash which resounded for miles around, a fissure, *twelve miles in length,* opened along the flanks of the disturbed mountain. The fissure extended nearly to the summit of Etna. It was very deep—how deep is unknown—but only six feet in width. Along its whole length there was emitted a most vivid light. Then, after a brief interval, five similar fissures opened one after another, emitting enormous volumes of smoke, and giving vent to bellowing sounds which could be heard at a distance of more than forty miles.

At length the eruption commenced in earnest. The volume of lava which was poured forth was greater than any that has ever been known to flow from the mountain during historical times. According to the estimate of Ferrara, no less than 140 millions of cubic yards of lava were poured down the sides of the mountain. The current, after melting down the foundations of a hill called Mompiliere, overflowed no fewer than fourteen towns and villages, some of which had as many as three thousand and four thousand inhabitants. Alarmed at the progress of the sea of lava which threatened to overwhelm their city, the Catanians upreared a rampart of enormous strength and sixty feet in height. So stoutly was this bulwark established that the lava was unable to break it or to burn it down. The molten sea gradually accumulated, until at length it rose above the summit of the rampart, from which it poured in a fiery cascade, and destroyed the nearer part of the city. 'The wall was not thrown down, however,' says Sir Charles Lyell, 'but was discovered long afterwards by excavations made in the rock by the Prince of Biscari ; so that the traveller may now see the solid lava curling over the top of the rampart as if still in the very act of falling. The current had performed a course of fifteen miles before it entered the sea, where it was still six hundred yards broad and forty feet deep. It covered some territories in the environs of Catania, which had never before been visited by the lavas of Etna. While moving on, its surface was in general a mass of solid rock ; and its mode of advancing, as is usual with lava-streams, was by the occasional fissuring of the solid walls. A gentle-man of Catania, named Pappalardo, desiring to secure the city from the approach of the threatening torrent, went out with a party of fifty men whom he had dressed in skins to protect them from the heat, and armed with iron crows and hooks. They broke open one of the solid walls which flanked the current near Belpasso, and immediately forth issued a rivulet of melted matter which took the direction of Paterno ; but the inhabitants of that town, being alarmed for their safety, took up arms and put a stop to further operations.'

In the eruption of 1755 a singular circumstance oc-curred. From the Val del Bove, usually dry and arid, there flowed a tremendous volume of water forming a stream two miles broad, and in some places 34 feet deep. It flowed in the first part of its course at the rate of two miles in three minutes. It is said to have been salt, and many supposed it had been in some way drawn from the sea, since its volume exceeded that of all the snow on the mountain. It has, however, since been found that vast reservoirs of snow and ice are accumulated in different parts of the mountain beneath the lava. The snow was melted by the heat of the rising lava, and was made salt by vaporous exhalations.

Of the singular solidity of the walls of an advancing lava-stream, Recupero has related a remarkable instance. During the eruption of 1766, he and his guide had ascended one of those minor cones which lie, as we have said, on the flanks of the mountain, and from the summit of this hill they watched with feelings of awe the slow advance of a fiery river two miles and a half in breadth. Suddenly they saw a fissure opening in the solid walls which encircled the front of the current of lava ; and then, from out this fissure, two streams of lava leapt forth and ran rapidly towards the hill on which the observers were standing. They had just time to make their escape, when, turning round, they saw the hill surrounded by the burning lava. Fifteen minutes later the foundations of the hill had been melted down, and the whole mass floated away upon the lava, with which it presently became completely incorporated.

It would be a mistake, however, to suppose that such an occurrence as the one we have just related is often observed. On the contrary, it seems that when burning lava comes into contact with rocky matter, the latter is usually very little affected. It is only when fresh portions of incandescent lava are successively brought into contact with fusible rocks that these can be completely melted. Sir Charles Lyell quotes a remarkable story in illustration of the small effects which are produced by lava when there is not a continual supply of fresh material in an incandescent state. ' On the site of Mompiliere, one of the towns overflowed in the great eruption of 1669, an excavation was made in 1704 ; and by immense labour the workmen reached, at the depth of 35 feet, the gate of the principal church, where there were three statues held in high veneration. One of these, together with a bell, some money, and other articles, was extracted in a good state of preservation from beneath a great arch formed by the lava.' This will seem the more extraordinary when it is remembered that eight years after the eruption the lava was still so hot at Catania, that it was impossible to hold the hand in some of the fissures.

Among the most remarkable of the eruptions of Etna which have taken place in recent times are those of 1811 and 1819.

In 1811, according to Gemmelaro, the great crater gave vent, at first, to a series of tremendous detonations, from which it was judged that the dome of the mountain had become completely filled with molten lava, which was seeking to escape. At length a violent shock was experienced, and from what followed it would seem that by this shock the whole internal framework of the mountain had been rent open. For, first a stream of lava began to pour out from a gap in the cone not far from the summit. Then another stream burst out at an opening directly under the first, and at some distance from it. Then a third opening appeared, still lower down ; then a fourth, and so on, until no less than seven openings had been formed in succession, all lying in the same vertical plane. From the way in which these openings appeared, and the peculiarity that each stream of lava had ceased to flow before the next lower one burst forth, it is supposed that the internal framework of the mountain had been rent open gradually, from the summit downwards, so as to suffer the internal column of lava to subside to a lower and lower level, by escaping through the successive vents. This, at least, is the opinion which Scrope has expressed on the subject, in his treatise on ' Volcanoes.'

The eruption of 1819 was in some respects even more remarkable. I have already mentioned the Val del Bove, which breaks in upon the dome of Etna upon the eastern side. In the eruption of 1819 the whole of this great valley was covered by a sea of burning lava. Three large caverns had opened not far from the fissures, out of which the lava had flowed in 1811 ; and from these, flames, smoke, red-hot cinders, and sand were flung out with singular impetuosity. Presently another cavern opened lower down, but still no lava flowed from the mountain. At length a fifth opening formed, yet lower, and from this a torrent of lava poured out, which spread over the whole width of the Val del Bove, and flowed no less than four miles in the first two days. This torrent of lava was soon after enlarged by the accession of enormous streams of burning matter flowing from the three caverns which had formed in the first instance. The river of lava at length reached the head of the Colonna Valley, where there is a vast and almost vertical precipice, over which the lava streamed in a cataract of fire. But there was a peculiarity about the falling lava which gave to the scene a strange and awful character. As the burning cascade rushed down, it became hardened through the cooling effects due to its contact with the rocky face of the precipice. Thus, the matter which had flowed over the head of the valley like a river of fire fell at the foot of the precipice in the form of solid masses of rock. The crash with which the falling crags struck the bottom of the valley is described as inconceivably awful. At first, indeed, the Catanians feared that a new eruption had burst out in that part of the mountain, since the air was filled with clouds of dust, produced by the abrasion of the face of the precipice as the hardened masses swept over it.

The length of time during which the lava of 1819 continued to flow down the slopes of the great valleys is well worth noticing. Mr. Scrope saw the current advancing at the rate of a yard per hour nine months after the occurrence of the eruption. The mode of its advance was remarkable. As the mass slowly pushed its way onward, the lower portions were arrested by the resistance of the ground, and thus the upper part would first protrude itself, and then, being unsupported, would fall over. The fallen mass would then in its turn be covered by a mass of more liquid lava, which poured over it from above. And thus 'the current had all the appearance of a huge heap of rough and large cinders rolling over and over upon itself by the effect of an extremely slow propulsion from behind. The contraction of the crust as it solidified, and the friction of the scoriform cakes against one another, produced a crackling sound. Within the crevices a dull red heat might be seen by night, and vapour issuing in considerable quantity was visible by day.'

The circumstance that Etna uprears its head high above the limit of perpetual snow has a remarkable bearing on the characteristics of this volcano. The peculiarity is touched on by Pindar in the words already quoted, in which he speaks of Etna as 'the nurse of everlasting frost concealing within deep caverns the fountains of unapproachable fire.' It will be readily conceived that the action of molten lava upon the enormous masses of snow, which lie upon the upper part of the mountain, must be calculated to produce —under special circumstances—the most remarkable and, unfortunately, the most disastrous effects. It does not always happen that fire and ice are thus brought into dangerous contact. But records are not wanting of catastrophes produced in this way. In 1755, for example, a tremendous flood was occasioned by the flow of the two streams of lava from the highest crater. The whole mountain was at the time (March 2nd) covered with snow, and the torrent of lava formed by the union of the two streams was no less than three miles in width. It will be readily conceived that the flow of such a mass of molten fire as this over the accumulated snows of the past winter produced the most disastrous effects. 'A frightful inundation resulted,' says Sir Charles Lyell, 'which devastated the sides of the mountain for eight miles in length, and afterwards covered the lower flanks of Etna (where they were less steep), together with the plains near the sea, with great deposits of sand, scoriæ, and blocks of lava.'

In connection with this part of the subject I may mention the singular and apparently paradoxical circumstance that, in 1828, a large mass of ice was found, which had been preserved for many years from melting by the fact that a current of red-hot lava had flowed over it. We might doubt the occurrence of so strange an event, were it not that the fact is vouched for by Sir Charles Lyell, who visited the spot where the ice had been discovered. He thus relates the circumstances of the discovery :—'The extraordinary heat experienced in the South of Europe, during the summer and autumn of 1828, caused the supplies of snow and ice which had been preserved in the spring of that year for the use of

x

Catania, and the adjoining parts of Sicily, and the island of Malta, to fail entirely. Great distress was consequently felt for want of a commodity regarded in those countries as one of the necessaries of life rather than an article of luxury, and the abundance of which contributes in some of the larger cities to the salubrity of the water and the general health of the community. The magistrates of Catania applied to Signor Gemmelaro, in the hope that his local knowledge of Etna might enable him to point out some crevice or natural grotto on the mountain where drift snow was still preserved. Nor were they disappointed ; for he had long suspected that a small mass of perennial ice at the foot of the highest cone was part of a large continuous glacier covered by a lava-current. Having procured a large body of workmen, he quarried into this ice, and proved the superposition of the lava for several hundred yards, so as completely to satisfy himself that nothing but the subsequent flowing of the lava over the ice could account for the position of the glacier ' (in other words, the ice had not accumulated in a cavern of moderate extent accidentally formed beneath overhanging lava masses). ' Unfortunately for the geologist,' adds Lyell, ' the ice was so extremely hard, and the excavation so expensive, that there is no probability of the operations being renewed.'

This strange phenomenon is explained, in all likelihood, by the fact that the drift of snow over which the lava flowed had become covered with a layer of volcanic sand before the descent of the molten matter. The effect of sand in resisting the passage of heat is well known. Nasmyth the inventor of the steam-hammer illustrated this property in a remarkable manner, by pouring eight tons of molten iron into a cauldron one-fourth of an inch thick, lined with a layer of sand and clay somewhat more than half an inch thick. When the fused metal had been twenty minutes in the cauldron the outside was still so cool that the palm of the hand could be applied to it without inconvenience. And lava consolidates so quickly that there must soon have been formed over the snow a solid covering, strong enough to resist the effects of the fresh molten matter which was continually streaming over it. In this way we may readily conceive, as Sir Charles Lyell has remarked, that a glacier 10,000 feet above the sea level would endure as long as the snows of Mont Blanc, unless heated by volcanic heat from below.

It is worthy of notice that in the Antarctic seas there is an island called Deception Island, which is almost entirely composed, according to the authority of Lieut. Kendall, of alternate layers of ice and volcanic ashes.

One of the most perplexing subjects to geologists is the existence of so remarkable a valley as the Val del Bove, breaking the contour of the dome of Etna nearly to the summit. It must be remembered that there are few subjects which have been more carefully examined than the question of the formation of valleys and ravines. The primary agent recognised by geologists is the action of subterranean forces in upheaving and depressing the land. In this way, doubtless, all the principal valleys have been formed. But fluviatile influences have also to be considered : and a valley which exists upon the flank of a mountain may, in nearly every instance, be ascribed to the action of running water.

In the case of the Val del Bove, however, we are forced to come to a different conclusion. If this valley had been formed by the action of running water in some long-past era of the mountain's history, the chasm would have deepened as it approached the base. On the contrary, the precipices which bound the Val del Bove are loftiest at the upper extremity, and gradually diminish in height as we approach the lower regions of the mountain.

Nor can we imagine that the valley has been formed by a landslip. The dimensions of the depression are altogether too great for such an explanation to be available. And, passing over this circumstance, we are met by the consideration that, if the land which once filled this valley had 'slipped' (in the ordinary sense of the term), we should see the traces of the movement, and be able to detect the existence of the removed mass. Not only is there no evidence of a motion of this sort, but the slightest examination of the valley at once disposes of the supposition that such a motion can at any time have taken place.

It remains only that we suppose the valley to have been caused by the bodily subsidence of the whole mass which had formerly filled up what is now wanting to the dome-shaped figure of the mountain. And the subsidence must have taken place in a sudden manner,—not necessarily in a single shock, but certainly not by a slow process of sinking. For the mass which has sunk is sharply separated from the rest, so that the precipitous walls of the valley exhibit the structure of the mountain's frame, to a depth of from 3,000 to 4,000 feet below the summit of the cone. In other words, a portion of the crust has been separated from the rest and has then sunk bodily down, leaving the remainder unchanged.

When we consider the dimensions of the valley, such an event becomes very startling. 'The Val del Bove,' says Lyell, ' is a vast amphitheatre, four or five miles in diameter, surrounded by nearly vertical precipices.' One might almost be prepared to doubt that such a valley as this could be formed in the manner described, were it not that within recent times we have had evidence of the occurrence of similar events. During a violent earthquake and volcanic eruption which took place in Java in 1822, the face of the mountain Galongoon was totally changed, 'its summits broken down, and one side, which had been covered with trees, became an enormous gulf in the form of a semicircle. This cavity was about midway between the summit and the plain, and surrounded by steep rocks.' Yet more remarkable was the great subsidence which took place in the year 1772 on Papendayang, the largest volcano in the island of Java. On that occasion, ' an extent of ground fifteen miles in length and six in breadth, covered by no less than forty villages, was engulfed, and the cone of the mountain lost 4,000 feet of its height.'

There is nothing unreasonable, therefore, in supposing that some such event may have resulted in the formation of the strange valley which mars the dome-shaped figure of Mount Etna, although no such events have been witnessed in the neighbourhood in recent times.

One singular feature of the valley remains to be mentioned. The vertical face of the precipices which bound it are broken by what, at a distant view, appear to be dark buttresses, strangely diversified in figure, and of tremendous altitude. On a closer inspection, however, these strange objects are seen to be composed of lava jutting out through the face of the cliffs. Being composed of harder materials than the cliffs, they waste away less rapidly, and thus it is that they are seen to stand out like buttresses. Now, we would invite the close attention of the reader to this part of our subject, because, as it seems to us, it illustrates in a singularly interesting manner the mode in which volcanic cones are affected during eruption.

We have seen that in the eruption of 1811 there was evidence of a perpendicular rent having taken place in the internal framework of Etna, and in 1669 a fissure was formed which extended right through the outer crust. In one case lava was forced through the rent, and burst out at the side of the mountain. In the other, the brilliant light which was emitted indicated the presence of molten lava deep down in the fissure. Now, when we combine these circumstances with the *dykes* seen in the Val del Bove, and with the similar appearances seen round the ancient crater of Vesuvius, we can come, as it appears to me, to but one conclusion. Before and during an eruption, the lava which is seeking for exit must be forced with such tremendous energy against the internal framework of the mountain's dome, as to fracture and rend the crust, either in one or two enormous fissures, or in a multitude of smaller ones. It does not follow that all or any of the fissures would be visible, because the outer surfaces of the crust may not be rent. Into the fissures thus formed the lava is forced by the pressure from below, and, there solidifying, the crust of the dome remains as strong, after the liquid lava has sunk to its usual level, as it was before the eruption. When we see dykes situated as in the Val del Bove, we learn that the fissures caused by the pressure of the lava extend far down the flanks of a volcanic mountain. That they are numerous is evidenced by the fact that those seen in the Val del Bove amount, according to Sir Charles Lyell, to 'thousands in number.'

And perhaps we may understand from such considerations as these the manner in which the Val del Bove itself was formed. For a wide strip of country between two great fissures might be so waved and shaken by the action of the sea of molten lava beneath as to be fractured cross-wise ; and then, on the subsidence of the lava, the whole mass below the fracture would sink down bodily. We gain an extended conception of the energy of the forces which are at work during volcanic eruptions, when we see that they thus have power to rend the whole framework of a mountain.

Among recent eruptions of Mount Etna, one of the most singular was that of the year 1852, which began so suddenly that a party of Englishmen, who were ascending the mountain, and had nearly reached the foot of the highest cone, were only able to escape with great difficulty. The eruption which had commenced so abruptly did not cease with corresponding rapidity, but continued with but few slight intermissions, for fully nine months.

The eruption in progress as I write has not yet attained any remarkable degree of energy, though possibly before these lines appear, another story may have to be told. In the last week of May a fissure opened on the north side of the mountain, 'and thence volumes of smoke and flame were seen to issue from it. From the crater itself, a great cloud of black ashes has been poured forth, rendering the mountain invisible and obscuring the rays of the sun' (by which the writer must surely mean obstructing their passage), 'even at a distance of many miles. These ashes have been carried far and wide, and have even covered the ground as far away as Reggio, on the adjacent coast of Calabria. Three new craters have opened in the direction of Randazzo, on the north side of the mountain, and the lava is running rapidly towards the town of Francavilla, where great alarm is felt, though that town is situated beyond the river Alcantara, and on the very outskirts of the region usually threatened by eruptions. On the opposite side of the mountain, Palermo and the adjacent villa of Santa Maria di Licodia are reported to be greatly alarmed.' But at present the direction of the disturbance is towards the north, and the chief danger lies therefore also in that direction. The new craters, and the fissure with which the eruption began, lie all on the northern side of the mountain. 'The stream of lava, which is estimated to be 70 mètres' (about 75 yards) 'in width, is flowing in a direction somewhere between Francavilla and Randazzo, and seems to have reached the high road which encircles the mountain, and connects the latter town with the villages Linguaglosso and Piedimonte. These villages are inshrouded in a canopy of ashes, and almost total darkness prevails in them. None of the ordinary concomitants of a great eruption seem to be absent. Balls of fire, or what are taken for such, are hurled into the air from the new craters and fissures, and, having reached a great height, they burst with a loud crash. Reports like the rolling of artillery are heard in the night, while night and day alike the stream of lava flows stealthily and irresistibly on, until by the latest accounts it has reached to within a few miles of Linguaglossa.'

Whether the eruption now in progress will attain the dimensions of the more remarkable of those which have preceded it, remains to be seen. As the last took place ten years ago, and was considerable, though following one which has occurred but three-and-a-half years earlier, it seems not unlikely that the present may be an important eruption.

What we know already respecting it, tends to confirm the belief of Sir Charles Lyell, that, if the earth's internal fires are diminishing in intensity, the diminution takes place very slowly. A process of change may be going on which will result one day in the cessation of all subterranean movements. But the rate at which such a process is going on is so slow at present as to be imperceptible. We cannot point to a time within the historical era, or even within that far wider range of duration which is covered by geological records, at which the earth's internal forces were decidedly superior in energy to those at present in action. Nor is this to be regarded as of evil import, but altogether the reverse. The work achieved by subterranean action, destructive though its immediate effects may often appear, is absolutely necessary to the welfare and happiness of the human race. It is to the reproductive energy of the earth's internal forces that we are indebted for the existence of continents and islands on which warm-blooded animals can live. 'Had the primeval world been constructed as it now exists,' says Sir John Herschel, ' time enough has elapsed, and force enough directed to that end has been in activity, to have long ago destroyed every vestige of land.' So that, raising our thoughts from present interests to the future fortunes of the human race, we may agree with Sir Charles Lyell that the most promising evidence of the permanence of the present order of things consists in the fact that the energy of subterranean movements is always uniform, when considered with reference to the whole of the earth's globe.

WEATHER FORECASTS.

A FEW years ago attention was called to the circumstance that whereas, in the United States, daily weather forecasts appeared whereof rather more than four-fifths were correct, our English weather reports were limited to announcements of the weather which had prevailed the day before, except in a few cases where storms or transient disturbances were predicted with a fair share of success. At that time it seemed to be the general opinion of British meteorologists that such weather warnings as were then and are still issued in America could not be given in this country. Mr. Scott, the director of the Meteorological Office, said only four years ago that the results attained in the United States ' furnished no precedent for us,' because ' the area covered by the telegraphic system there is so much larger than in Western Europe, irrespective of the fact' that ' the system is military and provided on a most liberal scale with funds.' Since that time a system of daily weather forecasting has been arranged, which has been almost as successful as the American system, notwithstanding the serious difficulties with which the meteorologists of Western Europe have to contend. Our meteorologists have learned to recognise certain rules of the weather, which, though not invariable, are yet fulfilled in a large proportion of cases. They have learned to indicate the weather phenomena at any given time in such a way that these rules can be applied quickly and correctly—correctly, it will be understood, in this sense, that the result· indicated is correctly described as the most probable though the forecast accordingly made may not be fulfilled by the event. Those little maps which appeared in *The Times* and other newspapers for many months before forecasts began to be made illustrate well the general principle on which weather predictions for the British Isles or for Western Europe, depend. Compare even the simplest of these charts with a table of meteorological statistics for fifty or sixty stations, and the value of the graphic method is at once recognised. The clearest head could not, after hours of study, deduce any law from the most complete and elaborate table of meteorological statistics. But it is by no means difficult to construct a chart from such a table, and the chart shows at a glance the state of the weather for the whole region over which meteorological stations are distributed. We see the lines of equal barometrical pressure (that is, of equal atmospheric density), the regions of low pressure around which the winds usually blow (as the wind-arrows show in cyclonic circulations), the areas of high pressure, or anti-cyclones as they are called, and we learn whether the general pressure over the whole region is above or below the average; the direction and force of the winds are indicated simply and clearly; the temperatures are shown; and we see also where rain is falling, so learning whether the area of low pressure is, as usual, wet, and, if so, in what degree, or whether it is simply cloudy, and the nature of the clouds prevailing there and elsewhere. A single map thus teaches a good deal. But yet more is learned when the map for a given time is compared with the series of preceding maps. For we thus learn in what way the areas of low barometric pressure are travelling—whether, as usual, from a southerly or westerly to a northerly or easterly point, or (as occasionally happens) from a northerly or easterly to a southerly or westerly point. We note whether as they travel they are gathering or losing moisture; whether the wind is increasing or diminishing in force at given distances from the cyclone centre; whether the curves of equal barometric pressure are drawing closer (which indicates sharp pressure gradients or rapid change of pressure) or drawing apart (which indicates that pressure is becoming more equable). We note, also, how temperature is changing with the progress of the area or areas of low or of high pressure, whether the skies are clearing, or darkening, and so forth. From such indications the probable progress of weather changes during the next few hours can be inferred, with more or less confidence, according as the changes over the region of observation have been steady or the reverse during the preceding hours or days. In some cases it becomes possible to forecast with tolerable confidence the progress of the weather during more than twenty-four hours ; in others, though forecasts may be issued very little reliance can be placed upon them, simply because the circumstances of the preceding changes indicate that the atmosphere is in an exceptionally variable condition. It is to be noticed, also, that when the skies are generally overcast the chances of correct prediction are considerably diminished for this reason, simply that the upper air-currents, which have a most important influence in producing weather changes, cannot at such times be studied, our only means of determining their direction and rate consisting in the observation of the movements taking place in the higher cloud-regions. It is also a great assistance to the meteorologist to know the nature of the higher clouds above different parts of the region where observations are made, for some of the most important weather changes depend principally on the temperature of the upper air-currents, and this can only be inferred from the appearance of the clouds which travel or are formed in those higher regions.

So many of our weather changes travel. from S.W. to N.E., or from some southerly or westerly towards some northerly or easterly point, that the prediction of weather changes in the British Isles is rendered much more difficult than it would be if there were a number of available stations towards the south-west instead of a wide extent of ocean, from which only imperfect meteorological information can reach us. Even in the most frequented seas ships are widely enough scattered. Not one in a hundred can give any information to meteorologists which can be of use in predicting weather, because most ships are not sailing for ports near enough for any meteorological information to reach them in good time for use in forecasts. In fact, Mr. Scott remarks, that even as regards the climatology of the sea we can get only imperfect information. 'The endeavour to give a correct account of the climate of any district of the sea presents,' he says, 'much the same prospect of success as we should have, were we set to determine the climate of the different parts of France, from observations made by English tourists in their railway journeys through the length and breadth of the land.' But, if this is the case as regards climate, how much more hopeless must be the attempt to get weather indications from sea regions. We might form a fair idea of the climate of a district of France by combining together the reports of a great number of railway tourists, because time would help us. But time would be against us in the attempt to learn from such reports what weather changes, if any, were travelling towards us from France. Before the reports of a sufficient number of travellers could be received and analysed, the weather changes would have come and gone, and the reports would have become useless. In fact, when we consider that the prediction of weather has only been rendered possible (as all meteorologists admit) by the facilities of communication afforded by the electric telegraph, and that it is impossible to communicate telegraphically with ships at sea (unless a ship chances to be laying a submarine cable) we perceive that the presence of a wide expanse of ocean on that side of a land region, from which most weather changes travel, must render satisfactory prediction exceedingly difficult. In fact it is impossible, usually, to make satisfactory forecasts for the western parts of Ireland. In the United States also, it is noticed that the predictions for the eastern and northern States are on the whole more correct than those for the western and southern States.

We may here consider those American predictions of European weather which have been made during the last few years with a fair degree of success. The first storm predicted by the *New York Herald* arrived as threatened, though not quite in the way expected, for instead of arriving from the south-west it came from the north. After that, other telegrams were received, which for the most part were justified by the event, though they have nearly all been characterised by the same defects—they have been too vague as to time, and they have given no means of determining in what direction the gale, when it arrived, would blow. There are those, indeed, who deny that any storms have really crossed the Atlantic as predicted, and consider the apparent fulfilment of some among the predictions of the *New York Herald* as merely accidental. Still, there can be little doubt that the predictions are made in all good faith, and are based on real evidence as to the condition of the Atlantic. It would be interesting to know how these forecasts are arrived at. As General Strachan has remarked, ' Our American friends are not very willing to " show their hands," as the saying is.' However, we may surmise how it is done. They have active agents who make extracts of the logs of all the steamers directly they arrive in New York, and by means of these extracts they can follow up all the storms which occur in our parallels. Thus it may often happen that information of storms is obtained by the *Herald* before they have had time to reach Western Europe. The *Herald* at once flashes the news by telegraph. We get the telegram surely and speedily, and the storm, if it does not vanish in due time, shortly afterwards. It is singular and illustrates strikingly the way in which storms travel usually from the south-west (though the wind may first begin to blow from other quarters) that we should thus receive news from America brought thither by ships sailing towards the south-west or meeting the storm. No ship sailing towards Europe ever brings news of an approaching storm, for the storm

reaches us first. It will be observed, too, how completely
the prediction of weather depends on telegraphic communication. If we are ever to have effective weather reports
from the Atlantic, it can only be by arranging some system
of communication like that by which, during the voyages of
cable-laying ships, we have had hourly news of their progress
and of the weather prevailing in the parts they are traversing.
But we can see no hope at present of any such system being
devised; certainly, none could be arranged with our present
means of submarine communication. The American storm-
warnings, though sometimes fulfilled, are not altogether
satisfactory. As we have said, some meteorologists doubt
whether storms ever have traversed the Atlantic from
America to Europe ; and Professor Loomis, the American
meteorologist, has shown that only a small proportion of the
storms which reach Western Europe from the Atlantic can
be identified with the disturbances which had previously been
recognised either in America or in the western parts of the
North Atlantic.

It must be admitted that the prediction of weather
changes is making progress. Already it has falsified Arago's
well-known saying, ' Jamais, quels que puissent être les
progrès des sciences, les savants soucieux de leur réputation
ne se hasarderont à prédire les temps,' and has passed
beyond the range indicated by Leverrier, who considered
that science could not hope for more in this direction than
the recognition of the progress of a storm and the issue of
useful storm-signals. But there still remains room for
further progress, and good reason to believe that further
progress will be achieved. Not only are our meteorologists
learning to recognise more and more clearly the laws
according to which atmospheric movements and changes of
condition proceed, and so deriving more and more satisfactory information from the observations already made, but
they are extending the range of observation, and they are
establishing stations in regions whence effective information
can be obtained instead of merely increasing the number of

stations in regions already occupied. They also recognise now more clearly than of yore the necessity of care in selecting stations—for weather-study, as distinguished from climatology—where the conditions are such that the indications are general, not peculiar to the place. 'Geographical position and freedom from conditions which will affect the character of the observations, especially of wind, are here,' says the Director of the Meteorological Office, ' of paramount importance. If an opportunity occurs of obtaining a report from a new station which will give us earlier and surer intimation of coming changes of weather, we reject ruthlessly offers of observations from the most ably-served observatory in the district,' meaning in the district already occupied. What we specially want at present, however, for satisfactory weather prediction, is the establishment of stations at a distance, so that rapidly-approaching weather changes may be recognised before they are actually upon us. In this connection we may call special attention to the proposal of Count Wilczek and Lieutenant Weyprecht, that a system of observatories should be established at suitable points around the polar regions. They indicate, as suitable parts of the northern hemisphere, the north coasts of Spitzbergen and of Novaya Zemlya, the neighbourhood of the North Cape, the Mouth of the Lena, New Siberia, Point Barrow, on the North East of Behring Strait, the west coast of Greenland and the east coast of Greenland in about 75 deg. north latitude. For the southern polar region they name the neighbourhood of Cape Horn, Kerguelen, or Macdonald Islands, and some one of the groups south of the Auckland Islands. Mr. Scott points out that one good station on Spitzbergen or Jan Mayen would be worth as much as ten in Western Europe, and therefore it can readily be understood that if the far-seeing scheme of Wilczek and Weyprecht were carried out, a great advance would before long be noted in the accuracy of weather forecasts, and possibly a considerable increase in the range of time over which our meteorologists could extend their predictions.

The possibility of foretelling weather for two days as satisfactorily as we can now make forecasts for one day, would give
far more than twofold value to the system of prediction.
We have hitherto said nothing on a subject which at the
present time is attracting more serious attention than the daily
forecasting of weather—the possibility, namely, of anticipating
the probable character of approaching seasons.   Unfortunately, we have but too good reason for saying little on
this subject, since there is little to be said, and nothing that
can be regarded as promising.   We have lately passed
through (or rather we are now passing through) an altogether
exceptional period of cold and wet weather.   If there ever
has been an occasion when approaching weather should
have afforded some evidence of its character it would seem
to have been in the autumn of 1878, yet there was no
circumstance in the weather prevailing from Midsummer,
1878, until the beginning of November, which suggested
the approach of one of the longest and altogether the
bitterest spells of cold weather ever experienced in Western
Europe.   So of the recent heavy and long-continued
rainfalls, and of those experienced in 1872, in the autumn of
1875, and last year.   Not a sign was noted by meteorologists
of the approach of those plagues of water.   Some have
told us that there are weather cycles corresponding with the
sun-spot period; but not the slightest connection can
be traced between the sun-spot changes and either our
temperature or our rainfall.   The heavy rainfall of 1875
occurred when spots were numerous, the deluges of 1878
and of the present year when spots were few or absent
altogether.   The long continued cold of the year 1879
occurred when spots have been few, but among the
series of long cold spells (some even longer than the one
now in progress has yet lasted) some of the most remarkable have occurred when spots were most numerous,
others when, as in 1879, spots were few, and others
in almost every part of the sun-spot cycle.   Nor can
we form any opinion as to the probable duration of

any spell of cold or of wet weather. We may say now—what was said by Mr. Scott four years ago, but unfortunately we may now say it with far more point, 'as to the prediction of weather' for a long time in advance, 'it has not been shown to be feasible to forecast weather even for one short week, except on the principle, which affords us scanty consolation, that weather when once established takes a long time to change.' . . . 'This does not mean that the chances are in favour of the weather never changing, but are only against its changing on a definite day, and increase with the length of time the existing weather has lasted.'

SOME STRANGELY FULFILLED
DREAMS.

So far as can be judged by ordinary methods of interpretation, it would seem that in the days when the history of
Joseph was written, and again in the time of Daniel, no
doubt was entertained respecting the supernatural origin of
all dreams. Joseph's brothers, according to the narrative,
took it for granted that Joseph's dreams indicated something
which was to happen in the future. Whether they questioned
the validity of his own interpretation is not altogether clear.
They hated him after his first dream, and envied him we are
told, after his second ; which shows they feared he might
be right in his interpretation ; but, on the other hand, they
conspired together to slay him, which suggests that they
entertained some doubts on the subject. In fact, we are
expressly told that when they conspired against him, they
said, ' Behold, this dreamer cometh ; come now therefore,
and let us slay him,' and so forth, ' and we shall see what
will become of his dreams.' Jacob, moreover, though he had
' observed ' Joseph's ' saying ' about the dream (after rebuking
him for telling the story), seems to have taken Joseph's
death for granted : ' Joseph is without doubt rent in pieces.'
Possibly in those days, even as now, dreams were noticed
when they were fulfilled, and forgotten when, as it seemed,
they remained unfulfilled.

In like manner, when the butler and baker of Pharaoh
dreamed each man his dream in one night, they were sad
(that is, serious) the morning after : for they could not

understand what the dreams meant. But Joseph said, ' Do not interpretations belong to God?' Doubtless this was the accepted belief in the days when the history of Joseph was written. It is singular that the butler, though he forgot Joseph till Pharaoh's dreams reminded him of his fellow-prisoner, seems to have associated the power of interpreting the two dreams with the power of bringing about the events supposed to be portended by the dreams. ' It came to pass, as he interpreted to us, so it was ; me he restored unto mine office, him he hanged.' It is just thus that, in our own time, persons who believe in the claims of fortune-tellers to predict the future, commonly believe also that fortune-tellers can to some degree control the future also.

Pharaoh's dreams were rather more fortunate to Joseph than either his own or those of the chief butler and baker. (It is noteworthy how the dreams of the story run in pairs.) In fact, one might be led to surmise that he inherited something of the ingenuity shown by his father's mother—referring to an arrangement, a year or two before Joseph entered the world, in which his mother showed to no great advantage, according to modern ideas. Be this as it may, it was certainly a clever thought of Joseph to sug-gest that the unfavourable weather he had predicted might be provided against by appointing a man discreet and wise to look after the interests of Egypt. Whom was Pharaoh likely to appoint but the person who had predicted the seven bad harvests? Even so, in these our own times, another Joseph told the British Pharaoh who lately ruled over India that years of famine in India can be predicted, and their effects prevented by appointing a man discreet and wise to look after the interests of India. And it is curious enough that this modern Joseph seems to have turned his thoughts to his ancient namesake, putting forward the idea that the seven good years and the seven bad years were years of many sun-spots, followed by years of few sun-spots. Nay, so strangely do these coincidences sometimes run on all-fours, that the younger Joseph has adopted the idea that

Y 2

the pyramids of Egypt (which were once thought to be Joseph's store-houses) were ' astronomical instruments.' Now, it is certain, though this he has not noticed, that before the upper half (in height) of the great pyramid was set on, the great ascending gallery might have been used all the year round for observing the sun at noon ; and that by using a dark screen at its uppermost or southern extremity, and admitting the sun's light only through a small opening in this curtain, a large and well-defined image of the sun could have been obtained without any telescope, an image showing any large spots which might be present on the sun's disc. It would be a pleasant theory (and all the better suited for association with the sun-spot-weather theory, in having no valid evidence in its favour) to suggest that Joseph really ascertained the approach of good and bad harvests by solar observations. His advice was that the fifth part of the land of Egypt should be taken up—that is, stored up—in the seven plenteous years : but the Astronomer-Royal for Scotland assures us that the numbers five and seven are symbolised repeatedly in the great pyramid. Could anything clearer be desired ?

But although I have been allowing fancy to lead me far away from facts, I think it may safely be inferred from the story of Pharaoh's dreams that the prediction of good and bad harvests was one of the qualities which the Pharaohs chiefly valued in their wise men, whether magi or astrologers.

The story of Nebuchadnezzar's dream is still more singular. I suppose the usual service expected by the kings of Babylon from their soothsayers included the interpretation of all dreams which had left a strong impression on the king's mind—dreams like the night visions of Eliphaz the Temanite, bringing fear and trembling, making all the bones to shake. It does not seem to have entered into the ordinary course of their duties to tell the king first what he had dreamed (when he had forgotten), and afterwards what the dream might signify. Indeed, though it is not a very un-

common occurrence to forget a dream, yet a dream which
has been forgotten does not generally leave a very strong
impression, and therefore would not require interpretation.
It happened otherwise with Nebuchadnezzar. His spirit
was troubled, and his sleep broke from him, because of his
dream, but what he had dreamt he could not remember.
His action hereupon was somewhat crazy : but we must remember there was madness in his blood. He told the
Chaldæans, that ' if they would not make known to him his
dream and the interpretation thereof, they should be cut in
pieces, and their houses made a dunghill.' This was precisely the way, one would imagine, to cause them to invent
a dream for him (he could not have detected the truth very
well), and to have devised a suitable interpretation, pleasing
in the king's eyes—which to persons of their ingenuity
should not have been very difficult.[1]

However, we must not further consider these more
ancient dreams, but turn at once to the examination of some
of those remarkable dreams of modern times which have
been regarded as showing that dreams are really sent in some
cases as forewarnings, or at any rate as foreshadowings of
real events. I propose to consider these narratives with
special reference to the theory that dreams which seem to
be fulfilled are fulfilled only by accident : so many dreams
occurring and so many events, that it would in fact be
stranger that no such fulfilments should be recognised than
that some among them should seem exceedingly striking.

There is one dream story which can hardly be explained
by the coincidence theory, if true in all its particulars. It
is related by Dr. Abercrombie as deserving of belief, though

---

[1] A great deal in the art of dream-interpretation for the rich and
powerful must obviously have depended on ingenuity in making things
pleasant. Thus, when an Eastern potentate dreamt that all his teeth
fell out, and was told that he was to lose all his relatives, he slew the
indiscreet interpreter ; but when another and a cleverer interpreter told
him the dream promised long life, and that he would survive all his
relatives, he made the man who thus pleasantly interpreted the omen
many rich and handsome presents.

I must confess that for my own part I cannot but think the actual facts must have undergone considerable modification before the story reached its present form. Certainly the case does not illustrate the occurrence of dreams, as a warning, effective or otherwise according to circumstances, for the dream happened simultaneously with the event to which it was supposed to relate. The story runs as follows (Dr. Abercrombie gives the story in a somewhat, but not essentially, different form):

On the night of May 11, 1812, Mr. Williams, of Scorrior House, near Redruth, in Cornwall, woke his wife, and in great agitation told her of a strange dream he had just had. He dreamt he was in the lobby of the House of Commons, and saw a man shoot with a pistol a gentleman who had just entered the lobby, who was said to be the Chancellor. His wife told him not to trouble himself about the dream, but to go to sleep again. He followed her advice, but presently woke her again, saying he had dreamt the same dream. Yet a third time was the dream repeated; after which he was so disturbed that, despite his wife's entreaties that he would trouble himself no more about the House of Commons, but try to sleep quietly, he got up and dressed himself. This was between one and two o'clock in the morning. At breakfast, Mr. Williams could talk of nothing but the dream; and early the same morning he went to Falmouth, where he told the dream to all of his acquaintance whom he met. Next day, Mr. Tucker, of Trematon Castle, accompanied by his wife, a daughter of Mr. Williams, went to Scorrior House on a visit. Mr. Williams told Mr. Tucker the circumstances of his dream. Mr. Tucker remarked that it could only be in a dream that the Chancellor would be found in the lobby of the House of Commons. Mr. Tucker asked what sort of man the Chancellor seemed to be, and Mr. Williams minutely described the man who was murdered in his dream. Mr. Tucker replied, 'Your description is not at all that of the Chancellor, but is very exactly that of Mr. Perceval, the Chancellor of the

Exchequer.' He asked if Mr. Williams had ever seen Mr. Perceval, and Mr. Williams replied that he had never seen him or had any communication of any sort with him; and further, that he had never been in the House of Commons in his life. At this moment they heard the·sound of a horse galloping to the door of the house ; immediately after a son of Mr. Williams entered the room, and said that he had galloped from Truro, having seen a gentleman there who had come by that evening's mail from town, who had been in the lobby of the House of Commons on the evening of the 11th, when a man called Bellingham had shot Mr. Perceval. After the astonishment which this intelligence created had a little subsided, Mr. Williams described most minutely the appearance and dress of the man whom he had seen in his dream fire the pistol at the Chancellor, as also the appearance and dress of the Chancellor. About six weeks after, Mr. Williams, having business in town, went in company with a friend to the House of Commons, where, as has been already observed, he had never before been. Immediately that he came to the steps of the entrance of the lobby, he said, ' This place is as distinctly within my recollection, in my dream, as any room in my own house,' and he made the same observation when he entered the lobby. He then pointed out the exact spot where Bellingham stood when he fired, and also that which Mr. Perceval had reached when he was struck by the ball, where he fell. The dress both of Mr. Perceval and Bellingham agreed with the description given by Mr. Williams, even to the most minute particulars.

So runs the story. Of course, like the 'well-authenticated' ghost stories, this one is confirmed by a number of particulars which are open to no other disadvantage than that of depending, like the rest of the story, on the narrator himself. It would be utterly absurd to base any theory respecting dreams on a story of this sort. The fact that on the night in question Mr. Williams dreamt about a murder in the House of Commons depends on his own assertion and his wife's confirmation. The details of the dream, the description of Perceval and Bellingham, Mr. Williams' ignorance respecting Mr. Perceval's appearance and the arrangement of the rooms in the House of Commons, these and a number of other matters essential to the significance of the story, depend on 'trustworthy witnesses,' whose evidence has in point of fact never been taken. All these points are like the details which appear in the papers the first few days after the occurrence of some 'tragic event.' They may be true or not, but they are apt to undergo considerable alteration when the witnesses are actually examined.

If we accepted the story precisely as it stands, we should be led to some rather startling results. In the first place, the coincidences are too numerous to be explained as merely accidental. Mr. Williams, or any other among the millions who slept and dreamt on the night of the murder, might be readily enough believed to have had a startling dream about the murder of some member of Parliament high in office. Nor could the triple repetition of such a dream be surprising ; for a dream which has produced a great effect on the mind is apt to be repeated. But that the event itself of Perceval's murder should be represented precisely as it occurred to a man who did not know Perceval or Bellingham from Adam, involves a multiplicity of relations which could not conceivably be all fulfilled simultaneously. We should have to admit, if we accepted the story as it stands, that there was something, I will not say supernatural or preternatural, but outside the range of known natural laws, in the dreams of Mr. Williams of Scorrior House.

Now, the case does not fall under precisely the same category as those numerous stories told of the appearance of persons, at the moment of their death, to friends or relatives at a distance. In the first place, most of these stories are themselves open to grave doubt. The persons who relate them are by their own account of highly sensitive and readily excitable temperament, and we do not look for perfectly uncoloured narratives from such persons. But even if we accept the general theory that under certain conditions the mind of a dying person may affect in some way the mind of a person at a distance who is in some way in sympathy with the moribund, we can hardly extend the theory to include strangers. It may not be utterly incredible, perhaps, that some physical mode of communication exists by wh'ch one brain may receive the same impressions which affect another—though I must confess I cannot see my own way to believe anything of the sort. But we can hardly imagine that the brain of a sleeping person in no way connected with a dying man could be affected by such brain-waves. Every story of the kind, truthful or otherwise, has described an impression produced on some dear friend or relative ; so that we should be justified in thinking (if we believe these stories at all) that brain-waves are especially intended for the benefit of close friends or near of kin. It would be a new and startling thing if any man might have a vision of any other person who chanced to be dying ; and considering that not a minute passes without several deaths, while there are some 1,500 millions of living persons, scarcely a day might be expected to pass without some one or other of the multitudinous deaths of the day finding some one or other brain among the 1,500 millions in the proper frame for receiving the visionary communication by the brain-wave method.

Nor is it easy to imagine a religiously supernatural inter-pretation of the story. The dream was certainly not sent as a warning, for when Williams dreamt his dream, Perceval was either being murdered, or was already dead. The event could produce no beneficial influence on mankind generally, or on the English people specially, or the Cornish folk still more specially. The number of persons who could be certain that Mr. Williams was telling the truth (always on our present assumption that this was the case) were very few — in fact, only Mr. and Mrs. Williams, Mr. Tucker, and perhaps one or two friends who remembered that the details

of the murder were communicated before the news could
have reached Mr. Williams. One does not readily see how
Williams himself was to be beneficially influenced by his
remarkable experience. Most of those who heard the story
would sit in the seat of the scornful, and receive no benefit
but harm. The idea generally entertained, and most probably by Williams as well as the rest, would be simply this,
that if it was worth while to let a miraculous vision of
Perceval's murder appear to anyone, it would have been
well to have let the vision appear before the event, and to
some one not living quite so far from town. Not, indeed,
that the warning might save Perceval ; for in reality it is a
bull of the broadest sort to imagine that a *true* vision of a
murder can prevent the murder. But a warning dream
might serve useful purpose without preventing the event
it indicated. If a man dreamt that he was to die in a
week, and believed the dream, he would have no hope from
the advice of his doctor, or from any other precautions
he might make against death ; yet he would usefully employ
the week in arranging his affairs. But it could be of no
earthly use to Perceval, or anyone else, that a vision of his
death should appear in triplicate to some one down in
Cornwall on the very night when the tragedy occurred in
London.

I imagine that the true explanation of the story is somewhat on this wise ; Williams probably had three startling
dreams about a murder ; told them to his wife in the way
related, and on the following morning to several friends.
News presently came of the murder of Perceval on the night
when Williams had had these dreams ; and gradually he
associated the events of his dreams with the circumstances
of the murder. When six weeks later he visited the scene
of the murder, he mistook his recollection of things told him
about Perceval, the lobby of the House of Commons, &c.,
for the recollection of things seen in his dreams. The story
actually related probably assumed form and substance after
Williams's visit to London. In perfect good faith, he, his

wife, and his friends may have given to the story the form it finally assumed. Of course, the explanation is rendered a little easier if we suppose Mr. Williams and his wife were not unwilling to colour their story a little. If a phonograph could have received the first account of the dream as imparted to Mrs. Williams on the night of May 11, I fancy the instrument might have repeated a tale somewhat unlike that which adorns the 'Royal Book of Dreams,' and Dr. Abercrombie's treatise on the Intellectual Powers. But without any intentional untruthfulness a story of this kind is apt to undergo very noteworthy modifications.

Dr. Abercrombie himself vouches for the truth of the two following stories, that is to say, he vouches for his belief in both stories : ' A Scotch clergyman who lived near Edinburgh dreamt one night, while on a visit in that town, that he saw a fire, and one of his children in the midst of it. On awaking, he instantly got up and returned home with the greatest speed. He found his house on fire, and was just in time to assist one of his children who in the alarm had been left in a place of danger.' The second story runs as follows :— Two sisters had been for some days attending a sick brother, and one of them had borrowed a watch from a friend, her own being under repair. The sisters were sleeping together in a room communicating with that of their brother, when the elder awoke in a state of great agitation, and roused the other to tell her that she had had a frightful dream. ' I dreamt,' she said, ' that Mary's watch stopped, and that when I told you of the circumstance you replied, " Much worse than that has happened ; for ——'s breath has stopped also," ' naming their sick brother. The watch, however, was found to be going correctly, and the brother was sleeping quietly. The dream recurred the next night ; and on the following morning, one of the sisters having occasion to seal a note, went to get the watch from a writing-desk in which she had deposited it, when she found it had stopped. She rushed into her brother's room in alarm, remembering the dream, and found that he had been suddenly seized with a fit of suffocation,

and had expired. (Abercrombie, 'Intellectual Powers,'
pp. 289, 302.)

With regard to the first of these stories, I would remark
that we find in it what is not always to be found in stories
of dream warnings, a reason and use in the dream, assuming
always that the story is true and that the dream really was
sent as a warning.   It is possible, of course, that the story
was embellished by the Scotch clergyman who related it to
Abercrombie.   If the story be true in all its details, it remains possible that the agreement between the dream and
the event was a mere coincidence.   On the first point, I
shall say only that some men, and even some clergymen,
have been quite capable of improving a story of this sort,
with the desire perhaps of impressing on their hearer the
anxious care which Providence takes in their special behalf.
On the second point, it should be always remembered that
among the many millions of strange dreams which might be
fulfilled, some few are certain to be fulfilled, and it is of these
dreams that we hear, not of those, though they are millions
of times more numerous, which are not fulfilled.   If, however, we accept the story precisely as related, and believe
that the fulfilment of the dream was not accidental, we have
at least a reasonable case of dream warning.   We cannot,
indeed, perceive why in this case Providence should interfere when so many similar cases happen without interference
of any sort.   And to the logical mind the idea will certainly
suggest itself that if special interpositions of Providence
can occur in such cases, they might be expected to be greatly
more numerous than they are.   But considering the case
apart from others, we cannot cavil at the action of Providence
in this case.   The danger, however, of approval in such
cases will be manifest if we consider that by parity of reasoning we ought to be dissatisfied when lamentable events
happen which dream warnings might have prevented.

With regard to the second of the above stories I venture
to express entire want of faith.   The action of the sister,
who, finding the watch had stopped, rushed in alarm into

her brother's room, showed that she was weak-minded and superstitious ; and we cannot expect exact statements of facts from weak-minded and superstitious persons. If the story were accepted as related, the case would differ altogether from the former. We can understand that Providence might interfere to warn a father of his child's danger in time to save the child ; but we can not reasonably believe that a double dream should be specially sent to indicate that when a certain watch had stopped a certain man would be found dead. If the events happened as told the coincidence was strange, but that is all. It seems to me altogether more probable, however, that the story was inexactly related to Dr. Abercrombie.

I have said that cases in which dreams are not fulfilled are usually forgotten. Occasionally, however, such dreams are preserved on account of some peculiarity in the circumstances. The following case, related by Abercrombie, is almost as singular as if the dream warning had been fulfilled by the event. A young man who was at an academy a hundred miles from home, dreamt that he went to his father's house in the night, tried the front door, but found it locked ; got in by a back door, and finding nobody out of bed, went directly to the bedroom of his parents. He then said to his mother, whom he found awake, ' Mother, I am going a long journey, and am come to bid you good-bye.' On this she answered, in much agitation, ' Oh, dear son, thou art dead !' He instantly awoke, and thought no more of his dream, until a few days after he received a letter from his father, inquiring very anxiously after his health, in consequence of a frightful dream his mother had had on the same night in which the dream now mentioned occurred to him. She dreamt that she heard some one attempt to open the front door, then go to the back door, and at last come into her bedroom. She then saw it was her son, who came to the side of her bed, and said, ' Mother, I am going a long journey, and I am come to bid you good-bye,' on which she exclaimed, ' Oh, dear son, thou art dead !' But nothing unusual happened to either of the parties.

This case, if correctly related by the young man, would afford some evidence in favour of the theory that mind can act on mind at a distance. But we have to trust wholly in the veracity of the unknown young man ; and it is barely possible that after reading his mother's letter he invented the account of his own dream. Or the story may have been told years after the event, and the facts related may have differed very widely from what actually happened. We know that memory often plays strange tricks in such cases.

At any rate, there was in this case no forewarning of any event, unless we suppose that the dream was sent to mother and son simultaneously, to prevent the son from undertaking a long journey at that time—assuming further that, if he had undertaken such a journey, he would have died upon the way. But anyone who could take this view of the matter would believe anything.

This unfulfilled dream, the circumstances of which, if accurately known, might probably be readily explained, reminds me of a dream or vision related by Dickens in a letter to Forster, and of the explanation which Dickens suggested in relation to it. The original narrative is so charming that I shall make no apology for quoting it without change or abridgment. 'Let me tell you,' he wrote from Genoa on September 30, 1843, 'of a curious dream I had last Monday night, and of the fragments of reality I can collect which helped to make it up. I have had a return of rheumatism in my back and knotted round my waist like a girdle of pain, and had lain awake nearly all that night under the infliction, when I fell asleep and dreamed this dream. Observe that throughout I was as real, animated, and full of passion as Macready (God bless him !) in the last scene of Macbeth. In an indistinct place, which was quite sublime in its indistinctness, I was visited by a spirit. I could not make out the face, nor do I recollect that I desired to do so. It wore a blue drapery, as the Madonna might wear in a picture by Raphael ; and bore no resemblance to anyone I have ever seen except in stature. I think (but I

am not sure) that I recognised the voice. Anyway, I knew
it was poor Mary's spirit. I was not at all afraid, but in a
great delight, so that I wept very much, and stretching out
my arms to it called it 'dear.' At this I thought it recoiled ;
and I felt immediately that, not being of my gross nature,
I ought not to have addressed it so familiarly. ' Forgive
me ! ' I said, ' we poor living creatures are only able to express ourselves by looks and words. I have used the word
most natural to *our* affections ; and you know my heart.' It
was so full of compassion and sorrow for me—which I knew
spiritually, for, as I have said, I did not perceive its emotions
by its face—that it cut me to the heart ; and I said, sobbing,
' Oh ! give me some token that you have really visited me ! '
' Form a wish,' it said. I thought, reasoning with myself, if
I form a selfish wish it will vanish, so I hastily discarded
such hopes and anxieties of my own as came into my mind,
and said, ' Mrs. Hogarth is surrounded with great distresses '
—observe, I never thought of saying ' your mother,' as to a
mortal creature—'will you extricate her ? ' ' Yes.' ' And
her extrication is to be a certainty to me that this has really
happened ? ' ' Yes.' ' But answer me one other question,'
I said, in an agony of entreaty lest it should leave me :
' What is the true religion ? ' As it paused a moment without replying, I said ' Good God ! ' in such an agony of haste,
lest it should go away, 'you think, as I do, that the form of
religion does not so greatly matter, if we try to do good ?—
or,' I said, observing that it still hesitated, and was moved
with the greatest compassion for me, ' perhaps the Roman
Catholic is the best? perhaps it makes one think of God
oftener, and believe in Him more steadily ? ' ' For *you*,'
said the spirit, full of such heavenly tenderness for me that
I felt as if my heart would break—'for *you*, it is the best ! '
Then I awoke with the tears running down my face, and
myself in exactly the condition of the dream. It was just
dawn. I called up Kate, and repeated it three or four
times over, that I might not unconsciously make it plainer
or stranger afterwards. It was exactly this, free from all

hurry, nonsense, or confusion whatever. Now, the strings
I can gather up leading to this were three. The first you
know forms the main subject of my former letter. The
second was, that there is a great altar in our bedroom, at
which some family who once inhabited this palace had mass
performed in old time ; and I had observed within myself,
before going to bed, that there was a mark in the wall above
the sanctuary, where a religious picture used to be ; and I had
wondered within myself what the subject might have been,
and what the face was like. Thirdly, I had been listening to
the convent bells (which ring at intervals in the night), and
so had thought, no doubt, of Roman Catholic services. And
yet for all this, put the case of that wish being fulfilled by
any agency in which I had no hand, and I wonder whether
I should regard it as a dream, or an actual vision.'

The promise of the dream-spirit was not fulfilled in this
respect. If it had chanced that some agency other than
Dickens's own had, at that time, relieved Mrs. Hogarth
from her anxieties, we can hardly doubt that he would have
regarded the vision as real. He was, indeed, rather prone
to recognise something beyond the natural in events which,
to say the least, admitted of a quite natural interpretation.
The story of his dream, I may remark in passing, is
interesting as showing how the thoughts of the dreamer's
own mind are in a dream assigned to the visionary persons
created also in reality out of the dreamer's mind. The
spirit in Dickens's dream expressed precisely his own views
about religion, and hesitated precisely where (as he elsewhere
tells us) he himself hesitated. But where, in his own mind,
he thought only that the Roman Catholic religion might be
the best for him, the vision said simply that it was so.
Had the dream promise been fulfilled, Dickens would probably have followed the supposed teaching of the dream-
spirit. Or even if no test had been suggested to his mind
in the dream, and the spirit had seemed to speak only of
religion, he would probably have concluded that for him the
Roman Church was the best. He would have felt, as

Eliphaz the Temanite did, that this thing was secretly brought to him. It is indeed singular how closely in some respects the dream of Eliphaz the Temanite resembled that which Charles Dickens the Englishman dreamed, three or four thousand years later. 'In thoughts from the visions of the night,' says Eliphaz, 'when deep sleep falleth upon men. Fear came upon me, and trembling, which made all my bones to shake. Then a spirit passed before my face, the hair of my flesh stood up. *It stood still, but I could not discern the form thereof: an image was before mine eyes, there was silence, and I heard a voice, saying,* Shall mortal man be more just than God? shall a man be more pure than his maker?' Fear possessed Eliphaz, instead of the delight which filled the heart of Dickens in the supposed presence of the departed dear one. But, like Dickens, the Temanite could hear a voice only, not discerning the form of the vision; and again, to him as to Dickens, the supposed vision repeated only what was in the dreamer's own mind.

Twenty years later Dickens had a dream which was fulfilled, at least to his own satisfaction. 'Here,' he wrote on May 30, 1863, 'is a curious case at first hand. On Thursday night last week, being at the office here,' in London, 'I dreamed that I saw a lady in a red shawl with her back towards me, whom I supposed to be E. On her turning round I found that I didn't know her, and she said, "I am Miss Napier." All the time I was dressing next morning I thought, "What a preposterous thing to have so very distinct a dream about nothing! And why Miss Napier? for I never heard of any Miss Napier." That same Friday night I read. After the reading came into my retiring-room Mary Boyle and her brother, and *the* lady in the red shawl, whom they present as "Miss Napier." These are all the circumstances exactly told.' This was probably a case of unconscious cerebration. Dickens had no doubt really seen the lady, and been told that she was Miss Napier, when his attention was occupied with other matters. There would be nothing unusual in his dreaming about a person whom he had thus seen without noticing. Of course it was an odd coincidence that the lady of whom he had thus dreamed should be introduced to him soon after—possibly the very day after. But such coincidences are not infrequent. To suppose that Dickens had been specially warned in a dream about so unimportant a matter as his introduction to Miss Napier would be absurd ; for, fulfilled or unfilled, the dream was, as Dickens himself described it, a very distinct dream about nothing.

Far different in this respect was the strange dream which President Lincoln had the night before he was shot. If the story was truly told by Mr. Stanton to Dickens, the case is one of the most curious on record. Dickens told it thus in a letter to John Forster: 'On the afternoon of the day on which the President was shot, there was a cabinet council, at which he presided. Mr. Stanton, being at the time commander-in-chief of the Northern troops that were concentrated about here, arrived rather late. Indeed, they were waiting for him, and on his entering the room, the President broke off in something he was saying, and remarked, " Let us proceed to business, gentlemen." Mr. Stanton then noticed with surprise that the President sat with an air of dignity in his chair, instead of lolling about in the most ungainly attitudes, as his invariable custom was; and that instead of telling irrelevant and questionable stories, he was grave, and calm, and quite a different man. Mr. Stanton, on leaving the council with the Attorney-General, said to him, " That is the most satisfactory cabinet meeting I have attended for many a long day. What an extraordinary change in Mr. Lincoln ! " The Attorney-General replied, " We all saw it before you came in. While we were waiting for you, he said, with his chin down on his breast, ' Gentlemen, something very extraordinary is going to happen, and that very soon.' To which the Attorney-General had observed, 'Something good, sir, I hope?' when the President answered very gravely, ' I don't know—I don't know. But it will happen, and shortly, too.' As they were all impressed

by his manner, the Attorney-General took him up again.
'Have you received any information, sir, not yet disclosed
to us?' 'No,' answered the President, 'but I have had a
dream. And I have now had the same dream three times.
Once on the night preceding the battle of Bull Run. Once
on the night preceding such another' (naming a battle also
not favourable to the North). His chin sank on his breast
again, and he sat reflecting. 'Might one ask the nature of
this dream, sir?' said the Attorney-General. 'Well,' replied
the President without lifting his head or changing his attitude, ' I am on a great broad rolling river—and I am in a
boat—and I drift !—and I drift !—but this is not business,'
—suddenly raising his face, and looking round the table as
Mr. Stanton entered—'let us proceed to business, gentlemen.'" Mr. Stanton and the Attorney-General said, as they
walked on together, it would be curious to notice whether
anything ensued on this, and they agreed to notice. He
was shot that night.' Here the dream itself was not remarkable ; it was such a one as might readily be dreamed by a
man from the Western States who had been often on broad
rolling rivers. Nor was its recurrence remarkable. The
noteworthy point was the occurrence of this dream three
several times, and (as may be presumed from the effect
which the dream produced on its third recurrence) those
three times only, on the night preceding a great misfortune for the cause of the North. However, there is
nothing in the story which cannot be attributed to merely
casual coincidence, though the coincidence was sufficiently
curious. As three years had elapsed from the time of
Lincoln's death when Stanton told Dickens the story, it is
possible that the account may have been incorrect in some
details.

It is, indeed, in this way that probably most of the more
wonderful dream stories are to be explained. The tricks
played by the memory in such matters would be perfectly
amazing if they were not so familiar. For instance, Dr.
Carpenter states that a lady had frequently asserted that

she had seen a table move at the command of a medium
when no one was near it. At length someone had sufficient
hardihood to challenge this assertion—made, it will be understood, in perfectly good faith ; and to satisfy the doubter
of its truth, the lady turned to a note-book in which she had
described the circumstances of the event at the time of its
occurrence. There she found it stated, not as her memory
had falsely told her, that no one was near the table, but that
the hands of six persons were touching it !

It is possible that in the following recent and certainly
most remarkable case of a fulfilled dream, the exact circumstances, had they been recorded, would have been found to
be not precisely those which the narrator believed them to be.

In the *Daily Telegraph* some months ago, in an
obituary notice of General Richard Taylor, son of a former
President of the United States (General Zachary Taylor),
and one of the Southern generals during the Civil War, the
following curious narrative was related :—

‘ On the morning of the day when the City and Suburban
Handicap was won by “ Aldrich,” a little-fancied outsider,
it so chanced that General Taylor travelled down to Epsom
in company with Lord Vivian, and heard from him that it
was his intention to back Lord Rosebery's horse, because
he had dreamt that he saw the primrose and rose-hoops
borne to victory in the race which they were on their road
to witness. Acting upon this hint, General Taylor took
1,000 to 30 about “Aldrich,” and was not a little elated at the
success of what he justly called “ a leap in the dark.” But
for the accident which caused “Lemnos,” another much-backed
candidate for the race, to fall at Tattenham Corner, there is
little probability that the dream of Lord Vivian would have
found the interpretation upon which General Taylor counted.’

The story probably came from one who had heard the
actual circumstances as related by Lord Vivian himself at
the time of their occurrence. The narrator's recollection of
what he had heard, and Lord Vivian's recollection of the
event itself, may both have been to some degree defective,

That one or other was in fault is manifest when we compare with the above account Lord Vivian's own statement a day or two later. He wrote as follows to the editor of the *Daily Telegraph* :—

' In your " leader" on General Taylor, in this day's paper, you introduce an anecdote relative to a dream of mine. The facts are these : I did dream, on the morning of the race for the City and Suburban Handicap, that I had fallen asleep in the weighing-room of the stand of Epsom, prior to that race, and that after it had been run I was awakened by a gentleman—the owner of another horse in the race --who informed me that " The Teacher" had won. Of this horse, so far as my recollections serve me, I had never before heard. On reaching Victoria Station, the first person I saw was the gentleman who had appeared to me in my dream, and I mentioned it to him, observing that I could not find any horse so named in the race. He replied, "' There is a horse now called ' Aldrich,' which was previously called ' The Teacher.' " The dream so vividly impressed me that I declared my intention of backing " Aldrich" for 100*l*., and was in course of doing this, when I was questioned by his owner as to "why I backed this horse.". I replied, " Because I had dreamt he had won the race." To this I was answered, " As against your dream, I will tell you this fact : I tried the horse last week with a hurdle-jumper, and he was beaten a distance ") I afterwards learnt that the trial horse was " Lowlander " !). I thanked my informant, and discontinued backing " Aldrich." General Taylor, who had overheard what passed, asked me if I did not intend backing the horse again for myself, to win him 1,000*l*. by him. This I did by taking for him 1,000 to 30 about " Aldrich." Such is the true account of my dream, and of General Taylor's profit from it.'

The difference between this account and that in the *Daily Telegraph* may not seem intrinsically important ; but it is noteworthy as indicating the probability that in other details there may have been changes (unintentional, of course).

The *Spectator* made the following remarks (very much to
the point, I think,) on this case :

' Lord Vivian's letter adds very much to the inexplicable
element in the story. In the shape in which the *Daily Telegraph* originally put it, there was nothing at all in the dream
but what it was quite reasonable for anyone to explain as a
somewhat remarkable coincidence between a dream of the
event and the event as it actually resulted, the best offered
being, however, a practical proof that the dream, as alleged,
• had occurred, and had greatly influenced the mind of the
dreamer and one of his companions before the prediction
was fulfilled.   But Lord Vivian's testimony that, instead of
dreaming of " Aldrich " as the winner, the friend seen in his
dream had mentioned a horse whose name was utterly unknown to him—at least, unknown to him in his waking state
—and of whose running he had no knowledge, and that the
name so dreamed of proved to have been the former name
of a horse actually in the race, supplies a very excellent
reason why he should have been sufficiently struck by his
dream to intend acting upon it, until he was discouraged by
hearing of the horse's defeat by a hurdle-jumper, and why
General Richard Taylor insisted that if Lord Vivian did not
bet on " Aldrich " on his own account, he should still bet on
him on behalf of General Richard Taylor.   In truth, Lord
Vivian has supplied the only really striking feature in the
story.   Everybody would be disposed to explain it at once
as a case of coincidence, but for the bit of fresh knowledge
apparently supplied in the dream, and verified in fact before
the chief prediction of the dream had been tested.   Now,
here we have exceedingly good evidence, not only of a successful prediction of an unlikely event—for that is nothing,
and occurs every day—but of its prediction after a fashion
which appears to have been beyond the scope of the dreamer's
power.   That he should have dreamt of the winning of
the race by a horse of name quite unknown to him would
of course have been nothing.   But that after such a dream
a friend should have been able to point out a horse actually

running in the race, to which the unknown name had actually belonged, was clearly a practical verification of the informing character of the dream, and makes the coincidence—if coincidence it were—of the complete fulfilment of all the important predictions of the dream, one far more extraordinary than the fulfilment of any simple anticipation. Is there any explanation possible of the really curious part of the story, the discernment that a horse which had been called " The Teacher " was to run in the race, although Lord Vivian could not recall ever having heard of such a horse, without recourse to hypothesis of an unverified and as yet purely conjectural kind ? '

The writer of the article in the *Spectator* proceeds to offer such an explanation :—' Supposing Lord Vivian to have really had something to do with the horse called " The Teacher," and to have been told in a moment of almost complete inattention that it had been rechristened " Aldrich," it is barely possible—we do not say it is at all likely—that this association may have revived in sleep, without presenting any of the appearance of a memory. In his waking hours, his mind may have dwelt on Lord Rosebery as a coming power on the Turf, and that may have turned his attention to the name of Lord Rosebery's horse. This name may, in sleep, have revived the half-obliterated association of old days, and the name of " The Teacher " may have come back. And then the imposing character of this name may have suggested a dream in which the dreamer was solemnly told that " The Teacher " had won the race. Such, we say, is a possible, though not at all probable, explanation of this strange dream, supposing it related with perfect accuracy. Certain it is, that our memories are often so much transformed in our sleeping state, that they hardly comport themselves as memories at all, but rather as brand-new experiences, when they are really due to the laws of association, though of association so completely stripped of all its most familiar elements as to look stranger than a totally new impression.'

Of course this explanation, even if accepted, gives no

account of the fulfilment of the dream despite the heavy
antecedent probability against 'Aldrich' winning. Unless we
set this down to mere coincidence, we should either have to
believe that Lord Vivian was specially favoured with a vision
by which —if only he were clever enough to avail himself of
the information—he might win much money on a horse-race
(a somewhat questionable proceeding if he were assured that
the information were trustworthy, and a somewhat foolish proceeding if he were not), or else we must suppose that, in his
sleep, information which he had once had (but had forgotten)
about the horse's qualities showed him what in his waking
hours he could not have ascertained, that the horse really
had a better chance than bettors imagined. Possibly persons
who bet on horse-races give their minds (or what they regard as such) so entirely to that absorbing though not very
ennobling pursuit, that they often dream about horses winning races. As their name is legion, and their dreams
would therefore be multitudinous, the wonder rather is, perhaps, that we do not oftener hear of seemingly remarkable
fulfilments of such dreams, than that one or two cases of the
kind should be recorded. Certainly there is little in this
case to encourage special faith in dreams about racing.
However ready the believer in dreams may be to regard
dream warnings as supernatural, he can hardly regard information about horse-races as communicated from above. If
they came from the contrary direction, it would be unsafe to
accept them with blind confidence, remembering to whom
the parentage of falsehood has been, on excellent authority,
attributed.

SUSPENDED ANIMATION.

Some time since an article appeared in the *Times*, quoted from the *Brisbane Courier* (an Australian paper of good credit), stating that one Signor Rotura had devised a plan by which animals might be congealed for weeks or months without being actually deprived of life, so that they might be shipped from Australia for English ports as dead meat, yet on their arrival here be restored to full life and activity. Many regarded this account as intended to be received seriously, though a few days later an article appeared, the opening words of which implied that only persons from the north of the Tweed should have taken the article *au grand sérieux*. Of course it was a hoax; but it is worthy of notice that the editor of the *Brisbane Courier* had really been misled, as he admitted a few weeks later, with a candour which did him credit.[1]

[1] Many fail to see a joke when it is gravely propounded in print, who would at once recognise it as such, were it uttered verbally, with however serious a countenance. Possibly this is due to the necessary absence in the printed account of the indications by which we recognise that a speaker is jesting—as a certain expression of countenance, or a certain intonation of voice, by which the grave utterer of a spoken jest conveys his real meaning. In a paper which recently appeared in the *Gentleman's Magazine*, Mr. Foster (Thomas of that ilk) propounded very gravely the theory that our Nursery Rhymes have in reality had their origin in Nature Myths. He explained, for instance, that the rhymes relating to Little Jack Horner were originally descriptive of sunrise in winter: Little Jack is the sun in winter, the Christmas pie is the cloud-covered sky; the thumb represents the sun's first ray piercing

This wonderful discovery, however, besides being worth publishing as a joke (though rather a mischievous one, as will presently be shown), did good service also by eliciting from a distinguished physician certain statements respecting the possibility of suspending animation, which otherwise might have remained for some time unpublished. I propose here to consider these statements, and the strange possibilities which some of them seem to suggest. In the first place, however, it may be worth while to recall the chief statements in the clever Australian story, as some of Dr. Richardson's statements refer specially to that narrative. I shall take the opportunity of indicating certain curious features of resemblance between the Australian story, which really had its origin in America (I am assured that it was published a year earlier in a New York paper), and an American hoax which acquired a wide celebrity some forty years ago, the so-called Lunar Hoax. As it is certain that the two stories came from different persons, the resemblance referred to seems to suggest that the special mental qualities (defects *bien entendu*) which cause some to take delight in such inventions, are commonly associated with a characteristic style of writing. If Buffon was right, indeed, in saying, *Le style c'est de l'homme même*, we can readily understand that clever hoaxers should thus have a style peculiar to themselves.

It can hardly be considered essential to the right comprehension of scientific experiments that a picturesque account should be given of the place where the experiments were made. The history of the wonderful Australian discovery opens nevertheless as follows :—'Many of the readers of the *Brisbane Courier* who know Sydney Harbour

through the clouds ; and Jack's rejoicing means the brightness of full sunlight. So also the rhymes beginning Hey Diddle Diddle are shown to be of deep and solemn import, all in manifest burlesque of some recent extravagant interpretations of certain ancient stories by Goldziher, Steinthal, and others. Yet this fun was seriously criticised by more than half the critics, by some approvingly, by some otherwise.

will remember the long inlet opposite the heads known as Middle Harbour, which, in a succession of land-locked reaches, stretches away like a chain of lakes for over twenty miles. On one of these reaches, made more than ordinarily picturesque by the bold headlands that drop almost sheer into the water, stand, on about an acre of grassy flat, fringed by white beach on which the clear waters of the harbour lap, two low brick buildings. Here, in perfect seclusion, and with a careful avoidance of publicity, is being conducted an experiment, the success of which, now established beyond any doubt, must have a wider effect upon the future prosperity of Australia than any project ever contemplated.' It was precisely in this tone that the author of the 'Lunar Hoax'[1] opened his account of those 'recent discoveries in astronomy which will build an imperishable monument to the age in which we live, and confer upon the present generation of the human race a proud distinction through all future time.' 'It has been poetically said,' he remarks— though probably he would have found some difficulty in saying where or by whom this had been said,—'that the stars of heaven are the hereditary regalia of man, as the intellectual sovereign of the animal creation; he may now fold the zodiac around him with a loftier consciousness of his mental supremacy' (a sublime idea, irresistibly suggestive of the description which an American humourist gave of a certain actor's representation of the death of Richard III., 'he wrapped the star-spangled banner around him, and died like the son of a hoss").

It next becomes necessary to describe the persons engaged in pursuing the experiments by which the art of freezing animals alive is to be attained. 'The gentlemen engaged in this enterprise are Signor Rotura, whose researches into the botany and natural history of South America have rendered his name eminent; and Mr. James Grant, a pupil of the late Mr. Nicolle, so long associated

[1] For a full account of this clever hoax the reader is referred to my 'Myths and Marvels of Astronomy.'

with Mr. Thomas Mort in his freezing process. Next to
the late Mr. Nicolle, Mr. James Grant can claim pre-eminence of knowledge in the science of generating cold, and
his freezing chamber at Woolhara has long been known as
the seat of valuable experiments originated in his, Mr.
Nicolle's, lifetime.' Is it merely an accident, by the way,
or is it due to the circumstance that exceptional powers of
invention in general matters are often found in company
with singular poverty of invention as to details, that two of
the names here mentioned closely resemble names connected with the Lunar Hoax? It was Nicollet who in
reality devised the Lunar Hoax, though Richard Alton
Locke, the reputed author, probably gave to the story its
final form ; and, again, the story purported to come from
Dr. Grant, of Glasgow. In the earlier narrative, again, as
in the later, due care was taken to impress readers with the
belief that those who had made the discovery, or taken part
in the work, were worthy of all confidence. Sir W. Herschel
was the inventor of the optical device by which the inhabitants of the moon were to be rendered visible, a plan which
'evinced the most profound research in optical science, and
the most dexterous ingenuity in mechanical contrivance.
But his son, Sir John Herschel, nursed and cradled in the
observatory, and a practical astronomer from his boyhood,
determined upon testing it at whatever cost.' Among his
companions he had ' Dr. Andrew Grant, Lieutenant Drum-
mond of the Royal Engineers, and a large party of the
best English mechanics.'

The accounts of preliminary researches, doubts, and
difficulties are in both cases very similar in tone. ' It
appears that five months ago,' says the narrator of the
Australian hoax, 'Signor Rotura called upon Mr. Grant to
invoke his assistance in a scheme for the transmission of
live stock to Europe. Signor Rotura averred that he had
discovered a South American vegetable poison, allied to the
well-known *woolara* (*sic*) that had the power of perfectly
suspending animation, and that the trance thus produced

continued until the application of another vegetable essence caused the blood to resume its circulation and the heart its functions. So perfect, moreover, was this suspension of life that Signor Rotura had found in a warm climate decomposition set in at the extremities after a week of this living death, and he imagined that if the body in this inert state were reduced to a temperature sufficiently low to arrest decomposition, the trance might be kept up for months, possibly for years. He frankly owned that he had never tried this preserving of the tissues by cold, and could not confidently speak as to its effect upon the after-restoration of the animal operated on. Before he left Mr. Grant he had turned that gentleman's doubts into wondering curiosity by experimenting on his dog.' The account of this experiment I defer for a moment till I have shown how closely in several respects this portion of the Australian hoax resembles the corresponding part of the American story. It will be observed that the great discovery is presented as simply a very surprising development of a process which is strictly within the limits, not only of what is possible, but of what is known. So also in the case of the Lunar Hoax, the amazing magnifying power by which living creatures in the moon were said to have been rendered visible, was presented as simply a very remarkable development of the familiar properties of the telescope. In both cases, the circumstances which in reality limit the possible extension of the properties in question were kept conveniently concealed from view. In both cases, doubts and difficulties were urged with an apparent frankness intended to disarm suspicion. In both cases, also, the inventor of the new method by which difficulties were to be overcome is represented as in conference with a man of nearly equal skill, who urges the doubts naturally suggested by the wonderful nature of the promised achievements In the Lunar Hoax, Sir John Herschel and Sir David Brewster are thus represented in conference. Herschel asks whether the difficulty arising from deficient illumination may not be overcome by effecting a transfusion of artificial light through the focal image. Brewster, startled at the novel thought, as he well might be, hesitatingly refers 'to the refrangibility of rays and the angle of incidence,' which is effective though glorious in its absurdity. (Yet it has been gravely asserted that this nonsense deceived Arago.) 'Sir John, grown more confident, adduced the example of the Newtonian reflector, in which the refrangibility was arrested by the second speculum and the angle of incidence restored by the third' (a bewilderingly ridiculous statement). '"And," continued he, "why cannot the illuminated microscope, say the hydro-oxygen, be applied to render distinct, and if necessary even to magnify, the focal object?" Sir David sprang from his chair in an ecstasy of conviction, and leaping half-way to the ceiling' (from which we may infer that he was somewhat more than *tête montée*), ' exclaimed, "Thou art the man !"'

The method devised in each case being once accepted as sound, the rest of course readily follows. In the case of the Lunar Hoax a number of discoveries are made which need not here be described [1] (though I shall take occasion presently to quote some passages relating to them which closely resemble in style certain passages in the Australian narrative). In the later hoax, the illustrative experiments are forthwith introduced. Signor Rotura, having so far persuaded Mr. Grant of the validity of the plan as to induce him to allow a favourite dog to be experimented upon, ' injected two drops of his liquid, mixed with a little glycerine, into a small puncture made in the dog's ear. In three or four minutes, the animal was perfectly rigid, the four legs stretched backward, eyes wide open, pupils very much dilated, and exhibiting symptoms very similar to those caused by strychnine, except that there had been no previous struggle or pain. Begging his owner to have no apprehension for the life of his favourite animal, Signor Rotura lifted the dog carefully and placed him on a shelf in a cupboard,

---

[1] The most curious are given in the ninth essay of my work referred to in the preceding note.

where he begged he might be left till the following day,
when he promised to call at ten o'clock and revive the
apparently dead brute. Mr. Grant continually during that
day and night visited the cupboard, and so perfectly was life
suspended in his favourite—no motion of the pulse or heart
giving any indication of the possibility of revival—that he
confesses he felt all the sharpest reproaches of remorse at
having sacrificed a faithful friend to a doubtful and dangerous experiment. The temperature of the body, too, in
the first four hours gradually lowered to 25 degrees Fahrenheit below ordinary blood temperature, which increased his
fears as to the result; and by morning the body was as cold
as in natural death. At ten o'clock next morning, according
to promise, Signor Rotura presented himself, and laughing
at Mr. Grant's fears, requested a tub 'of warm water to be
brought. He tested this with the thermometer at 32 degrees
Fahrenheit' (which, being the temperature of freezing water,
can hardly be called warm), 'and in this laid the dog, head
under.' In reply to Mr. Grant's objections Signor Rotura
assured him that, as animation must remain entirely suspended until the administration of the antidote, no water
could be drawn into the lungs, and that the immersion of
the body was simply to bring it again to a blood-heat.
After about ten minutes of this bath the body was taken
out, and another liquid injected in a puncture made in the
neck. 'Mr. Grant tells me,' proceeds the veracious narrator,
'that the revival of Turk was the most startling thing he
ever witnessed; and having since seen the experiment made
upon a sheep, I can fully confirm his statement. The dog
first showed the return of life in the eye' (winking, doubtless, at the joke), 'and after five and a half minutes he
drew a long breath, and the rigidity left his limbs. In a few
minutes more he commenced gently wagging his tail, and
then slowly got up, stretched himself, and trotted off as
though nothing had happened.' From this moment Mr.
Grant had full faith in Signor Rotura's discovery, and promised him all the assistance in his power. They next

determined to try freezing the body. But the first two experiments were not encouraging. Mr. Grant fortunately did
not allow his favourite dog to be experimented upon further,
so a strange dog was put into the freezing-room at Mr.
Grant's works for four days, after having in the first place
had his animation suspended by Signor Rotura. Although
this animal survived so far as to draw a long breath, the
vital energies appeared too exhausted for a complete rally,
and the animal died. So also did the next two animals
experimented on, a cat and a dog. 'In the meantime,
however, Dr. Barker had been taken into their counsels, and
at his suggestion respiration was encouraged, as in the case
of persons drowned, by artificial compression and expansion
of the lungs. Dr. Barker was of opinion that, as the heart
in every case began to beat, it was a want of vital force to
set the lungs in proper motion that caused death. The
result showed his surmises to be entirely correct. A number
of animals whose lives had been sealed up in this artificial
death have been kept in the freezing chamber from one to
five weeks, and it is found that though the shock to the
system from this freezing is very great, it is not increased by
duration of time.'

I need not follow the hoaxer's account of the buildings
erected for the further prosecution of these researches.
One point, however, may be mentioned, which illustrates
the resemblance I have already mentioned as existing
between this Australian narrative and the Lunar Hoax. In
describing the works erected at Middle Harbour, the
Australian account carefully notes that the necessary funds
were provided by Mr. Christopher Newton, of Pitt Street.
In like manner, in the Lunar Hoax we are told that the
plate-glass required for the optical arrangement devised by
Sir J. Herschel was 'obtained, by consent be it observed,
from the shop-window of M. Desanges, the Jeweller to his
ex-majesty Charles X., in High Street.'

Now comes the culminating experiment, the circumstances of which are the more worthy of being carefully

noted, because it is distinctly stated by Dr. Richardson
that none of the experiments described in this narrative,
apocryphal though they may really be, can be regarded as
beyond the range of scientific possibilities :—' Arrived at
the works in Middle Harbour, I was taken into the building that contains Mr. Grant's apparatus for generating cold.
. . . . Attached to this is the freezing chamber, a small,
dark room, about eight feet by ten. Here were eighteen
sheep, four lambs, and three pigs, stacked on their sides in
a heap, *alive*, which Mr. Grant told me had been in their
present position for nineteen days, and were to remain there
for another three months. Selecting one of the lambs,
Signor Rotura put it on his shoulder, and carried it outside
into the other building, where a number of shallow cemented
tanks were in the floor, having hot and cold water taps
to each tank, with a thermometer hanging alongside. One
of these tanks are quickly filled, and its temperature tested
by the Signor, I meantime examining with the greatest
curiosity and wonder the nineteen-days-dead lamb. The
days of miracles truly seem to have come back to us, and
many of those stories discarded as absurdities seem to me
less improbable than this fact, witnessed by myself. There
was the lamb, to all appearance dead, and as hard almost
as a stone, the only difference perceptible to me between his
condition and actual death being the absence of dull glassi-
ness about the eye which still retained its brilliant transparency. Indeed, this brilliancy of the eye, which is height-
ened by the enlargement of the pupil, is very striking, and
lends a rather weird appearance to the bodies. The lamb
was gently dropped into the warm bath, and was allowed
to remain in it about twenty-three minutes, its head being
raised above the water twice for the introduction of the
thermometer into its mouth, and then it was taken out and
placed on its side on the floor, Signor Rotura quickly dividing the wool on its neck, and inserting the sharp point of
a small silver syringe under the skin and injecting the antidote. This was a pale green liquid, and, as I believe, a

decoction from the root of the *Astracharlis,* found in South America. The lamb was then turned on its back, Signor Rotura standing across it gently compressing its ribs with his knees and hands in such a manner as to imitate their natural depression and expansion during breathing. In ten minutes the animal was struggling to free itself, and when released skipped out through the door and went gambolling and bleating over the little garden in front. Nothing has ever impressed me so entirely with a sense of the marvellous. One is almost tempted to ask, in the presence of such a discovery, whether death itself may not ultimately be baffled by scientific investigation.' In the Lunar Hoax there is a passage resembling in tone the lively account of the lamb's behaviour when released. Herds of agile creatures like antelopes were seen in the moon, 'abounding in the acclivitous glades of the woods.' ' This beautiful creature afforded us,' says the narrator, ' the most exquisite amusement. The mimicry of its movements upon our white-painted canvas was as faithful and luminous as that of animals within a few yards of the *camera obscura.* Frequently, when attempting to put our fingers upon its beard, it would suddenly bound away, as if conscious of our earthly impertinence ; but then others would appear, whom we could not prevent nibbling the herbage, say or do to them what we would.' And again, a little further on : ' We fairly laughed at the recognition of so familiar an acquaintance as a sheep in so distant a land —a good large sheep, which would not have disgraced the farms of Leicestershire or the shambles of Leadenhall Market ; presently they appeared in great numbers, and on reducing the lenses we found them in flocks over a great part of the valley. I need not say how desirous we were of finding shepherds to these flocks, and even a man with blue apron and rolled-up sleeves would have been a welcome sight to us, if not to the sheep ; but they fed in peace, lords of their own pastures, without either protector or destroyer in human shape.'

Not less amusing, though more gravely written, is the

account of the benefits likely to follow from the use of the wonderful process for freezing animals alive. Cargoes of live sheep can be readily sent from Australia to Europe. Any that cannot be restored to life will still be good meat ; while the rest can be turned to pasture or driven alive to market. With bullocks the case would not be quite so simple, because of their greater size and weight, which would render them more difficult to handle with safety. The carcass being rendered brittle by freezing, they are so much the more liable to injury. ' It sounded odd to hear Mr. Grant and Signor Rotura laying stress upon the danger of breakage in a long voyage.' This one can readily imagine.

Some of the remoter consequences of the discovery are touched on by the narrator, though but lightly, as if he saw the necessity of keeping his wonders within reasonable limits. Signor Rotura, 'though he had never attempted his experiment on a human being,' which was considerate on his part, ' had no doubt at all as to its perfect safety.' He had requested Sir Henry Parkes to allow him to operate on the next felon under capital sentence. This, by the way, was a compromising statement on our hoaxer's part. It requires very little aquaintance with our laws to know that no one could allow a felon condemned to death to be experimented on in this or in any other manner. Such a man is condemned to die, and to die without any preliminary tortures, bodily or mental, other than those inseparable from the legally adopted method of bringing death about. He can neither be allowed to remain alive after an experiment, and necessarily free (because he has not been condemned to other punishment than the death penalty), nor can he be first experimented upon and then hanged. So that that single sentence in the narrative should have shown every one that it was a hoax, even if the inherent absurdity of many other parts of the story had not shown this very clearly. As to whether a temporary suspension of the vital faculties would affect the longevity of the patient, Signor Rotura expressed himself somewhat doubtful ; he believed,

however, that the duration of life might in this way be prolonged for years. 'I was anxious,' says the hoaxer, 'to
know if a period of, say, five years of this inertness were
submitted to, whether it would be so much cut out of one's
life, or if it would be simply five years of unconscious existence tacked on to one's sentient life. Signor Rotura could
give no positive answer, but he believes, as no change takes
place or can take place while this frozen trance continues,
no consumption, destruction, or reparation of tissue being
possible, it would be so many unvalued and profitless years
added to a lifetime.' Of some of the strange ideas suggested
by this conception I shall take occasion to speak further on ;
I must for the present turn, however from the consideration
of this ingenious hoax to discuss the scientific possibilities
which underlie the narrative, or at least some parts of the
narrative.

In the first place, it must be noticed that in the phenomena of hibernation we have what at a first view seems
closely to resemble the results of Signor Rotura's apocryphal
experiments. As I remarked in the *Times*, the idea under-
lying the Australian story is that the hibernation of animals
can be artificially imitated and extended, so that as certain
animals lie in a state of torpor and insensibility throughout
the winter months, all animals also may perhaps be caused
to lie in such a state for an indefinite length of time, if only
a suitable degree of cold is maintained, and some special
contrivance adopted to prevent insensibility from passing into
death. The phenomena of hibernation are indeed so surprising, when rightly understood, that inexperienced persons
might well believe in almost any wonders resulting from the
artificial production (which, be it remembered, is altogether
possible) of the hibernating condition, and the artificial extension of this condition to other animals than those which
at present hibernate, and to long periods of time. It has
been justly said, that if hibernation had only been noticed
among cold-blooded animals, its possibility in the case of
mammals would have seemed inconceivable. The first

news that the bat and hedgehog pass into the state of complete hibernation, would probably have been received as
either a daring hoax or a very gross blunder.

Let us consider what hibernation really is. When, as
winter approaches and their insect food disappears, the bat
and the hedgehog resign themselves to torpor, the processes
which we are in the habit of associating with vitality gradually
diminish in activity. The breathing becomes slower and
slower, the heart beats more and more slowly, more and
more feebly. At last the breathing ceases altogether. The
circulation does not wholly cease however. So far as is
known, the life of warm-blooded animals cannot continue
after the circulation has entirely ceased for more than a
certain not very considerable length of time.[1] The chemical
changes on which animal heat depends, and without which
there can be no active vitality, cease with the cession of
respiration. But dormant vitality is still maintained in
hibernation, because the heart's fibre, excited to contract by
the carbonised blood, continues to propel the blood through
the torpid body. This slow circulation of venous blood
continues during the whole period of hibernation. It is
the only vital process which can be recognised ; and it is
not easy to understand how the life of any warm-blooded
animal can be maintained in this way. The explanation
usually offered is that the material conveyed by the absorbents
suffices to counterbalance the process of waste occasioned
by the slow circulation. But this does not in reality touch
the chief difficulty presented by the phenomena of hibernation. So far as mere waste is concerned (as I have elsewhere
pointed out) the imagined Australian process is as effectual
as hibernation ; in that process, of course the circulation
would be as completely checked as the respiration ; thus
there would be no waste, and the absorbents (which would

[1] Few probably are aware how long some animals may remain without breathing and yet survive. Kittens and puppies have been brought
to life after being immersed in water for nearly three-quarters of an
hour.

also be absolutely dormant) would not have to do even that slight amount of work which they accomplish during hibernation. Science can only say that the known cases of hibernation among warm-blooded animals show that the vital forces may be reduced much lower without destroying life, than but for them we should have deemed conceivable.

But next let us consider what science has to say as to the artificial suspension of vitality. In Dr. Richardson's paper on this subject there is much which seems almost as surprising as anything in the Australian story. Indeed, he seems scarcely to have felt assured that that story really was a hoax. 'The statements,' he says, 'which, under the head of "A Wonderful Discovery," are copied from the *Brisbane Courier*, seem greatly to have astonished the reading public. To what extent the statements are true or untrue it is impossible to say. The whole may be a cleverly-written fiction, and certain of the words and names used seem, according to some readers, to suggest that view ; but be this so or not, I wish to indicate that some part at all events of what is stated might be true, and is certainly within the range of possibility.' 'The discovery,' he proceeds, 'which is described in the communication under notice, is not in principle new ; on the subject of suspension of animation I have myself been making experimental inquiries for twenty-five years at least, and have communicated to the scientific world many essays, lectures, and demonstrations, relating to it. I have twice read papers bearing on this inquiry to the Royal Society, once to the British Association for the Advancement of Science, two or three times in my lectures on Experimental and Practical Medicine, and published one in *Nature*. In respect to the particular point of the preservation of animal bodies for food, I dwelt on this topic in the lectures delivered before the Society of Arts, in April and May of last year (1878), explaining very definitely that the course of research in the direction of preservation must ultimately lead to a process by which we should keep the structures of animals in a form of suspended molecular life.' In other words, Dr. Richardson had indicated the possibility of doing precisely that which would have constituted the chief value of the Australian discovery, if this had been real.

Let us next consider what is known respecting the possibility of suspending a conscious and active life. This is first stated in general terms by Dr. Richardson as follows : —'If an animal perfectly free from disease be subjected to the action of some chemical agents or physical agencies which have the property of reducing to the extremest limit the motor forces of the body, the muscular irritability, and the nervous stimulus to muscular action, and if the suspension of the muscular irritability and of the nervous excitation be made at once and equally, the body even of a warm-blooded animal may be brought down to a condition so closely resembling death, that the most careful examination may fail to detect any signs of life.' This general statement must be carefully studied if the reader desires thoroughly to understand at once the power and the limits of the power of science in this direction. The motor forces, the muscular irritability, and the nervous stimulus to muscular action, can be reduced to a certain extent without destroying life, but not absolutely without destroying life. The reduction of the muscular irritability must be made at once and equally ; if the muscular irritability is reduced to its lowest limit while the nervous excitation remains unaltered, or is less reduced, death ensues ; and *vice versâ*, if the nervous excitation is reduced to its lowest limits while the muscular irritability remains unaltered, or is little reduced, death equally follows. Then it is to be noticed that though when the state of seeming death is brought about, the most careful examination may fail to detect any signs of life, it does not follow that science may not find perfectly sure means of detecting cases where life still exists but is at its very lowest. Of course all the ordinary tests, in which so many place complete reliance—a mirror placed close to the mouth, a finger on the pulse, hand or ear to the breast [1] over the heart,

---

[1] Objection has been taken to the italicised words in the following

and so forth—would be utterly inadequate, in such a case, to reveal any signs of life. That doctors have been deceived by cases of suspended vitality not artificially produced, but presenting similar phenomena, is well known. A case in point may not be out of place here, as illustrating well certain features of suspended animation, and showing the possibility that in *some* cases consciousness may remain, even when the most careful examination detects no traces of life. The case is described by Dr. Alexander Crichton, in his 'Inquiry into the Nature and Origin of Mental Derangement.' ' A young lady, who had seemed gradually to sink until she died, had been placed in her coffin, careful scrutiny revealing no signs of vitality. On the day appointed for her funeral, several hymns were sung before her door. She was conscious of all that happened around her, and heard her friends lamenting her death. She felt them put on the dead-clothes, and lay her in the coffin, which produced an

passage from ' No Thoroughfare ' (one of the parts certainly written by Dickens and not by Wilkie Collins) : ' The cry came up : " His heart still beats against mine. I warm him in my arms. I have cast off the rope, for the ice melts under us, and the rope would separate me from him ; but I am not afraid." .·. . . . The cry came up, "We are sinking lower, but his heart still beats against mine." . . . . The cry came up, " We are sinking still, and we are deadly cold. *His heart no longer beats against mine.* Let no one come down to add to our weight. Lower the rope only." . . . . The cry came up with a deathly silence, " Raise ! softly !" . . . . She broke from them all and sank over him on his litter, with both her loving hands upon *the heart that stood still.*' It has been supposed that Dickens wilfully departed here from truth, in order to leave the impression on the reader that Vendale was assuredly dead. That he wished to convey this impression is obvious. He often showed similar care to remove, if possible, all hope from the anxious reader's mind (markedly so in his latest and unfinished work, where nevertheless any one well acquainted with Dickens's manner knows not only that Drood is alive, but that disguised as Datchery he was to have watched Jasper to the end). But in reality, it has happened more than once that persons have been restored to life who have been found in snow-drifts not merely reduced to complete insensibility, but without any recognisable heart-beat. Dickens had probably heard of such cases when in Switzerland.

indescribable mental anxiety. She tried to cry but her mind was without power, and could not act on the body. It was equally impossible to her to stretch out her arms or to open her eyes or to cry, although she continually endeavoured to do so. The internal anguish of her mind was, however, at its utmost height when the funeral hymns began to be sung and when the lid of the coffin was about to be nailed on. The thought that she was to be buried alive was the first one which gave activity to her mind, and caused it to operate on her corporeal frame. Just as the people were about to nail on the lid, a kind of perspiration was observed to appear on the surface of the body. It grew greater every moment, and at last a kind of convulsive motion was observed in the hands and feet of the corpse. A few minutes after, during which fresh signs of returning life appeared, she at once opened her eyes, and uttered a most pitiable shriek.' In this case it was considered that the state of trance had been brought about by the excessive contractile action of the nervous centres. St. Augustine, by the way, remarks in his ' De Civitate Dei ' on the case of a certain priest called Restitutus (appropriately enough), who could when he wished withdraw himself from life in such sort that he did not feel when twitched or stung, but might even be burned without suffering pain except afterwards from the wound so produced. Not only did he not struggle or even move, but like a dead person he did not breathe, yet afterwards he said that he could hear the voices of those around him (if they spoke loudly) as if from a great distance (*de longinquo*).

To return, however, to Dr. Richardson's discussion of the artificial suspension of active life.

He recognises three degrees of muscular irritability, to which he has given the names of active efficient, passive efficient, and negative,—though doubtless he would recognise the probability that the line separating the first from the second may not always be easily traced, and that, though there is a most definite distinction between the second and the third, the actual position of the boundary line has not as yet been determined. In other words, so far as the first and second states are concerned, there are not two degrees only, but many. As regards the third or negative state, which is only another way of describing death, there is, of course, only one degree, though the evidence as to the existence of this state may be more or less complete and obvious. Dr. Richardson defines the active efficient state of muscular irritability as that 'represented in the ordinary living muscle in which the heart is working at full tension and all parts of the body are thoroughly supplied with blood, with perfection of consciousness in waking hours, and, in a word, full life.' The second, or passive efficient state, 'is represented in suspended animation, in which the heart is working regularly but at low tension, supplying the muscles and other parts with sufficient blood to maintain the molecular life, but no more.' The third of these states —the negative—' is represented when there is no motion whatever of blood through the body, as in an animal entirely frozen.'

With the first and third of these states I have in reality nothing to do, unless indeed it could be shown that the third or negative state can be produced without causing death. Perhaps in assuming, as I did above, that this state is identical with the state of the dead, I was, in fact, assuming what science has yet to demonstrate. I may at any rate, however, say without fear of valid contradiction, that science has as yet never succeeded in showing that this negative state may be attained even for a moment without death ensuing ; and the probability (almost amounting to certainty) is that death and this change of state have in every instance been simultaneous. Dr. Richardson speaks of the second stage as that in which animation is *usually* suspended ; but he does not show that the third stage can even possibly be attained without death.

The second stage, or stage of passive efficiency, closely resembles the third, ' but differs from it in that, under favouring circumstances, the whole of the phenomena of the active efficient stage may be perfectly resumed, the heart suddenly enlarging in volume from its filling with blood, and reanimating the whole organism by the force of its renewed stroke in full tension. So far as we have yet proceeded,' continues Dr. Richardson, 'the whole phenomena of restoration from death are accomplished during this stage,' meaning, it would seem, that in all instances of restoration the restoration has been from the second, never from the third stage. 'To those who are not accustomed to see them they are no doubt very wonderful, looking like veritable restorations from death. They surprise even medical men the first time they are witnessed by them.' He gives an interesting illustration. At a meeting of the British Medical Association at Leeds, 'a member of the Association was showing to a large audience the action of nitrous oxide gas, using a rabbit as the subject of his demonstration. The animal was removed from the narcotising chamber a little too late, for it had ceased to breathe, and it was placed on the table to all appearance dead.' 'At this stage,' he proceeds, 'I went to the table, and by use of a small pair of double-acting bellows restored respiration. In about four minutes there was revival of active irritability in the abdominal muscles, and two minutes later the animal leaped again into life, as if it had merely been asleep. There was nothing remarkable in the fact ; but it excited, even in so cultivated an audience as was then present, the liveliest surprise.'

But when we learn the condition necessary that a body which has once been reduced to the state of passive efficiency should be restored to active life, we recognise that even when science has learned how to reduce vitality to a minimum without destroying it, few will care to risk the process, either in their own persons or in the case of those dear to them. Besides the condition already indicated, that the muscular irritability and the nervous excitation must be simultaneously and equally reduced, it is essential that the blood, the muscular fluid, and the nervous fluid should all

three remain in what Dr. Richardson calls the aqueous condition, and not become what he calls pectous, a word which
we must understand to bear the same relation to the word
solid or crystalline that the word 'aqueous,' as used by Dr.
Richardson, bears to the word watery. If all three fluids
remain in the aqueous condition, 'the period during which
life may be restored is left undefined. It may be a very
long period, including weeks, and possibly months, granting
that decomposition of the tissues is not established, and
even after a limited process of decomposition, there may
be renewal of life in cold-blooded animals. But if pectous
change begins in any one of the structures I have named, it
extends like a crystallisation quickly through all the structures
and thereupon recovery is impossible, for the change in one
of the parts is sufficient to prevent the restoration of all.
Thus the heart may be beating, but the blood being pectous
it beats in vain ; or the heart may beat and the blood may
flow, but the voluntary muscles being pectous the circulating
action is vain ; or the heart may beat, the blood may flow,
and the muscles may remain in the aqueous condition, but
the nerves being pectous the circulating action is in vain ;
or sometimes the heart may come to rest, and the other parts
may remain susceptible, but the motion of the heart and
blood not being present to quicken them into activity, their
life is in vain.' Add to this, that the restoration of the
motor forces, of the muscular irritability, and of the nervous
excitation, must be as simultaneous and as equal as their
reduction had been, and we begin to recognise decided objections to the too frequent suspension of animation, even
when the most perfect artificial means have been devised
for bringing about that interesting result.

Although, however, we may not feel encouraged to believe that many will care to have experiments tried on themselves in this direction, we may still examine with interest
the results of experimental research and experience. These
agree in showing that there are means by which active life
may be suspended, while at the same time the aqueous con-

dition of the fluids mentioned above (the blood, the muscular fluid, and the nervous fluid, the two latter of which are for convenience called the colloidal animal fluids, and are derived from the blood) is retained.

The first and in some respects the most efficient of these means is cold. The blood and the colloidal fluids remain in the aqueous condition when the body is exposed to cold at freezing-point. 'At this same point all vital acts, excepting perhaps the motion of the heart' (it is Dr. Richardson, be it remembered, who thus uses the significant word 'perhaps'), 'may be temporarily arrested in an animal, and then some animals may continue apparently dead for long intervals of time, and may yet return to life under conditions favourable to recovery.' Dr. Richardson gives a singular illustration of this, describing an experiment which must have appeared even more surprising to those who witnessed it than that in which the rabbit was restored to life. 'In one of my lectures on death from cold,' he says, 'which I delivered in the winter session of 1867, some fish which during a hard frost had been frozen in a tank at Newcastle-on-Tyne, were sent up to me by rail. They were produced in the completely frozen state at the lecture, and by careful thawing many of them were restored to perfect life. At my Croomian lecture on muscular irritability after systemic death, a similar fact was illustrated from frogs. It would appear, indeed, that so far as cold-blooded animals are concerned, there is no recognisable limit to the time during which they may remain thus frozen yet afterwards recover. But, even in their case, much skill is required to make the recovery sure. 'If in thawing them the utmost care is not taken to thaw gradually, and at a temperature always below the natural temperature of the living animal, the fluids will pass from the frozen state through the aqueous into the pectous so rapidly that death from pectous change will be pronounced without perceiving any intermediate or life stage at all.' Naturally it is much more difficult to restore life in the case of warm-blooded animals. Indeed, Dr. Richardson

remarks, that in the case of the more complex and differently shielded organs of warm-blooded animals, it is next
to impossible to thaw equally and simultaneously all the
colloidal fluids. ' In very young animals it can be done.
Young kittens, a day or two old, that have been drowned in
ice-cold water, will recover after two hours' immersion almost
to a certainty, if brought into dry air at a temperature of 98
degrees Fahrenheit. The gentlest motion of the body will
be sufficient to re-start the respiration, and therewith the
life.'

Remarking on such cases as these, Dr. Richardson notes
that the nearest natural approach to the stage of passive
efficiency is seen in hibernating animals. He states, however, that in hibernation the complete state of passive
efficiency is not produced. He does not accept the opinion
of those who consider that in true hibernation breathing
ceases as above described. A slow respiration continues, he
believes, as well as that low stage of active efficiency of
circulation which we have already indicated. ' The hibernating animal sleeps only ; and while sleeping it consumes
or wastes ; and if the cold be prolonged it may die from
waking.' More decisive, because surer, is the evidence
derived from the possibility of waking the hibernating
animals by the common method used for waking a sleeper.
This certainly seems to show that animation is not positively
suspended.

He asks next the question whether an animal like a fish,
frozen equally through all its structures, is to be regarded as
actually dead in the strict sense of the word or not, seeing
that if it be uniformly and equally thawed it may recover
from this perfectly frozen state. ' In like manner,' he says,
' it may be doubted whether a healthy warm-blooded animal
suddenly and equally frozen through all its parts is dead,
although it is not recoverable.' If, as seems certainly to
be the case, the animal dies because in the very act of
trying to restore it some inequality in the process is almost
sure to determine a fatal issue, some vital centre passing

into the petrous state, the animal could not have been dead
before restoration was attempted ; for the dead cannot die
again. Albeit, the outlook is not encouraging, at any rate
so far as the use of cold alone for maintaining suspended
animation in full-grown warm-blooded animals is concerned.
Cold will, however, for a long time maintain ready for motion
active organs locally subject to it. Even after death this
effect of cold 'may be locally demonstrated,' Dr. Richardson
tells us, 'and has sometimes been so demonstrated to the
wonder of the world.' 'For instance, on January 17, in
the year 1803, Aldini, the nephew of Galvani, created the
greatest astonishment in London by a series of experiments
which he conducted on a malefactor, twenty-six years old,
named John Foster, who was executed at Newgate, and
whose body, an hour after execution, was delivered over to
Mr. Keate, Master of the College of Surgeons, for research.
The body had been exposed for an hour to an atmosphere
two degrees below freezing point,[1] and from that cause,
though Aldini does not seem to have recognised the fact,
the voluntary muscles retained their irritability to such a
degree that when Aldini began to pass voltaic currents
through the body, some of the bystanders seem to have
concluded that the unfortunate malefactor had come again
to life. It is significant also that Aldini in his report says
that his object was not to produce reanimation, but to obtain a practical knowledge how far galvanism might be
employed as an auxiliary to recover persons who were
accidently suffocated, *as though he himself were in some*

[1] Dr. Richardson will certainly excite the contempt of the northern
professor who rebuked me recently for speaking of heat when I should
have said temperature. 'An atmosphere two degrees below freezing-
point' is an expression as inadmissible, if we must be punctilious in
such matters, as the expressions 'blood heat,' 'a heat of ten degrees,'
and so forth. Possibly, however, it is not desirable to be punctilious
when there is no possibility of being misunderstood, especially as it may
be noticed (the Edinburgh professor has often afforded striking illustrations of the fact by errors of his own) that too great an effort to be
punctilious often results in very remarkable incorrectness of expression.

doubt,—that is, not in doubt only about the power of gal-vanism, but in doubt whether Foster had been restored to life for a while, or not ! Dr. Richardson has himself re-peated, on lower animals, these experiments of Aldini's, except that the animals on which he had experimented have passed into death under chloroform, not through suffocation. His object, in fact, was to determine the best treatment for human beings who sink under chloroform and other anæsthetics. He finds that in warm weather he fails to get the same results. Noticing this, he says, ' I experimented at and below the freezing-point, and then found that by the electrical discharge, and by injection of water heated to 130 degrees ' (again this terrible inexactness of expression) ' into the muscles through the arteries, active muscular movements could be produced in warm-blooded animals many hours after death. Thus, for lecture experiment, I have removed one muscle from the body of an animal that had slept to death from chloroform, and putting the muscle in a glass tube surrounded with ice and salt, I have kept it for several days in a condition for its making a final muscular con-traction, do some mechanical work, such as moving a long needle on the face of a dial, or discharging a pistol. In muscles so removed from the body and preserved ready for motion there is, however, only one final act. For as the blood and nervous supply are both cut off from it, there is nothing left in it but the reserved something that was fixed by the cold. But I do not see any reason why this should not be maintained in reservation for weeks or months, as easily as days, in a fixed cold atmosphere.'

Cold being, however, obviously insufficient of itself for the suspension of active life in warm-blooded animals, at least if such life is eventually to be restored, let us next consider some of the agencies which either alone or aided by cold may suspend without destroying life.

The first known of all such agencies was mandragora. Dioscorides describes a wine, called *morion*, which was made from the leaves and the root of mandragora, and possessed properties resembling those of chloral hydrate. That it must have been an effective narcotic is shown by the circumstance that painful operations were performed on patients subjected to its influence, without their suffering the least pain, or even feeling. The sleep thus produced lasted several hours. Dr. Richardson considers that the use of this agent was probably continued until the twelfth or thirteenth century. ' From the use of it doubtless came,' he says, ' the Shaksperean legend of Juliet.' He strangely omits to notice that Shakspeare elsewhere speaks of this narcotic by name, where Iago says of Othello :

> ' Not poppy, nor mandragora,
> Nor all the drowsy syrups of the world,
> Shall ever med'cine thee to that sweet sleep
> Which thou own'dst yesterday.'

Probably the use of mandragora as a narcotic may have continued much later than the thirteenth century. In earlier times it was certainly used as opium is now used, not for medicinal purposes, but to produce for a while an agreeable sensation of dreamy drowsiness. ' There were those,' says Dr. Richardson, in an interesting article on Narcotics in the *Contemporary Review*, ' who drank of it for taste or pleasure, and who were spoken of as ' mandragorites,' as we might speak of "alcoholists " or " chloralists." They passed into the land of sleep and dream, and waking up in scare and alarm were the screaming mandrakes of an ancient civilisation.' He has himself made the ' morion' of the ancients, dispensing the prescription of Dioscorides and Pliny. ' The same chemist, Mr. Hanbury,' he says, ' who first put chloral into my hands for experiment, also procured for me the root of the true mandragora. From that root I made the morion, tested it on myself, tried its effects, and re-proved, after a lapse perhaps of four or five centuries, that it had all the properties originally ascribed to it.'

The ' deadly nightshade' has similar properties. (In fact, morion was originally made from the *Atropa belladonna*, not from its ally the *Atropa mandragora*.) In 1851, Dr. Richardson attended two children who were poisoned for a time from eating the berries and chewing the leaves of the nightshade, which they had gathered near Richmond. They were brought home insensible, he says, 'and they lay in a condition of suspended life for seven hours, the greatest care being required to detect either the respiration or the movements of the heart; they nevertheless recovered.'

With the nitrite of amyl, Dr. Richardson has suspended the life of a frog for nine days, yet the creature was then restored to full and vigorous life. He has shown also that the same power of suspension, though in less degree, 'could be produced in warm-blooded animals, and that the heart of a warm-blooded animal would contract for a period of eighteen hours after apparent death.' The action of nitrite of amyl seems to resemble that of cold. In the pleasing language of the doctors, 'it prevents the pectous change of colloidal matter, and so prevents *rigor mortis*, coagulation of blood, and solidification of nervous centres and cords.' So long as this change is prevented, active life can be restored. But when in these experiments 'the pectous change occurred, all was over, and resolution into new forms of matter by putrefaction was the result.' From the analogy of some of the symptoms resulting from the use of nitrite of amyl with the symptoms of catalepsy, Dr. Richardson has 'ventured to suggest that under some abnormal conditions the human body itself, in its own chemistry, may produce an agent which causes the suspended life observed during the cataleptic condition.' The suggestion has an interest apart from the question of the possibility of safely suspending animation for considerable periods of time : it might be possible to detect the nature of the agent thus produced by the chemistry of the human body (if the theory is correct), and thus to learn how its power might be counteracted.

Chloral hydrate seems singularly efficient in producing the semblance of death,—so completely, indeed, as to deceive even the elect. Dr. Richardson states that at the meeting of the British Association at Exeter, some pigeons which had been put to sleep by the needle injection of a large dose of chloral, 'fell into such complete resemblance of death that they passed for dead among an audience containing many physiologists and other men of science. For my own part,' he proceeds, 'I could detect no sign of life in them, and they were laid in one of the out-offices of the museum of the infirmary as dead. In this condition they were left late at night, but in the following morning they were found alive, and as well as if nothing hurtful had happended to them.' Similar effects seem to be produced by the deadly poisons cyanogen gas and hydrocyanic acid, though in the following case, narrated by Dr. Richardson, the animal experimented upon (not with the idea of eventually restoring it to life) belonged to a race so specially tenacious of life that some may consider only one of its proverbial nine lives to have been affected. In the laboratory of a large drug establishment a cat, 'by request of its owner, was killed, as was assumed, instantaneously and painlessly by a large dose of Scheele's acid. The animal appeared to die without a pang, and, presenting every appearance of death, was laid in a sink to be removed on the next morning. At night the animal was lying still in form of death in the tank beneath a tap. In the morning it was found alive and well, but with the fur wet from the dropping of water from the tap.' This fact was communicated to Dr. Richardson by an eminent chemist under whose direct observation it occurred, in corroboration of an observation of his own similar in character.

Our old friend alcohol (if friend it can be called) possesses the power of suspending active vitality without destroying life, or at any rate without depriving the muscles of their excitability. Dr. Richardson records the case of a drunken man who, while on the ice at the 'Welsh Harp' lake, fell into the water through an opening in the ice, and was for more than fifteen minutes completely immersed.

He was extricated to all appearance dead, but under artificial respiration was restored to consciousness, though he did
not survive for many hours. On the whole, alcoholic suspension of life does not appear to be the best method available. To test it, the patient must first get ' very, very drunk,'
and even then, like the soldiers in the old song, must go on
drinking, lest the experiment should terminate simply in the
fiasco of a drunken sleep.

The last agent for suspending life referred to by Dr.
Richardson is pure oxygen. But he has not yet obtained
such information on the power of oxygen in this respect as
he hopes to do.

Summing up the results of the various experiments made
with narcotics and other agents for suspending life, Dr.
Richardson remarks that much is already known in the
world of science in respect to the suspension of animal life
by artificial means : ' cold, as well as various chemical agents,
has this power, and it is worthy of note that cold, together
with the agents named, is antiseptic, as though whatever
suspended living action, suspended also by some necessary
and correlative influence the process of putrefactive change.'
He points out that if the news from Brisbane were reliable,
it would be clear that what had been done had been effected
by the combination of one of the chemical agents above
named, or of a similar agent, with cold. The only question
which would remain as of moment is, not whether a new
principle has been developed, but whether in matter of
detail a new product has been discovered which, better
than any of the agents we already possess, destroys and
suspends animation. ' In organic chemistry,' he proceeds,
' there are, I doubt not, hundreds of substances which, like
mandragora and nitrite of amyl, would suspend the vital
process, and it may be a new experimenter has met with
such an agent. It is not incredible, indeed, that the Indian
Fakirs possess a vegetable extract or essence which possesses
the same power, and by means of which they perform their
as yet unexplained feat of prolonged living burial.' But he

is careful to note the weak points of the Australian story— viz., first, the statement that the method used is a secret, 'for men of true science know no such word ;' secondly, that the experimenter has himself to go to America to procure more supplies of his agents ; and, thirdly, that he requires two agents, one of which is an antidote to the other. As respects this third point, he asks very pertinently how an antidote can be absorbed and enter into the circulation in a body practically dead.

It is, of course, now well known that the whole story was a hoax, and a mischievous one. Several Australian farmers travelled long distances to Sydney to make inquiries about a method which promised such important results, only to find that there was not a particle of truth in the story.

OUR ASTRONOMERS ROYAL.

IN the sixteenth century men began to travel boldly across the ocean, whole fleets taking such journeys as until then had been undertaken now and then by some daring sea captain. It was early in August 1492 that Columbus had set sail, in a ship of not quite a hundred tons burden, across the wide Atlantic, and seventy days later, on Friday, October 12, 1492, he sighted an island of the Bahama group (most probably Cat Island, though some maintain the claims of Turks' Island), and supposing he had reached the Indies by a westerly route, gave to the insular region the name it still bears—the West Indies. Inexact measurements of the earth's globe, and imperfect means of determining his westerly range of travel, led to this utter misconception of the true position on the earth of the region to which his daring expedition had led him. So far as such occasional journeys were concerned, men might have continued to remain content with their imperfect astronomical knowledge. But when in the course of a few decades navigation extended, it became essential that seamen should have some means of determining their position on the ocean. Yet years passed, and though every sea captain could on any clear day or night determine with sufficient accuracy his latitude, or distance from the equator, no means had been devised for determining even roughly the longitude, or the distance east or west from any given point on the earth from which (as from Greenwich, Paris, or Washington in our own time) longitude may be measured,

The nature of the difficulty which in the sixteenth century, and still more in the seventeenth, exercised astronomers and seamen may be readily indicated. Imagine a captain in the open ocean without any knowledge of his position, but with instruments for determining the apparent positions of the heavenly bodies in the sky. Then on the first clear night he can observe the elevation of the pole star, and though the pole star is not actually at the pole of the heavens, the observation will give him a rough indication of his latitude. For the pole of the heavens is the point towards which the axis of the earth points, and it is easily seen that the nearer a place is on the equator (the great circle lying exactly midway between the ends of that axis) the nearer the visible pole of the heavens will be to the horizon. An observer who should pass uniformly from the equator to either pole of the earth, would find the pole of the heavens passing as uniformly from the horizon [1] to the point overhead. Its arc distance from the horizon would all the time exactly correspond to his arc distances from the equator. So that if the pole star were exactly at the pole of the heavens, an observer, by determining its apparent height, would at once determine his latitude, or distance from the equator. And though the pole star does not occupy that precise position, yet it moves only in a small circle around the true pole, and by noting it either when just above or just below the pole, or when exactly to the right or exactly to the left of the pole, the true position of the pole itself becomes known, simply because the distance of the pole star from the pole is known. In the southern seas, where there is no star very near the pole, the case is not so simple, but even there any star circling at a known distance around the pole would give the southerly latitude. But as a matter of fact the sun is usually observed for the latitude. For his distance north or south of the equator on any given day of

---

[1] I take no account here of the effects of the refractive or bending action of our own air on the rays of light from a star, but suppose the observation *corrected for refraction* as it is technically expressed.

the year is known, so that by observing him at noon when he is at his highest and due south, either just above or just below the highest point of the equator on the sky, we learn the apparent height of this highest point of the equator. A line to this point makes of course exactly a right angle with a line to the pole of the heavens ; and thus we learn the latitude as certainly in this way as we could by observing a star actually at the pole, if such a star there were ; and as it is always more convenient to observe in the daytime than at night, it is in this way usually that latitude is determined. Moreover, although instruments were less exact and ingenious in the sixteenth century than now, and the position of the sun day after day with respect to the equator was less exactly determined, this method was as available (so far as general principles were concerned) at that time as at present.

But how should an observer, placed as we have supposed in the open sea, determine how far east or west he was of any given place on the earth ? The aspect of the starlit heavens, and the daily motions of the sun and planets, are almost exactly the same at stations in the same latitude, however far apart they may be. The motions of the moon, on account of her relative proximity to the earth, are very slightly different at different stations in the same latitude, but the difference is so slight that without excellent instruments and the most perfect knowledge of the moon's motions, no observer could pretend to determine his longitude from observations of the moon even on land, far less from the unstable deck of a ship at sea. The real difference between two stations far apart in longitude, that is, in an east and west direction, is as great as the difference between two stations as far apart in latitude ; but whereas the latter difference is one which may be studied and determined at any time, the other is a difference depending entirely on the time. Thus if A and B are two observers far apart in a north and south direction, either can at any time determine the apparent elevation of the pole of the heavens as seen from his station, and so learn his latitude. The difference between these two elevations is the same all the time. If A could telegraph to B, and *vice versâ*, either would give the other at any time the same news about the position of their respective poles. But if two observers, C and D, were in the same latitude and at stations far apart in longitude, say C far to the east of D, though C and D at any given moment would have the stellar groups very differently arranged with respect to the horizon, yet the aspect seen by C at any given moment would be shown to D after a certain definite time interval had elapsed. It would be impossible for either C or D to tell how far east or west their respective positions were from Greenwich or other fixed point on the earth, or how far east C was from D, by mere observations of the heavenly bodies however carefully such observations might be made (apart always from those exact observations of the lunar movements to which I have referred above). But if C could telegraph to D describing the exact aspect of his skyscape at any moment, then D, by waiting till his skyscape presented the same aspect, could tell exactly how far west [1] he was from C. If, for instance, a quarter of a day elapsed, D would know he was a quarter of the way round the earth west (measuring along their common circle of latitude, or along the equator from the point due south of C to the point due south of D), or perhaps I shall be better understood by saying that in this case a quarter rotation of the earth round her axis has carried D's place to the position before occupied by C. Or, if D had a clock showing true time at C's station, and so knew the precise epoch when the heavens seen by C would have such and such an aspect, he would, by noting how much later his own skies assumed that aspect, become aware how far west his position was from C's. But if his timepiece had gone wrong, he would be *pro tanto* mistaken. Such a mistake to a captain at sea might mean that a coast which he supposed to be far to the west or east

---

[1] The earth rotates of course from west to east, and so causes all the heavenly bodies to apparently rotate from east to west.

of him would be close at hand, and in a short time he might
run his ship upon it and be destroyed.

For safe navigation in open ocean, then, special knowledge of the movements of the heavenly bodies is required.
Even to determine latitude well a seaman requires excellent
instruments, and carefully constructed tables of the motions
of the sun, moon, planets, and stars. For longitude he
requires still more thorough investigation of the moon's
movements (at least for long lasting ocean journeys), and in
addition he should have most accurate time measurers.
How accurately time should be measured for this purpose
will be inferred from the following considerations. At the
equator an hour corresponds to fifteen degrees of longitude,
or four minutes to one degree, or about $69\frac{1}{2}$ nautical miles ;
thus four seconds correspond to one nautical mile, and one
second to rather more than 500 yards. In latitude 60
degrees north these distances are diminished one half ; but
still so small an error as a second in time corresponds to
about 260 yards, and an error of seven seconds, such an
error as the best stationary clock might easily acquire in a
week, would correspond to an error as to position of more
than a geographical mile !

It will be readily understood that even in the sixteenth
century, when hundreds of ships crossed the Atlantic,
Pacific, and Indian Oceans, there was occasion for very
careful study of the celestial movements, very excellent
instruments, and very accurate time-measuring apparatus.
How much greater was the need in the seventeenth century,
when for every ship that had crossed the ocean in the days
of Henry VIII., there were hundreds on its broad bosom ?

It was thus that the necessity arose for national observatories, not intended, as many imagine, for the study of
astronomy as a science (though the science of astronomy is
undoubtedly advanced in a most important manner by such
observatories), but for the survey of the heavens and the
exact measurement of time. Precisely as navigation would
be unsafe unless the terrestrial globe were carefully surveyed,

and the true position of every coast line, nay, even of every rock and reef, accurately determined, as well as all changes which such coast lines, islands, rocks, reefs, &c., may undergo, so would navigation be unsafe unless the celestial globe, within which as it were the earth is suspended, had been carefully surveyed, and the true position of every star, the exact paths along which sun, moon, and planets travel, all accurately determined. And in passing it may be noticed that the work of a national observatory (where alone such survey of the heavens can be conducted) bears somewhat the same relation to the higher astronomical research, that the trigonometrical and topographical survey of the earth's surface bears to the profounder studies of the geologist, the biologist, and the paleontologist.

Yet it was not till the year 1674 that any definite scheme for systematic survey of the heavens, in the interests of navigation and commerce, was planned in this country. It had been pointed out by a Frenchman, Le Sieur de St. Pierre, that if the motion of the moon as supposed to be seen from the earth's centre could be accurately predicted, then a seaman who should at any moment observe the exact position of the moon in the heavens, would know the precise instant of terrestrial time (say the true London time) at that moment. Thence, as the difference of longitude between two stations is measurable by the difference of time [1] between those stations, the latitude of the ship could be exactly determined. Charles II., to whom the plan was proposed by Le Sieur de St. Pierre, referred it to a commission of officers and scientific men. One of these, Sir Jonas Moore,

---

[1] That is, the difference between the time of noon, or of the coming to the south of any known fixed star, at those two stations. It should not be necessary to explain this, because the words 'difference of time' can bear no other interpretation, seeing that it is the same moment of absolute time at any instant all over the world and throughout the universe. Yet repeatedly I have been asked what astronomers can mean by the time being different at different stations. A rough way of expressing their meaning is by saying that the time of day is different at different stations,

sought the opinion of Flamsteed on the subject, Flamsteed being well known at that time as a skilful astronomer. Flamsteed stated that in his opinion the knowledge of the moon's motions at that epoch was far too inexact for the purpose intended. He said that 'even the places of the stars in existing catalogues were grievously faulty.' It was as though a geographer should have said that none of the charts used by navigators showed the positions of coast lines with any approach to accuracy.

Charles II., who really showed a most commendable zeal for science in this matter, was much struck by Flamsteed's remark, and very sensibly pointed out that if astronomical knowledge were thus defective, the best thing to be done was to set to work at once, and zealously to correct the defect.

Under the auspices then of the king, of whom Rochester wrongly said that 'he never said a foolish thing and never did a wise one,' Greenwich Observatory was built, and in 1676 Flamsteed, who had been appointed Astronomical Observator,[1] at a salary of 100*l.* a year, entered into residence at the Observatory. The instruments which he principally used in his work as Astronomical Observator were not in use until 1689.

And here it may be asked how it was that a much greater man than Flamsteed, a man who reached the zenith of his fame during Flamsteed's tenure of the office of Astronomer Royal, but had already attained a widespread reputation when Greenwich Observatory was founded, was not appointed to be Astronomical Observator. Whether the office was ever offered to Sir Isaac Newton or not, I do not know, but most assuredly if it were so offered, it is most fortunate for science that the offer was not accepted. Probably Newton would not half so efficiently as Flamsteed

[1] This title is still retained in official documents, and is undoubtedly a more suitable title than that of Astronomer Royal, seeing that astronomical surveying, not astronomical research, is the chief duty of the office.

have executed the observations which this observer made, though men inferior to either might have executed those observations as well as Flamsteed or better. But certainly no one could have done Newton's work had he neglected it for the routine work at Greenwich. Yet we must not forget that without the systematic observations of Flamsteed, Newton would never have been able to place the theory of the universe on that firm basis whereon he established it in his 'Principia.' The architect, however great his genius, cannot complete his conceptions without the aid of the builder, any more than the builder can erect an edifice without the materials necessary for his work.

Flamsteed laboured at Greenwich under difficulties such as none of his successors have had to encounter. His salary, as already mentioned, was but one hundred pounds per annum, and even this pittance was often ill-paid. He had to buy or make his own instruments. To defray the expenses he thus incurred, he was obliged to take pupils. At first he observed with a sextant belonging to Sir Jonas Moore, who also lent him two clocks; some other instruments were lent him by the Royal Society. The sextant was of iron and seven feet in radius. The clocks were constructed by Tompion, the most celebrated clockmaker of his day. The pendulums were thirteen feet long, and swung a complete or double vibration in four seconds, that is, beat two second, so that their length was four times the length of a pendulum beating seconds, or about thirteen feet. They were so constructed that they required winding only once a year. Flamsteed also brought with him from Derby to Greenwich a quadrant three feet in diameter. With these instruments, strangely in contrast with those now in use, Flamsteed began his labours at Greenwich on October 29, 1676.

I need hardly say that I do not here propose to give any detailed account either of the methods followed by Flamsteed and his successors, or of the instruments they employed in their work. But it may be interesting to notice how utterly unlike was the plan first followed from that now universally employed. Flamsteed's first observation of the stars, or his survey of the heavens, was conducted much as a trigonometrical survey of a terrestrial tract is carried out. He measured with the sextant the apparent arc-distance separating a star from each of two stars (or from more than two) whose positions were already known, and thence calculated the position of the star. The method is very rough, and could lead but to imperfect results. At the present day astronomers follow an entirely different and far more satisfactory plan. A telescope is caused to swing so as to sweep the meridian, that is, the circle on the heavens passing from the south point of the horizon to the point over head and thence to the north point of the horizon. Every heavenly body visible in our northern heavens must in its daily rotation around the polar axis of the skies cross the meridian once at least. (If it is one of the stars within ' the circle of perpetual apparition,' or stars near enough to the pole not to set when due north, the heavenly body crosses the meridian twice, once above the pole and once below it, in each diurnal circuit.) The telescope then which sweeps the meridian serves to show at what elevation and at what time any heavenly body crosses that circle of the heavens, and thus shows the body's distance from the pole, and its rotational distance from any fixed circle through the poles from which the astronomer may find it convenient to measure such rotations. Whereas in the first method, the astronomer had to measure arcs in all imaginable directions ; he has by the modern method to measure only vertical arcs, and these always along one and the same semicircle from south to north. The superiority of the modern method,[1] as

---

[1] I speak of this method as modern, but there are reasons for regarding it, as in principle, exceedingly ancient. For in the great pyramid, which was manifestly intended for astronomical observation (though afterwards cased over so that none who came after its owner's death should use it for that purpose), we find the great ascending gallery, 150 feet in length and 28 feet in height, constructed so as to bear pre-

respects uniformity of procedure and of result, will be manifest to all. There are other not less important advantages which only the mathematician can fully appreciate.

Flamsteed retained the office of Astronomical Observator to the end of his life, which occurred on the last day of the year 1719. His first observation was made on October 29, 1676, but it was not until September 11, 1689, that he began regular observations of stars on the meridian with a mural arc, an instrument so constructed as to swing on the face of a vertical north and south wall (whence its name), and with a sweep of one hundred and forty degrees on the meridian.

The forty-three years of Flamsteed's tenure of the office did not pass without some unseemly quarrels, chiefly caused by the impatience with which contemporary astronomers awaited the publication of his results. We find him, in October 1700, writing thus to Dr. Smith, of Oxford :— 'Briefly, sir, I am ready to put the observations into the press as soon as they that are concerned shall afford me assistants to copy them and finish the calculations. But if none be afforded, both they and I must sit down contented, till I can finish them with such hands as I have ; when I doubt not but to publish them, as they ought to be, handsomely and in good order, and to satisfy the world, whilst I have been barbarously traduced by base and silly people, that I have spent my time much better than I should have done if, to satisfy them, I had published anything sooner and imperfect.'

The impatience of his contemporaries, however, caused him to depart from the course on which he had thus determined. He drew an estimate of the extent of the work which had to be prepared for the press. This estimate was

cisely on the meridian, a long arc of which it commanded ; while many of the details of this gallery are such as an astronomer intending it for the purpose indicated would have been certain to give to it, and such as on any other hypothesis appear to be without reasonable interpretation.

read at a meeting of the Royal Society on November 15, 1704, and was unanimously approved. Prince George of Denmark, Queen Anne's husband, undertook to pay all the expenses of publication, and a committee, consisting of Newton, Wren, and three others, was appointed to examine Flamsteed's manuscripts. The committee recommended that the observations should all be published. Flamsteed placed in their hands a copy of the observations so far made, but stipulated that no steps should be taken toward their publication. So at least he asserted afterwards; but it is clear the stipulation was not such as to prevent the work being sent to the printers as it was. When, however, he should have supplied the rest, Flamsteed broke his agreement with the committee, delaying the printing for no other purpose, so far as appears, but to obtain better terms.

In 1708 Prince George died, and a further delay ensued. But as Flamsteed himself showed no disposition to supply the required copy, complaints were made which led to the appointment of a board of visitors, consisting of the President of the Royal Society, and such other members of the Council of that Society as he should deem fit to take part with him in the work of supervision. They were authorised to demand of the Astronomical Observator, six months after the close of each successive year, a true and fair copy of his annual observations, and also to direct him to make such observations as they should consider desirable. They were also to inspect the instruments, and to see that these were maintained in proper and serviceable condition.

Professor Grant, in his excellent 'History of Physical Astronomy,' remarks on this important event in the annals of the Royal Observatory : 'The origin of the Board of Visitors is clearly traceable to the unfortunate misunderstanding that prevailed between Flamsteed on the one hand, and his scientific countrymen generally on the other. It has continued to exercise its functions to the present day. The salutary influence of such a board of inspection is indisputable, for while on the one hand it serves to prevent the application of the resources of the Observatory to any unwarrantable purposes, on the other it has the effect of periodically relieving the conscientious astronomer, from the responsibility attaching to the discharge of his onerous duties, and thereby operates as an encouragement of future exertion. It is gratifying to reflect that during the last hundred years, at least, it is only in the latter respect that the advantages resulting from the establishment of the Board of Visitors have been apparent.' [1]

In the spring of 1711 Flamsteed's observations were published in a folio volume. The incomplete catalogue of stars which Flamsteed had placed in the hands of the committee in 1704 appeared in this volume, notwithstanding his alleged stipulation that it should be regarded only as a pledge for his subsequent delivery of a complete catalogue into their hands. But there is no room for doubt that even if the stipulation were made as alleged, it was not binding under the circumstances. Had the complete catalogue been placed in the printer's hands in reasonable time, there would undoubtedly have been no excuse for the issue of the incomplete one ; but year after year had passed without any fulfilment of Flamsteed's agreement to complete the catalogue, and the course pursued by the Committee was the only one left open to them. If Flamsteed's stipulation could be regarded as under any and all conditions closing

[1] At the accession of William IV. a new warrant was issued, by which the constitution of the Board of Visitors was to some degree modified. The Royal Astronomical Society had then recently been formed, and received its charter at that time. As the new society was formed specially for the advancement of astronomy, whereas the Royal Society took all science (and more) as its province, and so might have for its president a man very slightly acquainted with astronomy, it was fitting that a share, at least in the supervision of the national Astronomical Observatory, should be assigned to the Society specially devoted to astronomy. Accordingly the two Societies—the Royal and the Astronomical—are, according to the new warrant, represented equally in the Board of Visitors.

this course against them, the incomplete catalogue had no value as a pledge.

The quarrels which arose between Flamsteed on the one part and Newton and Halley on the other, were first made matter of public discussion in 1835, by Mr. Francis Baily. Finding in Flamsteed's own manuscripts and autobiography a number of statements injurious to the characters of Newton and Halley, Mr. Baily unwisely published what he called an 'Account of the Life of Flamsteed,' which involved in effect an *ex parte* and unjust attack upon those eminent men. In 1837 Mr. Baily published a supplement, in which he stated that he had 'sought in vain for documents which might tend either to extenuate or explain the conduct of Newton and Halley.' He cannot have searched very carefully, for such documents existed precisely where one would have expected to find them, namely, among Sir Isaac Newton's papers. Among these papers Sir David Brewster discovered a series of letters and other documents, completely exculpating Newton and Halley from the charges rashly brought against them by Mr. Baily, and placing the character of Flamsteed, their calumniator, in a very unfavourable light. Apparently the sole cause of Flamsteed's delay in the first instance, and anger with Newton and Halley in the second, was a greed of money.

Albeit, Flamsteed did good work as Astronomical Observator. Professor Grant thus sums up his work : ' Flamsteed is universally admitted to have been one of the most eminent practical astronomers of the age in which he lived. His merits do not, indeed, appear at first sight so conspicuous as those of some of his illustrious contemporaries with whom he may be compared, although at the same time they are no less substantial. In carrying out views of practical utility, with a scrupulous attention to accuracy in the most minute details, in fortitude of resolution under adverse circumstances, and persevering adherence to continuity and regularity of observation throughout a long career, he has few rivals in any age or country. He was thus enabled to establish the fundamental points of practical astronomy upon a new basis, and to rear a super-structure which, for many years afterwards, served as a land-mark of vast importance to astronomers. . . : As first astronomer of the Royal Observatory of Greenwich, he set an example to his successors the beneficial influence of which cannot for a moment be doubted; nor while that noble establishment continues to maintain its proud pre-eminence [high position?] among the institutions devoted to practical astronomy, will the labours of its original director, prosecuted with such unwearied perseverance throughout a long career, despite the depressing influence of constitu-tional ill-health [and the unrelenting hostility of a powerful faction [1]], cease to be held in respectful remembrance by his countrymen.'

Flamsteed was succeeded by Halley. But as all Flam-steed's instruments were removed from Greenwich, no observations could be made till 1721. On October 1 in that year Halley made his first observation with a transit instru-ment said to have been made by Dr. Hooke.

A greater astronomer than Flamsteed, perhaps inferior only to Sir Isaac Newton (certainly inferior only to him among the English astronomers of his day), Halley was by no means so skilful in the practical work of a sky-surveying observatory. In the first place, Halley was in his sixty-fourth year when he accepted the appointment. As Professor Grant remarks, it is surprising, when we consider his age, ' that he should have undertaken the discharge of duties of

---

[1] This was written at a time when it was supposed that the attack made by Mr. Baily on Newton and Halley represented the true state of the case instead of being a mere *ex parte* statement. I believe the view I have expressed in my sketch of Flamsteed's life, in the *Encyclo-pædia Britannica*, is sound—viz., that the necessity for publishing Sir David Brewster's refutation was scarcely a less misfortune for science than was the original and most foolish blunder of Baily's in publishing his ill-considered attack. Scientific squabbles are degrading enough when they occur without being raked up a century afterwards.

so onerous a nature as those attached to the situation of
Astronomer Royal.' The habits of minute attention to details, required for successful work in practical astronomy, are
not readily acquired in advanced life. But Halley seems to
have had little original aptitude for such work, and indeed
to have undervalued (a common fault) the qualities he did
not possess. We may pay but little attention to Baily's
severe criticism of Halley's observations as not worth printing, because Baily may have been to some degree prejudiced
against Halley after reading Flamsteed's animadversions.
But Maskelyne had earlier told Delambre that Halley's observations (extending from October 1721 to December 31,
1739) were hardly better than Flamsteed's, a severe criticism
when the rapid progress of improvement in the instruments
of observation in those days is taken into account.

Halley died on January 14, 1742, in the eighty-sixth
year of his age. During more than twenty-four months
before his death he had made no observations,[1] a circumstance not to be wondered at when we consider how old he
was. What one does wonder at is that being too old to
discharge the duties of his situation he did not resign.

Bradley, who succeeded Halley as Astronomer Royal in
1742 (his nomination is dated February 2, 1742), was one
of the ablest, perhaps the very ablest, of all who have held
the office. While astronomy owes to him, as it does not to
any other Astronomer Royal, some of the greatest discoveries which have adorned the science, these were such as

---

[1] At a meeting of the Royal Society on March 2, 1727, Sir Isaac
Newton, then President, called attention to the circumstance that
Halley had not supplied the Board of Visitors, in accordance with the
authority given them, a true and fair copy, within six months after the
lapse of each successive year, of the observations made during such
year. He pointed out that the continued neglect of this regulation
might be detrimental to the public interest. Halley, who was present,
made the rather lame excuse that he thought it better to keep the observations in his own custody, so that he might finish the theory he
designed to build on them before others could reap the benefit of his
labours.

belonged to the field of his labours as a practical observer. His discovery of the aberration of light was indeed made before he accepted the situation of Astronomical Observator at Greenwich; but in the prosecution of the observations which led to that discovery he was fitting himself for the position he afterwards held. His more difficult and less striking, but in reality more important,[1] discovery of the nutation of the earth's axis was made while he was at Greenwich.

It will serve to indicate the general character of the work at Greenwich, as well as to show what progress practical astronomy was making, to consider—but we must do so very briefly—the nature of these discoveries.

For guidance in navigation and travelling generally, as well as in the measurement of time for civil and other purposes, the stars and other heavenly bodies are regarded by the astronomer as sky marks, whose observed direction gives certain information as to position or as to time. But that the information should be trustworthy, the causes which may lead to erroneous ideas as to a heavenly body's direction must be understood and their effects corrected. Speaking generally, it may be stated that, in the first place, *not a single star visible in the sky at any moment is really where it seems to be; and in the second, every star's position on the star vault is constantly, though slowly, changing.* As it is the specific office of an Astronomical Observator to learn precisely where the heavenly bodies are, he must manifestly find out all the circumstances which might cause him to be deceived. Some of the sources of error are sufficiently obvious. A rough instrument, such as an ingenious schoolboy could construct in an hour or two, would suffice to indicate the deceptive effect of our own air, whose refractive action on rays of light causes every star to appear somewhat higher in the heavens than it really is. Other sources of error are less easily ascertained. Again, though the reeling of the earth like a gigantic top, under the attractions of the sun and

[1] More important in its bearing on physical astronomy, though less important as regards practical observation.

moon, does not cause any star to appear in a direction in which it does not actually lie, yet by constantly changing the position of every star with respect to the poles of the heavens (more correctly by constantly changing the position of these poles on the star sphere), this motion causes a steady though slow change in the calculated position of every star. So also does the slow motion of each star or sun along its own special path in space.

The aberration of light is a displacement of the former kind, nutation a displacement of the latter kind. Light streams forth in all directions with enormous velocity from each star, while the earth rushes with enormous velocity round the sun. The latter velocity, though enormous, is but small compared with the former. Yet it has to be taken into account in determining the direction whence the light of a star comes, just as the velocity of a ship propelled otherwise than by a stern wind, has to be taken into account in determining the direction in which the wind is blowing.[1]

[1] It is worthy of mention that Bradley was led to the interpretation of the aberration of the fixed stars by the recognition of precisely this analogous phenomenon. Dr. Robison, of Edinburgh, relates the story in his article on *Seamanship.* The following account is from Dr. Thomson's *History of the Royal Society* : 'When Bradley despaired of being able to account for the phenomena which he had observed, a satisfactory explanation of it occurred all at once to him when he was not in search of it. He accompanied a pleasure party in a sail upon the River Thames. The boat in which they were was provided with a mast, which had a vane upon the top of it. It blew a moderate wind, and the party sailed up and down the river for a considerable time. Dr. Bradley remarked that every time the boat put about, the vane at the top of the boat's mast shifted a little as if there had been a slight change in the direction of the wind. He observed this three or four times without speaking; at last he mentioned it to the sailors, and expressed his surprise that the wind should shift so regularly every time they put about. The sailors told him the wind had not shifted, but that the apparent change was owing to the change in the direction of the boat, and assured him that the same thing invariably happened in all cases. Bradley was quickly able to interpret the phenomena, and found in its interpretation that of the aberration of the fixed stars.

With a wind blowing from the side (the nautical reader will excuse my avoidance of technical terms) the forward motion of the ship causes the apparent wind to come from a point nearer that towards the ship is travelling than is the point from which the real wind is blowing. In other words, the wind is made to appear less favourable than it really is. We may, in fact, regard the motion of the ship as producing a wind of equal velocity blowing dead against the ship's course, and this wind has to be combined with the real wind to give the direction of the apparent wind. The light coming from a star with a velocity of more than 180,000 miles per second has similarly to be combined with the effects of the earth's forward motion at the rate of about 18 miles per second ; and the apparent direction from which the star's rays seem to come (in other words, the apparent position of the star) is nearer to that point on the star-sphere towards which the earth is travelling than in the actual position of the star. So that just as an exactly head wind and an exactly stern wind are the only winds not affected in apparent direction by a ship's motion, so a star lying exactly in the direction towards which, and a star lying exactly in the direction from which, the earth is moving, would be the only stars in the heavens seen precisely in their true position (so far at least as aberration is concerned). The greatest possible displacement due to this cause occurs in the case of stars situated anywhere on the great circle lying between the two points just named, where there is no displacement. It is not great, simply because the earth's velocity in her orbit is but about the ten thousandth part of the velocity of light.[1] Still it is not one of those exceedingly minute quantities which tax the astronomer's means of instrumental observation. It amounts, in fact, to about the ninetieth part of the apparent diameter of the moon.

[1] If we take along the circumference of a circle an arc equal in length to about the ten thousandth part of the radius, and draw radii to the two ends of this minute arc, the angle between these radii will correspond to the maximum apparent displacement of a star due to aberration.

Even if we only consider the effect of such a displacement as this, if undetected, to the seaman, it appears by no
means of small importance. Supposing a star on the equator,
and displaced on account of aberration either eastwards or
westwards by the greatest amount which this cause of displacement can produce, or about 20½ seconds of arc. Then
since 15 degrees of arc on the heavens correspond to one
hour of diurnal rotation, it follows that 15 minutes of arc
correspond to one minute of time, and 15 seconds of arcs to
one second of time. Thus 20 seconds of arc correspond to 1¼
seconds of time, and an error of this amount would be equivalent in the determination of a ship's longitude to an error of
more than 620 yards. But in reality the effect of neglecting
such a correction as that due to aberration is not to be measured in this way by its direct action. Indirectly, regarding
the stars as skymarks by which the movements of sun, moon,
and planets are measured, the correction due to aberration
becomes of yet greater importance.

It should be noticed that Bradley's great discovery
might have been based on Flamsteed's observations alone.
For though Flamsteed himself failed to detect the aberration
of the fixed stars, he made his observations so carefully and
well, that from the simple study of his various observations of the several stars at different seasons, the amount
of displacement caused by aberration can be determined
almost as exactly as from the best observations of recent
times.

The nutation of the fixed stars is a displacement smaller
in amount, and not affecting the direction in which the stars
appear to lie, but the position of the earth from which we
see them. The reeling motion of the earth detected by
Hipparchus (though Ptolemy usually gets the credit of the
discovery) is caused by the perturbing action of the sun and
moon on the earth's spheroidal globe. Were the earth a
perfect sphere, there would be no such motion. Nutation
may be described as a quivering of the earth as she thus
reels. Were the disturbing action of the sun and moon

constant, this reeling would be uniform ; but as the moon's path round the earth varies in position (in inclination, shape, &c.), the disturbing action varies, and thus the reeling varies in rate, and the slope of the reeling earth's axis varies also, or the axis of the reeling earth may be said to quiver. In reality there is a small and relatively rapid reeling super-added to the great slow reeling. The axial slope of the small reel—so to describe what corresponds to the inclina-tion of a reeling top's axis to the vertical, amounts only to about $9\frac{1}{4}$ seconds, and each reel is accomplished in about $18\frac{1}{2}$ years, whereas the slope of the great precessional reel amounts to about $23\frac{1}{2}$ degrees, and each reel requires about 25,900 years. Thus the pole of the heavens revolves in 25,900 years in a great circle 47 degrees in diameter, while it also revolves around the mean position due to this pre-cessional reeling in a circle—really an oval—$18\frac{1}{2}$ seconds in diameter, in a period of about $18\frac{1}{2}$ years. All the stars are affected, so far as their position with respect to the poles is concerned, by these motions. The nutation thus intro-duces a correction of all stellar positions, which must be taken into account in all observations of the stars.

I have considered these discoveries by Bradley because, as I have said, they are the most important of all the dis-coveries (almost the only important discoveries) made by astronomers carrying out the systematic work of practical observation, in other words attending to the business which they are paid to do.

Bradley's last observation at Greenwich was made on July 16, 1762. He was succeeded by Dr. Bliss, Savilian Professor of Geometry at Oxford, who had few of the qualifications necessary for the office of Astronomical Obser-vator. He died early in 1765, his last observation having been made on March 15 in that year.

Bliss was succeeded by Maskelyne, whose first observa-tion was made on May 7, 1765. He used the same instru-ments as Bradley, but he adopted a system better calculated to lead to trustworthy and valuable results. He limited his observations to a select number of stars (besides, of course, the sun, moon, and planets). He observed these stars on every available occasion, and based on these observations a catalogue, which, though containing but thirty-six stars, was far more accurate than any previously formed. This plan of observation he continued throughout the whole period of his tenure of office, his first observation being made, as already mentioned, on May 7, 1765, his last on December 31, 1810. His actual period of office was slightly greater than 45¾ years, and has been surpassed only by the period during which Sir G. Airy held the office.

We owe to Maskelyne the establishment of the 'Nautical Almanac,' which first appeared in 1767. It cannot be said that the Royal Observatory had fairly begun even to fulfil the purpose for which it was established until the 'Nautical Almanac' appeared. During his entire period of office Maskelyne superintended the publication of the almanac.

When Maskelyne was made Astronomer Royal, there was no very eminent English astronomer to whom persons ignorant of the special duties of the office might have thought that the position should have been offered. Sir W. Herschel was teaching music until 1766, when he was appointed organist at Halifax, and his earliest regular observations were made in 1776. It need hardly be said that later, during at least the last twenty years of Maskelyne's life, there could be no comparison between him and Sir W. Herschel as astronomers. Maskelyne was the more precise surveyor, but his name is associated with none of the great discoveries which constitute the glory of astronomy. Of William Herschel it has been justly said, *cœlorum perrupit claustra*; he burst the bonds of the heavens, he penetrated beyond the limits that had before restrained men's views, and searched boldly into the depths of the universe. Of Maskelyne we can only say that he helped to assign the true position of certain celestial skymarks. But then this was the duty which Maskelyne was engaged to do ; he did it honestly and well.

Eleven days after Maskelyne's last observation had been made, his successor, John Pond, made his first observation January 11, 1811. Although his name is little known, indeed, scarcely known at all outside the ranks of professional astronomers, he was one of the ablest of his class. He extended Maskelyne's method of sidereal astronomy to more than 1,000 stars, his catalogue being 'generally admitted,' says Prof. Grant, 'to be one of the most accurate productions of the kind that has ever been given to the world.' Fine instruments by Troughton were employed by him, and in the course of a controversy with Brinkley as to the distances of the fixed stars he invented a method of observing stars by reflection at the surface of mercury which notably increased the accuracy of certain orders of observations.

During Pond's tenure of the office the career of Sir W. Herschel came to its end, and that of his almost equally distinguished son began. When Pond retired from office, in the autumn of 1835, Sir John Herschel was already recognised as England's greatest astronomer. Fortunately for science, no one was so ill-advised as to propose that this eminent man, already deeply engaged in the researches which have rendered his name illustrious, should be appointed to the office rendered vacant by Pond's retirement. (Fortunately for science, at least, on the assumption—doubtless incorrect—that if he had been offered the appointment, he would have left his congenial field of labours to accept others of far less scientific importance, for which he was far less fitted.) A successor to Pond was sought for among men already working in the same field, that is, already engaged in the work of exact surveying of the heavens. A most fortunate choice was made in the selection of George Biddell Airy, who, during his tenure of office (the longest hitherto by a few weeks, as compared with the next, Maskelyne's), has done more than any of his predecessors, save perhaps Bradley, to give to Greenwich its present high position among national observatories. He was already eminent in his special department of astronomical work, having ably

directed the Cambridge Observatory during seven years.
He had there introduced two features, unknown till then in
the work of public observatories, viz., the reduction of all observations by the observer himself instead of subordinates,
and the systematic observation of the planets, a department
of astronomy long neglected at Greenwich.

Space does not remain for the description of the special
work of Sir G. Airy. What remains must be devoted to
some remarks on the mistaken ideas which many seem to
have formed respecting the duties of the office, and on the
unsuitable and in many cases preposterous selections made
by newspaper writers for a successor to Airy.

The late Professor De Morgan, in his 'Budget of Paradoxes,' relates an amusing story about Flamsteed, the first of
our Astronomers Royal. An old woman who had lost a
bundle of linen came to Flamsteed to learn its whereabouts,
being under the impression that it was one of the duties, if
not the chief duty, of an Astronomer Royal to answer such
questions as are customarily addressed, by ignorant persons,
to astrological charlatans. Flamsteed, proposing to amuse
himself at the old woman's expense, ' drew a circle, put a
square into it, and gravely pointed out a ditch near her
cottage, in which he said it would be found.' He meant,
says De Morgan, to have given the woman a little good
advice when she came back ; but unfortunately for his purpose, the bundle was found in the very place which he had
indicated. It is added, though De Morgan does not mention the fact, that Flamsteed determined thenceforth to have
nothing to do with astrology even in fun.

It would seem, from much that has been written about
the office of Astronomer Royal, that the general public are
scarcely better informed on the subject than the old lady
who mistook the Astronomer Royal of her time for a con-
juror. Persons were named as likely to succeed Airy who
would have been as ill-fitted for the office as a sea captain
for a generalship, a general for the command of a fleet, or an
historian for the office of prime minister. Even those who

have rightly apprehended that the office is one requiring special training, as well as original aptitude and capacity, have in many cases failed to note that such special training as observers in any great observatory may obtain, though fitting them for the charge of ordinary observatories, may not by any means fit them to take charge of a great national observatory.

It must not be supposed that I make these remarks in depreciation of any of those who were named as likely to succeed the Astronomer Royal in the office to which Mr. W. M. Christie, formerly first assistant at Greenwich, has been appointed. Most of those who were thus named were persons who, by their method of life and study, removed themselves from even the possibility of being thought of in connection with the office, and, as it were, declined to have it offered to them. There is one road, and only one, in which a man, fit as respects capacity, can put himself in the way of the office, and even that road eventually branches out into several, one only of which leads to the goal in question. A skilful mathematician, with first-rate working powers, who shall begin, from the time of taking a high degree at the university, to work in one of the subordinate offices at Greenwich, taking shortly (in virtue of his position as a mathematician) one of the chief of these subordinate offices, may later become one of those from whom a new Astronomer Royal can be selected. But such a one may become, after a few years at Greenwich, the head of some important Government observatory, a position of greater emolument and perhaps of greater dignity, but one which, should he occupy it many years, unfits him for the office which is justly regarded as the highest which a professional astronomer can occupy. The reason of this is not far to seek. The routine at Greenwich is necessarily unlike that at other observatories. Much of the work which must be done at Greenwich is by no means essential elsewhere, and in turn much of the work which can be done with great advantage at other observatories (we are speaking all the time, be it

understood, of Government observatories) would be entirely
out of place at Greenwich. Now, even though the system
at Greenwich were thoroughly stereotyped, which is far from
being the case, a few years' absence from Greenwich work
would render even the ablest astronomer less fit to take
charge of our great national observatory than one who had
been engaged in superintending such work during those
years. Seeing, however, that the system at Greenwich,
though to all intents and purposes fixed, does yet in details
undergo modifications—that, in fact, being a living organisa-
tion, it *grows*, we can readily see that even the most skilful
astronomer can only retain the fullest fitness for the office of
Astronomer Royal, by remaining at Greenwich, and by
working continuously under the direct supervision of the
actual holder of that office. When such a man, otherwise possessing the requisite capacity, succeeds to the position of Astronomer Royal, there is the greatest chance
that the change will cause no hitch, even for the shortest
period, in the work of the great national observatory, and
this, after all, is the point in which the public is most interested.

The fitness (in these respects) of the appointment recently made will therefore be readily understood, and it will
be seen also why several of those named by persons unac-
quainted with the requirements of the office were, for various
reasons, more or less unsuited for the post. The greatest
master living of the mathematics of astronomy, although at
the head of an important observatory, would not only have
been in all probability a less efficient Astronomer Royal than
one who had been working for years at Greenwich, but
his transference to the office (had he been willing to accept
it) would have been a serious loss to science, because in the
office of Astronomer Royal he would have been unable to
continue those researches in which he has few or no equals.
One of the greatest professors (if not actually the greatest)
of pure mathematics could as ill be spared from his special
labours, even if he possessed the knowledge of routine work

essential in the chief of our national observatory. It should hardly be necessary to say that the indefatigable director of the 'Nautical Almanac,' although for a long time the head (and a most skilful and successful head) of a fine private observatory, would be ill placed as chief at Greenwich if for no other reason for this, that he is the fittest man living for the post he actually holds.

Again there are men who, by their telescopic researches in what may be called the physics of astronomy, by spectroscopic observations and discoveries, by their analysis of the great mass of observations gathered by others, and in other ways, are deservedly regarded as having notably advanced our astronomical knowledge, who would yet be altogether unfit to take charge even of the commonest routine work at Greenwich ; and even though they could, would only do so at the expense of more important work for which they are pre-eminently fitted. Most of these, indeed, are independent workers in astronomy, who are not willing (and have through the whole course of their lives shown that they are unwilling) to accept what would be to them the comparative slavery of a salaried office.

One astronomer indeed, and only one of those who were mentioned as likely to succeed the Astronomer Royal, could have taken his place without loss to the public, either, on the one hand, because of unfitness for the post, or, on the other, because no one else could so well do work given up that the office might be taken. I refer to an astronomer who has quite recently left the charge of one of our most important colonial observatories to take a leading astronomical office at Oxford. That astronomer had for several years held the position of chief assistant at Greenwich, and had the Astronomer Royal resigned four or five years ago, would almost certainly have succeeded him. But, as I have already pointed out, an absence of several years from Greenwich diminishes an astronomer's fitness for the special duties (in particular the superintendence of routine work) belonging to the office of Astronomer Royal. Without

400 FAMILIAR SCIENCE STUDIES.

touching in any way upon the question of relative capacity, zeal, or energy, I may say that in all probability the public interests were better served by the appointment to this office of the younger man who has during the last few years held the position of chief assistant at Greenwich.

I have touched on the erroneous ideas which many persons entertain respecting the duties of an Astronomer Royal. I may conveniently conclude by noting the admirable way in which the actual duties of the office have been discharged by the venerable astronomer who has so long held that important position. If we do not find his name associated with striking discoveries respecting the sun and moon, planets, stars, and comets, it has been because the duties of his office have been inconsistent with the researches by which alone such discoveries can be effected. An Airy has no *right* to undertake such work as has ennobled the names of a Newton or a Herschel. His duty to the nation, in whose service he has taken office, requires that he should devote his energies first and chiefly to the control and superintendence of that systematic observatory work which is so important to the nation as forming the very basis of our commercial system. Not only the property, but the lives of millions depend more or less directly on the accuracy and completeness with which that system is carried out. I may add what may seem to some a common-place consideration, which presents, however, the common-sense practical view of the matter, that the nation pays a certain sum yearly to the Astronomer Royal for the performance of certain work, and therefore has a right (each one of us has a right) to claim that that work and no other shall be done—no other work at least which would prevent that work from being well and thoroughly done. An Astronomer Royal who should devote any large portion of his time to independent researches, such as the Herschels, Huggins, Lassell, Draper, and other private astronomers have undertaken, might become very eminent for his discoveries in physical astronomy, but it would be at the expense of the country in whose service he had accepted office, in the opinion of all right-minded men his distinction would be to his discredit. The Astronomer Royal who has just completed his long term of office has achieved—though his official career has not been absolutely without mistakes—a worthier reputation, in this, that he has worked with such zeal and energy in the duties properly belonging to his office, that even the hardest-working professional astronomer might well hesitate to succeed him in a position always important, but which he has made most arduous.

PHOTOGRAPHS OF A GALLOPING HORSE.

ABOUT two years ago I heard for the first time of a photographic achievement which seemed to me at the time scarce credible, and which I was presently assured by one of our ablest English photographers was absolutely outside the bounds of possibility,—to wit, the photographic presentation of a galloping horse. Of instantaneous photography, so called, I had of course heard, and I had seen the process in operation. But I knew that the actual exposure in what is called instantaneous photography is not less than a second, even in that arrangement which was called some ten or twelve years ago pistolgraphy. Again, I knew that the sun had been photographed in a period certainly not exceeding the 1,000th part of a second. But the shortness of the exposure in that case was a necessity instead of involving a difficulty ; for the brightness of the solar image is such that an exposure of the tenth or even the hundredth part of a second would suffice to entirely 'burn out' the details of the photographic picture. To photograph a galloping horse, however, with distinctness, requires on the one hand an exposure of much less than a second, or even than the tenth or hundredth part of a second ; while, on the other hand, the luminosity of the image cannot, under any circumstances, be greater than that which, when ordinary photographs are taken, involves an exposure of several seconds at least.

As to the first point, it is easy to see that an exposure

of a second would result in entirely blurring the outlines of the horse's limbs. A galloping horse advances ordinarily at the rate of a mile in less that two minutes. In the photographs of which I had heard, the rate mentioned was a mile in 1m. 40s., or thirty-six miles per hour. Taking the last-named rate, or a mile in a 100 seconds, the galloping horse advances one hundredth part of a mile, or nearly eighteen yards, in a second, and therefore, as a horse at rest occupies a width of less than three yards, it is hardly necessary to say the picture obtained from an exposure of one second would be a mere confused blur. The image obtained in the tenth of a second would be no better, as the blurring would correspond to a width of nearly two yards. In the hundredth part of a second the image would be blurred to a width corresponding to more than half a foot—so that, although the picture of the horse as a whole might be perhaps just recognisable as a horse, the limbs would be confused beyond recognition. To get a picture which should show the limbs of a galloping horse with anything like distinctness, the blurring should not exceed a width corresponding to one inch in the life-size image of a horse. Now in what precedes I have only taken into account the forward motion of the horse as a whole ; but in considering the definition of the limbs we have to remember that these are not only advancing with the body, but are moved also in relation to the body, and that when the limbs are being thrown forward, this forward motion is added to the advancing motion of the body. Now the forward motion of the limbs varies in rate, from nothing when the limbs are farthest forward and farthest back, to a maximum somewhere near the middle of their forward sweep. This maximum cannot be less than the advancing motion of the horse, and is probably much greater.[1] As we must add this forward motion to the ad-

---

[1] In the case of a carriage, we get in the motion of the wheels what corresponds to the relative motion of the horse's limbs. In this case, we know that the relative forward motion of the top of the wheel, and the relative backward motion of the bottom of the wheel are each

vancing motion of the horse as a whole, we get for the maximum forward motion of a limb (meaning now the full forward motion, not only the motion relatively to the body) twice the advancing motion of the horse. We have seen that with an exposure of one second the blurring of the body of the horse would have a width corresponding to half a foot in the life-size image of a horse. The blurring of the limbs would vary from nothing to a width corresponding to a foot. That the blurring then, should nowhere exceed a width corresponding to an inch, the exposure should not exceed the 1,200th part of a second in duration. As a matter of fact, satisfactory pictures were not obtained until the exposure had been reduced to the 2,000th part of a second, and in later pictures the exposure has been reduced to the 5,000th part of a second.

And here, in passing, I may answer an objection which will occur perhaps to many readers. I remember that after mentioning in a lecture at Sydney, New South Wales, the brief exposure of Janssen's solar negatives, I was asked by one of the chief photographers of New South Wales, who had been present, how I could venture to speak of an exposure of the 1,600th part of a second, when no means could possibly be devised for measuring so short a period of time. I was able to reply that not only had Janssen been able in the most satisfactory manner to measure the exposure of his plates to the solar image, but that science had been able to measure periods of time so short as the 100,000th, and even the 200,000th part of a second. Nay, Wheatstone claims, and not without good reason, that, when attempting to determine the duration of a lightning flash, he measured periods very much shorter even than this. It sounds at first hearing altogether incredible, and indeed absurd, that men should pretend to measure by optical and mechanical means (for so has the task been achieved) a period which is a very small fraction of the duration of a

equal to the advancing motion of the carriage, so that the top of the wheel is advancing twice as fast as the carriage, while the bottom of the wheel is momentarily at rest.

luminous impression on the eye. Yet in reality this has been done by taking advantage of the very circumstance which seems at first sight to render it impossible. The method is so ingenious, and at the same time so simple, that it will be well to consider it here as an introduction to the less minute subdivisions of time involved in the processes which form the subject of this essay.

Conceive a rather large disc of ebony, round the edge of which are inlaid radiating lines of silver wire, exceedingly fine. Say, for instance, that there are 1,600 equidistant radiating lines, or in each quadrant 400, so that each centigrade degree (100 to the quadrant) is divided into four parts. If each wire is the hundredth of an inch in thickness, and the disc is one foot in diameter, the black space between the ends of the wires will be one-hundredth and a quarter (of a hundredth) in width. Now, suppose this disc set in rapid rotation, making, for instance, a hundred rotations per second. Then, in the 160,000th part of a second, one of the radiating wires will be carried to the position which, at the beginning of that short period, had been occupied by its next neighbour. But the forward edge of a wire will be carried to the position which had been occupied by the backward (or following) edge in a shorter time still—manifestly in five-ninths of the short period; for the breadth of the black space between the wires is five-ninths of the distance from centre to centre of successive wires. Thus, if the disc is whirling in darkness, and is suddenly lit up by a flash of lightning, and the flash lasts five-ninths of the 160,000th part of a second, or lasts one 288,000th of a second, the disc will appear as if bordered by a continuous ring of silver ; for during that time every part of the edge will have been occupied by lightning-lit silver, and as the eye retains a luminous impression for fully one-tenth of a second, the light from every part of the edge of the disc will appear to form a single image, in which the spokes of wire will not be separately discernible. If the lightning flash lasted half that time, the black spaces would be discernible, but would seem to be but half their real width, half their width being cut off during the continuance of

the flash. If the flash lasted a fourth of the above-mentioned
time, only one-fourth of the width of the black space would
be cut off, so that its width would appear but three-fourths
of what it really was, and so forth for yet shorter periods.
But this will suffice to show that Wheatstone could measure
by this method, as he claimed, the millionth part of a second.
For manifestly the eye could readily detect the diminution
of the black spaces by a full fourth of its amount, and this
reduction (on our assumptions as to the size of the disc and
the rate of its rotation) would be produced if a lightning
flash lasted but one 1,152,000th, or less than the millionth
part of a second. Thus, when Wheatstone stated, as the
result of his experiments, that a lightning flash does not last
the millionth part of a second, he was not (as some rashly
asserted) announcing over-confidently what could not by any
possibility have been established by evidence, but was, in
fact, simply asserting what he had satisfactorily proved.
Yet how wonderful it seems at first that science should be
able to say, as it did in this case, that a luminous appearance,
visible for fully the tenth of a second, lasts in reality less than
the 20,000th, or even than the 100,000th, part of that time.[1]

We see, then, that it is not only possible, but an easy
matter, to measure periods of time much shorter than the
1,000th or 10,000th part of a second. But it might still
seem marvellous, and in fact it is, that science should be

[1] Within a few hours of writing the above lines, I witnessed at the
observatory of Dr. Henry Draper, of New York, a very simple experiment illustrating the instantaneous character of the electric spark, and also
the intermittance of a luminosity which, as judged by the eye, appears
persistent. While the electric discharge was taking place in a series of
rapidly following sparks, the hand held steadily in front of the light
appeared to be quite steadily illuminated ; but if the hand was rapidly
fluttered about, a multitude of distinct images of the hand were seen,
producing an appearance as of a multiform hand with multitudinous
(and ever varying) fingers attached to it,—the explanation being that
the hand was successively visible and invisible, and many successive
images were seen in different positions during each tenth of a second of
the duration of luminous impressions.

able so to arrange matter that in such a minute period of time an image should be taken which shall be clear and well defined in all its details. Yet this has been achieved, and some of the results of the application of this process have now to be considered.

In the best paintings of horse-races, charges, the hunting-field, and so forth, we have what may be regarded as a conventional view of the horse at full gallop. He is shown with the two fore legs thrown well forward and the two hind legs thrown well back—in the attitude, in fact, which is indicated by the French expression *ventre à terre*, applied to an animal at full gallop. Anyone who has watched a race or a charge of galloping horses, will certainly be prepared to affirm that this attitude is one of those which a horse assumes in galloping. It is, of course, to some degree absurd that this one attitude, which is only (even on this assumption) assumed at certain definite instants by the horse at full gallop, should be presented as the only or almost the only attitude recognisable in a group of galloping horses. Still, the idea generally entertained by those who study pictures of the kind is that this attitude is the most characteristic, and the one best suited for delineation. Accordingly, paintings and drawings of galloping horses which present this attitude and no other, are amongst those most admired by the artistic world.

So soon, however, as we test by instantaneous photography the movements of a horse, we find that this admired and presumedly characteristic attitude is not one which really characterises the gallop. Not only is this the case, but the attitude is actually never assumed at all by a horse either in this or in any other gait. And, on the other hand, we find that positions are assumed by the galloping horse which no one would for a moment have supposed possible.

The positions shown in Mr. Muybridge's photographs are eleven, and these include all the movements made in one complete stride. It requires some care to distinguish

the movements of the different legs. Let us follow the
movements *seriatim*.

The first position to the series is that shown in Fig. 1.
Here the horse seems to be balanced on one fore leg, the
two hind legs being thrown into the position often shown
in drawings of a leaping horse. The other fore leg is thrown
back in a position suggestive of rest rather than of the violent
action of a galloping horse's limbs. The four legs are numbered so that their subsequent motions may be followed. It
must be remembered that this picture does not belong to the
initial series of movements by which a trot or a canter is
changed into a gallop. The animal thus photographed was
in full gallop all the time. In this position the fore leg

FIG. 1.

marked 1 appears to bear the entire weight of the body, but,
in reality, it does not (although the contrary has been maintained). The body has been propelled forwards and slightly
upwards somewhat earlier, as will presently appear, and
fore foot 1 is in reality scarcely supporting the body at all,
but simply adding to the propulsive motion, the body need-
ing for the moment little support.

Fig. 2 shows the horse twenty-seven inches further forward. (It may be noticed in passing that Fig. 11 shows a
position of the body between the positions shown in Fig. 1
and Fig. 2.) The fore leg marked 1 has continued to propel the body forward until this leg had become so aslant
(see Fig. 11) that the hoof has to leave the ground, and is
thrown back as shown in Fig. 2. Fore leg 2 has been

carried forward, the hoof rising and the leg becoming more sharply bent. Both hind legs have been thrown forward, but leg 4 more than leg 3, so that the hoofs are rather nearer together than in Fig. 2.

In the interval between the positions shown in Figs. 1

FIG. 2.

and 2 there had been propulsion, though not very forcibly, only one leg touching the ground, and that only during a. portion of the time. As the pictures are made at equal distances of 27 inches apart, the time between Fig. 1 and Fig. 2 is to some degree diminished by the additional velo-

FIG. 3.

city due to this propulsive motion. On the other hand, as all four limbs are in the air during the interval of time between Figs. 2 and 3, there has not been, in this case, any propulsive action, and the body of the horse has therefore been all the time, though but slightly, losing forward velocity. We note a considerable alteration in the position of

all four limbs.   Fore leg 1 has been thrown forward, so far
as the upper part of the limb is concerned, but the lower
part of the limb has been thrown upward.   Fore leg 2 has
been thrown forward, and is now slightly less bent.   Hind
leg 3 seems, at first sight, scarcely changed in position ; but,
in reality, it has been thrown forward and then backward to
nearly the position it had when Fig. 2 was taken.   Hind
leg 4 has been thrown further forward.

Between Fig. 3 and Fig. 4 the body has been entirely
in the air until just before Fig. 4 was taken, when hind leg
3 had just touched the ground.   Thus the interval in time,
as there had been no propulsive motion, has been rather
greater between Figs. 3 and 4 than between Figs. 2 and 3,

FIG. 4.

and greater still than between Figs. 1 and 2.   A correspondingly greater change has taken place in the position of the
limbs.   Fore leg 1 has been curled up under the body, the
upper part of the limb being thrown forward.   Fore leg 2
has been thrown more markedly forward and partly unbent.
Hind leg 3 has been set down by being thrown backward,
and hind leg 4 has been thrown forward nearly to the
farthest.   In this position the body is advancing almost at
its slowest—though, of course, it will be understood that in
saying this I do not mean to describe the rate of advance
as greatly reduced.   The body has been only carried forward seven feet four inches from the position it had in Fig.
1, and its rate of advance has scarcely been reduced at all.
Nevertheless, such reduction as the rate of advance does

undergo during the swift gallop of the horse attains its maximum at about this position.

In Fig. 4 the fore legs have changed notably in position. Fore leg 1 has been thrown upward (so far as the upper half is concerned) and forward. Fore leg 2 has been thrown forward in preparation for the work which this leg will have to do after the hind legs have done theirs. Of the hind legs, No. 3, which in the position of Fig. 4 had just begun the work of propulsion, has driven the body well forward, so that this limb has become nearly upright. The other hind leg seems to be nearly in the same position as in Fig. 4, but in reality it is now being carried backwards, whereas, in the former position, it was travelling forwards. This leg is the

FIG. 5.

one which is next to take the work of propulsion. Notice that 1 is the *left* fore leg and 2 the right. Between the work of these two legs, both hind legs do their work of propulsion : the left fore leg's work is followed by that of the right hind leg, then the left hind leg does its work and next the right fore leg.

In the position shown in Fig. 6 both hind legs are at work, giving to the body its strongest propulsion both forwards and upwards, but chiefly forwards. Hind leg 3 has nearly done its work ; hind leg 4 has little more than begun. Fore leg 1 has been thrown upwards and forwards, slightly unbending. Fore leg 2 has been straightened into a position which no one would imagine to be ever assumed by a horse's leg. However, one can at once see that the attitude is indicative of the energy which is about to be put into the backward stroke given by this fore limb. In considering this picture, and indeed all those in which a hoof touches the ground, it must be borne in mind that the attitude is not one assumed by the horse for any definite period of time, however short. It is difficult to dispossess oneself of the notion that this is the case, and the absurdity of some of the attitudes in our series of pictures arises chiefly from this mistaken conception. Regarding these attitudes as simply *passed* through during the horse's rapid rush forward in swift gallop, they no longer appear so absurd ; though, even as thus viewed, there is some difficulty in imagining that attitudes so unlike those which the eye can recognise

FIG. 6.

as a horse gallops past, should be assumed once in each stride. In Fig. 6 we see the horse in that part of his action which is most energetic in the galloping gait. At this stage of his stride, and at this stage only, those two legs are at work in propelling the horse forward which have the greatest propulsive power. Strictly speaking, the stride should be regarded as commenced from this attitude ; and I should so have dealt with the series of pictures had it chanced that they represented precisely one stride. Since, however, Fig. 11 shows a position about a foot in advance of that shown in Fig. 1, but about as much behind that shown in Fig. 2, the series only runs by equal intervals from Fig. 1 to Fig. 11, and it was necessary therefore to commence with Fig. 1, though that really belongs to the middle of a stride.

In Fig. 7 two feet are shown touching the ground, one a
fore foot, the other a hind foot. Leg 2, which in the last
figure was preparing for propulsive action, is here fully engaged in it. But the two hind legs have already given a
strong propulsive impetus to the body, and hind leg 4 is still
urging the body forward. It is only necessary to compare
these two legs to see how much more powerful the propulsive
action of the hind legs must be than is that of the fore legs.
I would venture to predict that if ever an experimental test
is applied by which the propulsive action of the fore and
hind legs is compared, the former will be found at least
three times as effective as the latter. It will be remembered that 2 is the right foreleg and that 4 is the left hind

FIG. 7.

foot. We notice, further, that the gallop is not a symmetrical gait, as the trot is. For in the trot right and left fore
legs work in similar ways with left and right hind legs respectively. But we see, from the series of figures illustrating
the gallop, that whereas the right fore leg works with the left
hind leg, the left fore leg does not work with the right hind
leg. Each of these legs—the left fore leg and the right
hind leg—does its work alone, except that the right hind leg
during a part of its work receives help from the other hind
leg, but at no time from either fore leg. Such at least is
the case illustrated in our series of figures ; of course, the
gallop can equally be executed when the right and left fore
legs do the work which the left and right fore legs are here
represented as doing, the hind legs also interchanging their

work. In fact, the illustrations would have appeared precisely as they do if the work of the two fore legs, as of the two hind legs, had thus been interchanged.

In Fig. 8 the two hind legs are both thrown back, and are, for the moment, in a position not very unlike that in which these limbs are commonly represented in pictures of a galloping horse. But the fore limbs are posed as the fore limbs of a horse never were shown in a picture. Fore leg 2 is at work urging the horse forward, or rather it is maintaining and increasing the forward motion given by the energetic action of the hind legs. Fore leg 1 has been straightened from the position shown in Fig. 7, but it is to be noticed¸that in the interval between the positions shown in

FIG. 8.

Figs 7 and 8 this leg has reached its highest motion upward, and is now on its way downward. Notice also that the fore legs are always more or less bent when rising, but as they are brought downwards to give their stroke, they are straightened, even from the beginning of this downward motion. Compare, for instance, the pose of fore leg 2 in Figs. 5 and 6, and again the fore leg 1 in Figs. 7 and 8. Notice also that each leg remains straight in sweeping round through about a right angle, fore leg 2 from the position of Fig. 6 to that of Fig. 9, and fore leg 1 from the position of Fig. 8 to that of Fig. 11.

In Fig. 9, fore leg 2 is shown doing the last part of its work of propulsion, while fore leg 1 is just about to begin its work. The hind legs are so nearly in the same position

in the picture that it is not easy to tell which is which.
However, a little consideration will show that the leg whose
hock shows highest is, as marked, fore leg 3, or the right.
For notice that in Fig. 3 the right fore leg (3) has nearly the
same position as the left fore leg (4) in Fig. 5. In Fig. 4 and
Fig. 6 these legs have respectively nearly the same positions.
So have they in Figs 5 and 7; in Figs. 6 and 8, though
here the slight difference in time between the action of the
right fore leg in one picture and the left fore leg in the next
picture but one, is shown by the right fore leg being on the
ground in Fig. 6, while the left fore leg has just been lifted
from the ground in Fig. 8. We infer, then, that the left
fore leg in Fig. 9 has nearly the same position as the right

FIG. 9.

fore leg (3) in Fig. 7, in other words is nearly straight.
Therefore the other, or more bent leg in Fig. 9, is the right
fore leg (3). We see, in fact, that just as the fore legs
begin to straighten just after they begin to descend for their
propulsive stroke, so the fore legs continue nearly straight
after their propulsive stroke, until just before they reach
their greatest height. In Fig. 9 hind leg 4 is travelling backwards and passing hind leg 3, which has just begun to travel
forwards, precisely as in Fig. 3 hind leg 4, travelling forwards,
is passing hind leg 3 travelling backwards. The vigorous
action of fore leg 2, and the vigorous attitude—preparative
for action of fore leg 1, form very striking characteristics of
Fig. 9. Nothing could serve better to show how the fore
legs do their work than this picture, and yet nothing could

be more unlike the conventional position of the fore legs of a galloping horse in pictures. The hind legs look more as shown in the pictures, yet neither are these as any artist who valued his reputation would care to show them in a painting.

FIG. 10.

In the next position we see the hind legs thrown into an attitude familiar enough in drawings of galloping and leaping horses. Hind leg 3 has been advanced somewhat from the position it had in Fig. 9. Fore leg 1 has commenced the work of propulsion, while fore leg 2 has completed its work

FIG. 11.

and has already become considerably bent, and the foot is well raised from the ground.

Finally, in Fig. 11, we see the end of the stride begun so far as the left fore foot is concerned from the position shown in Fig. 1. As already mentioned, the stride may more properly be regarded as beginning with the action of the hind legs. But we must consider the stride actually photographed. In Fig. 11 we see the fore leg nearly at the end of its work in adding to the forward motion of the body. Fore leg 2 has been carried forward to a position somewhat in advance of that shown in Fig. 1. So also both the hind legs are in advance of the position there shown.

Fig. 12 simply shows the horse standing at rest.

In considering this series of pictures separately, we are struck by the absolute want of resemblance between nearly all of them and the attitudes we are in the habit of regarding as belonging to the galloping horse. The second and third figures alone seem at all natural, though even these would scarcely be regarded as admissible into a painting represent-

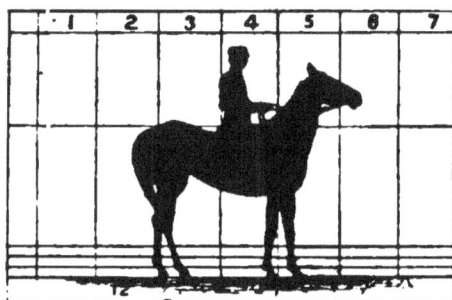

FIG. 12.

ing a charge or race. Notice further that these two are the only pictures in which no leg of the horse touches the ground. In all the other nine at least two of the legs seem absurdly posed, in several three seem so, while in two all four legs have a preposterous appearance.

Yet it is found that so soon as the pictures, instead of being studied separately and with steady gaze, are submitted in rapid succession to the eye, each remaining but a fraction of a second in view—in other words, when they are studied in a manner more nearly corresponding to that in which the actual movements of a galloping horse are seen—the views which had appeared separately absurd become merged into a view showing the horse as he actually appears in the gallop. By arranging them uniformly round the outside of a rather large disc, only a small portion of the upper part of which can be seen at a single view, and setting this disc in rapid rotation, so that picture after picture comes into view and remains in view but a moment, we are able to see the horse galloping as in nature, stride succeeding stride, and every circumstance of the motion, even to the waving of the tail and mane, being truthfully and therefore naturally presented.

Mr. Muybridge himself considers that since these views are severally truthful, however absurd they may appear to those accustomed to study the usual artistic pictures of galloping horses, we should infer that pictures such as these ought to replace the conventional attitudes which have been so long in vogue. Here I must confess that, admirer though I am of his work, I am altogether at issue with him. A picture should represent what we see, and he would be the first to admit that the eye cannot properly be said to see any one of the attitudes he has shown to be really assumed by the galloping horse. He might reply to this that neither can the eye be said to see, nor can it see, any of the attitudes shown by artists, for the simple reason that these attitudes have no real existence in nature. But a picture to be true must show what the eye seems to see. Even in such matters as colouring and shading, the artist has to depart from what nature really presents. In order to produce an appearance of reality, he must modify the colours and the shades until in some cases they are utterly unlike those actually existing. Now if this is the case where at any rate the objects depicted are at rest, so that one would say the representation if really correct should, when duly studied, appear to be truthful, how much more may we expect it to be the case where the object represented is moving so rapidly that the eye cannot detect the real nature of the attitudes successively assumed ! We might, indeed, antici- pate that in such a case no drawing could possibly represent the appearance of the moving object. In many cases this is actually so. But in others, as in that of a carriage rapidly advancing, we know that the appearances recognised by the eye can be readily enough represented. Now take such a case as this. At any instant of time the wheel of a rapidly advancing carriage has its spokes in some definite position, and we might draw them in such a position, and regard the wheel when so drawn as correctly represented. But we know that if it were so drawn the carriage would appear to be at rest ; and that to convey the idea of rapid motion, the wheels of a carriage must be represented as it really appears to the eye, with the spokes blended together into confused discs. When the wheels are so drawn, and accessories drawn in so as to suggest the idea of rapid motion, as post-boys leaning forward and flourishing their whips, the dust rising around the wheels, and so forth, we obtain a picture which conveys the idea of a rapidly advancing carriage. The mere fact, then, that a galloping horse assumes such attitudes as are shown in our series of figures is no argument in favour of the introduction of such attitudes into a drawing of a race or charge. One might as reasonably represent cannon balls in mid-air, in a battle scene, as we see in some of the illustrations of Froissart's 'Chronicles.' Cannon balls and musket balls are certainly in the air during a brisk exchange of missiles, but as no one can see them they have no proper place in a picture. On the other hand, it is difficult to understand how the conventional attitudes of a galloping horse came to be employed ; for they certainly are not seen during a charge or race, though the idea conveyed may be that such attitudes are not only assumed by the galloping horse, but are actually characteristic of his actions. It may perhaps be, that the attitudes approaching those seen in the pictures are retained longer than the others which seem unnatural. Thus the general effect is, we may assume, that conveyed by the pictures. And yet it is strange, if this be so, that the hind legs do not pass through those positions which seem natural at the same time that the fore legs are passing through their natural attitudes. Thus the positions of the hind legs in Figs. 8, 9, 10, and 11, are not unlike those shown in the pictures, but in all these figures the fore legs are in positions which seem altogether unnatural. On the

other hand, in Figs. 2, 3, 4, and 5, the fore legs are in
natural positions; while the hind legs are in positions
more or less unnatural. (Of course, in using the words
natural and unnatural, I refer only to the conventional ideas
as to the action of the galloping horse ; all the positions of
the eleven figures are really natural, though they are unfamiliar to the eye.) So that, in fact, it seems as though the
conventional attitudes of a galloping horse were obtained
by combining the position of the fore legs in one part of
the stride with that of the hind legs in another. Yet though
this seems strange, it is after all akin to the circumstance
that in picturing a rapidly rotating wheel we show the spokes
in a number of positions which they do not simultaneously
occupy. As in the case of the rotating wheel so in that of
the galloping horse, the movements are too quick to be
followed by the eye, and so several positions really occupied
at different times are combined together into a single impression. Where the movements are slower, so that the eye
can recognise the several positions pretty clearly, the features
of different positions would not be thus combined. For
instance, an artist's pictures of a trotting horse, even when
the pace to be represented is very rapid, do not differ much
from those obtained by instantaneous photography. Of
twelve such photographs obtained by Mr. Muybridge only
two seem to differ—and those not greatly—from such views
as might be given in a picture of a trotting match. So again
the pictures of a walking horse, of a man walking at full
speed, and of a man running at moderate speed, all closely
resemble such drawings as an artist would make. But in
the case of a man running at full speed, and still more in
that of a man taking a high leap, the attitudes are such as
have never been shown in any picture, such in fact as have
never been seen, simply because, though all the attitudes are
of necessity really assumed, they are assumed for so brief
an interval of time, and so rapidly exchanged for others
quite unlike them, that the eye is not cognisant even of their
momentary existence. We may note also, as another reason

why some of the attitudes of a leaping or swiftly running man seem unnatural (and of course the same reasoning applies to a galloping horse), that they are attitudes which cannot be maintained even for a single second, but are only passed through in the course of a certain series of energetic actions ; so that the pictures look like ill-drawn representatiòns of impossible attitudes.

The great value of such pictures lies in the evidence which they afford as to the real nature of the movements involved in particular gaits or exercises, as for the horse in the gallop, canter, run, or trot, and for the man in the high leap (running or standing), the long leap, the run, the swift walk, and so forth. They serve to correct some erroneous ideas as to the nature of such movements, ideas even entertained (in the case of exercises for men) by those who are most skilled in leaping or running. For instance, Mr. Muybridge informed me that the most skilful runners are positive that, in running swiftly, they bring the toes to the ground before the heel ; and certainly most runners, if not all, would think so : but the instantaneous pictures show that in rapid running the heel comes first to the ground. This was shown in every case, even where the runner had been told beforehand that the photographs would put to the test his own confidently expressed opinion that he brought the toes to the ground first. In pictures of a very swift runner at full speed, the toes appear thrown ridiculously upwards, just as absurdly as the hoofs of the fore feet of the horse appear in Figs. 6 and 8 of our series. (On consideration, I am inclined to think the evidence on which Mr. Muybridge depends is open to some degree of question. His views show, as I have myself had the opportunity of noting, that the toes are pointed upwards as the foot descends, till at any rate it is quite near to the ground ; but so far as I recollect, they do not show that at the last there is not a rapid motion of the forward part of the foot, bringing the toes down before the heel. Note, for instance, how in Fig. 7 the hoof, which had been pointed upwards in the previous position, Fig. 6, has come down to the ground before the fetlock, which in Fig. 8 has reached the ground ; and, still more to the purpose, note how in Fig. 9 we see the hoof before reaching the ground already thrown far downward of the position, relatively to the fetlock, which it had had in Fig. 8. Mr. Muybridge, by the way, asserts that all animals bring the heels to the ground, in rapid running, before the toes : this, of course, would relate only to the hind feet, and is not supported by the views of our series, even if the fetlock be regarded as the heel. But in reality the fetlock corresponds to the ball of the foot, not to the heel, the heel corresponding to the horse's hock, which never touches the ground at all, except when the animal rears till he is absolutely upright.)

I should like to see Mr. Muybridge's method applied to a number of other movements, which so far as I know he has not yet tested ; in particular to the movements of a man's body and limbs in rowing, first in heavier boats, then in lapsteaked gigs, then in racing boats : and in steady pulling, as well as in the fiercest spurts.

Mr. Muybridge claims that in his later photographs the exposure, as tested by the distinctness of the outlines, cannot be more than the 5,000th part of a second. If this is really so it would be possible by this method to secure a picture, though not a sharply defined one, of a cannon ball, even at the beginning of its flight. For such a ball travels at a rate of less than 500 yards per second, so that in the 5,000th part of a second it travels but the tenth of a yard, or less than four inches. Even in the 2,000th part of a second a cannon ball would fly but about nine inches at the beginning of its course, and much less at the close of its first flight, supposing the cannon so inclined that the range would be nearly the maximum.

LONDON : PRINTED BY
SPOTTISWOODE AND CO., NEW-STREET SQUARE
AND PARLIAMENT STREET

CHATTO & WINDUS'S
LIST OF BOOKS.

NEW FINE-ART WORK.   Large 4to, bound in buckram, 21*s.*

Abdication, The; or, Time Tries All.

An Historical Drama.   By W. D. SCOTT-MONCRIEFF.   With Seven Etchings by JOHN PETTIE, R.A., W. Q. ORCHARDSON, R.A., J. MAC WHIRTER, A. R.A., COLIN HUNTER, R. MACBETH. and TOM GRAHAM.

Crown 8vo, Coloured Frontispiece and Illustrations, cloth gilt, 7*s.* 6*d.*

Advertising, A History of.

From the Earliest Times.   Illustrated by Anecdotes, Curious Specimens, and Notices of Successful Advertisers.   By HENRY SAMPSON.

Crown 8vo, cloth extra, with 639 Illustrations, 7*s.* 6*d.*

Architectural Styles, A Handbook of.

From the German of A. ROSENGARTEN by W. COLLETT-SANDARS.

Crown 8vo, with Portrait and Facsimile, cloth extra, 7*s.* 6*d.*

Artemus Ward's Works:

The Works of CHARLES FARRER BROWNE, better known as ARTEMUS WARD.   With Portrait, Facsimile of Handwriting, &c.

Crown 8vo, cloth extra, 7*s.* 6*d.*

Bankers, A Handbook of London;

With some Account of their Predecessors, the Early Goldsmiths; together with Lists of Bankers from 1677 to 1876.   By F. G. HILTON PRICE.

Bardsley (Rev. C. W.), Works by:

English Surnames: Their Sources and Significations.   By CHARLES WAREING BARDSLEY, M.A.   Crown 8vo, cloth extra, 7*s.* 6*d.*

Curiosities of Puritan Nomenclature.   By CHARLES W. BARDSLEY.   Crown 8vo, cloth extra, 7*s.* 6*d.*

Crown 8vo, cloth extra, Illustrated, 7*s.* 6*d.*

Bartholomew Fair, Memoirs of.

By HENRY MORLEY.   New Edition, with One Hundred Illustrations.

Imperial 4to, cloth extra, gilt and gilt edges, 21s. per volume.

Beautiful Pictures by British Artists :

A Gathering of Favourites from our Picture Galleries. In Two Series.
The FIRST SERIES including Examples by WILKIE, CONSTABLE,
TURNER, MULREADY, LANDSEER, MACLISE, E. M. WARD, FRITH,
Sir JOHN GILBERT, LESLIE, ANSDELL, MARCUS STONE, Sir NOEL
PATON, FAED, EYRE CROWE, GAVIN O'NEIL, and MADOX BROWN.
The SECOND SERIES containing Pictures by ARMITAGE, FAED,
GOODALL, HEMSLEY, HORSLEY, MARKS, NICHOLLS, Sir NOEL
PATON, PICKERSGILL, G. SMITH, MARCUS STONE, SOLOMON,
STRAIGHT, E. M. WARD, and WARREN.
All engraved on Steel in the highest style of Art. Edited, with
Notices of the Artists, by SYDNEY ARMYTAGE, M.A.

" This book is well got up, and good engravings by Jeens, Lumb Stocks, and others, bring back to us Royal Academy Exhibitions of past years."—TIMES.

Small 4to, green and gold, 6s. 6d. ; gilt edges, 7s. 6d.

Bechstein's As Pretty as Seven,

And other German Stories. Collected by LUDWIG BECHSTEIN. With
Additional Tales by the Brothers GRIMM, and 100 Illustrations by
RICHTER.

One Shilling Monthly, Illustrated.

Belgravia for 1882.

A New Serial Story, entitled "All Sorts and Conditions of Men,"
written by WALTER BESANT and JAMES RICE, Authors of " Ready-
Money Mortiboy," &c., and Illustrated by FRED. BARNARD, will be
begun in the JANUARY Number of BELGRAVIA ; this Number will
contain also the First Chapters of a New Novel, entitled " The
Admiral's Ward," by Mrs. ALEXANDER, Author of "The
Wooing o't." &c. ; and the first of a series of Twelve Papers, entitled
" About Yorkshire," by KATHARINE S. MACQUOID, illustrated by
T. R. MACQUOID.

** The FORTY-FIFTH Volume of BELGRAVIA, elegantly bound in crimson cloth, full gilt side and back, gilt edges, price 7s. 6d., is now ready.—Handsome Cases for binding volumes can be had at 2s. each.

Demy 8vo, with Illustrations, 1s.

Belgravia Annual.

With Stories by WILKIE COLLINS, F. W. ROBINSON, DUTTON COOK,
PERCY FITZGERALD, J. ARBUTHNOT WILSON, HENRY W. LUCY
D. CHRISTIE MURRAY, JAMES PAYN, and others.   [*Nov.* 10.

Folio, half-bound boards, India Proofs, 21s.

Blake (William) :

Etchings from his Works. By W. B. SCOTT. With descriptive Text.

Crown 8vo, cloth extra, gilt, with Illustrations, 7s. 6d.

Boccaccio's Decameron ;

or, Ten Days' Entertainment. Translated into English, with an Introduction by THOMAS WRIGHT, Esq., M.A., F.S.A. With Portrait, and
STOTHARD'S beautiful Copperplates.

Demy 8vo, Illustrated, uniform in size for binding.

Blackburn's (Henry) Art Handbooks:

Academy Notes, 1875. With 40 Illustrations. 1s.
Academy Notes, 1876. With 107 Illustrations. 1s.
Academy Notes, 1877. With 143 Illustrations. 1s.,
Academy Notes, 1878. With 150 Illustrations. 1s.
Academy Notes, 1879. With 146 Illustrations. 1s.
Academy Notes, 1880. With 126 Illustrations. 1s.
Academy Notes, 1881. With 128 Illustrations. 1s.
Grosvenor Notes, 1878. With 68 Illustrations. 1s.
Grosvenor Notes, 1879. With 60 Illustrations. 1s.
Grosvenor Notes, 1880. With 56 Illustrations. 1s.
Grosvenor Notes, 1881. With 74 Illustrations. 1s.
Pictures at the Paris Exhibition, 1878. 80 Illustrations. 1s.
Pictures at South Kensington. With 70 Illustrations. 1s.
The English Pictures at the National Gallery. 114 Illusts. 1s.
The Old Masters at the National Gallery. 128 Illusts. 1s. 6d.
Academy Notes, 1875-79. Complete in One Volume, with
nearly 600 Illustrations in Facsimile. Demy 8vo, cloth limp, 6s.
A Complete Illustrated Catalogue to the National Gallery.
With Notes by H. BLACKBURN, and 242 Illusts. Demy 8vo, cloth limp, 3s.

UNIFORM WITH "ACADEMY NOTES."

Royal Scottish Academy Notes, 1878. 117 Illustrations. 1s.
Royal Scottish Academy Notes, 1879. 125 Illustrations. 1s.
Royal Scottish Academy Notes, 1880. 114 Illustrations. 1s.
Royal Scottish Academy Notes, 1881. 104 Illustrations. 1s.
Glasgow Institute of Fine Arts Notes, 1878. 95 Illusts. 1s.
Glasgow Institute of Fine Arts Notes, 1879. 100 Illusts. 1s.
Glasgow Institute of Fine Arts Notes, 1880. 120 Illusts. 1s.
Glasgow Institute of Fine Arts Notes, 1881. 108 Illusts. 1s.
Walker Art Gallery Notes, Liverpool, 1878. 112 Illusts. 1s.
Walker Art Gallery Notes, Liverpool, 1879. 100 Illusts. 1s.
Walker Art Gallery Notes, Liverpool, 1880. 100 Illusts. 1s.
Royal Manchester Institution Notes, 1878. 88 Illustrations. 1s.
Society of Artists Notes, Birmingham, 1878. 95 Illusts. 1s.
Children of the Great City. By F. W. LAWSON. 1s.

Bowers' (G.) Hunting Sketches:

Canters in Crampshire. By G. BOWERS. I. Gallops from
Gorseborough. II. Scrambles with Scratch Packs. III. Studies with
Stag Hounds. Oblong 4to, half-bound boards, 21s.
Leaves from a Hunting Journal. By G. BOWERS. Coloured in
facsimile of the originals. Oblong 4to, half-bound, 21s.

Crown 8vo, cloth extra, gilt, 7s. 6d.

Brand's Observations on Popular Antiquities,

chiefly Illustrating the Origin of our Vulgar Customs, Ceremonies, and
Superstitions. With the Additions of Sir HENRY ELLIS. An entirely
New and Revised Edition, with fine full-page Illustrations.

Bret Harte, Works by:

Bret Harte's Collected Works. Arranged and Revised by the Author. Complete in Five Vols., crown 8vo, cloth extra, 6*s.* each.

Vol. I. COMPLETE POETICAL AND DRAMATIC WORKS. With Steel Plate Portrait, and an Introduction by the Author.

Vol. II. EARLIER PAPERS—LUCK OF ROARING CAMP, and other Sketches —BOHEMIAN PAPERS—SPANISH and AMERICAN LEGENDS.

Vol. III. TALES OF THE ARGONAUTS—EASTERN SKETCHES.

Vol. IV. GABRIEL CONROY.

Vol. V. STORIES—CONDENSED NOVELS, &c.

The Select Works of Bret Harte, in Prose and Poetry. With Introductory Essay by J. M. BELLEW, Portrait of the Author, and 50 Illustrations. Crown 8vo, cloth extra, 7*s.* 6*d.*

An Heiress of Red Dog, and other Stories. By BRET HARTE. Post 8vo, illustrated boards, 2*s.*; cloth limp, 2*s.* 6*d.*

The Twins of Table Mountain. By BRET HARTE. Fcap. 8vo, picture cover, 1*s.*; crown 8vo, cloth extra, 3*s.* 6*d.*

The Luck of Roaring Camp, and other Sketches. By BRET HARTE. Post 8vo, illustrated boards, 2*s.*

Jeff Briggs's Love Story. By BRET HARTE. Fcap. 8vo, picture cover, 1*s.*; cloth extra, 2*s.* 6*d.*

Small crown 8vo, cloth extra, gilt, with full-page Portraits, 4*s.* 6*d.*

Brewster's (Sir David) Martyrs of Science

Small crown 8vo, cloth extra, gilt, with Astronomical Plates, 4*s.* 6*d.*

Brewster's (Sir D.) More Worlds than One,

the Creed of the Philosopher and the Hope of the Christian.

A HANDSOME GIFT-BOOK.—Small 4to, cloth extra, profusely Illustrated, 6*s.*

Brushwood.

By T. BUCHANAN READ. Illustrated from Designs by FREDERICK DIELMAN.

THE STOTHARD BUNYAN.—Crown 8vo, cloth extra, gilt, 7*s.* 6*d.*

Bunyan's Pilgrim's Progress.

Edited by Rev. T. SCOTT. With 17 beautiful Steel Plates by STOTHARD, engraved by GOODALL; and numerous Woodcuts.

Demy 8vo, cloth extra, 7*s.* 6*d.*

Burton's Anatomy of Melancholy:

A New Edition, complete, corrected and enriched by Translations of the Classical Extracts.

Crown 8vo, cloth extra, gilt, with Illustrations, 7*s.* 6*d.*

Byron's Letters and Journals.

With Notices of his Life. By THOMAS MOORE. A Reprint of the Original Edition, newly revised, with Twelve full-page Plates.

Demy 8vo, cloth extra, 14*s.*

Campbell's (Sir G.) White and Black:

Travels in the United States. By Sir GEORGE CAMPBELL, M.P.

Demy 8vo, cloth extra, with Illustrations, 7s. 6d.

Caravan Route (The) between Egypt and
Syria. By His Imperial and Royal Highness the ARCHDUKE LUDWIG
SALVATOR of AUSTRIA. With 23 full-page Illustrations by the Author.

Post 8vo, cloth extra, 1s. 6d.

Carlyle (Thomas) On the Choice of Books.
With a Life of the Author by R. H. SHEPHERD. Entirely New and
Revised Edition.

Crown 8vo, cloth extra, 7s. 6d.

Century (A) of Dishonour:
A Sketch of the United States Government's Dealings with some of
the Indian Tribes.

Crown 8vo, cloth extra, with Illustrations, 7s. 6d.

Chap-Books.—A History of the Chap-Books
of the Eighteenth Century. By JOHN ASHTON. With nearly 400
Illustrations, engraved in facsimile of the originals.   [*In the press.*

** A few Large-Paper copies will be carefully printed on hand-made
paper, for which early application should be made.

Large 4to, half-bound, profusely Illustrated, 28s.

Chatto and Jackson.—A Treatise on Wood
Engraving: Historical and Practical. By WILLIAM ANDREW CHATTO
and JOHN JACKSON. With an Additional Chapter by HENRY G.
BOHN; and 450 fine Illustrations. A reprint of the last Revised Edition.

Small 4to, cloth gilt, with Coloured Illustrations, 10s. 6d.

Chaucer for Children:
A Golden Key. By Mrs. H. R. HAWEIS. With Eight Coloured
Pictures and numerous Woodcuts by the Author.

Demy 8vo, cloth limp, 2s. 6d.

Chaucer for Schools.
By Mrs. HAWEIS, Author of "Chaucer for Children."

Crown 8vo, cloth limp, with Map and Illustrations, 2s. 6d.

Cleopatra's Needle:
Its Acquisition and Removal to England. By Sir J. E. ALEXANDER.

Crown 8vo, cloth extra, gilt, 7s. 6d.

Colman's Humorous Works:
"Broad Grins," "My Nightgown and Slippers," and other Humorous
Works, Prose and Poetical, of GEORGE COLMAN. With Life by G.
B. BUCKSTONE, and Frontispiece by HOGARTH.

Post 8vo, cloth limp, 2s. 6d.
Convalescent Cookery:
A Family Handbook. By CATHERINE RYAN.

Conway (Moncure D.), Works by:
Demonology and Devil-Lore. By MONCURE D. CONWAY,
M.A. Two Vols., royal 8vo, with 65 Illustrations, 28s.
A Necklace of Stories. By MONCURE D. CONWAY, M.A.
Illustrated by W. J. HENNESSY. Square 8vo, cloth extra, 6s.
The Wandering Jew. By MONCURE D. CONWAY, M.A. Crown
8vo, cloth extra, 6s.
Thomas Carlyle. By MONCURE D. CONWAY, M.A. With
Illustrations. Crown 8vo, cloth extra, 6s.

Two Vols., crown 8vo, cloth extra, 21s.
Cook (Dutton).—Hours with the Players.
By DUTTON COOK.

Post 8vo, cloth limp, 2s. 6d.
Copyright.—A Handbook of English and
Foreign Copyright in Literary and Dramatic Works. Being a concise Digest of the Laws regulating Copyright in the Chief Countries
of the World, together with the Chief Copyright Conventions existing
between Great Britain and Foreign Countries. By SIDNEY JERROLD,
of the Middle Temple, Esq., Barrister-at-Law.

Crown 8vo, cloth extra, 7s. 6d.
Cornwall.—Popular Romances of the West
of England; or, The Drolls, Traditions, and Superstitions of Old
Cornwall. Collected and Edited by ROBERT HUNT, F.R.S. New
and Revised Edition, with Additions, and Two Steel-plate Illustrations
by GEORGE CRUIKSHANK.

Crown 8vo, cloth extra, gilt, with 13 Portraits, 7s. 6d.
Creasy's Memoirs of Eminent Etonians;
with Notices of the Early History of Eton College. By Sir EDWARD
CREASY, Author of "The Fifteen Decisive Battles of the World."

Crown 8vo, cloth extra, with Etched Frontispiece, 7s. 6d.
Credulities, Past and Present.
By WILLIAM JONES, F.S.A., Author of "Finger-Ring Lore," &c.

Crown 8vo, cloth extra, 6s.
Crimes and Punishments.
Including a New Translation of Beccaria's "Dei Delitti e delle Pene."
By JAMES ANSON FARRER.

Crown 8vo, cloth gilt, Two very thick Volumes, 7s. 6d. each.

Cruikshank's Comic Almanack.

Complete in TWO SERIES: The FIRST from 1835 to 1843; the SECOND from 1844 to 1853. A Gathering of the BEST HUMOUR of THACKERAY, HOOD, MAYHEW, ALBERT SMITH, A'BECKETT, ROBERT BROUGH, &c. With 2,000 Woodcuts and Steel Engravings by CRUIKSHANK, HINE, LANDELLS, &c.

Two Vols., crown 8vo, cloth extra, with Illustrations, 24s.

Cruikshank (The Life of George).

In Two Epochs. By BLANCHARD JERROLD, Author of "The Life of Napoleon III.," &c. With numerous Illustrations, and a List of his Works. [*In preparation.*]

Two Vols., demy 4to, handsomely bound in half-morocco, gilt, profusely Illustrated with Coloured and Plain Plates and Woodcuts, price £7 7s.

Cyclopædia of Costume;

or, A Dictionary of Dress—Regal, Ecclesiastical, Civil, and Military—from the Earliest Period in England to the reign of George the Third. Including Notices of Contemporaneous Fashions on the Continent, and a General History of the Costumes of the Principal Countries of Europe. By J. R. PLANCHÉ, Somerset Herald.

The Volumes may also be had *separately* (each Complete in itself) at £3 13s. 6d. each:

Vol. I. THE DICTIONARY.
Vol. II. A GENERAL HISTORY OF COSTUME IN EUROPE.

Also in 25 Parts, at 5s. each. Cases for binding, 5s. each.

"*A comprehensive and highly valuable book of reference. . . . We have rarely failed to find in this book an account of an article of dress, while in most of the entries curious and instructive details are given. . . . Mr. Planché's enormous labour of love, the production of a text which, whether in its dictionary form or in that of the 'General History,' is within its intended scope immeasurably the best and richest work on Costume in English. . . . This book is not only one of the most readable works of the kind, but intrinsically attractive and amusing.*"—ATHENÆUM.

"*A most readable and interesting work—and it can scarcely be consulted in vain, whether the reader is in search for information as to military, court, ecclesiastical, legal, or professional costume. . . . All the chromo-lithographs, and most of the woodcut illustrations—the latter amounting to several thousands —are very elaborately executed; and the work forms a livre de luxe which renders it equally suited to the library and the ladies' drawing-room.*"—TIMES.

Demy 8vo, cloth extra, 12s. 6d.

Doran's Memories of our Great Towns.

With Anecdotic Gleanings concerning their Worthies and their Oddities. By Dr. JOHN DORAN, F.S.A.

Two Vols., crown 8vo, cloth extra, 21s.

Drury Lane, Old:

Fifty Years' Recollections of Author, Actor, and Manager. By EDWARD STIRLING.

Demy 8vo, cloth, 16s.

Dutt's India, Past and Present;

with Minor Essays on Cognate Subjects. By SHOSHEE CHUNDER DUTT, Rái Báhádoor.

Crown 8vo, cloth boards, 6s. per Volume.

Early English Poets.

Edited, with Introductions and Annotations, by Rev. A. B. GROSART.

1. **Fletcher's (Giles, B.D.) Complete Poems:** Christ's Victorie in Heaven, Christ's Victorie on Earth, Christ's Triumph over Death, and Minor Poems. With Memorial-Introduction and Notes. One Vol.

2. **Davies' (Sir John) Complete** Poetical Works, including Psalms I. to L. in Verse, and other hitherto Unpublished MSS., for the first time Collected and Edited. Memorial-Introduction and Notes. Two Vols.

3. **Herrick's (Robert) Hesperides,** Noble Numbers, and Complete Collected Poems. With Memorial-Introduction and Notes, Steel Portrait, Index of First Lines, and Glossarial Index, &c. Three Vols.

4. **Sidney's (Sir Philip) Complete** Poetical Works, including all those in "Arcadia." With Portrait, Memorial-Introduction, Essay on the Poetry of Sidney, and Notes. Three Vols.

Imperial 8vo, with 147 fine Engravings, half-morocco, 36s.

Early Teutonic, Italian, and French Masters

(The). Translated and Edited from the Dohme Series, by A. H. KEANE, M.A.I. With numerous Illustrations.

*"Cannot fail to be of the utmost use to students of art history."—*TIMES.

Crown 8vo, cloth extra, gilt, with Illustrations, 6s.

Emanuel On Diamonds and Precious

Stones; their History, Value, and Properties; with Simple Tests for ascertaining their Reality. By HARRY EMANUEL, F.R.G.S. With numerous Illustrations, Tinted and Plain.

Crown 8vo, cloth extra, with Illustrations, 7s. 6d.

Englishman's House, The:

A Practical Guide to all interested in Selecting or Building a House, with full Estimates of Cost, Quantities, &c. By C. J. RICHARDSON. Third Edition. With nearly 600 Illustrations.

Crown 8vo, cloth extra, with nearly 300 Illustrations, 7s. 6d.

Evolution, Chapters on;

A Popular History of the Darwinian and Allied Theories of Development. By ANDREW WILSON, Ph.D., F.R.S. Edin. &c. [*In preparation.*

Crown 8vo, cloth extra, 6s.

Evolutionist (The) At Large.

By GRANT ALLEN.

By the same Author. Crown 8vo, cloth extra, 6s.

Vignettes from Nature.

By GRANT ALLEN.   [*In preparation.*

Folio, cloth extra, £1 11s. 6d.

Examples of Contemporary Art.

Etchings from Representative Works by living English and Foreign Artists. Edited, with Critical Notes, by J. COMYNS CARR.

"*It would not be easy to meet with a more sumptuous, and at the same time a more tasteful and instructive drawing-room book.*"—NONCONFORMIST.

Crown 8vo, cloth extra, with Illustrations, 6s.

Fairholt's Tobacco :

Its History and Associations ; with an Account of the Plant and its Manufacture, and its Modes of Use in all Ages and Countries. By F. W. FAIRHOLT, F.S.A. With Coloured Frontispiece and upwards of 100 Illustrations by the Author.

Crown 8vo, cloth extra, 7s. 6d.

Familiar Allusions :

A Handbook of Miscellaneous Information ; including the Names of Celebrated Statues, Paintings, Palaces, Country Seats, Ruins, Churches, Ships, Streets, Clubs, Natural Curiosities, and the like. By WILLIAM A. WHEELER, Author of "Noted Names of Fiction;" and CHARLES G. WHEELER. [*In the press.*

Crown 8vo, cloth extra, with Illustrations, 4s. 6d.

Faraday's Chemical History of a Candle.

Lectures delivered to a Juvenile Audience. A New Edition. Edited by W. CROOKES, F.C.S. With numerous Illustrations.

Crown 8vo, cloth extra, with Illustrations, 4s. 6d.

Faraday's Various Forces of Nature.

New Edition. Edited by W. CROOKES, F.C.S. Numerous Illustrations.

Crown 8vo, cloth extra, with Illustrations, 7s. 6d.

Finger-Ring Lore :

Historical, Legendary, and Anecdotal. By WM. JONES, F.S.A. With Hundreds of Illustrations of Curious Rings of all Ages and Countries.

"*One of those gossiping books which are as full of amusement as of instruction.*"—ATHENÆUM.

Gardening Books :

A Year's Work in Garden and Greenhouse : Practical Advice to Amateur Gardeners as to the Management of the Flower, Fruit, and Frame Garden. By GEORGE GLENNY. Post 8vo, cloth limp, 2s. 6d.

Our Kitchen Garden : The Plants we Grow, and How we Cook Them. By TOM JERROLD, Author of "The Garden that Paid the Rent," &c. Post 8vo, cloth limp, 2s. 6d.

Household Horticulture : A Gossip about Flowers. By TOM and JANE JERROLD. Illustrated. Post 8vo, cloth limp, 2s. 6d.

My Garden Wild, and What I Grew there. By FRANCIS GEORGE HEATH. Crown 8vo, cloth extra, 5s.

One Shilling Monthly.

Gentleman's Magazine (The), for 1882.

The JANUARY Number of this Periodical will contain the First Chapters of a New Serial Story, entitled "Dust," by JULIAN HAWTHORNE, Author of "Garth," &c. "Science Notes," by W. MATTIEU WILLIAMS, F.R.A.S., will also be continued monthly.

** *Now ready, the Volume for* JANUARY *to* JUNE, 1881, *cloth extra, price* 8*s.* 6*d.; and Cases for binding, price* 2*s. each.*

Demy 8vo, illuminated cover, 1*s.*

Gentleman's Annual, The.

Containing Two Complete Novels.   [*Nov.* 15.

THE RUSKIN GRIMM.—Square 8vo, cloth extra, 6*s.* 6*d.* ; gilt edges, 7*s.* 6*d.*

German Popular Stories.

Collected by the Brothers GRIMM, and Translated by EDGAR TAYLOR. Edited with an Introduction by JOHN RUSKIN. With 22 Illustrations after the inimitable designs of GEORGE CRUIKSHANK. Both Series Complete.

"*The illustrations of this volume . . . are of quite sterling and admirable art, of a class precisely parallel in elevation to the character of the tales which they illustrate; and the original etchings, as I have before said in the Appendix to my 'Elements of Drawing,' were unrivalled in masterfulness of touch since Rembrandt (in some qualities of delineation, unrivalled even by him). . . . To make somewhat enlarged copies of them, looking at them through a magnifying glass, and never putting two lines where Cruikshank has put only one, would be an exercise in decision and severe drawing which would leave afterwards little to be learnt in schools.*"—*Extract from Introduction by* JOHN RUSKIN.

Post 8vo, cloth limp, 2*s.* 6*d.*

Glenny's A Year's Work in Garden and

Greenhouse : Practical Advice to Amateur Gardeners as to the Management of the Flower, Fruit, and Frame Garden. By GEORGE GLENNY.

"*A great deal of valuable information, conveyed in very simple language. The amateur need not wish for a better guide.*"—LEEDS MERCURY.

Crown 8vo, cloth gilt and gilt edges, 7*s.* 6*d.*

Golden Treasury of Thought, The:

An ENCYCLOPÆDIA OF QUOTATIONS from Writers of all Times and Countries. Selected and Edited by THEODORE TAYLOR

New and Cheaper Edition, demy 8vo, cloth extra, with Illustrations, 7*s.*6*d.*

Greeks and Romans, The Life of the,

Described from Antique Monuments. By ERNST GUHL and W. KONER. Translated from the Third German Edition, and Edited by Dr. F. HUEFFER. With 545 Illustrations.

Square 16mo (Tauchnitz size), cloth extra, 2s. per volume.

Golden Library, The :

Ballad History of England. By W. C. BENNETT.

Bayard Taylor's Diversions of the Echo Club.

Byron's Don Juan.

Emerson's Letters and Social Aims.

Godwin's (William) Lives of the Necromancers.

Holmes's Autocrat of the Breakfast Table. With an Introduction by G. A. SALA.

Holmes's Professor at the Breakfast Table.

Hood's Whims and Oddities. Complete. With all the original Illustrations.

Irving's (Washington) Tales of a Traveller.

Irving's (Washington) Tales of the Alhambra.

Jesse's (Edward) Scenes and Occupations of Country Life.

Lamb's Essays of Elia. Both Series Complete in One Vol.

Leigh Hunt's Essays : A Tale for a Chimney Corner, and other Pieces. With Portrait, and Introduction by EDMUND OLLIER.

Mallory's (Sir Thomas) Mort d'Arthur : The Stories of King Arthur and of the Knights of the Round Table. Edited by B. MONTGOMERIE RANKING.

Pascal's Provincial Letters. A New Translation, with Historical Introduction and Notes, by T. M'CRIE, D.D.

Pope's Poetical Works. Complete.

Rochefoucauld's Maxims and Moral Reflections. With Notes, and an Introductory Essay by SAINTE-BEUVE.

St. Pierre's Paul and Virginia, and The Indian Cottage. Edited, with Life, by the Rev. E. CLARKE.

Shelley's Early Poems, and Queen Mab, with Essay by LEIGH HUNT.

Shelley's Later Poems : Laon and Cythna, &c.

Shelley's Posthumous Poems, the Shelley Papers, &c.

Shelley's Prose Works, including A Refutation of Deism, Zastrozzi St. Irvyne, &c.

White's Natural History of Selborne. Edited, with Additions, by THOMAS BROWN, F.L.S.

Crown 8vo, cloth extra, gilt, with Illustrations, 4s. 6d.

Guyot's Earth and Man;

or, Physical Geography in its Relation to the History of Mankind. With Additions by Professors AGASSIZ, PIERCE, and GRAY ; 12 Maps and Engravings on Steel, some Coloured, and copious Index.

Hake (Dr. Thomas Gordon), Poems by :

Maiden Ecstasy. Small 4to, cloth extra, 8s.

New Symbols. Crown 8vo, cloth extra, 6s.

Legends of the Morrow. Crown 8vo, cloth extra, 6s.

Medium 8vo, cloth extra, gilt, with Illustrations, 7s. 6d.

Hall's (Mrs. S. C.) Sketches of Irish Character.

With numerous Illustrations on Steel and Wood by MACLISE, GILBERT, HARVEY, and G. CRUIKSHANK.

"*The Irish Sketches of this lady resemble Miss Mitford's beautiful English sketches in 'Our Village,' but they are far more vigorous and picturesque and bright.*"—BLACKWOOD'S MAGAZINE.

Haweis (Mrs.), Works by:

The Art of Dress. By Mrs. H. R. HAWEIS. Illustrated by the Author. Small 8vo, illustrated cover, 1s.; cloth limp, 1s. 6d.

*"A well-considered attempt to apply canons of good taste to the costumes of ladies of our time. . . . . Mrs. Haweis writes frankly and to the point, she does not mince matters, but boldly remonstrates with her own sex on the follies they indulge in. . . . . We may recommend the book to the ladies whom it concerns."—*ATHENÆUM.

The Art of Beauty. By Mrs. H. R. HAWEIS. Square 8vo, cloth extra, gilt, gilt edges, with Coloured Frontispiece and nearly 100 Illustrations, 10s. 6d.

The Art of Decoration. By Mrs. H. R. HAWEIS. Square 8vo, handsomely bound and profusely Illustrated, 10s. 6d.

*** *See also* CHAUCER, *p.* 5 *of this Catalogue.*

Crown 8vo, cloth extra, 5s.

Heath (F. G.)—My Garden Wild,

And What I Grew there. By FRANCIS GEORGE HEATH, Author of "The Fern World," &c.

SPECIMENS OF MODERN POETS.—Crown 8vo, cloth extra, 6s.

Heptalogia (The); or, The Seven against Sense.

A Cap with Seven Bells.

*"The merits of the book cannot be fairly estimated by means of a few extracts; it should be read at length to be appreciated properly, and, in our opinion, its merits entitle it to be very widely read indeed."—*ST. JAMES'S GAZETTE.

Cr. 8vo, bound in parchment, 8s.; Large-Paper copies (only 50 printed), 15s.

Herbert.—The Poems of Lord Herbert of

Cherbury. Edited, with an Introduction, by J. CHURTON COLLINS.

· Complete in Four Vols., demy 8vo, cloth extra, 12s. each.

History of Our Own Times, from the Accession

of Queen Victoria to the General Election of 1880. By JUSTIN McCARTHY, M.P.

*"Criticism is disarmed before a composition which provokes little but approval. This is a really good book on a really interesting subject, and words piled on words could say no more for it."—*SATURDAY REVIEW.

New Work by the Author of " A HISTORY of OUR OWN TIMES."

Four Vols. demy 8vo, cloth extra, 12s. each.

History of the Four Georges.

By JUSTIN McCARTHY, M.P.   [*In preparation.*

Crown 8vo, cloth limp, with Illustrations, 2s. 6d.

Holmes's The Science of Voice Production

and Voice Preservation : A Popular Manual for the Use of Speakers and Singers. By GORDON HOLMES, L.R.C.P.E.

Crown 8vo, cloth extra, gilt, 7s. 6d.

Hood's (Thomas) Choice Works,

In Prose and Verse. Including the CREAM OF THE COMIC ANNUALS. With Life of the Author, Portrait, and Two Hundred Illustrations.

Square crown 8vo, cloth extra, gilt edges, 6s.

Hood's (Tom) From Nowhere to the North

Pole : A Noah's Arkæological Narrative. With 25 Illustrations by W. BRUNTON and E. C. BARNES.

" *The amusing letterpress is profusely interspersed with the jingling rhymes which children love and learn so easily. Messrs. Brunton and Barnes do full justice to the writer's meaning, and a pleasanter result of the harmonious co-operation of author and artist could not be desired.*" —TIMES.

Crown 8vo, cloth extra, gilt, 7s. 6d.

Hook's (Theodore) Choice Humorous Works,

including his Ludicrous Adventures, Bons-mots, Puns, and Hoaxes: With a new Life of the Author, Portraits, Facsimiles, and Illustrations.

Crown 8vo, cloth extra, 7s.

Horne's Orion:

An Epic Poem in Three Books. By RICHARD HENGIST HORNE. With a brief Commentary by the Author. With Photographic Portrait from a Medallion by SUMMERS. Tenth Edition.

Crown 8vo, cloth extra, 7s. 6d.

Howell's Conflicts of Capital and Labour

Historically and Economically considered. Being a History and Review of the Trade Unions of Great Britain, showing their Origin, Progress, Constitution, and Objects, in their Political, Social, Economical, and Industrial Aspects. By GEORGE HOWELL.

" *This book is an attempt, and on the whole a successful attempt, to place the work of trade unions in the past, and their objects in the future, fairly before the public from the working man's point of view.*"—PALL MALL GAZETTE.

Demy 8vo, cloth extra, 12s. 6d.

Hueffer's The Troubadours:

A History of Provencal Life and Literature in the Middle Ages. By FRANCIS HUEFFER.

Crown 8vo, cloth extra, 6s.

Janvier.—Practical Keramics for Students.

By CATHERINE A. JANVIER.

" *Will be found a useful handbook by those who wish to try the manufacture or decoration of pottery, and may be studied by all who desire to know something of the art.*"—MORNING POST.

A NEW EDITION, Revised and partly Re-written, with several New Chapters and Illustrations, crown 8vo, cloth extra, 7s. 6d.

Jennings' The Rosicrucians:

Their Rites and Mysteries. With Chapters on the Ancient Fire and Serpent Worshippers. By HARGRAVE JENNINGS. With Five full-page Plates and upwards of 300 Illustrations.

Jerrold (Tom), Works by:

Household Horticulture : A Gossip about Flowers. By TOM and JANE JERROLD. Illustrated. Post 8vo, cloth limp, 2s.6d.

Our Kitchen Garden : The Plants we Grow, and How we Cook Them. By TOM JERROLD, Author of "The Garden that Paid the Rent," &c. Post 8vo, cloth limp, 2s. 6d.

"The combination of hints on cookery with gardening has been very cleverly carried out, and the result is an interesting and highly instructive little work. Mr. Jerrold is correct in saying that English people do not make half the use of vegetables they might ; and by showing how easily they can be grown, and so obtained fresh, he is doing a great deal to make them more popular."—DAILY CHRONICLE.

Two Vols. 8vo, with 52 Illustrations and Maps, cloth extra, gilt, 14s.

Josephus, The Complete Works of.

Translated by WHISTON. Containing both "The Antiquities of the Jews" and "The Wars of the Jews."

Small 8vo, cloth, full gilt, gilt edges, with Illustrations, 6s.

Kavanaghs' Pearl Fountain,

And other Fairy Stories. By BRIDGET and JULIA KAVANAGH. With Thirty Illustrations by J. MOYR SMITH.

"Genuine new fairy stories of the old type, some of them as delightful as the best of Grimm's ' German Popular Stories.' . . . . For the most part the stories are downright, thorough-going fairy stories of the most admirable kind. . . . Mr. Moyr Smith's illustrations, too, are admirable."—SPECTATOR.

Square 8vo, cloth extra, with Illustrations, 6s.

Knight (The) and the Dwarf.

By CHARLES MILLS. With numerous Illustrations by THOMAS LINDSAY.

Crown 8vo, illustrated boards, with numerous Plates, 2s. 6d.

Lace (Old Point), and How to Copy and

Imitate it. By DAISY WATERHOUSE HAWKINS. With 17 Illustrations by the Author.

Crown 8vo, cloth extra, gilt, with Portraits, 7s. 6d.

Lamb's Complete Works,

In Prose and Verse, reprinted from the Original Editions, with many Pieces hitherto unpublished. Edited, with Notes and Introduction, by R. H. SHEPHERD. With Two Portraits and Facsimile of a Page of the "Essay on Roast Pig."

"A complete edition of Lamb's writings, in prose and verse, has long been wanted, and is now supplied. The editor appears to have taken great pains to bring together Lamb's scattered contributions, and his collection contains a number of pieces which are now reproduced for the first time since their original appearance in various old periodicals."—SATURDAY REVIEW.

Crown 8vo, cloth extra, with numerous Illustrations, 10s. 6d.

Lamb (Mary and Charles):

Their Poems, Letters, and Remains. With Reminiscences and Notes by W. CAREW HAZLITT. With HANCOCK's Portrait of the Essayist, Facsimiles of the Title-pages of the rare First Editions of Lamb's and Coleridge's Works, and numerous Illustrations.

"*Very many passages will delight those fond of literary trifles; hardly any portion will fail in interest for lovers of Charles Lamb and his sister.*"—STANDARD.

Small 8vo, cloth extra, 5s.

Lamb's Poetry for Children, and Prince

Dorus. Carefully Reprinted from unique copies.

"*The quaint and delightful little book, over the recovery of which all the hearts of his lovers are yet warm with rejoicing.*"—A. C. SWINBURNE.

Crown 8vo, cloth extra, 6s.

Lares and Penates;

Or, The Background of Life. By FLORENCE CADDY.

"*The whole book is well worth reading, for it is full of practical suggestions. . . . . We hope nobody will be deterred from taking up a book which teaches a good deal about sweetening poor lives as well as giving grace to wealthy ones.*"—GRAPHIC.

Crown 8vo, cloth, full gilt, 6s.

Leigh's A Town Garland.

By HENRY S. LEIGH, Author of "Carols of Cockayne."

"*If Mr. Leigh's verse survive to a future generation—and there is no reason why that honour should not be accorded productions so delicate, so finished, and so full of humour—their author will probably be remembered as the Poet of the Strand.*"—ATHENÆUM.

SECOND EDITION.—Crown 8vo, cloth extra, with Illustrations, 6s.

Leisure-Time Studies, chiefly Biological.

By ANDREW WILSON, F.R.S.E., Lecturer on Zoology and Comparative Anatomy in the Edinburgh Medical School.

"*It is well when we can take up the work of a really qualified investigator, who in the intervals of his more serious professional labours sets himself to impart knowledge in such a simple and elementary form as may attract and instruct, with no danger of misleading the tyro in natural science. Such a work is this little volume, made up of essays and addresses written and delivered by Dr. Andrew Wilson, lecturer and examiner in science at Edinburgh and Glasgow, at leisure intervals in a busy professional life. . . . Dr. Wilson's pages teem with matter stimulating to a healthy love of science and a reverence for the truths of nature.*"—SATURDAY REVIEW.

Crown 8vo, cloth extra, with Illustrations, 7s. 6d.

Life in London;

or, The History of Jerry Hawthorn and Corinthian Tom. With the whole of CRUIKSHANK'S Illustrations, in Colours, after the Originals.

Crown 8vo, cloth extra, 6s.
Lights on the Way:
Some Tales within a Tale.   By the late J. H. ALEXANDER, B.A.
Edited, with an Explanatory Note, by H. A. PAGE, Author of
"Thoreau : A Study."

Crown 8vo, cloth extra, with Illustrations, 7s. 6d.
Longfellow's Complete Prose Works.
Including "Outre Mer," "Hyperion," "Kavanagh," "The Poets
and Poetry of Europe," and "Driftwood." With Portrait and Illustrations by VALENTINE BROMLEY.

Crown 8vo, cloth extra, gilt, with Illustrations, 7s. 6d.
Longfellow's Poetical Works.
Carefully Reprinted from the Original Editions.   With numerous
fine Illustrations on Steel and Wood.

Crown 8vo, cloth extra, 5s.
Lunatic Asylum, My Experiences in a.
By a SANE PATIENT.
*" The story is clever and interesting, sad beyond measure though the subject
be. There is no personal bitterness, and no violence or anger. Whatever may
have been the evidence for our author's madness when he was consigned to an
asylum, nothing can be clearer than his sanity when he wrote this book; it is
bright, calm, and to the point."*—SPECTATOR.

Demy 8vo, with Fourteen full-page Plates, cloth boards, 18s.
Lusiad (The) of Camoens.
Translated into English Spenserian verse by ROBERT FFRENCH DUFF,
Knight Commander of the Portuguese Royal Order of Christ.

Mallock's (W. H.) Works:
Is Life Worth Living? By WILLIAM HURRELL MALLOCK.
New Edition, crown 8vo, cloth extra, 6s.
*" This deeply interesting volume. . . . . It is the most powerful vin-
dication of religion, both natural and revealed, that has appeared since Bishop
Butler wrote, and is much more useful than either the Analogy or the Ser-
mons of that great divine, as a refutation of the peculiar form assumed by
the infidelity of the present day. . . . . Deeply philosophical as the book
is, there is not a heavy page in it. The writer is 'possessed,' so to speak,
with his great subject, has sounded its depths, surveyed it in all its extent,
and brought to bear on it all the resources of a vivid, rich, and impassioned
style, as well as an adequate acquaintance with the science, the philosophy,
and the literature of the day."*—IRISH DAILY NEWS.

The New Republic; or, Culture, Faith, and Philosophy in an
English Country House. By W. H. MALLOCK. Post 8vo, cloth limp, 2s. 6d.

The New Paul and Virginia; or, Positivism on an Island. By
W. H. MALLOCK. Post 8vo, cloth limp, 2s. 6d.

Poems. By W. H. MALLOCK. Small 4to, bound in parchment, 8s.

A Romance of the Nineteenth Century. By W. H. MALLOCK.
Second Edition, with a Preface. Two Vols., crown 8vo, 21s.

Macquoid (Mrs.), Works by:

In the Ardennes. By KATHARINE S. MACQUOID. With 50 fine Illustrations by THOMAS R. MACQUOID. Uniform with "Pictures and Legends." Square 8vo, cloth extra, 10s. 6d.

"This is another of Mrs. Macquoid's pleasant books of travel, full of useful information, of picturesque descriptions of scenery, and of quaint traditions respecting the various monuments and ruins which she encounters in her tour. . . . To such of our readers as are already thinking about the year's holiday, we strongly recommend the perusal of Mrs. Macquoid's experiences. The book is well illustrated by Mr. Thomas R. Macquoid."—GRAPHIC.

Pictures and Legends from Normandy and Brittany. By KATHARINE S. MACQUOID. With numerous Illustrations by THOMAS R. MACQUOID. Square 8vo, cloth gilt, 10s. 6d.

Through Normandy. By KATHARINE S. MACQUOID. With 90 Illustrations by T. R. MACQUOID. Square 8vo, cloth extra, 7s. 6d.

"One of the few books which can be read as a piece of literature, whilst at the same time handy in the knapsack."—BRITISH QUARTERLY REVIEW.

Through Brittany. By KATHARINE S. MACQUOID. With numerous Illustrations by T. R. MACQUOID. Sq. 8vo, cloth extra, 7s. 6d.

"The pleasant companionship which Mrs. Ma qu id offers, while wandering from one point of interest to another, seems to throw a renewed charm around each oft-depicted scene."—MORNING POST.

Mark Twain's Works:

The Choice Works of Mark Twain. Revised and Corrected throughout by the Author. With Life, Portrait, and numerous Illustrations. Crown 8vo, cloth extra, 7s. 6d.

The Adventures of Tom Sawyer. By MARK TWAIN. With 100 Illustrations. Small 8vo, cloth extra, 7s. 6d. CHEAP EDITION, illustrated boards, 2s.

A Pleasure Trip on the Continent of Europe : The Innocents Abroad, and The New Pilgrim's Progress. By MARK TWAIN. Post 8vo, illustrated boards, 2s.

An Idle Excursion, and other Sketches. By MARK TWAIN. Post 8vo, illustrated boards, 2s.

The Prince and the Pauper. By MARK TWAIN. With nearly 200 Illustrations. Crown 8vo, cloth extra, 7s. 6d. Uniform with "A Tramp Abroad." [*In the press.*

The Innocents Abroad ; or, The New Pilgrim's Progress : Being some Account of the Steamship "Quaker City's" Pleasure Excursion to Europe and the Holy Land, with descriptions of Countries, Nations, Incidents, and Adventures, as they appeared to the Author. With 234 Illustrations. By MARK TWAIN. Crown 8vo, cloth extra, 7s. 6d. Uniform with "A Tramp Abroad."

A Tramp Abroad. By MARK TWAIN. With 314 Illustrations. Crown 8vo, cloth extra, 7s. 6d.

"The fun and tenderness of the conception, of which no living man but Mark Twain is capable, its grace and fantasy and slyness, the wonderful feeling for animals that is manifest in every line, make of all this episode of Jim Baker and his jays a piece of work that is not only delightful as mere reading, but also of a high degree of merit as literature. . . . The book is full of good things, and contains passages and episodes that are equal to the funniest of those that have gone before."—ATHENÆUM

Crown 8vo, cloth extra, with Illustrations, 2s. 6d.

Madre Natura v. The Moloch of Fashion.

By LUKE LIMNER. With 32 Illustrations by the Author. FOURTH EDITION, revised and enlarged.

Handsomely printed in facsimile, price 5s.

Magna Charta.

An exact Facsimile of the Original Document in the British Museum, printed on fine plate paper; nearly 3 feet long by 2 feet wide, with the Arms and Seals emblazoned in Gold and Colours.

Post 8vo, cloth limp, 2s. 6d. per volume.

Mayfair Library, The:

The New Republic. By W. H. MALLOCK.

The New Paul and Virginia. By W. H. MALLOCK.

The True History of Joshua Davidson. By E. LYNN LINTON.

Old Stories Re-told. By WALTER THORNBURY.

Thoreau: His Life and Aims. By H. A. PAGE.

By Stream and Sea. By WILLIAM SENIOR.

Jeux d'Esprit. Edited by HENRY S. LEIGH.

Puniana. By the Hon. HUGH ROWLEY.

More Puniana. By the Hon. HUGH ROWLEY.

Puck on Pegasus. By H. CHOLMONDELEY-PENNELL.

The Speeches of Charles Dickens.

Muses of Mayfair. Edited by H. CHOLMONDELEY-PENNELL.

Gastronomy as a Fine Art. By BRILLAT-SAVARIN.

The Philosophy of Handwriting. By DON FELIX DE SALAMANCA.

Curiosities of Criticism. By HENRY J. JENNINGS.

Literary Frivolities, Fancies, Follies, Frolics. By W. T. DOBSON.

Pencil and Palette. By ROBERT KEMPT.

Latter-Day Lyrics. Edited by W. DAVENPORT ADAMS.

Original Plays by W. S. GILBERT. FIRST SERIES. Containing: The Wicked World—Pygmalion and Galatea—Charity—The Princess—The Palace of Truth—Trial by Jury.

Original Plays by W. S. GILBERT. SECOND SERIES. Containing: Broken Hearts — Engaged — Sweethearts — Dan'l Druce — Gretchen—Tom Cobb—The Sorcerer—H.M.S. Pinafore—The Pirates of Penzance.

Carols of Cockayne. By HENRY S. LEIGH.

The Book of Clerical Anecdotes. By JACOB LARWOOD.

The Agony Column of "The Times," from 1800 to 1870. Edited, with an Introduction, by ALICE CLAY.

The Cupboard Papers. By FIN-BEC.

Pastimes and Players. By ROBERT MACGREGOR.

Melancholy Anatomised: A Popular Abridgment of "Burton's Anatomy of Melancholy."

Quips and Quiddities. Selected by W. DAVENPORT ADAMS.

Leaves from a Naturalist's Note-Book. By ANDREW WILSON, F.R.S.E.

The Autocrat of the Breakfast-Table. By OLIVER WENDELL HOLMES. Illustrated by J. GORDON THOMSON.

Balzac's "Comédie Humaine" and its Author. With Translations by H. H. WALKER.

. *Other Volumes are in preparation.*

Small 8vo, cloth limp, with Illustrations, 2s. 6d.

Miller's Physiology for the Young;

Or, The House of Life: Human Physiology, with its Applications to the Preservation of Health. For use in Classes and Popular Reading. With numerous Illustrations. By Mrs. F. FENWICK MILLER.

"*An admirable introduction to a subject which all who value health and enjoy life should have at their fingers' ends.*"—ECHO.

Milton (J. L.), Works by:

The Hygiene of the Skin. A Concise Set of Rules for the Management of the Skin; with Directions for Diet, Wines, Soaps, Baths, &c. By J. L. MILTON, Senior Surgeon to St. John's Hospital. Small 8vo, 1s.; cloth extra, 1s. 6d.

The Bath in Diseases of the Skin. Small 8vo, 1s.; cloth extra, 1s. 6d.

Square 8vo, cloth extra, with numerous Illustrations, 7s. 6d.

North Italian Folk.

By Mrs. COMYNS CARR. Illustrated by RANDOLPH CALDECOTT.

"*A delightful book, of a kind which is far too rare. If anyone wants to really know the North Italian folk, we can honestly advise him to omit the journey, and read Mrs. Carr's pages instead. . . Description with Mrs. Carr is a real gift. . It is rarely that a book is so happily illustrated.*"—CONTEMPORARY REVIEW.

NEW NOVELS.

A NEW NOVEL BY OUIDA.

The Title of which will shortly be announced. 3 vols., crown 8vo.

SOMETHING IN THE CITY.

By GEORGE AUGUSTUS SALA. 3 vols. crown 8vo.

GOD AND THE MAN.

By ROBERT BUCHANAN, Author of "The Shadow of the Sword," &c. 3 vols. crown 8vo. With 11 Illustrations by FRED. BARNARD.

THE COMET OF A SEASON.

By JUSTIN MCCARTHY, M.P., Author of "Miss Misanthrope." 3 vols., crown 8vo.

JOSEPH'S COAT.

By DAVID CHRISTIE MURRAY, Author of "A Life's Atonement," &c. With 12 Illustrations by FRED. BARNARD.

PRINCE SARONI'S WIFE, and other Stories.

By JULIAN HAWTHORNE. 3 vols., crown 8vo.

A HEART'S PROBLEM.

By CHARLES GIBBON, Author of "Robin Gray," &c. 2 vols. crown 8vo.

THE BRIDE'S PASS.

By SARAH TYTLER, 2 vols., crown 8vo.

Crown 8vo, cloth extra, with Vignette Portraits, price 6s. per Vol.

Old Dramatists, The:

Ben Jonson's Works.
With Notes, Critical and Explanatory, and a Biographical Memoir by WILLIAM GIFFORD. Edited by Colonel CUNNINGHAM. Three Vols.

Chapman's Works.
Now First Collected. Complete in Three Vols. Vol. I. contains the Plays complete, including the doubtful ones; Vol. II. the Poems and Minor Translations, with an Introductory Essay

by ALGERNON CHARLES SWINBURNE. Vol. III. the Translations of the Iliad and Odyssey.

Marlowe's Works.
Including his Translations. Edited, with Notes and Introduction, by Col. CUNNINGHAM. One Vol.

Massinger's Plays.
From the Text of WILLIAM GIFFORD. With the addition of the Tragedy of "Believe as you List." Edited by Col. CUNNINGHAM. One Vol.

O'Shaughnessy (Arthur) Works by:

Songs of a Worker. By ARTHUR O'SHAUGHNESSY. Fcap. 8vo, cloth extra, 7s. 6d.

Music and Moonlight. By ARTHUR O'SHAUGHNESSY. Fcap. 8vo, cloth extra, 7s. 6d.

Lays of France. By ARTHUR O'SHAUGHNESSY. Crown 8vo, cloth extra, 10s. 6d.

Crown 8vo, red cloth extra, 5s. each.

Ouida's Novels.—Library Edition.

Held in Bondage.	By OUIDA.	Pascarel.	By OUIDA.
Strathmore.	By OUIDA.	Two Wooden Shoes.	By OUIDA.
Chandos.	By OUIDA.	Signa.	By OUIDA.
Under Two Flags.	By OUIDA.	In a Winter City.	By OUIDA.
Idalia.	By OUIDA.	Ariadne.	By OUIDA.
Cecil Castlemaine.	By OUIDA.	Friendship.	By OUIDA.
Tricotrin.	By OUIDA.	Moths.	By OUIDA.
Puck.	By OUIDA.	Pipistrello.	By OUIDA.
Folle Farine.	By OUIDA.	A Village Commune.	By OUIDA.
Dog of Flanders.	By OUIDA.		

*** Also a Cheap Edition of all but the last two, post 8vo, illustrated boards, 2s. each.

Post 8vo, cloth limp, 1s. 6d.

Parliamentary Procedure, A Popular Handbook of. By HENRY W. LUCY.

Large 4to, cloth extra, gilt, beautifully Illustrated, 31s. 6d.

Pastoral Days;

Or, Memories of a New England Year. By W. HAMILTON GIBSON. With 76 Illustrations in the highest style of Wood Engraving.

"*The volume contains a prose poem, with illustrations in the shape of wood engravings more beautiful than it can well enter into the hearts of most men to conceive.*"—SCOTSMAN.

LIBRARY EDITIONS, mostly Illustrated, crown 8vo, cloth extra, 3s. 6d. each.

Piccadilly Novels, The.

𝔓opular 𝔖torie𝔰 b𝔶 t𝔥e 𝔅e𝔰t 𝔄ut𝔥or𝔰.

Maid, Wife, or Widow? By Mrs. ALEXANDER.

Ready-Money Mortiboy. By W. BESANT and JAMES RICE.

My Little Girl. By W. BESANT and JAMES RICE.

The Case of Mr. Lucraft. By W. BESANT and JAMES RICE.

This Son of Vulcan. By W. BESANT and JAMES RICE.

With Harp and Crown. By W. BESANT and JAMES RICE.

The Golden Butterfly. By W. BESANT and JAMES RICE.

By Celia's Arbour. By W. BESANT and JAMES RICE.

The Monks of Thelema. By W. BESANT and JAMES RICE.

'Twas in Trafalgar's Bay. By W. BESANT and JAMES RICE.

The Seamy Side. By WALTER BESANT and JAMES RICE.

Antonina. By WILKIE COLLINS.

Basil. By WILKIE COLLINS.

Hide and Seek. W. COLLINS.

The Dead Secret. W. COLLINS.

Queen of Hearts. W. COLLINS.

My Miscellanies. W. COLLINS.

The Woman in White. By WILKIE COLLINS.

The Moonstone. W. COLLINS.

Man and Wife. W. COLLINS.

Poor Miss Finch. W. COLLINS.

Miss or Mrs.? By W. COLLINS.

The New Magdalen. By WILKIE COLLINS.

The Frozen Deep. W. COLLINS.

The Law and the Lady. By WILKIE COLLINS.

The Two Destinies. By WILKIE COLLINS.

The Haunted Hotel. By WILKIE COLLINS.

The Fallen Leaves. By WILKIE COLLINS.

Jezebel's Daughter. W. COLLINS.

Deceivers Ever. By Mrs. H. LOVETT CAMERON.

Juliet's Guardian. By Mrs. H. LOVETT CAMERON.

Felicia. M. BETHAM-EDWARDS.

Olympia. By R. E. FRANCILLON.

The Capel Girls. By EDWARD GARRETT.

Robin Gray. CHARLES GIBBON.

For Lack of Gold. By CHARLES GIBBON.

In Love and War. By CHARLES GIBBON.

What will the World Say? By CHARLES GIBBON.

For the King. CHARLES GIBBON.

In Honour Bound. By CHARLES GIBBON.

Queen of the Meadow. By CHARLES GIBBON.

In Pastures Green. By CHARLES GIBBON.

Under the Greenwood Tree. By THOMAS HARDY.

Garth. By JULIAN HAWTHORNE.

Ellice Quentin. By JULIAN HAWTHORNE.

Thornicroft's Model. By Mrs. A. W. HUNT.

Fated to be Free. By JEAN INGELOW.

Confidence. HENRY JAMES, Jun.

The Queen of Connaught. By HARRIETT JAY.

The Dark Colleen. By H. JAY.

Number Seventeen. By HENRY KINGSLEY.

Oakshott Castle. H. KINGSLEY.

Patricia Kemball. By E. LYNN LINTON.

The Atonement of Leam Dundas. By E. LYNN LINTON.

The World Well Lost. By E. LYNN LINTON.

Under which Lord? By E. LYNN LINTON.

With a Silken Thread. By E. LYNN LINTON.

The Waterdale Neighbours. By JUSTIN McCARTHY.

PICCADILLY NOVELS—*continued.*

My Enemy's Daughter. By JUSTIN McCARTHY.

Linley Rochford. By JUSTIN McCARTHY.

A Fair Saxon. J. McCARTHY.

Dear Lady Disdain. By JUSTIN McCARTHY.

Miss Misanthrope. By JUSTIN McCARTHY.

Donna Quixote. J. McCARTHY.

Quaker Cousins. By AGNES MACDONELL.

Lost Rose. By KATHARINE S. MACQUOID.

The Evil Eye. By KATHARINE S. MACQUOID.

Open! Sesame! By FLORENCE MARRYAT.

Written in Fire. F. MARRYAT.

Touch and Go. By JEAN MIDDLEMASS.

A Life's Atonement. By D. CHRISTIE MURRAY.

Whiteladies. Mrs. OLIPHANT.

The Best of Husbands. By JAMES PAYN.

Fallen Fortunes. JAMES PAYN.

Halves. By JAMES PAYN.

Walter's Word. JAMES PAYN.

What He Cost Her. J. PAYN.

Less Black than we're Painted. By JAMES PAYN.

By Proxy. By JAMES PAYN.

Under One Roof. JAMES PAYN.

High Spirits. By JAMES PAYN.

Her Mother's Darling. By Mrs. J. H. RIDDELL.

Bound to the Wheel. By JOHN SAUNDERS.

Guy Waterman. J. SAUNDERS.

One Against the World. By JOHN SAUNDERS.

The Lion in the Path. By JOHN SAUNDERS.

The Way We Live Now. By ANTHONY TROLLOPE.

The American Senator. By ANTHONY TROLLOPE.

Diamond Cut Diamond. By T. A. TROLLOPE.

NEW VOLUMES OF "THE PICCADILLY NOVELS."

Put Yourself in his Place. By CHARLES READE.

A Confidential Agent. By JAMES PAYN. With 12 Illustrations.

The Violin-Player. By BERTHA THOMAS.

Queen Cophetua. By R. E. FRANCILLON.

The Leaden Casket. By Mrs. ALFRED HUNT.

Carlyon's Year. By J. PAYN.

The Ten Years' Tenant, and other Stories. By WALTER BESANT and JAMES RICE.

A Child of Nature. By ROBERT BUCHANAN.

Cressida. By BERTHA THOMAS.

From Exile. By JAMES PAYN.

Sebastian Strome. By JULIAN HAWTHORNE.

The Black Robe. By WILKIE COLLINS.

Archie Lovell. By Mrs. ANNIE EDWARDES.

"My Love!" By E. LYNN LINTON.

Lost Sir Massingberd. By JAMES PAYN.

The Chaplain of the Fleet. By WALTER BESANT and JAMES RICE.

Proud Maisie. By BERTHA THOMAS.

The Two Dreamers. By JOHN SAUNDERS.

What She Came through. By SARAH TYTLER.

Crown 8vo, cloth extra, 6s.

Planché.—Songs and Poems, from 1819 to 1879.

By J. R. PLANCHÉ. Edited, with an Introduction, by his Daughter, Mrs. MACKARNESS.

Post 8vo, illustrated boards, 2s. each.

Popular Novels, Cheap Editions of.

[WILKIE COLLINS' NOVELS and BESANT and RICE'S NOVELS may also be had in cloth limp at 2s. 6d. *See, too, the* PICCADILLY NOVELS, *for Library Editions.*]

Confidences. HAMILTON AÏDÉ.

Carr of Carrlyon. H. AÏDÉ.

Maid, Wife, or Widow? By Mrs. ALEXANDER.

Ready-Money Mortiboy. By WALTER BESANT and JAMES RICE.

With Harp and Crown. By WALTER BESANT and JAMES RICE.

This Son of Vulcan. By W. BESANT and JAMES RICE.

My Little Girl. By the same.

The Case of Mr. Lucraft. By WALTER BESANT and JAMES RICE.

The Golden Butterfly. By W. BESANT and JAMES RICE.

By Celia's Arbour. By WALTER BESANT and JAMES RICE.

The Monks of Thelema. By WALTER BESANT and JAMES RICE.

'Twas in Trafalgar's Bay. By WALTER BESANT and JAMES RICE.

Seamy Side. BESANT and RICE.

Grantley Grange. By SHELSLEY BEAUCHAMP.

An Heiress of Red Dog. By BRET HARTE.

The Luck of Roaring Camp. By BRET HARTE.

Gabriel Conroy. BRET HARTE.

Surly Tim. By F. E. BURNETT.

Deceivers Ever. By Mrs. L. CAMERON.

Juliet's Guardian. By Mrs. LOVETT CAMERON.

The Cure of Souls. By MAC-LAREN COBBAN.

The Bar Sinister. By C. ALLSTON COLLINS.

Antonina. By WILKIE COLLINS.

Basil. By WILKIE COLLINS.

Hide and Seek. W. COLLINS.

The Dead Secret. W. COLLINS.

Queen of Hearts. W. COLLINS.

My Miscellanies. W. COLLINS.

Woman in White. W. COLLINS.

The Moonstone. W. COLLINS.

Man and Wife. W. COLLINS.

Poor Miss Finch. W. COLLINS.

Miss or Mrs.? W. COLLINS.

New Magdalen. W. COLLINS.

The Frozen Deep. W. COLLINS.

Law and the Lady. W. COLLINS.

Two Destinies. W. COLLINS.

Haunted Hotel. W. COLLINS.

Fallen Leaves. By W. COLLINS.

Leo. By DUTTON COOK.

A Point of Honour. By Mrs. ANNIE EDWARDES.

Archie Lovell. Mrs A. EDWARDES

Felicia. M. BETHAM-EDWARDS.

Roxy. By EDWARD EGGLESTON.

Polly. By PERCY FITZGERALD.

Bella Donna. P. FITZGERALD.

Never Forgotten. FITZGERALD.

The Second Mrs. Tillotson. By PERCY FITZGERALD.

Seventy-Five Brooke Street. By PERCY FITZGERALD.

Filthy Lucre. By ALBANY DE FONBLANQUE.

Olympia. By R. E. FRANCILLON.

The Capel Girls. By EDWARD GARRETT.

Robin Gray. By CHAS. GIBBON.

For Lack of Gold. C. GIBBON.

What will the World Say? By CHARLES GIBBON.

In Honour Bound. C. GIBBON.

The Dead Heart. By C. GIBBON.

In Love and War. C. GIBBON.

For the King. By C. GIBBON.

Queen of the Meadow. By CHARLES GIBBON.

Dick Temple. By JAMES GREENWOOD.

Every-day Papers. By ANDREW HALLIDAY.

Paul Wynter's Sacrifice. By Lady DUFFUS HARDY.

Under the Greenwood Tree. By THOMAS HARDY.

POPULAR NOVELS—*continued*.

Garth. By JULIAN HAWTHORNE.
Golden Heart. By TOM HOOD.
The Hunchback of Notre Dame.
By VICTOR HUGO.
Thornicroft's Model. By Mrs.
ALFRED HUNT.
Fated to be Free. By JEAN
INGELOW.
Confidence. By HENRY JAMES,
Jun.
The Queen of Connaught. By
HARRIETT JAY.
The Dark Colleen. By H. JAY.
Number Seventeen. By HENRY
KINGSLEY.
Oakshott Castle. H. KINGSLEY.
Patricia Kemball. By E. LYNN
LINTON.
Leam Dundas. E. LYNNLINTON.
The World Well Lost. By E.
LYNN LINTON.
Under which Lord? By E.
LYNN LINTON.
The Waterdale Neighbours.
By JUSTIN McCARTHY.
Dear Lady Disdain. By the same.
My Enemy's Daughter. By
JUSTIN McCARTHY.
A Fair Saxon. J. McCARTHY.
Linley Rochford. McCARTHY.
Miss Misanthrope. McCARTHY.
Donna Quixote. J. McCARTHY.
The Evil Eye. By KATHARINE
S. MACQUOID.
Lost Rose. K. S. MACQUOID.
Open! Sesame! By FLORENCE
MARRYAT.
Harvest of Wild Oats. By
FLORENCE MARRYAT.
A Little Stepson. F. MARRYAT.
Fighting the Air. F. MARRYAT.
Touch and Go. By JEAN
MIDDLEMASS.
Mr. Dorillion. J. MIDDLEMASS.
Whiteladies. By Mrs. OLIPHANT.
Held in Bondage. By OUIDA.
Strathmore. By OUIDA.
Chandos. By OUIDA.
Under Two Flags. By OUIDA.
Idalia. By OUIDA.

Cecil Castlemaine. By OUIDA.
Tricotrin. By OUIDA.
Puck. By OUIDA.
Folle Farine. By OUIDA.
A Dog of Flanders. By OUIDA.
Pascarel. By OUIDA.
Two Little Wooden Shoes. By
Signa. By OUIDA. [OUIDA.
In a Winter City. By OUIDA.
Ariadne. By OUIDA.
Friendship. By OUIDA.
Moths. By OUIDA.
Lost Sir Massingberd. J. PAYN.
A Perfect Treasure. J. PAYN.
Bentinck's Tutor. By J. PAYN.
Murphy's Master. By J. PAYN.
A County Family. By J. PAYN.
At Her Mercy. By J. PAYN.
A Woman's Vengeance. J. PAYN.
Cecil's Tryst. By JAMES PAYN.
The Clyffards of Clyffe. J. PAYN.
Family Scapegrace. J. PAYN.
The Foster Brothers. J. PAYN.
Found Dead. By JAMES PAYN.
Gwendoline's Harvest. J. PAYN.
Humorous Stories. J. PAYN.
Like Father, Like Son. J. PAYN.
A Marine Residence. J. PAYN.
Married Beneath Him. J. PAYN.
Mirk Abbey. By JAMES PAYN.
Not Wooed, but Won. J. PAYN.
Two Hundred Pounds Reward.
By JAMES PAYN.
Best of Husbands. By J. PAYN.
Walter's Word. By J. PAYN.
Halves. By JAMES PAYN.
Fallen Fortunes. By J. PAYN.
What He Cost Her. J. PAYN.
Less Black than We're Painted.
By JAMES PAYN.
By Proxy. By JAMES PAYN.
Under One Roof. By J. PAYN.
High Spirits. By JAS. PAYN.
Paul Ferroll.
Why P. Ferroll Killed his Wife.
The Mystery of Marie Roget.
By EDGAR A. POE.

POPULAR NOVELS—*continued.*

Put Yourself in his Place By CHARLES READE.
Her Mother's Darling. By Mrs. J. H. RIDDELL.
Gaslight and Daylight. By GEORGE AUGUSTUS SALA.
Bound to the Wheel. By JOHN SAUNDERS.
Guy Waterman. J. SAUNDERS.
One Against the World. By JOHN SAUNDERS.
The Lion in the Path. By JOHN and KATHERINE SAUNDERS.
A Match in the Dark. By A. SKETCHLEY.

Tales for the Marines. By WALTER THORNBURY.
The Way we Live Now. By ANTHONY TROLLOPE.
The American Senator. Ditto.
Diamond Out Diamond. Ditto.
A Pleasure Trip in Europe. By MARK TWAIN
Tom Sawyer. By MARK TWAIN.
An Idle Excursion. M. TWAIN.
Sabina. By Lady WOOD.
Castaway. By EDMUND YATES.
Forlorn Hope. EDMUND YATES.
Land at Last. EDMUND YATES.

Fcap. 8vo, picture covers, 1s. each.

Jeff Briggs's Love Story. By BRET HARTE.
The Twins of Table Mountain. By BRET HARTE.
Mrs. Gainsborough's Diamonds. By JULIAN HAWTHORNE.
Kathleen Mavourneen. By the Author of "That Lass o' Lowrie's."
Lindsay's Luck. By the Author of "That Lass o' Lowrie's."
Pretty Polly Pemberton. By Author of "That Lass o' Lowrie's."
Trooping with Crows. By Mrs. PIRKIS.
The Professor's Wife. By LEONARD GRAHAM.

Crown 8vo, cloth extra, 6s.

Payn.—Some Private Views.

Being Essays contributed to *The Nineteenth Century* and to *The Times.* By JAMES PAYN. Author of "High Spirits," "By Proxy," "Lost Sir Massingberd," &c. [*Nearly ready.*

Two Vols. 8vo, cloth extra, with Portraits, 10s. 6d.

Plutarch's Lives of Illustrious Men.

Translated from the Greek, with Notes, Critical and Historical, and a Life of Plutarch, by JOHN and WILLIAM LANGHORNE.

Crown 8vo, cloth extra, with Portrait and Illustrations, 7s. 6d.

Poe's Choice Prose and Poetical Works.

With BAUDELAIRE's "Essay."

Crown 8vo, cloth extra, 7s. 6d.

Primitive Manners and Customs.

By JAMES A. FARRER.

Small 8vo, cloth extra, with 130 Illustrations, 3s. 6d.

Prince of Argolis, The:

A Story of the Old Greek Fairy Time. By J. MOYR SMITH.

Crown 8vo, cloth extra, gilt, 7s. 6d.

Pursuivant of Arms, The;

or, Heraldry founded upon Facts. By J. R. PLANCHE, Somerset Herald. With Coloured Frontispiece and 200 Illustrations.

Proctor's (R. A.) Works:

Easy Star Lessons. With Star Maps for Every Night in the Year, Drawings of the Constellations, &c. By RICHARD A. PROCTOR. Crown 8vo, cloth extra, 6s.

Familiar Science Studies. By RICHARD A. PROCTOR. Crown 8vo, cloth extra, 7s. 6d.   [*In the press,*

Saturn and its System. By RICHARD A. PROCTOR. New and Revised Edition, demy 8vo, cloth extra, 10s. 6d.   [*In preparation.*

Myths and Marvels of Astronomy. By RICH. A. PROCTOR, Author of "Other Worlds than Ours," &c. Crown 8vo, cloth extra, 6s.

Pleasant Ways in Science. By R. A. PROCTOR. Cr. 8vo, cl. ex. 6s.

Rough Ways made Smooth: A Series of Familiar Essays on Scientific Subjects. By R. A. PROCTOR. Crown 8vo, cloth extra, 6s.

Our Place among Infinities: A Series of Essays contrasting our Little Abode in Space and Time with the Infinities Around us. By RICHARD A. PROCTOR. Crown 8vo, cloth extra, 6s.

The Expanse of Heaven: A Series of Essays on the Wonders of the Firmament. By RICHARD A. PROCTOR. Crown 8vo, cloth, 6s.

Wages and Wants of Science Workers. By RICHARD A. PROCTOR. Crown 8vo, 1s. 6d.

Crown 8vo, cloth extra, with Illustrations, 7s. 6d.

Rabelais' Works.

Faithfully Translated from the French, with variorum Notes, and numerous characteristic Illustrations by GUSTAVE DORE.

Crown 8vo, cloth gilt, with numerous Illustrations, and a beautifully executed Chart of the various Spectra, 7s. 6d.

Rambosson's Popular Astronomy.

By J. RAMBOSSON, Laureate of the Institute of France. Translated by C. B. PITMAN. Profusely Illustrated.

Second Edition, Revised, Crown 8vo, 1,200 pages, half-roxburghe, 12s. 6d.

Reader's Handbook (The) of Allusions, References, Plots, and Stories. By the Rev. Dr. Brewer.

Crown 8vo, cloth extra, 6s.

Richardson's (Dr.) A Ministry of Health, and other Papers. By BENJAMIN WARD RICHARDSON, M.D., &c.

Rimmer (Alfred), Works by:

Our Old Country Towns. With over 50 Illustrations. By ALFRED RIMMER. Square 8vo, cloth extra, gilt, 10s. 6d.

Rambles Round Eton and Harrow. By ALFRED RIMMER. With 50 Illustrations by the Author. Square 8vo, cloth gilt, 10s. 6d.

About England with Dickens. With Illustrations by ALFRED RIMMER and C. A. VANDERHOOF, Sq. 8vo, cloth gilt, 10s. 6d. [*In the press.*

Handsomely printed, price 5s.

Roll of Battle Abbey, The;

or, A List of the Principal Warriors who came over from Normandy with William the Conqueror, and Settled in this Country, A.D. 1066-7. With the principal Arms emblazoned in Gold and Colours.

Two Vols., large 4to, profusely Illustrated, half-morocco, £2 16s.

Rowlandson, the Caricaturist.

A Selection from his Works, with Anecdotal Descriptions of his Famous Caricatures, and a Sketch of his Life, Times, and Contemporaries. With nearly 400 Illustrations, mostly in Facsimile of the Originals. By JOSEPH GREGO, Author of "James Gillray, the Caricaturist; his Life, Works, and Times."

Crown 8vo, cloth extra, profusely Illustrated, 4s. 6d. each.

"Secret Out" Series, The.

The Pyrotechnist's Treasury; or, Complete Art of Making Fireworks. By THOMAS KENTISH. With numerous Illustrations.

The Art of Amusing: A Collection of Graceful Arts, Games, Tricks, Puzzles, and Charades. By FRANK BELLEW. 300 Illustrations.

Hanky-Panky: Very Easy Tricks, Very Difficult Tricks, White Magic, Sleight of Hand. Edited by W. H. CREMER. 200 Illusts.

The Merry Circle: A Book of New Intellectual Games and Amusements. By CLARA BELLEW. Many Illustrations.

Magician's Own Book: Performances with Cups and Balls, Eggs, Hats, Handkerchiefs, &c. All from Actual Experience. Edited by W. H. CREMER. 200 Illustrations.

Magic No Mystery: Tricks with Cards, Dice, Balls, &c., with fully descriptive Directions; the Art of Secret Writing; Training of Performing Animals, &c. Coloured Frontispiece and many Illustrations.

The Secret Out: One Thousand Tricks with Cards, and other Recreations; with Entertaining Experiments in Drawing-room or "White Magic." By W. H. CREMER. 300 Engravings.

Crown 8vo, cloth extra, 6s.

Senior's Travel and Trout in the Antipodes.

An Angler's Sketches in Tasmania and New Zealand. By WILLIAM SENIOR ("Red Spinner"), Author of "By Stream and Sea."

Shakespeare:

Shakespeare, The First Folio. Mr. WILLIAM SHAKESPEARE'S Comedies, Histories, and Tragedies. Published according to the true Originall Copies. London, Printed by ISAAC IAGGARD and ED. BLOUNT, 1623.—A Reproduction of the extremely rare original, in reduced facsimile by a photographic process—ensuring the strictest accuracy in every detail. Small 8vo, half-Roxburghe, 7s. 6d.

Shakespeare, The Lansdowne. Beautifully printed in red and black, in small but very clear type. With engraved facsimile of DROESHOUT's Portrait. Post 8vo, cloth extra, 7s. 6d.

Shakespeare for Children: Tales from Shakespeare. By CHARLES and MARY LAMB. With numerous Illustrations, coloured and plain, by J. MOYR SMITH. Crown 4to, cloth gilt, 10s. 6d.

Shakespeare Music, The Handbook of. Being an Account 350 Pieces of Music, set to Words taken from the Plays and Poems of Shakespeare, the compositions ranging from the Elizabethan Age to the Present Time. By ALFRED ROFFE. 4to, half-Roxburghe, 7s.

Shakespeare, A Study of. By ALGERNON CHARLES SWINBURNE. Crown 8vo, cloth extra, 8s.

Crown 8vo, cloth extra, gilt, with 10 full-page Tinted Illustrations, 7*s.* 6*d.*
Sheridan's Complete Works,
with Life and Anecdotes.   Including his Dramatic Writings, printed from the Original Editions, his Works in Prose and Poetry, Translations, Speeches, Jokes, Puns, &c. ; with a Collection of Sheridaniana.

Crown 8vo, cloth extra, with 100 Illustrations, 7*s.* 6*d.*
Signboards:
Their History.   With Anecdotes of Famous Taverns and Remarkable Characters.   By JACOB LARWOOD and JOHN CAMDEN HOTTEN.

Crown 8vo, cloth extra, gilt, 6*s.* 6*d.*
Slang Dictionary, The:
Etymological, Historical, and Anecdotal.   An ENTIRELY NEW EDITION, revised throughout, and considerably Enlarged.

Exquisitely printed in miniature, cloth extra, gilt edges, 2*s.* 6*d.*
Smoker's Text-Book, The. By J. HAMER, F.R.S.L.

Crown 8vo, cloth extra, 5*s.*
Spalding's Elizabethan Demonology:
An Essay in Illustration of the Belief in the Existence of Devils, and the Powers possessed by them.   By T. ALFRED SPALDING, LL.B.

Crown 4to, uniform with "Chaucer for Children," with Coloured Illustrations, cloth gilt, 10*s.* 6*d.*
Spenser for Children.
By M. H. TOWRY.   Illustrations in Colours by WALTER J. MORGAN.

A New Edition, small crown 8vo, cloth extra, 5*s.*
Staunton.—Laws and Practice of Chess;
Together with an Analysis of the Openings, and a Treatise on End Games.   By HOWARD STAUNTON.   Edited by ROBERT B. WORMALD.

Crown 8vo, cloth extra, 9*s.*
Stedman's Victorian Poets:
Critical Essays.   By EDMUND CLARENCE STEDMAN.

Post 8vo, cloth extra, 5*s.*
Stories about Number Nip,
The Spirit of the Giant Mountains. Retold for Children, by WALTER GRAHAME.   With Illustrations by J. MOYR SMITH.

Two Vols., crown 8vo, cloth extra, 21*s.*
Stories from the State Papers.
By ALEX. CHARLES EWALD, F.S.A., Author of "The Life of Prince Charles Stuart," &c.   With an Autotype Facsimile.

Two Vols., crown 8vo, with numerous Portraits and Illustrations, 24*s.*
Strahan.—Twenty Years of a Publisher's
Life.   By ALEXANDER STRAHAN.   [*In the press.*

Crown 8vo, cloth extra, with Illustrations, 7s. 6d.

Strutt's Sports and Pastimes of the People

of England; including the Rural and Domestic Recreations, May Games, Mummeries, Shows, Processions, Pageants, and Pompous Spectacles, from the Earliest Period to the Present Time. With 140 Illustrations. Edited by WILLIAM HONE.

Crown 8vo, with a Map of Suburban London, cloth extra, 7s. 6d.

Suburban Homes (The) of London:

A Residential Guide to Favourite London Localities, their Society, Celebrities, and Associations. With Notes on their Rental, Rates, and House Accommodation.

Crown 8vo, cloth extra, with Illustrations, 7s. 6d.

Swift's Choice Works,

In Prose and Verse. With Memoir, Portrait, and Facsimiles of the Maps in the Original Edition of "Gulliver's Travels."

Swinburne's Works:

The Queen Mother and Rosamond. Fcap. 8vo, 5s.

Atalanta in Calydon.
A New Edition. Crown 8vo, 6s.

Chastelard.
A Tragedy. Crown 8vo, 7s.

Poems and Ballads.
FIRST SERIES. Fcap. 8vo, 9s. Also in crown 8vo, at same price.

Poems and Ballads.
SECOND SERIES. Fcap. 8vo, 9s. Also in crown 8vo, at same price.

Notes on "Poems and Ballads." 8vo, 1s.

William Blake:
A Critical Essay. With Facsimile Paintings. Demy 8vo, 16s.

Songs before Sunrise.
Crown 8vo, 10s. 6d.

Bothwell:
A Tragedy. Crown 8vo, 12s. 6d.

George Chapman:
An Essay. Crown 8vo, 7s.

Songs of Two Nations.
Crown 8vo, 6s.

Essays and Studies.
Crown 8vo, 12s.

Erechtheus:
A Tragedy. Crown 8vo, 6s.

Note of an English Republican on the Muscovite Crusade. 8vo, 1s.

A Note on Charlotte Brontë.
Crown 8vo, 6s.

A Study of Shakespeare.
Crown 8vo, 8s.

Songs of the Springtides. Cr. 8vo, 6s.

Studies in Song.
Crown 8vo, 7s.

MR. SWINBURNE'S NEW DRAMA.—Crown 8vo, cloth extra, 8s.
Mary Stuart: A Tragedy, in Five Acts. By ALGERNON CHARLES SWINBURNE. [*In the press.*

Demy 8vo, cloth extra, Illustrated, 21s.

Sword, The Book of the:

Being a History of the Sword, and its Use, in all Times and in all Countries. By Captain RICHARD BURTON. With numerous Illustrations. [*In preparation.*

Medium 8vo, cloth extra, with Illustrations, 7s. 6d.

Syntax's (Dr.) Three Tours,

In Search of the Picturesque, in Search of Consolation, and in Search of a Wife. With the whole of ROWLANDSON'S droll page Illustrations, in Colours, and Life of the Author by J. C. HOTTEN.

Four Vols. small 8vo, cloth boards, 30*s*.

Taine's History of English Literature.
Translated by HENRY VAN LAUN.

*** Also a POPULAR EDITION, in Two Vols. crown 8vo, cloth extra, 15*s*.

Crown 8vo, cloth gilt, profusely Illustrated, 6*s*.

Tales of Old Thule.
Collected and Illustrated by J. MOYR SMITH.

One Vol. crown 8vo, cloth extra, 7*s*. 6*d*.

Taylor's (Tom) Historical Dramas:
"Clancarty," "Jeanne Darc," "'Twixt Axe and Crown," "The Fool's Revenge," "Arkwright's Wife," "Anne Boleyn," "Plot and Passion."

*** The Plays may also be had separately, at 1*s*. each.

Crown 8vo, cloth extra, with Coloured Frontispiece and numerous Illustrations, 7*s*. 6*d*.

Thackerayana:
Notes and Anecdotes. Illustrated by a profusion of Sketches by WILLIAM MAKEPEACE THACKERAY, depicting Humorous Incidents in his School-life, and Favourite Characters in the books of his every-day reading. With Hundreds of Wood Engravings, facsimiled from Mr. Thackeray's Original Drawings.

Crown 8vo, cloth extra, gilt edges, with Illustrations, 7*s*. 6*d*.

Thomson's Seasons and Castle of Indolence.
With a Biographical and Critical Introduction by ALLAN CUNNINGHAM, and over 50 fine Illustrations on Steel and Wood.

Crown 8vo, cloth extra, with numerous Illustrations, 7*s*. 6*d*.

Thornbury's (Walter) Haunted London.
A New Edition, Edited by EDWARD WALFORD, M.A., with numerous Illustrations by F. W. FAIRHOLT, F.S.A.

Crown 8vo, cloth extra, with Illustrations, 7*s*. 6*d*.

Timbs' Clubs and Club Life in London.
With Anecdotes of its famous Coffee-houses, Hostelries, and Taverns. By JOHN TIMBS, F.S.A. With numerous Illustrations.

Crown 8vo, cloth extra, with Illustrations, 7*s*. 6*d*.

Timbs' English Eccentrics and Eccentricities: Stories of Wealth and Fashion, Delusions, Impostures, and Fanatic Missions, Strange Sights and Sporting Scenes, Eccentric Artists, Theatrical Folks, Men of Letters, &c. By JOHN TIMBS, F.S.A. With nearly 50 Illustrations.

Demy 8vo, cloth extra, 14*s*.

Torrens' The Marquess Wellesley,
Architect of Empire. An Historic Portrait. *Forming Vol. I. of* PROCONSUL and TRIBUNE: WELLESLEY and O'CONNELL: Histori Portraits. By W. M. TORRENS, M.P. In Two Vols.

Demy 8vo, cloth extra, with Illustrations, 9*s*.

Tunis : the Land and the People.

By ERNST VON HESSE-WARTEGG. With many fine full-page Illustrations. [*In the press.*

Crown 8vo, cloth extra, with Coloured Illustrations, 7*s*. 6*d*.

Turner's (J. M. W.) Life and Correspondence:

Founded upon Letters and Papers furnished by his Friends and fellow-Academicians. By WALTER THORNBURY. A New Edition, considerably Enlarged. With numerous Illustrations in Colours, facsimiled from Turner's original Drawings.

Two Vols., crown 8vo, cloth extra, with Map and Ground-Plans, 14*s*.

Walcott's Church Work and Life in English

Minsters ; and the English Student's Monasticon. By the Rev. MACKENZIE E. C. WALCOTT, B.D.

Large crown 8vo, cloth antique, with Illustrations, 7*s*. 6*d*.

Walton and Cotton's Complete Angler ;

or, The Contemplative Man's Recreation : being a Discourse of Rivers, Fishponds, Fish and Fishing, written by IZAAK WALTON ; and Instructions how to Angle for a Trout or Grayling in a clear Stream, by CHARLES COTTON. With Original Memoirs and Notes by Sir HARRIS NICOLAS, and 61 Copperplate Illustrations.

The Twenty-second Annual Edition, for 1881, cloth, full gilt, 50*s*.

Walford's County Families of the United

Kingdom. By EDWARD WALFORD, M. A. Containing Notices of the Descent, Birth, Marriage, Education, &c., of more than 12,000 distinguished Heads of Families, their Heirs Apparent or Presumptive, the Offices they hold or have held, their Town and Country Addresses, Clubs, &c.

Crown 8vo, cloth extra, 3*s*. 6*d*. per volume.

Wanderer's Library, The :

Merrie England in the Olden
Time. By GEORGE DANIEL. With Illustrations by ROBT. CRUIKSHANK.

The Old Showmen and the Old
London Fairs. By THOMAS FROST.

The Wilds of London. By
JAMES GREENWOOD.

Tavern Anecdotes and Sayings ;
Including the Origin of Signs, and Reminiscences connected with Taverns, Coffee Houses, Clubs, &c. By CHARLES HINDLEY. With Illusts.

Circus Life and Circus Celebrities. By THOMAS FROST.

The Lives of the Conjurers.
By THOMAS FROST.

The Life and Adventures of a
Cheap Jack. By One of the Fraternity. Edited by CHARLES HINDLEY.

The Story of the London Parks.
By JACOB LARWOOD. With Illusts.

Low-Life Deeps. An Account
of the Strange Fish to be found there. By JAMES GREENWOOD.

Seven Generations of Executioners : Memoirs of the Sanson
Family (1688 to 1847). Edited by HENRY SANSON.

The World Behind the Scenes.
By PERCY FITZGERALD.

London Characters. By HENRY
MAYHEW. Illustrated.

The Genial Showman : Life
and Adventures of Artemus Ward. By E. P. HINGSTON. Frontispiece.

Wanderings in Patagonia ; or,
Life among the Ostrich Hunters. By JULIUS BEERBOHM. Illustrated.

Summer Cruising in the South
Seas. By CHARLES WARREN STODDARD. Illustrated by WALLIS MACKAY.

Carefully printed on paper to imitate the Original, 22 in. by 14 in., 2s.

Warrant to Execute Charles I.

An exact Facsimile of this important Document, with the Fifty-nine Signatures of the Regicides, and corresponding Seals.

Beautifully printed on paper to imitate the Original MS., price 2s.

Warrant to Execute Mary Queen of Scots.

An exact Facsimile, including the Signature of Queen Elizabeth, and a Facsimile of the Great Seal.

Crown 8vo, cloth limp, with numerous Illustrations, 4s. 6d.

Westropp's Handbook of Pottery and Porce-

lain; or, History of those Arts from the Earliest Period. By HODDER M. WESTROPP. With numerous Illustrations, and a List of Marks.

Post 8vo, cloth limp, 2s. 6d.

What shall my Son be ?

Hints for Parents on the Choice of a Profession or Trade for their Sons. By FRANCIS DAVENANT, M.A.

SEVENTH EDITION.   Square 8vo, 1s.

Whistler v. Ruskin: Art and Art Critics.

By J. A. MACNEILL WHISTLER.

A VERY HANDSOME VOLUME.— Large 4to, cloth extra, 31s. 6d.

White Mountains (The Heart of the):

Their Legend and Scenery. By SAMUEL ADAMS DRAKE. With nearly 100 Illustrations by W. HAMILTON GIBSON, Author of "Pastoral Days."   [*Nearly ready.*

Crown 8vo, cloth limp, with Illustrations, 2s. 6d.

Williams' A Simple Treatise on Heat.

By W. MATTIEU WILLIAMS, F.R.A.S., F.C.S.

Small 8vo, cloth extra, Illustrated, 6s.

Wooing (The) of the Water-Witch:

A Northern Oddity. By EVAN DALDORNE. Illust. by J. MOYR SMITH.

Crown 8vo, half-bound, 12s. 6d.

Words, Facts, and Phrases:

A Dictionary of Curious, Quaint, and Out-of-the-Way Matters. By ELIEZER EDWARDS.

Crown 8vo, cloth extra, with Illustrations, 7s. 6d.

Wright's Caricature History of the Georges.

(The House of Hanover.) With 400 Pictures, Caricatures, Squibs, Broadsides, Window Pictures, &c. By THOMAS WRIGHT, M.A., F.S.A.

Large post 8vo, cloth extra, gilt, with Illustrations, 7s. 6d.

Wright's History of Caricature and of the

Grotesque in Art, Literature, Sculpture, and Painting. By THOMAS WRIGHT, F.S.A. Profusely Illustrated by F. W. FAIRHOLT, F.S.A.

J. OGDEN AND CO., PRINTERS, 172, ST. JOHN STREET, E.C.

www.ingramcontent.com/pod-product-compliance
Lightning Source LLC
Chambersburg PA
CBHW031823270326
41932CB00008B/519